PENGUIN CLASSICS

THE FABLE OF THE BEES

BERNARD MANDEVILLE (1670–1733) was a native of Rotterdam in Holland. He attended the Erasmian school there and went to the University of Leyden, where he qualified as a doctor of medicine. Within a few years he settled in London, where he practised medicine and acquired great skill in the English language as a writer and conversationalist.

In 1705 he published a doggerel poem called *The Grumbling Hive: or, Knaves Turn'd Honest*. It was reprinted anonymously in 1714 along with *An Enquiry into the Origin of Moral Virtue*, and a series of remarks, under the title *The Fable of the Bees, or Private Vices, Public Benefits*. An expanded edition appeared in 1723, with an *Essay on Charity and Charity Schools, A Search into the Nature of Society*, and further remarks. In 1724 Mandeville enlarged the book again by adding *A Vindication of the Book*.

The Grand Jury of Middlesex presented this work as a public nuisance, and it was denounced in the *London Journal* and attacked by numerous people, although Doctor Johnson found it a source of illumination. To many it gave great offence; it was also highly popular.

Mandeville wrote many other pieces, largely in the same satirical vein.

PHILLIP HARTH has taught since 1965 at the University of Wisconsin, Madison, where he is Merritt Y. Hughes Professor of English and a senior member of the Institute for Research in the Humanities. He taught earlier at Northwestern University, and was a visiting professor at the University of Virginia in 1973. He is the author of *Swift and Anglican Rationalism* (1961) and *Contexts of Dryden's Thought* (1968), and has edited *New Approaches to Eighteenth-Century Literature* (1974).

T0200931

THE
FABLE
OF THE
BEES

Bernard Mandeville

Edited with an introduction by
PHILLIP HARTH

PENGUIN BOOKS

PENGUIN BOOKS

Published by the Penguin Group
Penguin Books Ltd, 27 Wrights Lane, London W8 5TZ, England
Penguin Books USA Inc., 375 Hudson Street, New York, New York 10014, USA
Penguin Books Australia Ltd, Ringwood, Victoria, Australia
Penguin Books Canada Ltd, 10 Alcorn Avenue, Toronto, Ontario, Canada M4V 3B2
Penguin Books (NZ) Ltd, 182–190 Wairau Road, Auckland 10, New Zealand

Penguin Books Ltd, Registered Offices: Harmondsworth, Middlesex, England

First published in Pelican Books 1970
Reprinted in Penguin Classics 1989

026

Printed and bound in Great Britain by Clays Ltd, Elcograf S.p.A.
Set in Linotype Granjon

www.greenpenguin.co.uk

MIX
Paper | Supporting
responsible forestry
FSC
www.fsc.org   FSC® C018179

Penguin Books is committed to a sustainable
future for our business, our readers and our planet.
This book is made from Forest Stewardship
Council™ certified paper.

Contents

Introduction

INTELLECTUAL works which have won lasting recognition usually owe their importance to the influence they have exerted, at least for a time, on sympathetic readers. The *Discourse on Method*, *An Essay Concerning Human Understanding*, and *The Origin of Species* all had to fight their way against the lethargy and even hostility which await most new ideas, but they succeeded, nevertheless, in winning acceptance and changing the course of men's thinking. In some cases, of which the *Discourse Concerning Method* is an instance, this acceptance was followed by rejection from a later generation; yet the effect of an idea, once it has been adopted, is beyond calculation. In some form, modified almost beyond recognition, it survives the change in fashion which overtakes thoughts as well as things.

A few intellectual works, however, owe their importance far more to the controversy they excited and the opprobrium they earned than to any proselytes they were able to win. One thinks particularly of three works of this kind whose notoriety is the best measure of their influence: *The Prince*, the *Leviathan*, and *The Fable of the Bees*. By acting as irritants which contemporary readers found impossible to ignore, each of these books stimulated men to re-examine their ways of thought in order to justify their exasperation. In England, indeed, for a period of 200 years the authors of these three books appeared as successive embodiments of the Faust legend. Machiavelli for the Elizabethans, Hobbes for the subjects of Charles II, and Mandeville for eighteenth-century Englishmen became, each in his turn, a continuing figure of the perverse seeker after knowledge who serves the

7

Father of Lies. For John Brown, author of the famous *Estimate*, Hobbes and Mandeville were 'Detested Names! yet sentenc'd ne'er to die; / Snatch'd from Oblivion's Grave by Infamy!'[1] John Wesley, reading *The Fable of the Bees* for the first time, wrote in his journal: 'Till now I imagined there had never appeared in the world such a book as the works of Machiavel. But de Mandeville goes far beyond it.'[2] To an anonymous eighteenth-century poet, indeed, his contemporary was Anti-Christ: 'And, if GOD-MAN Vice to abolish came, / Who Vice commends, MAN-DEVIL be his Name.'[3]

Surprisingly little is known about the private life of the man who gained so much notoriety through his writings. Bernard Mandeville was born in Rotterdam in 1670, attended the Erasmian School there, and entered the University of Leyden in 1685, where he pursued the study of philosophy and medicine. In 1691 he received the degree of Doctor of Medicine and began practice as a specialist in the 'hypochondriack and hysterick passions', or what would be called today nervous diseases. Within a few years Mandeville resolved to learn the English language, visited London for this purpose, and decided to settle there. Resuming the practice of medicine, he married an Englishwoman in 1699 and remained a successful and respected London physician until his death in 1733. But his ambition to master the English language, which had first brought him to his adopted land, had meanwhile offered him the opportunity of following a second career as a writer, and it was in this role that he was to win lasting fame.

Mandeville's first appearance as an English writer was in the modest role of translator. In 1703 he published *Some Fables after the Easie and Familiar Method of Monsieur de la Fontaine*, all but two of which were renditions, in doggerel verse, of selections from the famous *Fables*, some of which had already been translated in another version by John Dennis, who was later to become a violent antagonist

of Mandeville's. The next year, 1704, Mandeville brought
out two further books of verse translation from the French.
The first of these, *Aesop Dress'd or A Collection of Fables
Writ in Familiar Verse*, included English versions of ten
additional fables by La Fontaine along with those he had
already published the previous year. The second, *Typhon:
or the Wars between the Gods and Giants*, was a translation
into English verse of the first canto of Scarron's burlesque
poem, which, like the *Fables*, already existed in an earlier
English version.

With these publications Mandeville's brief career as a
translator ended as abruptly as it had begun. It had been
hack work, probably undertaken to supplement his income
at a time when he was still building his medical practice,
but the exercise it afforded in turning verse fables and
burlesque poetry into English also determined the bent of
Mandeville's earliest efforts as an original author. In his first
book he had included, along with his translations of twenty-
seven of La Fontaine's fables, two of his own, 'The Carp'
and 'The Nightingale and the Owl', which exposed some of
the follies connected with pride. His next original work was
somewhat more ambitious. It appeared as an anonymous
sixpenny pamphlet in 1705 and was called *The Grumbling
Hive: or, Knaves Turn'd Honest*. As in his previous efforts,
he again followed in the footsteps of La Fontaine, producing
a moral fable which exposed a favourite folly of mankind.
With this little poem Mandeville created the nucleus from
which was to grow his greatest work, *The Fable of the Bees*.

As an independent poem *The Grumbling Hive* seems to
have attracted little attention from Mandeville's adopted
countrymen, and for nearly a decade he busied himself with
other matters: writing *A Treatise of the Hypochondriack
and Hysterick Passions*, carrying on his practice as a speci-
alist in these popular ailments, and publishing a small col-
lection of poems as well as *The Virgin Unmask'd*, an

amusing series of prose dialogues 'betwixt an Elderly Maiden Lady, and her Niece'. But he must also have been giving considerable thought at this time to the subject of *The Grumbling Hive*, for in 1714, nine years after the poem had first appeared, he reissued it along with a series of twenty prose remarks under the title of *The Fable of the Bees: or, Private Vices, Publick Benefits*.

The poem was all but submerged by the weight of the commentary accompanying it, and Mandeville admitted that 'the Censorious that never saw the *Grumbling Hive*, will tell me, that whatever I may talk of the Fable, it not taking up a Tenth part of the Book, was only contriv'd to introduce the *Remarks*'. The proportions were certainly curious, and they were to grow more so as he continued over the years to expand and add to the remarks and to include independent essays, one of which, 'An Enquiry into the Origin of Moral Virtue', was already to be found in the first edition. Mandeville seems to have been indifferent to the book's form. He eventually described it as 'a Rhapsody void of Order or Method'. Yet he also referred to it as a satire on a number of occasions and insisted that the purpose of the entire book, like that of the poem from which it grew, was to expose the follies of his countrymen and to lash their vices. Its form, rare in English literature, is actually that of a Menippean Satire, mingling verse with prose and, in the predominant prose section, combining straightforward discourse with parables, fables, and illustrative anecdotes.

The 1714 edition of *The Fable of the Bees* was less than half the length to which it would eventually grow. After another interval of nine years, marked by the appearance of his *Free Thoughts on Religion, the Church, and National Happiness*, Mandeville published in 1723 a new edition of *The Fable of the Bees*, which had been greatly expanded. Besides adding two new remarks and enlarging a number of others, he now filled out what had become a sizable volume with two further independent essays: 'An Essay on Charity and Charity-Schools' and 'A Search into the Nature of Society'.

The following year, 1724, *The Fable of the Bees* reached its final form. In this new edition Mandeville added the finishing touches to his work by including 'A Vindication of the Book'. This marks the last and most important stage in the history of *The Fable of the Bees*, in which its author was to find himself, in the last decade of his life, the centre of one of the most heated controversies of the century. In spite of the acerbity of *The Grumbling Hive* and the undisguised ridicule to which Mandeville had treated his adopted countrymen in the first edition of *The Fable of the Bees*, it was only with the enlarged edition of 1723 that his satire attracted public notice.

Then, quite suddenly, the *Fable* became the target of a furious onslaught in the press, the pulpit, and even the courts. In July of 1723 the book was presented as a public nuisance by the Grand Jury of Middlesex and later in the same month, on the 27th, a virulent attack on the *Fable* was published in the *London Journal* by someone who styled himself 'Theophilus Philo-Britannus'. Mandeville lost no time in answering these two charges. On 10 August he published his vindication of the *Fable* in the *London Journal*, answering the accusations of both the Grand Jury and Theophilus Philo-Britannus. Later in the year he reissued his defence, along with the presentment of the Grand Jury and the attack on him in the *London Journal*, in a sixpenny pamphlet. It was the contents of this pamphlet which he added to the *Fable* in 1724 as 'A Vindication of the Book'.

But Mandeville could not halt the attacks upon his book, nor could he stop himself from continuing his hopeless effort to justify himself and to pacify his aroused countrymen. During the five years following the appearance of the 'Vindication' no less than ten books were published attacking *The Fable of the Bees*, by such important divines, philosophers and critics as William Law, John Dennis, Francis Hutcheson, Archibald Campbell, and Isaac Watts. During the same period the book was the subject of numerous attacks in pastoral letters, sermons, and letters to the press, and it was again presented by the Grand Jury of Middlesex in 1728. Mandeville could be silent no longer, and in 1729 he published *The Fable of the Bees, Part II*. This sizable volume is a sequel to *The Fable of the Bees* only in the sense that it continues to explore the subjects he had first raised in the *Fable*, as do all of Mandeville's later books. 'As in this Volume I have not alter'd the Subject, on which a former, known by the Name of *the Fable of the Bees*, was wrote,' he explained in the preface to his new book, 'and the same unbiass'd Method of searching after Truth and enquiring into the Nature of Man and Society, made use of in that, is continued in this, I thought it unnecessary to look out for another Title.' But the new book lacks the sustained satirical tone of the *Fable*, and its form is entirely different. It consists of a series of six dialogues between 'Cleomenes', the spokesman for Mandeville, and his friend 'Horatio'. One can make as good a case, therefore, for its being the forerunner of Mandeville's *Enquiry into the Origin of Honour, and the Usefulness of Christianity in War* (1732) as for its being a sequel to *The Fable of the Bees*, since in the *Enquiry* the same two characters engage in further dialogues. Nevertheless, the preface to *The Fable of the Bees, Part II*, as well as the first and third dialogues of the book, contain a new defence of the *Fable* which tries to answer the charges brought against it since the previous vindication, without attempting to deal with its individual opponents, now grown too numerous for individual attention. 'I once thought to have taken this Opportunity of presenting [the reader] with a List of the Adversaries that have appeared in Print against me,' Mandeville declared in the preface to his new book, 'but as they are in nothing so considerable as they are in their Numbers, I was afraid it would have look'd like Ostentation, unless I would have answered them all, which I shall never attempt.'

Mandeville also refers in this same preface to 'a Defence of the *Fable of the Bees*, in which I have stated and endeavour'd to solve all the Objections that might reasonably be made against it, as to the Doctrine contain'd in it, and the Detriment it might be of to others,' written two years earlier and still in manuscript. He continued to withhold this defence and it seems never to have appeared in print. Meanwhile, the objections which he promised to answer continued to multiply, and in 1732 a particularly formidable antagonist appeared in the person of George Berkeley. In the second dialogue of *Alciphron: or, The Minute Philosopher*, the bishop launched an attack on the *Fable* which Mandeville seems to have found particularly galling. The same year, and but a few months before his death, Mandeville returned for the last time to the vindication of his book. *A Letter to Dion*, addressed to Berkeley and concerned with answering the particular charges levelled against himself in *Alciphron*, is in many ways the most able and spirited of all Mandeville's defences of *The Fable of the Bees*.

Yet it was no more successful in quieting his enemies than had been his earlier attempts. The chorus of voices raised against the *Fable* continued to swell after Mandeville's death and persisted for the remainder of the century. Though 'Mandevil could prate no more', in the words of *The Dunciad*,[4] the repeated abuse of the man and his book provided a common theme uniting people of various faiths and different schools of thought. Seventy-five years after the appearance of the *Fable* even Gibbon, for all his hostility towards cherished beliefs, could find no greater commendation of William Law, the friend of his family, than that 'on the appearance of the fable of the Bees he drew his pen against the licentious doctrine that private vices are public benefits, and morality as well at Religion', he added, 'must joyn in his applause.'[5]

With such notoriety in his adopted country, it was not long before Mandeville's book became a *cause célèbre* on the Continent as well. It was translated into both French and German and in France it was ordered to be burned by the common hangman. As foreign interest in the *Fable* increased, the attacks multiplied, and by the close of the century allusions to Mandeville had become as common in Continental books as they were in the writings of Englishmen.

Seldom has a satirist earned so much abuse while pursuing his traditional avocation of condemning vice and ridiculing folly. When Mandeville described himself to Berkeley as 'an Author, who dares to expose Vice' and who discloses 'the false Pretences, which are made to Virtue',[6] he spoke no more than the truth, for the pride, hypocrisy, and ineradicable selfishness of his countrymen are a constant burden of *The Fable of the Bees*. But when he went on to complain to the bishop that this was 'the true Cause of the Malice, and all the Clamours against me' and to declare that 'my reprehending, lashing and ridiculing Vice and Insincerity, have procured me infinitely more Enemies than all the pretended Encouragement to Vice and Immorality they can meet with,' he was being less than candid.[7] The role of the moral satirist is akin to that of the preacher, and as long as he is content to denounce vices for violating accepted morality, he can launch his jeremiads as safely from the press as from the pulpit. But this was not Mandeville's method. He condemned not only the vices of pride and hypocrisy which he found all about him, but also some of his countrymen's most cherished beliefs, which, he suggested, were responsible for these vices and represented the principal follies he set out to expose. It was his refusal to accept the conventional norms of the moral satirist and his insistence on substituting others of his own that earned him the enmity of his contemporaries. Most of the complaints against him can be reduced to three charges. By examining each of these separately, we can come to understand Mandeville's position in *The Fable of the Bees*.

THE DEFENCE OF VICE

'Vice and Luxury have found a Champion and a Defender, which they never did before,' John Dennis wrote of Mandeville in 1724.

There have, indeed, been several champions for Infidelity, Champions for Deism, for Arianism, for Socinianism, and for a Thousand Sorts of whimsical and fanatical Enthusiasm: Yet all these Champions have declared loudly for Moral Virtue, and all of them, the Deist only excepted, have declared for Revealed Religion; But a Champion for Vice and Luxury, a serious, a cool, a deliberate Champion, that is a Creature intirely new, and has never been heard of before in any Nation, or any Age of the World.[8]

Setting aside the hyperbole characteristic of 'furious Dennis', as Pope called him in *The Dunciad*, this charge is a common one among Mandeville's critics. It was encouraged by the famous paradox which he adopted in 1714 as the subtitle of the *Fable*, 'Private Vices, Publick Benefits', and which, then as well as now, has been associated with his name by thousands who have never opened *The Fable of the Bees*. But the foundation for this charge was laid nine years earlier in *The Grumbling Hive*, with which we ought to begin.

In his verse fable, Mandeville describes a flourishing beehive which is like the England of his own day in every respect, even to the unique advantage of being 'happily governed by a limited Monarchy'. The most noticeable characteristic of this beehive, or nation, is its addiction to vice, especially to 'Fraud, Luxury, and Pride'. Its population includes, in the first place, large numbers of avowed criminals:

> As Sharpers, Parasites, Pimps, Players,
> Pick-Pockets, Coiners, Quacks, Sooth-Sayers.

But the crimes of such individuals as these, if more open, are hardly less serious than those practised by their more respected neighbours:

> These were called Knaves; but, bar the Name,
> The grave Industrious were the Same.
> All Trades and Places knew some Cheat,
> No Calling was without Deceit.

The lawyers in this kingdom bilk their clients, the physicians are only interested in extorting fees from patients whom they cannot cure, while the clergy, ignorant and lazy, pursue the methods of Tartuffe. Similarly, the merchants defraud their customers, the judges accept bribes, and the ministers of the crown rob the public treasury. Finally, the entire population, without exception, gratify their pride and indulge their appetite for luxury.

Up to a point this sounds very much like any Juvenalian satire that rails against the vices of the age to the applause of all good citizens. But there are several important differences which indicate, from the outset of his career, Mandeville's refusal to adopt conventional satiric norms. In the first place, instead of condemning the bees for their vices, he goes to great lengths to show that the happiness and prosperity of the hive depend directly on these very faults.

> Thus every Part was full of Vice,
> Yet the whole Mass a Paradice,

he declares in a line which was the forerunner of his more famous phrase, 'Private Vices, Publick Benefits'. The explanation for this paradox is that full employment, which is the basis of national prosperity, and a brisk trade, which is necessary to its continuance, are the immediate consequence of immorality. The commission of crime, for example, is responsible for keeping whole multitudes at work : lawyers, gaolers, turnkeys, sergeants, bailiffs, tipstaffs, locksmiths,

> and all those Officers,
> That squeeze a Living out of Tears.

As for the vices of luxury, avarice, prodigality, pride, envy, and vanity displayed by the more respectable members of the community, these promote trade by creating wants which it is the business of merchants, tradesmen, and manufacturers to supply.

Furthermore, the denouement of Mandeville's fable seems at first sight to betray the expectations we bring to a moral fable, in which the vicious are punished for their crimes. Under ordinary circumstances we might expect that the wicked bees, in spite of temporary prosperity, would ultimately come to grief as a result of their numerous sins. But while misfortune does become their lot, this reversal comes about when the knaves are suddenly turned honest. With the ensuing absence of crimes that create employment and of vices that foster trade, the professions decay, commerce dwindles, thousands of unemployed emigrate, and the hive's prosperity comes to an end.

The members of this wicked community do, therefore, become the victims of divine chastisement, but for a totally unexpected reason. These creatures, at the height of their prosperity, have been accustomed to deplore with apparent aversion the vices of the hive from which all of them derive some benefit. 'Good Gods, had we but Honesty!' is the everlasting complaint of this wicked, flourishing, yet grumbling hive. And it is to punish their hypocrisy that

> *Jove*, with Indignation moved,
> At last in Anger swore, he'd rid
> The bawling Hive of Fraud, and did.

Their fate is to have their insincere petition granted and to be forced to accept as a blessing the honest poverty which is their secret aversion. 'Then leave Complaints,' advises the 'Moral' to the poem,

> Fools only strive
> To make a Great an honest Hive.

As Mandeville was to explain later, the satire of *The Grumbling Hive* was written

to expose the Unreasonableness and Folly of those, that desirous of being an opulent and flourishing People, and wonderfully greedy after all the Benefits they can receive as such, are yet always murmuring at and exclaiming against those Vices and Inconveniencies, that from the beginning of the World to this present Day, have been inseparable from all Kingdoms and States that ever were fam'd for Strength, Riches and Politeness at the same time.

In defending the necessity of vice both in *The Grumbling Hive* and in numerous remarks in *The Fable of the Bees*, Mandeville is concerned exclusively with its importance to one particular kind of state. 'What Country soever in the Universe is to be understood by the Bee-Hive represented here,' he explained later, 'it is evident . . . that it must be a large, rich and warlike Nation'; and in the remarks themselves he repeatedly describes this kind of state in such terms as 'a populous, rich, wide, extended Kingdom', 'a large stirring Nation', 'a trading Country'. He is concerned, in other words, with the great world powers of his day and with those economic conditions which 'are requisite to aggrandize and enrich a Nation'. He recognizes another kind of state, however, which he describes in such terms as 'a frugal and honest Society', 'a small, indigent State or Principality', a 'pitiful Commonwealth'. Such countries are exempt from his concern and have no need for the vices he describes. There is considerable justice, therefore, to Mandeville's reiterated assertion that he is not championing vice for its own sake when he insists on its importance to the emerging capitalist economy. If he argues that the economic prosperity of great nations is dependent on the vices of their inhabitants, he avoids expressing any open preference for rich countries over poor ones. He gives the recipe for national greatness without recommending the product.

There are really two different kinds of vice which Mandeville considers inseparable from national prosperity. The first kind, which he describes by the general term 'fraud', receives the greatest emphasis in *The Grumbling Hive*. Most of the vices described there are such 'cheats' as robbery, swindling, extortion, bribery, embezzlement, and other ways of plundering money which, when detected, are regarded as violations of the law. So prevalent is this kind of vice among the bees that the appearance of the single virtue opposed to it, honesty, is sufficient to rid the hive of its evils, but also of its prosperity, since the elimination of so many occupations concerned with the prevention or punishment of dishonesty gives rise to unemployment and subsequent emigration.

By the time he published *The Fable of the Bees*, however, Mandeville seems to have come to consider such crimes as unavoidable evils which accompany prosperity without necessarily promoting it. Only in Remark *G* does he discuss the economic advantages of dishonesty, when he argues that even highwaymen encourage trade by spending lavishly what they have stolen. More often he alludes to such vices as 'Inconveniencies' which are present in every 'great and flourishing Nation'. So in Remark *A* he shows that such socially undesirable occupations as are followed by card-sharpers, pickpockets, and counterfeiters are inevitable in a society large enough to include the lazy and the fickle and varied enough to provide such people with opportunities of gaining a dishonest livelihood. But the consequence need not be anarchy. Even in *The Grumbling Hive* 'Vice is beneficial found' only 'When it's by Justice lopt, and bound.' Let the laws be rigorously enforced and crimes punished with alacrity, Mandeville urges, but do not dream of eradicating the drones to be found in every flourishing hive. Such loathsome vices, he explains in the preface to the *Fable*, are like the dirt and litter that filled the streets of eighteenth-century London. Wise men will bear such inconveniences cheerfully, for

when once they come to consider, that what offends them is the result of the Plenty, great Traffick and Opulency of that mighty City, if they have any Concern in its Welfare, they will hardly ever wish to see the Streets of it less dirty.

A second kind of vice, which receives rather scant attention in *The Grumbling Hive*, is referred to there as 'pride and luxury'. A few stanzas mention its prominence among the bees and the disastrous consequences of its disappearance, but it is overshadowed in the poem by the attention given to fraud and its antithesis, honesty. By the time he came to publish *The Fable of the Bees*, however, Mandeville had arrived at the realization that national greatness depends much less on crime than on other, more prevalent, vices which, while exempt from the law, are condemned by religion. Fully half the remarks in the *Fable* are concerned with this subject. Some, such as Remarks *I*, *K*, and *M*, argue the importance of avarice, prodigality, pride, and similar sins in insuring that the demand for consumer goods will always equal or exceed the supply. Others, such as Remarks *L*, *P*, and *Y*, insist that luxury, although accounted a sin, is responsible for most of the consumption which creates full employment and increases national wealth. Still others, such as Remarks *Q*, *S*, *V*, and *X*, suggest that frugality and the other ascetic virtues are the true enemies of national prosperity to a far greater degree than the honesty which destroyed the opulent hive. 'What I call Vices,' Mandeville was to explain later in *A Letter to Dion*, 'are the Fashionable Ways of Living, the Manners of the Age, that are often practis'd and preach'd against by the same People.'[9] A truly virtuous society, he argues repeatedly in the *Fable*, would be like that of the Spartans: frugal, abstemious, free of pride, luxury, prodigality, and the other vices, but also devoid of every comfort and pleasure that Englishmen have come to regard as no more than their due. Yet where is the man, he asks, who would be willing to pay such a price for virtue, or to forego the public benefits of vice? On every side, men dream of a Golden Age they could never endure for a single day, while they condemn the opulence that provides them with their most precious enjoyments.

Nothing Mandeville had to say on the subject of vice proved as offensive to so many as his identification of luxury with the national interest and his dismissal of frugality as 'an idle dreaming Virtue that employs no Hands, and therefore very useless in a trading Country'. To most of his countrymen luxury was the most glaring example of a private vice which, if it became prevalent, could lead to public disaster. Preachers were fond of reminding their congregations that every previous civilization had been destroyed by the growth of luxury among its citizens; the depravity of the late Roman empire and its subsequent fate offered a lasting reminder of the wages of self-indulgence. But the moralists were not alone in attacking luxury. They received strong support from many economists.

One of the most prominent aspects of the mercantilist

economics which prevailed until the time of Adam Smith was the concern for insuring, through government regulation, a favourable balance of trade with other nations. The economic goal of many mercantilist writers was a state of affairs in which, encouraged by restrictive tariffs, Great Britain would export more of her products to each country with which she traded than she found it expedient to import, so that foreign countries must be forced to make up the deficit with payments of gold and silver. In this hopeful situation the demand for British goods on the world market would be so great as to insure constant production and full employment at home, while at the same time domestic consumption of foreign products would be kept at a minimum, the consequence of which must be a steady annual flow of foreign bullion to British shores and an endless increase of the national wealth.

Some mercantilist writers even dreamt of an ideal market in which the traffic of goods would be all in one direction. 'If we export any value of our manufactures for the consumption of a foreign nation', a writer in *The British Merchant* assured his readers in 1713, 'and import thence no goods at all for our own consumption, it is certain the whole price of our own manufactures exported must be paid to us in money, and that all the money paid to us is our clear gain.'[10]

The theory was an attractive one and it easily lent itself to the attacks on luxury which moralists were accustomed to making. Luxury, they were quick to point out, encouraged a taste for costly delicacies which shunned the simplicity of domestic manufactures in favour of exotic products from foreign lands. Patriotism lent new overtones of disapproval to the word 'luxury' when it was coupled with the epithet 'foreign'. 'Haughty *Chloe*' in *The Grumbling Hive* boasts furniture 'Which th' *Indies* had been ransack'd for.' The wants of the fastidious must be supplied by contributions from every quarter of the globe, like the 'various Off'rings of the World' displayed on Belinda's dressing table in *The Rape of the Lock*, published the same year as *The Fable of the Bees*:

> This Casket *India*'s glowing Gems unlocks,
> And all *Arabia* breathes from yonder Box.
> The Tortoise here and Elephant unite,
> Transform'd to *Combs*, the speckled and the white.[11]

A nation of Chloes and Belindas, satisfying their own taste for luxury at the expense of the nation's economy, must jeopardize the favourable balance of trade by their insatiable demand for foreign products. The sanctions against luxury, like the rewards of frugality, were apparently economic as well as moral.

Mandeville, however, has nothing but contempt for the popular notion that economics and morality are natural allies. 'Religion is one thing and Trade is another', he declares in 'A Search into the Nature of Society'. So far are these two from any harmonious alliance that they actually contradict each other. The ideals proclaimed by religion and morality, he insists in Remark *Q*, would, if adopted, produce a 'State of slothful Ease and stupid Innocence' incompatible with national prosperity, since 'all the Cardinal Virtues together won't so much as procure a tolerable Coat or a Porridge Pot among 'em'. It is a popular fallacy, he points out in Remark *M*, to suppose 'that without Pride or Luxury, the same things might be eat, wore, and consumed, the same number of Handicrafts and Artificers employ'd, and a Nation be every way as flourishing as where those Vices are the most predominant.' A people must choose between moral virtue and economic greatness, Mandeville insists without presuming to direct their choice, and having decided in favour of one alternative, they ought not to lament the absence of the other.

Introduction

The mistake of the bullionists who condemn foreign luxury in hopes of achieving a favourable balance of trade, Mandeville argues in Remark *L*, is that they expect other nations to tolerate an unfavourable balance of trade with Great Britain which would soon lead them to national bankruptcy. No country can long afford to trade with the British at a disadvantage, paying with gold and silver for what they import because the British refuse to reciprocate by importing an equal number of foreign products. Faced with such a situation they must inevitably abandon the British market and turn to other nations which are willing to trade with them on equal terms. 'Buying is Bartering,' he reminds his readers,

and no Nation can buy Goods of others that has none of her own to purchase them with. . . . We know that we could not long continue to purchase the Goods of other Nations, if they would not take our Manufactures in Payment for them; and why should we judge otherwise of other Nations?

In rejecting the ideal of a favourable balance of trade, however, Mandeville does not abandon the mercantilist belief in the importance of government intervention. If a favourable balance of trade is impracticable, in his view, an unfavourable balance would create a gold drain which would be disastrous. To avoid such a calamity, the government must carefully regulate commerce by means of tariff laws.

Good Politicians, by dextrous Management, laying heavy Impositions on some Goods, or totally prohibiting them, and lowering the Duties on others, may always turn and divert the course of Trade which way they please,

he writes in Remark *L*.

But above all, they'll keep a watchful Eye over the Ballance of Trade in general, and never suffer that all the Foreign

Commodities together that are imported in one Year, shall exceed in value what of their own Growth or Manufacture is in the same exported to others.

To Mandeville, then, the balance of trade is as vital a matter of government concern as it is to the bullionist, but he attaches a different meaning to the term. It is not an excess in favour of exports by which Great Britain is left with a credit balance at the end of the year, but an equilibrium of trade between the British and their foreign customers. On these terms, the more his countrymen import from abroad, the more their neighbours can afford to buy from them; trade will increase and prosperity will follow. As long as

the Imports are never allow'd to be superior to the Exports, no Nation can ever be impoverish'd by Foreign Luxury; and they may improve it as much as they please, if they can but in proportion raise the Fund of their own that is to purchase it.

Mandeville's belief in the importance of government intervention is not limited, however, to the regulation of trade. 'Trade is the Principal, but not the only Requisite to aggrandize a Nation', he points out in the same remark. 'There are other Things to be taken Care of besides.' Here, as well as in Remarks *Q* and *Y*, he is careful to explain that the economic benefits to be derived from private vices are not a matter of spontaneous growth but of careful pruning. It is the care of the legislator and the vigilance of the magistrate that 'make a People potent, renown'd and flourishing'. Those vices which promote the prosperity of the nation must be condoned and encouraged. Others which need proper direction must be diverted into such channels as insure the maximum economic benefit for all. Still others, which grow into crimes and threaten harm to the community, must be rigorously discouraged and severely punished. But in all these cases the criteria of the politician must be those of economics and national policy rather than of religion and morality.

THE DISPARAGEMENT OF VIRTUE

'The Province you have chosen for your self,' William Law declared to Mandeville in 1726,

is to deliver Man from the *Sagacity* of Moralists, the Encroachments of Virtue, and to re-place him in the Rights and Privileges of Brutality; to recall him from the giddy Heights of rational Dignity, and Angelick likeness, to go to Grass, or wallow in the Mire.[12]

This charge that he denies mankind its most estimable qualities, virtue and reason, and tries to reduce it to the level of the beasts was frequently raised against Mandeville by hostile critics. The accusation does not refer to the stand he takes against such virtues as honesty and frugality which he finds detrimental to the economic well-being of a trading country. It was occasioned instead by a second thesis of Mandeville's which did not originate in *The Grumbling Hive*, but in 'An Enquiry into the Origin of Moral Virtue', the essay which stands alongside his earlier poem at the beginning of *The Fable of the Bees*.

Although the title of the book implies that it is concerned exclusively with the theme of *The Grumbling Hive*, this second thesis is equally important in the *Fable*, for it is the subject not only of the 'Enquiry' but of some of the remarks as well. All of the remarks are ostensibly notes to *The Grumbling Hive*, of course, and each of them is headed by a verse taken from the poem; but Mandeville has two ways of converting some of them into commentaries on the 'Enquiry' whenever it suits his convenience. In Remarks *N*, *O*, and *R* he employs the method of selecting a verse containing some word ('envy', 'pleasures', or 'honour') which he promptly extracts from its original context in the poem and uses as the subject of an essay related to the thesis of the 'Enquiry'. In Remarks *C* and *T* he uses another method of beginning with a brief commentary on some verse of the poem and then suddenly digressing into an essay which brings him back to the 'Enquiry'. Although such remarks are few in number they are among the longest in the book, occupying, in fact, half the space devoted to the remarks, so that the 'Enquiry' receives fully as much attention in the *Fable* as does *The Grumbling Hive*.

In this other part of *The Fable of the Bees* Mandeville continues to explore the benefits of vice, but in a different context. Instead of considering the economic advantages of vice to large, rich, and war-like nations as opposed to small, indigent communities, he is interested here in its use to any 'Civil Society, where Men are become taught Animals and great numbers of them have by mutual compact framed themselves into a Body Politick,' as distinct from the state of nature. 'All untaught Animals,' he begins his 'Enquiry', 'are only Sollicitous of pleasing themselves, and naturally follow the bent of their own Inclinations, without consider-ing the good or harm that from their being pleased will accrue to others.' Man is the most instinctively selfish of all animals, and therefore the least naturally sociable; yet he is also the most teachable and can therefore be made fit for society by education. His selfish passions are too powerful to be subdued by reason, it is true, but since they are not all of equal vigour, his weaker passions can be overcome by those which are stronger. The business of the moralist is to render man sociable by playing off his passions against each other.

The most inveterate of man's passions is his pride, and therefore his pursuit of honour is insatiable, while he will go to any length to avoid shame. If men are to be made fit for society they must learn to associate selfishness with shame and the pursuit of the public interest with honour.

Hence 'the Moralists and Philosophers of all Ages' invented the distinction between vice and virtue. They pursuaded their fellow men

to call every thing, which, without Regard to the Publick, Man should commit to gratify any of his Appetites, VICE; if in that Action there could be observ'd the least prospect, that it might either be injurious to any of the Society, or ever render himself less serviceable to others: And to give the Name of VIRTUE to every Performance, by which Man, contrary to the impulse of Nature, should endeavour the Benefit of others, or the Conquest of his own Passions, out of a Rational Ambition of being good.

Observing that those who were public-spirited and given the name of virtuous were held up to honour and praise while those who were selfish and labelled vicious were the objects of shame and detestation, men were forced by pride to curb their predatory impulses. Thus mankind owes its sociable qualities, Mandeville writes, not to nature, but to

the skilful Management of wary Politicians; and the nearer we search into human Nature, the more we shall be convinc'd, that the Moral Virtues are the Political Offspring which Flattery begot upon Pride.

'This was (or at least might have been) the manner after which Savage Man was broke,' he concludes. But he is less interested in speculating on the origin of society than in examining the degree to which, in his own day, civilized man is moved by new combinations of the same passions found in his savage state, and is no more swayed by reason now than in his former condition. Repeatedly Mandeville examines supposedly virtuous actions in which a man seems to 'endeavour the Benefit of others, or the Conquest of his own Passions, out of a Rational Ambition of being good' and shows that in reality they are only what he calls 'counterfeited' virtues because they were undertaken out of

self interest in order to indulge whatever passion was upper-
most at the moment. A soldier shows bravery under fire not
because his reason has mastered his fear, but because his
fear of shame is greater than his fear of death. The man
who saves 'an Innocent Babe ready to drop into the Fire'
obliges only himself, 'for to have seen it fall, and not strove
to hinder it, would have caused a Pain' which his self-
preservation compelled him to prevent. A man relieves a
beggar because his importunities are an annoyance which
can be most readily stopped with a coin. 'Thus thousands
give Money to Beggars from the same motive as they pay
their Corn-cutter, to walk Easy.' And so with all the other
supposedly virtuous actions Mandeville examines. None is
completely distinterested nor immune from some powerful
passion.

He is not suggesting, of course, that all human conduct
is vicious. None of the actions just described is 'injurious
to any of the Society' or renders the man who performs
them 'less serviceable to others'. Quite the contrary, in fact.
But if they deserve no blame, neither do they merit praise,
since those who performed them were only interested in
serving themselves. 'All this I have nothing against,' he ob-
serves in Remark *O*, 'but I see no Self denial, without which
there can be no Virtue.' Yet in revealing the 'Contradiction
in the Frame of Man' in whom 'the Theory of Virtue is so
well understood, and the Practice of it so rarely to be met
with', a discrepancy noticed by most moralists, Mandeville
parts company with the preacher by refusing to urge men
to greater effort. If they scarcely ever attain the lofty heights
they have been taught to aspire to, he suggests, this is be-
cause moral virtue is an impracticable ideal at odds with
human nature. It was inevitable that his attitude should
provoke most of his contemporaries, for it managed to
offend at the same time two schools of Christian moralists,
although for different reasons.

The older and more rigorous of these traditions was Mandeville's original target when he published the first edition of *The Fable of the Bees* in 1714. 'Most of the ancient Philosophers and grave Moralists, especially the Stoicks,' he pointed out, had condemned the passions as the source of discontent and had 'placed true Happiness in the calm Serenity of a contented Mind free from Guilt and Ambition; a Mind, that, having subdued every sensual Appetite, despises the Smiles as well as Frowns of Fortune.' The theory, subject to one important modification, had proved congenial to many Christian moralists. They agreed with the Stoics in condemning the passions, portrayed them as sinful appetites which are the legacy of fallen nature, and stressed the importance of bringing them under the control of reason. But, mindful of the dangers of Pelagianism, they insisted that reason was powerless to subdue the unruly passions without the assistance of religion. Aided by divine grace, the Christian could reduce his appetites to the government of reason and attain virtue. 'All our heady and disordered affections, which are the secret factors of sin and Satan', wrote Bishop Hall, the 'English Seneca' of the preceding century, 'must be restrained by a strong and yet temperate command of Reason and Religion.' The truly valiant Christian, he declared, 'is the master of himselfe, and subdues his passions to reason; and by this inward victory workes his owne peace.'[13]

Mandeville's quarrel with the pagan and Christian Stoics is not against their estimate of the passions. Both sides agree that these appetites are selfish and turbulent. What he rejects is the notion that men's passions can ever be controlled by reason, a weak and ineffectual faculty, in his view, which is no match against such sturdy rebels. 'I believe Man', he wrote in the 'Introduction' to *The Fable of the Bees*, 'to be a Compound of various Passions, that all of them, as they are provoked and come uppermost, govern him by turns, whether he will or no.' What is notably absent from this picture of human behaviour is the 'Rational Ambition of being good' which is an essential criterion for virtuous action according to the rigorists. 'Reason is our universal law, that obliges us in all places, and at all times,' Mandeville's antagonist William Law wrote in *A Serious Call to a Devout and Holy Life*, 'and no actions have any honour, but so far as they are instances of our obedience to reason.'[14] If that is the case, Mandeville replies, your virtue is a chimera of the imagination, demanding reason where there is only passion.

He was not alone in rejecting such rigoristic views. Many Christians of Mandeville's day rebelled against the dispassionate severity of moralists who preached an asceticism which was felt to be inconsistent with humanity. 'For two years I have been preaching after the model of your two practical treatises,' Wesley protested to Law in 1738, 'and all that heard have allowed that the law is great, wonderful, and holy. But no sooner did they attempt to fulfil it but they found that it is too high for man.'[15] The tradition which has come to be known as benevolism began long before the rise of Methodism, however. Since the middle of the seventeenth century Latitudinarian clergymen of the Church of England had been preaching this pleasant doctrine, and it had already gained wide popularity by the time *The Fable of the Bees* appeared. Reacting against the severities of Christian Stoicism, such churchmen insisted that the truly good man is not a coldly righteous individual who stifles his affections but one whose feelings spontaneously solicit him to virtue. 'Our Reason has but little to do in the forming of our minds, and bringing us to a Vertuous Religious Life,' wrote Bishop Hickman, a contemporary of Mandeville's, ' 'tis our Passions and Affections that must do the work.'[16]

Such a view, of course, is based on a very different estimate of the passions than the one we have been examining. These churchmen strongly reacted against the doctrine of total depravity which pictures human feelings as so many sinful appetites. Even worse, in their view, was Hobbes's attempt to reduce all human motivation to selfish passions directed toward our own gratification. Instead, they taught that man is naturally inclined to live in society and endowed with benevolent feelings towards his fellow creatures. The famous Isaac Barrow spoke for many of his church when he referred to

that general sympathy which naturally intercedes between all men, since we can neither see, nor hear of, nor imagine another's grief, without being afflicted ourselves. Antipathies may be natural to wild beasts; but to rational creatures they are wholly unnatural.[17]

The idea that man's sociableness arises from his natural feelings awakened a ready response among Englishmen and was propagated by the third Earl of Shaftesbury, who died the year before *The Fable of the Bees* made its initial appearance.

Mandeville did not respond to benevolism at first. His attention in 1714 was wholly taken up by his crusade against rigorism for exalting reason and emphasizing the conquest of the passions. A few years later, however, he read Shaftesbury's *Characteristics*, and when he added new essays and remarks to the *Fable* in 1723 it was clear that he had found a new target. 'The Generality of Moralists and Philosophers,' he begins 'A Search into the Nature of Society',

have hitherto agreed that there could be no Virtue without Self-denial, but a late Author, who is now much Read by Men of Sense is of a contrary Opinion, and imagines that Men without any trouble or violence upon themselves may be Naturally Virtuous.

This author's mistake is not that of the rigorists, who advocate an asceticism beyond human capacity, but it is just as great an error. 'This Noble Writer,' he explains,

(for it is the Lord *Shaftsbury* I mean in his Characteristicks) Fancies, that as Man is made for Society, so he ought to be born with a kind Affection to the whole, of which he is a part, and a propensity to seek the Welfare of it.

To be virtuous, he need only indulge his benevolent feelings.

Without modifying in any way the analysis of human behaviour he had presented nine years earlier in his 'Enquiry', Mandeville could now argue that men's actions are no more virtuous by the standards of the benevolist than by those of the rigorist. The newer ethics had rejected obedience to reason, which was the criterion of virtuous behaviour for Christian Stoics, and replaced it with disinterested feeling as the essential ingredient. Let a man 'in any particular, act ever so well,' Shaftesbury writes in the *Characteristics*,

if at the bottom it be that selfish affection alone which moves him, he is in himself still vicious. Nor can any creature be considered otherwise when the passion towards self-good, though ever so moderate, is his real motive in the doing that to which a natural affection for his kind ought by right to have inclined him.[18]

On those terms, Mandeville replies, all men must be vicious, for they are always and everywhere motivated by self-esteem.

As he clearly recognized, benevolism posed a more serious threat to his central thesis than rigorism; indeed, 'two Systems cannot be more opposite than his Lordship's and mine'. For if men are naturally sociable, civil societies are a spontaneous outgrowth of men's deepest instincts, whereas Mandeville insists that they are artful contrivances shaped from the most unlikely materials. His famous paradox applies in fact to men's social as well as their economic condition. It is from his vices of pride and self-love, man's most hateful and destructive qualities, that politicians have laboriously constructed a congenial society. 'The Power and Sagacity as well as Labour and Care of the Politician in civilising the Society,' Mandeville writes in Remark *N*,

> has been no where more conspicuous, than in the Happy Contrivance of playing our Passions against one another. By flattering our Pride and still encreasing the good Opinion we have of our selves on the one hand; and inspiring us on the other with a superlative Dread and mortal Aversion against Shame, the Artful Moralists have taught us chearfully to encounter ourselves, and if not subdue, at least so to conceal and disguise

these passions that we can live in harmony with each other.

The two theses of *The Fable of the Bees* are therefore really two angles of vision from which Mandeville considers the same problem. Considered as an economic state or as a civil society, it is the same Leviathan which the art of the governor has fashioned from discordant elements. This is the true sense, to which he returned in his final sentence, of 'the seeming Paradox, the Substance of which is advanc'd in the Title Page; that Private Vices by the dextrous Management of a skilful Politician may be turn'd into Publick Benefits'.

THE ATTACK ON CHARITY SCHOOLS

'The first Impression of the Fable of the Bees, which came out in 1714, was never carpt at, or publickly taken Notice of,' Mandeville wrote in his 'Vindication of the Book',

and all the Reason I can think on why this Second Edition should be so unmercifully treated, tho' it has many Precautions which the former wanted, is an Essay on Charity and Charity-Schools, which is added to what was printed before.

When the avalanche of attacks on the *Fable* began in 1723, they certainly were not addressed to this particular essay alone. But Mandeville may have been right in suggesting that it was his attack on the charity schools which triggered public reaction, for in this essay he assaulted an institution, more cherished than any system of ethics, in which a large sector of the British public had made a financial as well as an emotional investment.

What Mandeville called 'the Enthusiastick Passion for Charity-Schools' was one of those phenomena in which an entire nation eagerly adopts some project which it supports for a generation or two before turning its attention to a more novel interest. It began in the closing years of the seventeenth century, caught the public imagination at once, and had reached the peak of its success just at the moment Mandeville published his essay attacking it. The movement was popularly regarded as a panacea for the vice and destitution to which the children of the dependent poor were bred in eighteenth-century Britain. A large and growing population existing on marginal incomes were unable to support their numerous children, who were suffered to run the streets when they did not become a charge upon the parish. Bred up to no useful occupation and deprived of religious instruction, many turned to beggary and stealing, becoming an economic burden as well as a moral scandal to the rest of the nation.

The charity schools were designed to alleviate the sufferings of these children while instilling sound habits of religion and morality. Between the ages of seven and twelve or fourteen, they were fed and clothed by these institutions, drilled in their prayers and the church catechism, taught to read the Bible and *The Whole Duty of Man*, and given the rudiments of writing sufficient for copying passages from the Scriptures. On leaving the school they were apprenticed to some trade or entered service in a household. The immediate benefits expected from this course of instruction concerned the children's religious welfare, but economic advantages could be expected to follow also. A child who had acquired habits of sober diligence and honest effort from a charity school would not only escape the fate of Hogarth's Idle 'Prentice, but might be expected to reap some of the earthly rewards of his Industrious 'Prentice.

A typical charity school of the early eighteenth century was founded and maintained by the spontaneous enthusiasm of the members of a parish, who retained local management of the institution while following guide lines provided by the Society for Promoting Christian Knowledge. Unlike other foundations the charity schools did not enjoy an endowment and were supported by voluntary subscriptions from the parish members. The precarious means by which they were financed was actually one of the reasons for their popularity. Thousands of middle-class Englishmen who were in no position to endow a hospital or found a college could become one of the benefactors of a charity school at comparatively little cost. The broad basis of support for these institutions became a matter for frequent congratulation, testifying to the benevolent feelings of eighteenth-century Englishmen. Addison, writing in the *Guardian*, thought charity schools 'the glory of the age we live in',[19] while Steele in the *Spectator* proclaimed them 'the greatest Instances of publick Spirit the Age has produced'.[20]

For Mandeville, on the other hand, the charity school movement offered a practical application of both the theses of *The Fable of the Bees*. In the first place, the public spirit and open-handed charity supposedly inspiring the movement were to him a perfect example of self-interest masquerading behind counterfeited virtue. 'Pride and Vanity have built more Hospitals than all the Virtues together', he declares, and the same egoistic passions are 'the real Source of this present Folly' of charity schools. The conducting of these institutions satisfies the 'strong Inclination to Govern' found in all men at the same time that it offers them the opportunity to appear charitable at small expense to their purses or their private passions. Secondly, the charity-school movement was to Mandeville an egregious instance of the meddlesome interference of religion and morality in the affairs of economics which he everywhere deplored.

It was a common maxim of eighteenth-century mercantilism that people are the riches of a nation. By 'people' was meant the working poor, and by 'riches' the national wealth to which they contributed by their labour without receiving any considerable dividend in return. The more labourers there were in a nation, the more products manufactured; the more products, the greater the trade and the higher the profits. But a flourishing trade and large profits depended on the ability of manufacturers to keep their costs as low as possible. The mercantilists envisioned, therefore, a dense population of labourers who would be fully employed, but employed at the lowest possible wages so that their products could be offered at a competitive price on the foreign market.

The promoters of the charity-school movement had no intention of interfering with this system. Their purpose was not to rescue their charges from the necessitous condition into which they had been born, but to give them a religious upbringing which would reconcile them with their continued poverty. 'There must be drudges of labour (hewers of wood and drawers of water the Scriptures call them) as well as Counsellers to direct, and Rulers to preside,' the Bishop of Norwich preached in a charity-school sermon.

These poor children are born to be daily labourers, for the most part to earn their bread by the sweat of their brows. It is evident then that if such children are, by charity, brought up in a manner that is only proper to qualify them for a rank to which they ought not to aspire, such a child would be injurious to the Community.[21]

But no such outcome need be feared from the charity schools, whose products, rendered religious and obedient by their careful training, would cheerfully return to take up the hard lot for which nature had intended them.

To Mandeville, however, the hard economic necessity that demands a large working force in a trading nation was totally at odds with the 'unreasonable Vein of Petty Reverence for the Poor' running through the charity-school movement. 'In a Free Nation where Slaves are not allow'd of,' he agrees with the other mercantilist writers, 'the surest wealth consists in a multitude of Laborious Poor.' But while his countrymen were paying lip service to this maxim, they were busily contradicting it as they increased the number of charity schools.

Going to School in comparison to Working is Idleness, and the longer Boys continue in this easy sort of Life, the more unfit they'll be when grown up for downright Labour.

A child who has been taught to read and write will no longer be willing to undertake the 'Abundance of hard and dirty Labour' that must be done. The consequence must be an artificial overstocking of trades and a dearth of common labourers. Where the supply of necessary labour is scarce, wages must rise and foreign trade, the basis of national prosperity, decline. The 'two Engines' by which labour is made cheap, Mandeville writes, are 'discouraging Idleness' among the poor and 'bringing them up in Ignorance'. Where this is the case 'we must infallibly out-sell our Neighbours; and at the same time encrease our Numbers.

This is the Noble and Manly way of encountring the Rivals of our Trade, and by dint of Merit outdoing them at Foreign, Markets.' But the supporters of charity schools, like the foolish bees in *The Grumbling Hive*, have forgotten these truths and are pursuing economic disaster under the names of morality and religion.

THE SATIRE AGAINST HUMAN FOLLY

Some awareness of these matters of controversy between Mandeville and his contemporaries is necessary in order to understand *The Fable of the Bees* in its historical setting. It will not account, however, for the unmistakable appeal the book has for Mandeville's modern readers. The economic, ethical, and social theories Mandeville took for granted were not noticeably more enlightened than those of his contemporaries whom he attacked. He was no Bacon leading an assault on old-fashioned ideas in the name of progress. He accepted far more of the mercantilist economics of his time than he ever criticized, and his ethical attitudes look backwards to Hobbes and Bayle more often than they anticipate the moral philosophy of a later day. On social questions Mandeville was no liberal or humanitarian, and his attitude towards the poor was sometimes considered harsh even by the rough standards of his contemporaries. He took for granted a class society in which 'some Body must do the work' while another enjoys the fruits of his inferior's labour. He considered the poor a shiftless and idle lot who would work only intermittently if their wages ever rose above the level of mere subsistence to provide them with a discretionary income. He neither foresaw the welfare state nor would have welcomed the prospect if he had. In all these respects he was a man of his age and cannot claim—nor would he seek—the honours of a social reformer such as William Wilberforce or Hannah More.

Mandeville's true genius appears in his role as a critical, rather than a constructive, thinker. His uncompromising realism led him to adopt a tactic of exposure whose effectiveness owes less to his own economic and ethical theories than to his eye for the vulnerability of those he is attacking. He insisted that societies, like individuals, must make hard choices between clearly understood alternatives, and he noticed with amusement that most men have neither the intelligence to recognize their options nor the courage to sacrifice some of them in the course of adopting others. His repeated theme of human inconsistency—'the Contradiction in the Frame of Man'—expresses his recognition of a perennial human weakness temporarily embodied in those visions of a society both prosperous and virtuous, of human conduct entirely free of selfish passions, and of a panacea offered by the charity schools to which the men of his own time and place had succumbed. But his manner of exposing these contemporary expressions of age-old folly was not so much by dispassionate argument as by irony and ridicule. His opponents, encumbered by their heavy armour, were no match for a derisive satirist who exclaimed: 'Oh! the mighty Prize we have in view for all our Self-denial! can any Man be so serious as to abstain from Laughter?' But the same strategy that drove his contemporaries to distraction has become a source of enjoyment for later readers.

Mandeville's remarkable talent as a satirist emerges as fully in the prose remarks and essays as in the little poem at the beginning of *The Fable of the Bees*. They show him turning from verse to prose, not in order to abandon satire, but to exploit it with greater freedom. And there is scarcely a page of the *Fable* where those talents are not displayed in profuse variety. If he introduces a simile with an air of innocence, the effect is sudden deflation. So honour among great families, he explains in Remark *R*, 'is like the Gout, generally counted Hereditary, and all Lords Children are born with it'. Or in Remark *K* he sets out to 'compare the Body Politick (I confess the Simile is very low) to a Bowl of Punch' and continues for several pages, finding some equivalent in society for each ingredient:

I could compare the gaudy Trimming and splendid Equipage of a profuse Beau, to the glistning brightness of the finest Loaf Sugar; for as the one by correcting the sharpness prevents the injuries which a gnawing Sower might do to the Bowels, so the other is a pleasing Balsam that heals and makes amends for the smart, which the Multitude always suffers from the Gripes of the Avaricious; whilst the substances of both melt away alike, and they consume themselves by being beneficial to the several Compositions they belong to.

If Mandeville introduces an example to illustrate his thesis, it soon assumes dimensions of its own. It may become a vivid portrait, as in his characters of the 'cholerick City Captain', the 'beardless Ensign', and the 'wealthy Parson' in Remark *M*, of the 'worldly minded, voluptuous and ambitious Man' in Remark *O*, or of a 'Man of Honour' in Remark *R*. Just as often his example takes the form of a delightful anecdote, as those of Decio and Alcander, the two merchants in Remark *B*, of the unlucky highwayman in Remark *G*, of Florio and Cornaro in Remark *I*, and those of the two lazy sisters, the gentleman and the porter, and the idle man and his Uncle Gripe which follow one another in Remark *V*. At other time Mandeville will spend whole pages relating an amusing apologue, like the fable of the Roman merchant and the lion in Remark *P*, or the parable of small beer he tells in Remark *T*.

These are all instances of the narrative skill Mandeville could command for the purpose of his satire. But his dramatic talents are just as great. Although he is writing as an essayist, he makes frequent use of a device, as old as Horace, of imagining an interruption by an angry reader

or a meddlesome bystander. So, in Remark *G*, the apologist
for gin must be heard, while in Remark *T* an indignant
epicure suddenly interrupts him to defend the teachings of
Lord Shaftesbury. Sometimes his adversary is not easily
silenced and a lively dialogue ensues, as when Mrs Abigail
breaks into his discourse on the clergy in Remark *O* to cry:
'You unconscionable Wretch, with all your Suppositions
and Self denials!' But perhaps his dramatic talents are best
displayed in those 'Scenes of low Life' he delights in draw-
ing, such as the conversation between the 'spruce Mercer'
and a female customer in 'A Search into the Nature of
Society' or the skit, full of lively dialogue, in which he
portrays the various members of a parish going about the
establishment of a charity school.

These last are only a few of the 'digressions' Mandeville
enjoys introducing with a mock apology, begging 'my
Serious Reader that he would for a while abate a little of
his Gravity' or asking

pardon of my Reader for the tiresom Dance I am going to
lead him if he intends to follow me, and therefore I desire that
he would either throw away the Book and leave me, or else
arm himself with the Patience of *Job* to endure all the Imperti-
nencies of Low Life, the Cant and Tittle Tattle he is like to meet
with before he can go half a Street's length.

These digressions offer oblique support to his argument,
but they are also instances of Mandeville's incorrigible
playfulness, like the 'foolish Trifle' in 'An Essay on Charity
and Charity-Schools' where he allows his fancy full play in
imagining the vengeance he can expect if he succeeds in
banishing charity schools: he will be 'stuck full of useless
Penknives up to the Hilts', buried alive under 'a great
heap of Primers and spelling-Books', 'bruised to Death in
a Paper Mill', drowned in ink, and finally 'pelted and
knock'd o' the head with little squat Bibles clasp'd in
Brass and ready arm'd for Mischief'.

Introduction

If Mandeville was a philosopher, he was one like Dr Johnson's old school fellow Edwards, for whom 'cheerfulness was always breaking in'. Such an author cannot be judged solely on his merits as an economist or a moralist. Mandeville was the contemporary of Swift as well as Shaftesbury and the mention of his work should bring to mind the first of these writers as well as the second. Whatever its other claims on our attention, *The Fable of the Bees* is an outstanding ornament of the greatest age of English satire.

Notes to the Introduction

1 *Honour, a Poem* (London, 1743).
2 *The Journal of the Rev. John Wesley*, ed. Nehemiah Curnock (London, 1909–16), IV, 157 (entry for 14 April 1756).
3 *The Character of the Times Delineated* (London, 1732).
4 Bk II, l. 414.
5 *Memoirs of My Life*, ed. Georges A. Bonnard (London, 1966), p. 22.
6 *A Letter to Dion* (London, 1732), p. 8.
7 ibid., p. 36.
8 *Vice and Luxury Publick Mischiefs* (London, 1724), pp. xvi–xvii.
9 *Letter to Dion*, p. 31.
10 *The British Merchant*, 3rd edn (London, 1748), 1, 28. Quoted by Jacob Viner in *Studies in the Theory of International Trade* (New York and London, 1937), where the reader can find a full account of mercantilist views on the balance of trade.
11 Canto I, ll. 133–6.
12 *Remarks upon a Late Book, Entituled, The Fable of the Bees*, 3rd edn (London, 1726), p. 6.
13 *Heaven upon Earth and Characters of Vertues and Vices*, ed. Rudolf Kirk (New Brunswick, New Jersey, 1948), pp. 100 and 154. Christian rigorism was no longer as prevalent in the England of Mandeville's time, however, as it was on the Continent. For a persuasive argument that Mandeville was chiefly responding to Continental rigorism, especially French Jansenism, see Jacob Viner's illuminating introduction to the Augustan Reprint Society's facsimile edition of *A Letter to Dion* (Los Angeles, 1953).
14 *A Serious Call to a Devout and Holy Life*, ed. J. V. Moldenhawer (Philadelphia, 1948), p. 352.

15 *The Letters of John Wesley*, ed. John Telford (London, 1931), I, 239 (14 May 1738).

16 Charles Hickman, *Fourteen Sermons* (London, 1700), p. 272. Quoted by R. S. Crane in 'Suggestions toward a Genealogy of the "Man of Feeling"', *ELH, a Journal of English Literary History*, I (1934), 205–30, where the origins of benevolism are traced in full.

17 *Theological Works* (London, 1830), II, 141.

18 'An Inquiry concerning Virtue or Merit', *Characteristics*, ed. John M. Robertson (London, 1900), I, 249.

19 *Guardian* No. 105 (11 July 1713).

20 *Spectator* No. 294 (6 February 1712).

21 *A Sermon Preached by the Bishop of Norwich at the Anniversary Meeting of the Charity Schools in and about London and Westminster* (London, 1755). Quoted by M. G. Jones in *The Charity School Movement* (Cambridge, 1938), where the reader can find an excellent account of the subject.

The Text of the Present Edition

In this edition I have tried to offer a text which preserves as faithfully as possible Mandeville's spelling and punctuation and at the same time represents his final intention as to its wording. Since none of the editions in his lifetime or later aims at both these ideals, I have had to construct an eclectic text instead of presenting a facsimile of any extant edition.

Eighteenth-century compositors were allowed considerable freedom in altering the accidentals of a manuscript (spelling, punctuation, italicization and use of capitals) to suit their own taste or that of their printing house. The first edition of a book, set from the author's manuscript, can be expected to preserve a certain proportion of the author's characteristic spelling and punctuation along with modifications introduced by the compositor. Each successive edition, however, being normally set from a copy of the previous edition, introduces further modifications by the next compositor, so that the proportion of accidentals for which the author was responsible grows less with each reprinting. The first edition, therefore, while not an entirely faithful facsimile of what the author wrote, reproduces the general texture of his writing more closely than any reprint.

Compositors of the eighteenth century were fairly scrupulous, on the other hand, in trying to follow the actual wording of their author. The presence of a number of important substantive variants (substitution, addition, or deletion of words) in a later edition, therefore, is evidence usually of the author's revision. These variants represent for the most part deliberate alterations in the text which the

47

author wished to have included in future editions, although a few will be errors for which the compositor was unwittingly responsible. Any modern editor, then, who aims at preserving the general texture of the author's manuscript along with his final revisions must adopt the first edition as his copy text and incorporate into this text all substantive variants from later editions for which the author can be assumed to have been responsible. The task is compounded for Mandeville's editor, however, by the fact that *The Fable of the Bees* grew by stages over a period of nearly twenty years, so that no single edition is the 'first edition' of the entire book.

The Grumbling Hive was first published in 1705 and a pirated edition of no textual authority appeared the same year. I have used the Bodleian Library copy of the genuine first edition as my copy text for this poem as well as for the verses from the poem which appear at the head of each remark (and on three occasions in the body of the remarks as well). *The Fable of the Bees* was first published in 1714 and a second edition, which is a page-for-page reprint of the first, appeared the same year. Besides reprinting the poem, the first edition included 'The Preface', 'The Introduction', 'An Enquiry into the Origin of Moral Virtue', and twenty of the remarks. For all these prose pieces my copy text has been the Ashley Library copy of the first edition, now in the British Museum. The 'second edition' (really the third) appeared in 1723. Besides reprinting the material in the first edition from a copy of that edition, it included the following new material set from manuscript: Remarks N and T in their entirety, all but the first paragraph of Remarks G and Y, the greater part of Remark C as well as a paragraph in Remark L, 'An Essay on Charity and Charity-Schools', 'A Search into the Nature of Society', and the 'Index'. My copy text for this new material has been the Harvard University Library copy of the 1723 edition. The 'third edition' (really the fourth) appeared in 1724 and besides reprinting all the previous material from a copy of the 1723 edition included two new pages to 'The Preface' as well as the 'Vindication of the Book'. Since the addition to 'The Preface' was set from manuscript, I have taken this from a copy of the 1724 edition in my possession. The 'Vindication', however, while new to *The Fable of the Bees*, was set from a separate pamphlet which was in turn a reprint of material in the *Evening Post* for 11 July 1723 ('Presentment of the Grand Jury') and in the *London Journal* for 27 July 1723 ('Letter to Lord C.') and 10 August 1723 (Mandeville's letter of defence). I have therefore used copies of these issues in the Burney Collection, British Museum, as the copy text for the 'Vindication'.

Besides adding all this new material to the editions of 1714, 1723, and 1724, Mandeville in each case made substantial revisions in the parts which had been previously published, adding, deleting, and substituting words, phrases, and entire sentences. Although he did not add any new material to the next edition, 1725, he must have been responsible for introducing further revisions into the text, for the nature and frequency of the substantive variants in this edition can only be explained as due to the intervention of the author. The remaining editions of the *Fable* which appeared in his lifetime, those of 1728, 1729, and 1732 (set from a copy of the 1728 edition) were not, however, revised by Mandeville. These three editions contain far fewer substantive variants than any of the previous editions and all of them can be easily ascribed to the compositor. I have therefore ignored these three editions, while introducing into the text of the present edition all substantive variants from the editions of 1714, 1723, 1724, and 1725 which can be reasonably assumed to be authoritative, but omitting a few variants in each of these editions which I ascribe to the compositor.

The Text of the Present Edition

In choosing among substantive variants, I have had to assume the responsibility of deciding which ones were likely to have been made by Mandeville. Where the text was altered for the better by a later variant, the choice was an easy one. In the case of indifferent readings, I have thought it best to give Mandeville the benefit of the doubt and accept the change in the text. But where the variants were obvious errors or did not accord with what I judged to be Mandeville's usage, I have rejected them without scruple. On four occasions I have made unauthorized corrections in order to restore normal eighteenth-century usage. All page references in the text to other parts of the *Fable* have been silently altered to conform to the present edition. The results will not satisfy every reader in all cases, but I believe that the text presented here is closer to what Mandeville wrote than that of any previous edition.

I have annotated the text only to the extent of clarifying obscure allusions, defining words no longer in common usage, and translating Latin phrases and quotations as well as identifying the latter. Mandeville regularly names the authors of quotations which he gives in English, and I have not thought it necessary to specify the works from which they are taken, except for English authors. Those who wish to trace the sources of Mandeville's many quotations from Continental authors and of his individual ideas should consult F. B. Kaye's admirable annotation to the Clarendon Press edition of *The Fable of the Bees*. I have also noted all passages, of at least a sentence in length, which Mandeville added to the *Fable* in 1723 and 1724, so that the reader can trace the book's growth.

The Fable of the Bees facsimile title page of the first edition.

THE
FABLE
OF THE
BEES:
OR,
Private Vices,
Publick Benefits.

LONDON:
Printed for J. RORERTS, near the *Ox-ford Arms* in *Warwick Lane,* 1714.

THE
PREFACE

LAWS and Government are to the Political Bodies of Civil
Societies, what the Vital Spirits and Life it self are to the
Natural Bodies of Animated Creatures; and as those that
study the Anatomy of Dead Carkasses may see, that the
chief Organs and nicest Springs more immediately required
to continue the Motion of our Machine, are not hard Bones,
strong Muscles and Nerves, nor the smooth white Skin that
so beautifully covers them, but small trifling Films and
little Pipes that are either overlook'd, or else seem incon-
siderable to Vulgar Eyes; so they that examine into the
Nature of Man, abstract from Art and Education, may
observe, that what renders him a Sociable Animal, consists
not in his desire of Company, good Nature, Pity, Affability,
and other Graces of a fair Outside; but that his vilest and
most hateful Qualities are the most necessary Accomplish-
ments to fit him for the largest, and according to the World,
the happiest and most flourishing Societies.

The following Fable, in which what I have said is set
forth at large was printed above eight Years ago* in a Six-
penny Pamphlet call'd, *The Grumbling Hive*; *or Knaves
turn'd Honest*; and being soon after Pyrated, cry'd about
the Streets in a Half-penny Sheet. Since the first publishing
of it I have met with several that either wilfully or ignorantly
mistaking the Design, would have it, that the Scope of it
was a Satyr upon Virtue and Morality, and the whole wrote
for the Encouragement of Vice. This made me resolve,
whenever it should be reprinted, some way or other to in-

*This was wrote in 1714.[1]

1. This note was added in 1723. – Ed.

53

form the Reader of the real Intent this little Poem was wrote with. I do not dignify these few loose Lines with the Name of Poem, that I would have the Reader expect any Poetry in them, but barely because they are Rhime, and I am in reallity puzled what name to give them; for they are neither Heroick nor Pastoral, Satyr, Burlesque nor Heroi-comick; to be a Tale they want Probability, and the whole is rather too long for a Fable. All I can say of them is, that they are a Story told in Dogrel, which without the least design of being witty, I have endeavour'd to do in as easy and familiar a Manner as I was able: The Reader shall be welcome to call them what he pleases. 'Twas said of *Montagne*, that he was pretty well vers'd in the Defects of Mankind, but unacquainted with the Excellencies of Humane Nature: If I fare no worse, I shall think my self well used.

What Country soever in the Universe is to be understood by the Bee-Hive represented here, it is evident from what is said of the Laws and Constitution of it, the Glory, Wealth, Power and Industry of its Inhabitants, that it must be a large, rich and warlike Nation that is happily governed by a limited Monarchy. The Satyr therefore to be met with in the following Lines upon the several Professions and Callings, and almost every Degree and Station of People was not made to injure and point to particular Persons, but only to shew the Vileness of the Ingredients that all together compose the wholesome Mixture of a well order'd Society; in order to extol the wonderful Power of Political Wisdom, by the help of which so beautiful a Machine is rais'd from the most contemptible Branches. For the main design of the Fable, (as it is breefly explain'd in the Moral) is to shew the Impossibility of enjoying all the most elegant Comforts of Life that are to be met with in an industrious, wealthy and powerful Nation, and at the same time be bless'd with all the Virtue and Innocence that can be wish'd for in a

Golden Age; from thence to expose the Unreasonableness and Folly of those, that desirous of being an opulent and flourishing People, and wonderfully greedy after all the Benefits they can receive as such, are yet always murmuring at and exclaiming against those Vices and Inconveniencies, that from the beginning of the World to this present Day, have been inseparable from all Kingdoms and States that ever were fam'd for Strength, Riches and Politeness at the same time.

To do this, I first slightly touch upon some of the Faults and Corruptions the several Professions and Callings are generally charg'd with. After that I shew that those very Vices of every Particular Person by skilful Management were made subservient to the Grandeur and worldly Happiness of the whole. Lastly, by setting forth what of necessity must be the consequence of general Honesty and Virtue and National Temperance, Innocence and Content, I demonstrate that if Mankind could be cured of the Failings they are Naturally guilty of they would cease to be capable of being rais'd into such vast, potent and polite Societies, as they have been under the several great Common-wealths and Monarchies that have flourish'd since the Creation.

If you ask me why I have done all this, *cui bono*? And what Good these Notions will produce; truly besides the Reader's Diversion, I believe none at all; but if I was ask'd what Naturally ought to be expected from 'em, I wou'd answer, That in the first Place the People, who continually find Fault with others, by reading them, would be taught to look at home, and examining their own Consciences, be made asham'd of always railing at what they are more or less guilty of themselves; and that in the next, those who are so fond of the Ease and Comforts, and reap all the Benefits that are the Consequence of a great and flourishing Nation, would learn more patiently to submit to those Inconveniencies, which no Government upon Earth can remedy, when they should see the Impossibility of enjoying any great share of the first, without partaking likewise of the latter.

This I say ought naturally to be expected from the publishing of these Notions, if People were to be made better by any thing that could be said to them; but Mankind having for so many Ages remain'd still the same, notwithstanding the many instructive and elaborate Writings, by which their Amendment has been endeavour'd, I am not so vain as to hope for better success from so inconsiderable a Trifle.

Having allow'd the small Advantage this little Whim is likely to produce, I think my self oblig'd to shew, that it cannot be prejudicial to any; for what is published, if it does no good, ought at least to do no harm: In order to this I have made some Explanatory Notes, to which the Reader will find himself refer'd in those Passages that seem to be most liable to Exceptions.

The Censorious that never saw the *Grumbling Hive*, will tell me, that whatever I may talk of the Fable, it not taking up a Tenth part of the Book, was only contriv'd to introduce the *Remarks*; that instead of clearing up the doubtful or obscure Places, I have only pitch'd upon such as I had a Mind to expatiate upon; and that far from striving to extenuate the Errors committed before I have made Bad worse, and shewn my self a more bare-fac'd Champion for Vice, in the rambling Digressions, than I had done in the Fable itself.

I shall spend no time in answering these Accusations; where Men are prejudic'd, the best Apologies are lost; and I know that those who think it Criminal to suppose a necessity of Vice in any Case whatever, will never be reconcil'd to any part of the Performance; but if this be thoroughly examin'd all the Offence it can give, must result from the wrong Inferences that may perhaps be drawn from it, and which I desire no body to make. When I assert, that Vices are inseparable from great and potent Societies, and that it is impossible their Wealth and Grandeur should subsist without, I do not say that the particular Members of them who are guilty of any, should not be continually reprov'd, or not be punish'd for them when they grow into Crimes.

There are, I believe, few People in *London*, of those that are at any time forc'd to go a foot, but what could wish the Streets of it much cleaner than generally they are; whilst they regard nothing but their own Cloaths and private Conveniency; but when once they come to consider, that what offends them is the result of the Plenty, great Traffick and Opulency of that mighty City, if they have any Concern in its Welfare, they will hardly ever wish to see the Streets of it less dirty. For if we mind the Materials of all sorts that must supply such an infinite number of Trades and Handicrafts, as are always going forward; the vast quantity of Victuals, Drink and Fewel that are daily consum'd in it, and the Waste and Superfluities that must be produc'd from them; the multitudes of Horses and other Cattle that are always dawbing the Streets, the Carts, Coaches and more heavy Carriages that are perpetually wearing and breaking the Pavement of them, and above all the numberless swarms of People that are continually harrassing and trampling through every part of them. If, I say, we mind all these, we shall find that every Moment must produce new Filth, and considering how far distant the great Streets are from the River side, what Cost and Care soever be bestow'd to remove the Nastiness almost as fast as 'tis made, it is impossible *London* should be more cleanly before it is less flourishing. Now would I ask if a good Citizen, in consideration of what has been said, might not assert, that dirty Streets are a necessary Evil inseparable from the Felicity of *London* without being the least hindrance to the cleaning of Shoes, or

sweeping of Streets, and consequently without any Preju-
dice either to the *Blackguard*[2] or the *Scavingers*.

But if, without any regard to the Interest or Happiness of
the City, the Question was put, What Place I thought most
pleasant to walk in? No body can doubt but before the
stinking Streets of *London*, I would esteem a fragrant
Garden, or a shady Grove in the Country. In the same
manner, if laying aside all worldly Greatness and Vain
Glory, I should be ask'd where I thought it was most prob-
able that Men might enjoy true Happiness, I would prefer
a small peaceable Society, in which Men neither envy'd nor
esteem'd by Neighbours, should be contented to live upon
the Natural Product of the Spot they inhabit, to a vast
multitude abounding in Wealth and Power, that should
always be conquering others by their Arms Abroad, and
debauching themselves by Foreign Luxury at Home.[3]

Thus much I had said to the Reader in the First Edition;
and have added nothing by way of Preface in the Second.
But since that, a violent Out-cry has been made against the
Book, exactly answering the Expectation I always had of
the Justice, the Wisdom, the Charity, and Fair-dealing of
those whose Goodwill I despair'd of. It has been presented
by the Grand-Jury, and condemn'd by thousands who never
saw a word of it. It has been preach'd against before my
Lord Mayor; and an utter Refutation of it is daily expected
from a Reverend Divine, who has call'd me Names in the
Advertisements, and threatned to answer me in two
Months time for above five Months together.[4] What I have
to say for my self, the Reader will see in my Vindication
at the end of the Book, where he will likewise find the
Grand-Jury's Presentment, and a Letter to the Right

2. A shoeblack. – Ed.

3. The remainder of 'The Preface' was added in 1724. – Ed.

4. William Hendley, author of *A Defence of the Charity
Schools* (1724). – Ed.

Honourable Lord *C.* which is very Rhetorical beyond Argument or Connexion. The Author shews a fine Talent for Invectives, and great Sagacity in discovering Atheism, where others can find none. He is zealous against wicked Books, points at the Fable of the Bees, and is very angry with the Author: he bestows four strong Epithets on the Enormity of his Guilt, and by several elegant Innuendo's to the Multitude, as the Danger there is in suffering such Authors to live, and the Vengeance of Heaven upon a whole Nation, very charitably recommends him to their Care.

Considering the length of this Epistle, and that it is not wholly levell'd at me only, I thought at first to have made some Extracts from it of what related to my self; but finding, on a nearer Enquiry, that what concern'd me was so blended and interwoven with what did not, I was oblig'd to trouble the Reader with it entire; not without Hopes that, prolix as it is, the Extravagancy of it will be entertaining to those who have perused the Treatise it condemns with so much Horror.

THE

Grumbling Hive:

OR,

Knaves Turn'd Honest

A Spacious Hive well stock'd with Bees,
That lived in Luxury and Ease;
And yet as fam'd for Laws and Arms,
As yielding large and early Swarms;
Was counted the great Nursery
Of Sciences and Industry.
No Bees had better Government,
More Fickleness, or less Content.
They were not Slaves to Tyranny,
Nor ruled by wild Democracy;
But Kings, that could not wrong, because
Their Power was circumscrib'd by Laws.

These Insects lived like Men, and all
Our Actions they perform'd in small:
They did whatever's done in Town,
And what belongs to Sword, or Gown:
Tho' th'Artful Works, by nimble Slight
Of minute Limbs, 'scaped Human Sight;
Yet we've no Engines, Labourers,
Ships, Castles, Arms, Artificers,
Craft, Science, Shop, or Instrument;
But they had an Equivalent:
Which, since their Language is unknown,
Must be call'd, as we do our own.
As grant, that among other Things
They wanted Dice, yet they had Kings;
And those had Guards; from whence we may
Justly conclude, they had some Play;

Unless a Regiment be shewn
Of Soldiers, that make use of none.

    Vast Numbers thronged the fruitful Hive;
Yet those vast Numbers made 'em thrive;
Millions endeavouring to supply
Each other's Lust and Vanity;
Whilst other Millions were employ'd,
To see their Handy-works destroy'd;
They furnish'd half the Universe;
Yet had more Work than Labourers.
Some with vast Stocks, and little Pains
Jump'd into Business of great Gains;
And some were damn'd to Sythes and Spades,
And all those hard laborious Trades;
Where willing Wretches daily sweat,
And wear out Strength and Limbs to eat:
(*A.*) Whilst others follow'd Mysteries,
To which few Folks bind 'Prentices;
That want no Stock, but that of Brass,
And may set up without a Cross;[5]
As Sharpers, Parasites, Pimps, Players,
Pick-Pockets, Coiners, Quacks, Sooth-Sayers,
And all those, that, in Enmity
With down-right Working, cunningly
Convert to their own Use the Labour
Of their good-natur'd heedless Neighbour.
(*B.*) These were called Knaves; but, bar the Name,
The grave Industrious were the Same.
All Trades and Places knew some Cheat,
No Calling was without Deceit.

    The Lawyers, of whose Art the Basis
Was raising Feuds and splitting Cases,

    5. Without a groat to their name. – Ed.

Opposed all Registers, that Cheats
Might make more Work with dipt Estates;[6]
As were't unlawful, that one's own,
Without a Law-Suit, should be known.
They kept off Hearings wilfully,
To finger the refreshing Fee;
And to defend a wicked Cause,
Examin'd and survey'd the Laws;
As Burglars Shops and Houses do;
To find out where they'd best break through.

Physicians valued Fame and Wealth
Above the drooping Patient's Health,
Or their own Skill; The greatest Part
Study'd, instead of Rules of Art,
Grave pensive Looks, and dull Behaviour;
To gain th' Apothecary's Favour,
The Praise of Mid-wives, Priests and all,
That served at Birth, or Funeral;
To bear with th'ever-talking Tribe,
And hear my Lady's Aunt prescribe;
With formal Smile, and kind How d'ye,
To fawn on all the Family;
And, which of all the greatest Curse is,
T'endure th'Impertinence of Nurses.

Among the many Priests of *Jove*,
Hir'd to draw Blessings from Above,
Some few were learn'd and eloquent,
But Thousands hot and ignorant:
Yet all past Muster, that could hide
Their Sloth, Lust, Avarice and Pride;
For which they were as famed, as Taylors
For Cabbage; or for Brandy, Sailors:

6. Mortgaged estates. – Ed.

Some meagre look'd, and meanly clad
Would mystically pray for Bread,
Meaning by that an ample Store,
Yet lit'rally receiv'd no more;
And, whilst these holy Drudges starv'd,
The lazy Ones, for which they serv'd,
Indulg'd their Ease, with all the Graces
Of Health and Plenty in their Faces.

(C.)   The Soldiers, that were forced to fight,
If they survived, got Honour by't;
Tho' some, that shunn'd the bloody Fray,
Had Limbs shot off, that ran away:
Some valiant Gen'rals fought the Foe;
Others took Bribes to let them go:
Some ventur'd always, where 'twas warm;
Lost now a Leg, and then an Arm;
Till quite disabled, and put by,
They lived on half their Salary;
Whilst others never came in Play,
And staid at Home for Double Pay.

Their Kings were serv'd; but Knavishly
Cheated by their own Ministry;
Many, that for their Welfare slaved,
Robbing the very Crown they saved:
Pensions were small, and they lived high,
Yet boasted of their Honesty.
Calling, whene'er they strain'd their Right,
The slipp'ry Trick a Perquisite;
And, when Folks understood their Cant,
They chang'd that for Emolument;
Unwilling to be short, or plain,
In any thing concerning Gain:
(D.) For there was not a Bee, but would

Get more, I won't say, than he should;
But than he dared to let them know,
(*E.*) That pay'd for't; as your Gamesters do,
That, tho' at fair Play, ne'er will own
Before the Losers what they've won.

But who can all their Frauds repeat!
The very Stuff, which in the Street
They sold for Dirt t'enrich the Ground,
Was often by the Buyers found
Sophisticated with a Quarter
Of Good-for-nothing, Stones and Mortar;
Tho' Flail had little Cause to mutter,
Who sold the other Salt for Butter.

Justice her self, famed for fair Dealing,
By Blindness had not lost her Feeling;
Her Left Hand, which the Scales should hold,
Had often dropt 'em, bribed with Gold;
And, tho' she seem'd impartial,
Where Punishment was corporal,
Pretended to a reg'lar Course,
In Murther, and all Crimes of Force;
Tho' some, first Pillory'd for Cheating,
Were hang'd in Hemp of their own beating;
Yet, it was thought, the Sword she bore
Check'd but the Desp'rate and the Poor;
That, urged by mere Necessity,
Were tied up to the wretched Tree
For Crimes, which not deserv'd that Fate,
But to secure the Rich, and Great.

Thus every Part was full of Vice,
Yet the whole Mass a Paradice;
Flatter'd in Peace, and fear'd in Wars

67

They were th' Esteem of Foreigners,
And lavish of their Wealth and Lives,
The Ballance of all other Hives.
Such were the Blessings of that State;
Their Crimes conspired to make 'em Great;
(*F.*) And Vertue, who from Politicks
Had learn'd a Thousand cunning Tricks,
Was, by their happy Influence,
Made Friends with Vice: And ever since
(*G.*) The Worst of all the Multitude
Did something for the common Good.

This was the State's Craft, that maintain'd
The Whole, of which each Part complain'd:
This, as in Musick Harmony,
Made Jarrings in the Main agree;
(*H.*) Parties directly opposite
Assist each oth'r, as 'twere for Spight;
And Temp'rance with Sobriety
Serve Drunkenness and Gluttony.

(*I.*)   The Root of evil Avarice,
That damn'd ill-natur'd baneful Vice,
Was Slave to Prodigality,
(*K.*) That Noble Sin; (*L.*) whilst Luxury
Employ'd a Million of the Poor,
(*M.*) And odious Pride a Million more.
(*N.*) Envy it self, and Vanity
Were Ministers of Industry;
Their darling Folly, Fickleness
In Diet, Furniture, and Dress,
That strange ridic'lous Vice, was made
The very Wheel, that turn'd the Trade.
Their Laws and Cloaths were equally
Objects of Mutability;

For, what was well done for a Time,
In half a Year became a Crime;
Yet whilst they alter'd thus their Laws,
Still finding and correcting Flaws,
They mended by Inconstancy
Faults, which no Prudence could foresee.

    Thus Vice nursed Ingenuity,
Which join'd with Time, and Industry
Had carry'd Life's Conveniencies,
(O.) It's real Pleasures, Comforts, Ease,
(P.) To such a Height, the very Poor
Lived better than the Rich before;
And nothing could be added more:

    How vain is Mortal Happiness!
Had they but known the Bounds of Bliss;
And, that Perfection here below
Is more, than Gods can well bestow,
The grumbling Brutes had been content
With Ministers and Government.
But they, at every ill Success,
Like Creatures lost without Redress,
Cursed Politicians, Armies, Fleets,
Whilst every one cry'd, Damn the Cheats,
And would, tho' Conscious of his own,
In Others barb'rously bear none.

    One, that had got a Princely Store,
By cheating Master, King, and Poor,
Dared cry aloud; The Land must sink
For all it's Fraud; And whom d'ye think
The Sermonizing Rascal chid?
A Glover that sold Lamb for Kid.

The least Thing was not done amiss,
Or cross'd the Publick Business;
But all the Rogues cry'd brazenly,
Good Gods, had we but Honesty!
Merc'ry smiled at th'Impudence;
And Others call'd it want of Sence,
Always to rail at what they loved:
But *Jove*, with Indignation moved,
At last in Anger swore, he'd rid
The bawling Hive of Fraud, and did.
The very Moment it departs,
And Honesty fills all their Hearts;
There shews 'em, like th' Instructive Tree,
Those Crimes, which they're ashamed to see;
Which now in Silence they confess,
By Blushing at their Uglyness;
Like Children, that would hide their Faults,
And by their Colour own their Thoughts;
Imag'ning, when they're look'd upon,
That Others see, what they have done.

But, Oh ye Gods! What Consternation,
How vast and sudden was th'Alteration!
In half an Hour, the Nation round,
Meat fell a Penny in the Pound.
The Mask Hypocrisie's flung down,
From the great Statesman to the Clown;
And some, in borrow'd Looks well known,
Appear'd like Strangers in their own.
The Bar was silent from that Day;
For now the willing Debtors pay,
Ev'n what's by Creditors forgot;
Who quitted them, that had it not.
Those, that were in the Wrong, stood mute,
And dropt the patch'd vexatious Suit.

On which, since nothing less can thrive,
Than Lawyers in an honest Hive,
All, except those, that got enough,
With Ink-horns by their Sides troop'd off.

Justice hang'd some, set others free;
And, after Goal delivery,
Her Presence be'ng no more requir'd,
With all her Train, and Pomp retir'd.
First march'd some Smiths, with Locks and Grates,
Fetters, and Doors with Iron-Plates;
Next Goalers, Turnkeys, and Assistants:
Before the Goddess, at some distance,
Her chief and faithful Minister
Squire Catch,[7] the Laws great Finisher,
Bore not th' imaginary Sword,
But his own Tools, an Ax and Cord:
Then on a Cloud the Hood-wink'd fair
Justice her self was push'd by Air:
About her Chariot, and behind,
Were Sergeants, Bums of every kind,[8]
Tip-staffs, and all those Officers,
That squeeze a Living out of Tears.

Tho' Physick lived, whilst Folks were ill,
None would prescribe, but Bees of Skill;
Which, through the Hive dispers'd so wide,
That none of 'em had need to ride,
Waved vain Disputes; and strove to free
The Patients of their Misery;
Left Drugs in cheating Countries grown,
And used the Product of their own,

7. Jack Ketch, the proverbial hangman. – Ed.
8. Bailiffs. – Ed.

Knowing the Gods sent no Disease
To Nations without Remedies.

   Their Clergy rouz'd from Laziness,
Laid not their Charge on Journey-Bees;[9]
But serv'd themselves, exempt from Vice,
The Gods with Pray'r and Sacrifice;
All those, that were unfit, or knew,
Their Service might be spared, withdrew:
Nor was there Business for so many,
(If th' Honest stand in need of any.)
Few only with the High-Priest staid,
To whom the rest Obedience paid:
Himself, employ'd in holy Cares,
Resign'd to others State-Affairs:
He chased no Starv'ling from his Door,
Nor pinch'd the Wages of the Poor;
But at his House the Hungry's fed,
The Hireling finds unmeasur'd Bread,
The needy Trav'ler Board and Bed.

   Among the King's great Ministers,
And all th' inferiour Officers
The Change was great; (*Q*.) for frugally
They now lived on their Salary.
That a poor Bee should Ten times come,
To ask his Due, a trifling Sum,
And by some well-hir'd Clerk be made,
To give a Crown, or ne'er be paid;
Would now be call'd a down-right Cheat,
Tho' formerly a Perquisite.
All Places; managed first by Three,
Who watch'd each other's Knavery,
And often for a Fellow-feeling,

9. Curates. – Ed.

Promoted one another's Stealing;
Are happily supply'd by one;
By which some Thousands more are gone.

(R.)   No Honour now could be content,
To live, and owe for what was spent.
Liv'ries in Brokers Shops are hung,
They part with Coaches for a Song;
Sell stately Horses by whole Sets;
And Country-Houses to pay Debts.

Vain Cost is shunn'd as much as Fraud;
They have no Forces kept Abroad;
Laugh at th' Esteem of Foreigners,
And empty Glory got by Wars;
They fight but for their Country's Sake,
When Right or Liberty's at Stake.

Now mind the glorious Hive, and see,
How Honesty and Trade agree:
The Shew is gone, it thins apace;
And looks with quite another Face,
For 'twas not only that they went,
By whom vast Sums were Yearly spent;
But Multitudes, that lived on them,
Were daily forc'd to do the Same.
In vain to other Trades they'd fly;
All were o're-stock'd accordingly.

The Price of Land, and Houses falls;
Mirac'lous Palaces, whose Walls,
Like those of *Thebes*, were raised by Play,
Are to be lett; whilst the once gay,
Well-seated Houshold Gods would be

More pleased t'expire in Flames, than see
The mean Inscription on the Door
Smile at the lofty Ones they bore.
The Building Trade is quite destroy'd,
Artificers are not employ'd;
(S.) No Limner for his Art is famed;
Stone-cutters, Carvers are not named.

Those, that remain'd, grown temp'rate, strive,
Not how to spend; but how to live;
And, when they paid their Tavern Score,
Resolv'd to enter it no more:
No Vintners Jilt in all the Hive
Could wear now Cloth of Gold and thrive;
Nor *Torcol* such vast Sums advance,
For *Burgundy* and *Ortelans*;
The Courtier's gone, that with his Miss
Supp'd at his House on *Christmass* Peas;
Spending as much in Two Hours stay,
As keeps a Troop of Horse a Day.

The haughty *Chloe*, to live Great,
Had made her (*T*.) Husband rob the State:
But now she sells her Furniture,
Which th' *Indies* had been ransack'd for;
Contracts th' expensive Bill of Fare,
And wears her strong Suit a whole Year:
The slight and fickle Age is past;
And Cloaths, as well as Fashions last.
Weavers that join'd rich Silk with Plate,
And all the Trades subordinate,
Are gone. Still Peace and Plenty reign,
And every Thing is cheap, tho' plain:
Kind Nature, free from Gard'ners Force,
Allows all Fruits in her own Course;

But Rarities cannot be had,
Where Pains to get 'em are not paid.

 As Pride and Luxury decrease,
So by degrees they leave the Seas.
Not Merchants now; but Companies
Remove whole Manufacturies.
All Arts and Crafts neglected lie;
(*V.*) Content the Bane of Industry,
 Makes 'em admire their homely Store,
And neither seek, nor covet more.

 So few in the vast Hive remain;
The Hundredth part they can't maintain
Against th' Insults of numerous Foes;
Whom yet they valiantly oppose:
Till some well-fenced Retreat is found;
And here they die, or stand their Ground.
No Hireling in their Armies known;
But bravely fighting for their own,
Their Courage and Integrity
At last were crown'd with Victory.
They triumph'd not without their Cost;
For many Thousand Bees were lost.
Hard'ned with Toils, and Exercise
They counted Ease it self a Vice;
Which so improved their Temperance;
That, to avoid Extravagance,
They flew into a hollow Tree,
Blest with Content and Honesty.

The Moral

Then leave Complaints: Fools only strive
(X.) To make a Great an honest Hive.
(Y.) T' enjoy the World's Conveniencies,
Be famed in War, yet live in Ease
Without great Vices, is a vain
Eutopia seated in the Brain.
Fraud, Luxury, and Pride must live
Whilst we the Benefits receive.
Hunger's a dreadful Plague, no doubt,
Yet who digests or thrives without?
Do we not owe the Growth of Wine
To the dry shabby crooked Vine?
Which, whilst its Shutes neglected stood,
Choak'd other Plants, and ran to Wood;
But blest us with its Noble Fruit;
As soon as it was tied, and cut:
So Vice is beneficial found,
When it's by Justice lopt, and bound;
Nay, where the People would be great,
As necessary to the State
As Hunger is to make 'em eat.
Bare Vertue can't make Nations live
In Splendour; they, that would revive
A Golden Age, must be as free,
For Acorns, as for Honesty.

FINIS

THE
INTRODUCTION

One of the greatest Reasons why so few People understand themselves, is, that most Writers are always teaching Men what they should be, and hardly ever trouble their heads with telling them what they really are. As for my part, without any Compliment to the Courteous Reader, or my self, I believe Man (besides Skin, Flesh, Bones, &c. that are obvious to the Eye) to be a Compound of various Passions, that all of them, as they are provoked and come uppermost, govern him by turns, whether he will or no. To shew, that these Qualifications, which we all pretend to be asham'd of, are the great support of a flourishing Society, has been the subject of the foregoing Poem. But there being some Passages in it seemingly Paradoxical, I have in the Preface promised some explanatory Remarks on it; which, to render more useful, I have thought fit to enquire, how Man no better qualify'd, might yet by his own Imperfections be taught to distinguish between Virtue and Vice: And here I must desire the Reader once for all to take notice, that when I say Men, I mean neither Jews nor Christians; but meer Man, in the State of Nature and Ignorance of the true Deity.

AN

Enquiry into the
Origin of Moral Virtue

ALL untaught Animals are only Sollicitous of pleasing themselves, and naturally follow the bent of their own Inclinations, without considering the good or harm that from their being pleased will accrue to others. This is the Reason, that in the wild State of Nature those Creatures are fittest to live peaceably together in great Numbers, that discover the least of Understanding, and have the fewest Appetites to gratify, and consequently no Species of Animals is without the Curb of Government, less capable of agreeing long together in Multitudes than that of Man; yet such are his Qualities, whether good or bad, I shall not determine, that no Creature besides himself can ever be made sociable: But being an extraordinary selfish and headstrong as well as cunning Animal, however he may be subdued by superior Strength, it is impossible by force alone to make him tractable, and receive the Improvements he is capable of.

The chief Thing therefore, which Law-givers and other Wise Men, that have laboured for the Establishment of Society, have endeavour'd, has been to make the People they were to govern, believe, that it was more beneficial for every body to conquer than indulge his Appetites, and much better to mind the Publick than what seem'd his private Interest. As this has always been a very difficult Task, so no Wit or Eloquence has been left untried to compass it; and the Moralists and Philosophers of all Ages employ'd their utmost Skill to prove the truth of so useful an Assertion. But whether Mankind would have ever believ'd it or not, it is not likely that any body could have perswaded them to disapprove of their natural Inclinations, or prefer the good of

others to their own, if at the same time he had not shew'd
them an Equivalent to be enjoy'd as a Reward for the
Violence, which by so doing they of necessity must com-
mit upon themselves. Those that have undertaken to civilise
Mankind, were not ignorant of this; but being unable to
give so many real Rewards as would satisfy all Persons for
every individual Action, they were forc'd to contrive an
imaginary one, that as a general Equivalent for the trouble
of Self-denial should serve on all occasions, and without
costing any thing either to themselves or others, be yet a
most acceptable Recompence to the Receivers.

They thoroughly examin'd all the Strength and Frailties
of our Nature, and observing that none were either so
savage as not to be charm'd with Praise, or so despicable as
patiently to bear Contempt, justly concluded, that Flattery
must be the most powerful Argument that cou'd be used
to Human Creatures. Making use of this bewitching Engine,
they extoll'd the Excellency of our Nature above other
Animals, and setting forth with unbounded Praises the
Wonders of our Sagacity and vastness of Understanding,
bestow'd a thousand Encomiums on the Rationality of our
Souls, by the help of which we were capable of performing
the most noble Atchievements. Having by this artful way
of Flattery insinuated themselves into the Hearts of Men,
they began to instruct them in the Notions of Honour and
Shame; representing the one as the worst of all Evils, and the
other as the highest good to which Mortals could aspire :
Which being done, they laid before them how unbecoming
it was the Dignity of such sublime Creatures to be sollicitous
about gratifying those Appetites, which they had in common
with Brutes, and at the same time unmindful of those
higher qualities that gave them the pre-eminence over all
visible Beings. They indeed confess'd, that those impulses
of Nature were very pressing; that it was troublesome to
resist, and very difficult wholly to subdue them : But this

they only used as an Argument to demonstrate, how glorious the Conquest of them was on the one hand, and how scandalous on the other not to attempt it.

To introduce moreover an Emulation amongst Men, they divided the whole Species in two Classes, vastly differing from one another: The one consisted of abject, low minded People, that always hunting after immediate Enjoyment, were wholly incapable of Self-denial, and without regard to the good of others, had no higher Aim than their private Advantage; such as being enslaved by Voluptuousness, yielded without Resistance to every gross desire, and made no use of their Rational Faculties but to heighten their Sensual Pleasures. These vile grov'ling Wretches, they said, were the Dross of their kind, and having only the Shape of Men, differ'd from Brutes in nothing but their outward Figure. But the other Class was made up of lofty high-spirited Creatures, that free from sordid Selfishness, esteem'd the Improvements of the Mind to be their fairest Possessions; and setting a true value upon themselves, took no delight but in imbellishing that Part in which their Excellency consisted; such as despising whatever they had in common with irrational Creatures, opposed by the help of Reason their most violent Inclinations; and making a continual War with themselves to promote the Peace of others, aim'd at no less than the Publick Welfare and the Conquest of their own Passions.

Fortior est qui se quam qui fortissima Vincit Mœnia——[10]

These they call'd the true Representatives of their sublime Species, exceeding in worth the first Class by more

---

10. 'He who conquers himself is stronger than one who takes the greatest fortress.' Mandeville may be giving an inexact paraphrase of *Proverbs*, xvi, 32. – Ed.

degrees, than that it self was superior to the Beasts of the Field.

As in all Animals that are not too imperfect to discover Pride, we find, that the finest and such as are the most beautiful and valuable of their kind, have generally the greatest Share of it; so in Man, the most perfect of Animals, it is so inseparable from his very Essence (how cunningly soever some may learn to hide or disguise it) that without it the Compound he is made of would want one of the chiefest Ingredients: Which, if we consider, it is hardly to be doubted but Lessons and Remonstrances, so skillfully adapted to the good Opinion Man has of himself, as those I have mentioned, must, if scatter'd amongst a Multitude, not only gain the assent of most of them, as to the Speculative part, but likewise induce several, especially the fiercest, most resolute, and best among them, to endure a thousand Inconveniences, and undergo as many hardships, that they may have the pleasure of counting themselves Men of the second Class, and consequently appropriating to themselves all the Excellencies they have heard of it.

From what has been said we ought to expect in the first place, that the Heroes who took such extraordinary Pains to master some of their natural Appetites, and prefer'd the good of others to any visible Interest of their own, would not recede an Inch from the fine Notions they had receiv'd concerning the Dignity of Rational Creatures; and having ever the Authority of the Government on their side, with all imaginable Vigour assert the Esteem that was due to those of the second Class, as well as their superiority over the rest of their kind. In the second, that those who wanted a sufficient Stock of either Pride or Resolution, to buoy them up in mortifying of what was dearest to them, follow'd the sensual dictates of Nature, would yet be asham'd of confessing themselves to be those despicable Wretches that belong'd to the inferior Class, and were generally reckon'd

to be so little remov'd from Brutes; and that therefore in
their own Defence they would say, as others did, and hid-
ing their own Imperfections as well as they could, cry up
Self-denial and Publick spiritedness as much as any : For
it is highly probable, that some of them, convinced by the
real Proofs of Fortitude and Self-Conquest they had seen,
would admire in others what they found wanting in them-
selves; others be afraid of the Resolution and Prowess of
those of the second Class, and that all of them were kept
in awe by the Power of their Rulers, wherefore it is reason-
able to think, that none of them (whatever they thought in
themselves) would dare openly contradict, what by every
body else was thought Criminal to doubt of.

This was (or at least might have been) the manner after
which Savage Man was broke; from whence it is evident,
that the first Rudiments of Morality, broach'd by skilfull
Politicians, to render Men useful to each other as well as
tractable, were chiefly contriv'd; that the Ambitious might
reap the more Benefit from, and govern vast Numbers of
them with the greater Ease and Security. This Foundation
of Politicks being once laid, it is impossible that Man should
long remain uncivilis'd : For even those who only strove to
gratify their Appetites, being continually cross'd by others
of the same Stamp, could not but observe, that whenever
they check'd their Inclinations, or but follow'd them. with
more Circumspection, they avoided a world of Troubles,
and often escap'd many of the Calamities that generally
attended the too eager pursuit after Pleasure.

First, they receiv'd, as well as others, the benefit of those
Actions that were done for the good of the whole Society,
and consequently could not forbear wishing well to those
of the superior Class that perform'd them. Secondly, the
more intent they were in seeking their own Advantage,
without Regard to others, the more they were hourly

convinced, that none stood so much in their way as those that were most like themselves.

It being the Interest then of the very worst of them, more than any, to preach up Publick-spiritedness, that they might reap the Fruits of the Labour and Self-denial of others, and at the same time indulge their own Appetites with less disturbance, they agreed with the rest, to call every thing, which, without Regard to the Publick, Man should commit to gratify any of his Appetites, VICE; if in that Action there could be observ'd the least prospect, that it might either be injurious to any of the Society, or ever render himself less serviceable to others: And to give the Name of VIRTUE to every Performance, by which Man, contrary to the impulse of Nature, should endeavour the Benefit of others, or the Conquest of his own Passions, out of a Rational Ambition of being good.

It shall be objected, that no Society was ever any ways civilis'd before the major part had agreed upon some Worship or other of an over ruling Power, and consequently that the Notions of Good and Evil, and the Distinction between *Virtue* and *Vice*, were never the Contrivance of Politicians, but the pure effect of Religion. Before I answer this Objection, I must repeat what I have said already, that in this *Enquiry into the Origin of Moral Virtue* I speak neither of *Jews* or *Christians*, but Man in his State of Nature and Ignorance of the true Deity; and then I affirm, that the Idolatrous Superstitions of all other Nations, and the pitiful Notions they had of the Supreme Being were incapable of exciting Man to Virtue, and good for nothing but to awe and amuse a rude and unthinking Multitude. It is evident from History, that in all considerable Societies, how stupid or ridiculous soever Peoples received Notions have been, as to the Deities they worship'd, Human Nature has ever exerted itself in all its branches, and that there is no Earthly Wisdom or Moral Virtue, but at one time or other Men have excell'd in it in all Monarchies and Commonwealths, that for Riches and Power have been any ways remarkable.

The *Ægyptians* not satisfy'd with having Deify'd all the ugly Monsters they could think on, were so silly as to adore the Onions of their own sowing; yet at the same time their Country was the most famous Nursery of Arts and Sciences in the World, and themselves more eminently skill'd in the deepest Mysteries of Nature than any Nation has been since.

No States or Kingdoms under Heaven have yielded more or greater Paterns in all sorts of Moral Virtues than the *Greek* and *Roman* Empires, more especially the latter; and yet how loose, absurd, and ridiculous were their Sentiments as to Sacred Matters: For without reflecting on the extravagant Number of their Deities, if we only consider the infamous Stories they father'd upon them, it is not to be denied but that their Religion, far from teaching Men the Conquest of their Passions, and the way to Virtue, seem'd rather contriv'd to justify their Appetites, and encourage their Vices. But if we would know what made 'em excel in Fortitude, Courage and Magnanimity, we must cast our Eyes on the Pomp of their Triumphs, the Magnificence of their Monuments and Arches, their Trophies, Statues, and Inscriptions; the variety of their Military Crowns, their Honours decreed to the Dead, Publick Encomiums on the Living, and other imaginary Rewards they bestow'd on Men of Merit; and we shall find, that what carried so many of them to the utmost Pitch of Self-denial, was nothing but their Policy in making use of the most effectual Means that human Pride could be flatter'd with.

It is visible then that it was not any Heathen Religion or other Idolatrous Superstition, that first put Man upon crossing his Appetites and subduing his dearest Inclinations, but the skilful Management of wary Politicians; and the nearer we search into human Nature, the more we shall be convinc'd, that the Moral Virtues are the Political Offspring which Flattery begot upon Pride.

There is no Man of what Capacity or Penetration soever, that is wholly Proof against the witchcraft of Flattery, if artfully perform'd, and suited to his Abilities. Children and Fools will swallow Personal Praise, but those that are more cunning, must be manag'd with greater Circumspection; and the more general the Flattery is, the less it is suspected by those it is levell'd at. What you say in Commendation of a whole Town is receiv'd with Pleasure by all the Inhabitants: Speak in Commendation of Letters in general, and every Man of Learning will think himself in particular obliged to you. You may safely praise the Employment a Man is of, or the Country he was born in; because you give him an opportunity of screening the Joy he feels upon his own account, under the Esteem which he pretends to have for others.

It is common among cunning Men, that understand the Power which Flattery has upon Pride, when they are afraid they shall be impos'd upon to enlarge, tho' much against their Conscience, upon the Honour, fair Dealing and Integrity of the Family, Country, or sometimes the Profession of him they suspect; because they know that Men often will change their Resolution, and act against their Inclination, that they may have the Pleasure of continuing to appear in the Opinion of some what they are conscious not to be in reality. Thus Sagacious Moralists draw Men like Angels, in hopes that the Pride at least of some will put 'em upon copying after the beautiful Originals which they are represented to be.

When the Incomparable Sir *Richard Steele* in the usual Elegance of his easy Style, dwells on the Praises of his sublime Species, and with all the Embellishments of Rhetorick, sets forth the Excellency of Human Nature, it is impossible not to be charm'd with his happy Turns of Thought, and the Politeness of his Expressions. But tho' I have been often moved by the Force of his Eloquence, and ready to swallow the ingenious Sophistry with Pleasure, yet I could never be so serious but reflecting on his artful Encomiums, I thought on the Tricks made use of by the Women that would teach Children to be mannerly. When an awkward Girl before she can either Speak or Go, begins after many entreaties to make the first rude Essays of Curt'sying: The Nurse falls in an extasy of Praise; *There's a delicate Curt'sy! O fine Miss! There's a pretty Lady! Mama! Miss can make a better Curt'sy than her Sister* Molly! The same is eccho'd over by the Maids, whilst Mama almost hugs the Child to pieces; only Miss *Molly*, who being four Years older, knows how to make a very handsome Curt'sy, wonders at the Perverseness of their Judgment, and swelling with Indignation, is ready to cry at the Injustice that is done her, till being whisper'd in the Ear that it is only to please the Baby, and that she is a Woman; she grows Proud at being let into the Secret, and rejoycing at the Superiority of her Understanding, repeats what has been said with large Additions, and insults over the weakness of her Sister, whom all this while she fancies to be the only Bubble among them. These extravagant Praises would by any one, above the Capacity of an Infant, be call'd fulsome Flatteries, and, if you will, abominable Lies; yet Experience teaches us, that by the help of such gross Encomiums, young Misses will be brought to make pretty Curt'sies, and behave themselves womanly much sooner, and with less trouble, than they would without them. 'Tis the same with Boys, whom they'll strive to perswade, that all fine Gentlemen do as they are bid, and that none but Beggar Boys are rude, or dirty their Cloaths; nay, as soon as the wild Brat with his untaught Fist begins to fumble for his Hat, the Mother, to make him pull it off, tells him before he is two Years old, that he is a

Man; and if he repeats that Action when she desires him, he's presently a Captain, a Lord Mayor, a King, or something higher if she can think of it, till egg'd on by the force of Praise, the little Urchin endeavours to imitate Man as well as he can, and strains all his Faculties to appear what his shallow Noddle imagines he is believ'd to be.

The meanest Wretch puts an inestimable value upon himself, and the highest wish of the Ambitious Man is to have all the World, as to that particular, of his Opinion: So that the most insatiable Thirst after Fame that ever Heroe was inspired with, was never more than an ungovernable Greediness to engross the Esteem and Admiration of others in future Ages as well as his own; and (what Mortification soever this Truth might be to the second Thoughts of an *Alexander* or a *Cæsar*) the great Recompence in view; for which the most exalted Minds have with so much Alacrity, sacrifis'd their Quiet, Health, sensual Pleasures, and every inch of themselves, has never been any thing else but the Breath of Man, the Aerial Coyn of Praise. Who can forbear Laughing when he thinks on all the Great Men that have been so serious on the Subject of that *Macedonian* Madman, his Capacious Soul, that mighty Heart, in one Corner of which, according to *Lorenzo Gracian*, the World was so commodiously Lodged, that in the whole there was room for Six more? Who can forbear Laughing, I say, when he compares the fine things that have been said of *Alexander*, with the End he proposed to himself from his vast Exploits, to be proved from his own Mouth, when the vast Pains he took to pass the *Hydaspes* forc'd him to cry out? *Oh ye* Athenians, *could you believe what Dangers I expose my self to, to be praised by you!* [11] To define then the Reward of Glory in the amplest manner, the most that can be said of it, is, that it consists in a superlative Felicity which a

11 These sentences concerning Alexander the Great were added in 1723. – Ed.

Man, who is conscious of having perform'd a noble Action, enjoys in Self love, whilst he is thinking on the Applause he expects of others.

But here I shall be told, that besides the noisy Toils of War and publick Bustle of the Ambitious, there are noble and generous Actions that are perform'd in Silence; that Virtue being its own Reward, those who are really Good have a satisfaction in their Consciousness of being so, which is all the Recompence they expect from the most worthy Performances; that among the Heathens there have been Men, who when they did good to others, were so far from coveting Thanks and Applause, that they took all imaginable Care to be for ever conceal'd from those on whom they bestow'd their Benefits, and consequently that Pride has no hand in spurring Man on to the highest pitch of Self denial.

In Answer to this I say, that it is impossible to judge of a Man's Performance, unless we are thoroughly acquainted with the Principle and Motive from which he acts. Pity, tho' it is the most gentle and the least mischievous of all our Passions, is yet as much a Frailty of our Nature, as Anger, Pride, or Fear. The weakest Minds have generally the greatest Share of it, for which Reason none are more Compassionate than Women and Children. It must be own'd, that of all our Weaknesses it is the most amiable, and bears the greatest Resemblance to Virtue; nay, without a considerable mixture of it the Society could hardly subsist: But as it is an impulse of Nature, that consults neither the publick Interest nor our own Reason, it may produce Evil as well as Good. It has help'd to destroy the Honour of Virgins, and corrupted the Integrity of Judges, and whoever acts from it as a Principle, what good soever he may bring to the Society, has nothing to boast of but that he has indulged a Passion that has happened to be beneficial to the Publick. There is no Merit in saving an Innocent Babe ready to drop into the Fire: The Action is neither good nor bad, and what Benefit soever the Infant received, we only obliged our selves; for to have seen it fall, and not strove to hinder it, would have caused a Pain which Self-preservation compell'd us to prevent: Nor has a rich Prodigal, that happens to be of a commiserating Temper, and loves to gratify his Passions, greater Virtue to boast of when he relieves an Object of Compassion with what to himself is a trifle.

But such Men as without complying with any weakness of their own, can part from what they value themselves, and from no other Motive but their Love to Goodness, perform a worthy Action in Silence: Such Men, I confess, have acquir'd more refin'd Notions of Virtue than those I have hitherto spoke of; yet even in these (with which the World has yet never swarm'd) we may discover no small Symptoms of Pride, and the humblest Man alive must confess, that the Reward of a Virtuous Action, which is the Satisfaction that ensues upon it, consists in a certain Pleasure he procures to himself by Contemplating on his own Worth: Which Pleasure, together with the occasion of it, are as certain Signs of Pride, as looking pale and trembling at any imminent Danger, are the Symptoms of Fear.

If the too scrupulous Reader should at first View condemn these Notions concerning the Origin of Moral Virtue, and think them perhaps offensive to Christianity, I hope he'll forbear his Censures, when he shall consider, that nothing can render the unsearchable depth of the Divine Wisdom more conspicuous than that *Man*, whom Providence had designed for Society, should not only by his own Frailties and Imperfections be led into the Road to Temporal Happiness, but likewise receive, from a seeming Necessity of Natural Causes, a Tincture of that Knowledge, in which he was afterwards to be made perfect by the True Religion, to his Eternal Welfare.

REMARKS

PAGE 64. LINE 17. In the Education of *Youth*, in order to their getting of a *Livelihood* when they shall be arriv'd at *Maturity*, most People look out for some warrantable Employment or other, of which there are whole *Bodies* or *Companies*, in every large *Society* of *Men*. By this means all *Arts* and *Sciences*, as well as *Trades* and *Handicrafts* are perpetuated in the *Commonwealth*, as long as they are found useful; the Young Ones that are daily brought up to 'em, continually supplying the loss of the Old ones that die. But some of these Employments being vastly more Creditable than others, according to the great difference of the Charges required to set up in each of them, all prudent *Parents* in the choice of them chiefly consult their own *Abilities* and the *Circumstances* they are in. A Man that gives Three or Four Hundred Pounds with his *Son* to a great *Merchant*, and has not Two or Three Thousand Pounds to spare against he is out of his Time to begin the World with, is much to blame not to have brought his *Child* up to something that might be follow'd with less *Money*.

There are abundance of *Men* of a *genteel* Education, that have but very small *Revenues*, and yet are forc'd, by their Reputable *Callings*, to make a greater *Figure* than ordinary People of twice their *Income*. If these have any *Children*, it often happens, that as their *Indigence* renders them incapable of bringing them up to creditable *Occupations*, so their Pride makes 'em unwilling to put them out to any of

Remark (A)

the mean laborious *Trades*, and then, in hopes either of an Alteration in their *Fortune*, or that some Friends, or favourable *Opportunity* shall offer, they from time to time put off the disposing of them, till insensibly they come to be of *Age*, and are at last brought up to Nothing. Whether this Neglect be more barbarous to the Children, or prejudicial to the Society, I shall not determine. At *Athens* all *Children* were forc'd to assist their *Parents*, if they came to *Want*: But *Solon* made a Law, that no *Son* should be oblig'd to relieve his *Father*, who had not bred him up to any *Calling*.

Some *Parents* put out their *Sons* to good *Trades* very suitable to their then present Abilities, but happen to dye or fail in the World, before the Children have finish'd their *Apprenticeships*, or are made fit for the *Business* they are to follow: A great many young Men again on the other hand are handsomely provided for and set up for themselves, that yet (some for want of *Industry* or else a sufficient *Knowledge* in their *Callings*, others by indulging their *Pleasures*, and some few by *Misfortunes*) are reduced to Poverty, and altogether unable to maintain themselves by the Business they were brought up to. It is impossible but that the Neglects, Mismanagements and Misfortunes I named, must very frequently happen in Populous Places, and consequently great numbers of People be daily flung unprovided for into the wide World, how Rich and Potent a Commonwealth may be, or what Care soever a Government may take to hinder it. How must these People be dispos'd of? The Sea I know, and Armies, which the World is seldom without, will take off some. Those that are honest Drudges, and of a laborious Temper, will become *Journeymen* to the Trades they are of, or enter into some other Service: Such of them as study'd and were sent to the University, may become Schoolmasters, Tutors, and some few of them get into some Office or other: But what must become of the

Lazy that care for no manner of working, and the *Fickle* that hate to be confin'd to any Thing?

Those that ever took Delight in Plays and Romances, and have a spice of Gentility, will, in all probabilty, throw their Eyes upon the *Stage*, and if they have a good Elocution with tollerable Mein, turn *Actors*. Some that love their Bellies above any thing else; if they have a good Palate, and a little Knack at Cookery, will strive to get in with *Gluttons* and *Epicures*, learn to cringe and bear all manner of Usage, and so turn *Parasites*, ever flattering the Master, and making Mischief among the rest of the *Family*. Others, who by their own and Companion's Lewdness judge of People's Incontinence, will naturally fall to Intriguing, and endeavour to live by Pimping for such as either want Leisure or Address to speak for themselves. Those of the most abandon'd Principles of all, if they are sly and dextrous, turn Sharpers, Pick-pockets, or Coiners, if their Skill and Ingenuity give them leave. Others again, that have observ'd the Credulity of simple Women, and other foolish People, if they have Impudence and a little Cunning, either set up for Doctors, or else pretend to tell Fortunes; and every one turning the Vices and Frailties of others to his own Advantage, endeavours to pick up a Living the easiest and shortest way his Talent and Abilities will let him.

These are certainly the Bane of Civil Society; but they are Fools, who not considering what has been said, storm at the Remissness of the Laws that suffer them to live, whilst wise Men content themselves with taking all imaginable Care not to be circumvented by them; without quarrelling, at what no Humane Prudence can prevent.

Remark (B)

(B.) These were called Knaves; but, bar the Name,
The grave Industrious were the Same.

PAGE 64. LINE 27. This I confess is but a very indifferent Compliment to all the Trading part of the People. But if the Word *Knave* may be understood in its full Latitude, and comprehend every Body that is not sincerely honest, and does to others what he would dislike to have done to himself, I don't question but I shall make good the Charge. To pass by the innumerable Artifices, by which Buyers and Sellers outwit one another that are daily allowed of and practised among the fairest of *Dealers*; shew me the *Tradesman* that has always discover'd the Defects of his Goods to those that cheapen'd them; nay, where will you find one that has not at one time or other industriously conceal'd them to the detriment of the *Buyer*? Where is the Merchant that has never against his Conscience extoll'd his Wares beyond their Worth, to make them go off the better?

Decio a Man of great Figure, that had large Commissions for Sugar from several parts beyond Sea, treats about a considerable parcel of that Commodity with *Alcander*, an eminent *West India* Merchant; both understood the Market very well, but could not agree: *Decio* was a Man of Substance, and thought no Body ought to buy Cheaper than himself, *Alcander* was the same, and not wanting Money, stood for his Price. Whilst they were driving their Bargain at a Tavern near the *Exchange, Alcander*'s Man brought his Master a Letter from the *West Indies*, that inform'd him of a much greater quantity of Sugars coming for *England* than was expected. *Alcander* now wish'd for nothing more than to sell at *Decio*'s Price, before the News was publick; but being a cunning Fox, that he might not seem too precipitant, nor yet lose his Customer, he drops the Discourse they were upon, and putting on a Jovial Humour, commends the Agreeableness of the Weather, from whence falling upon the Delight he took in his Gardens, invites *Decio* to go along with him to his Country House, that was not above Twelve Miles from *London*. It was in the Month of *May*, and as it happen'd upon a *Saturday* in the Afternoon, *Decio*, who was a single Man, and would have no Business in Town before *Tuesday*, accepts of the others Civility, and away they go in *Alcander*'s Coach. *Decio* was splendidly entertain'd that Night and the Day following; the *Monday* Morning, to get himself an Appetite, he goes to take the Air upon a Pad of *Alcander*'s, and coming back meets with a Gentleman of his Acquaintance, who tells him News was come the Night before that the *Barbadoes* Fleet was destroy'd by a Storm, and adds, that before he came out it had been confirm'd at *Lloyd's* Coffee House, where it was thought Sugars would rise 25 *per Cent.* by Change time. *Decio* returns to his Friend, and immediately resumes the Discourse they had broke off at the Tavern: *Alcander*, who thinking himself sure of his Chap, did not design to have moved it till after Dinner, was very glad to see himself so happily prevented; but how desirous soever he was to sell, the other was yet more eager to buy; yet both of them afraid of one another, for a considerable time counterfeited all the Indifference imaginable; till at last *Decio* fired with what he had heard, thought delays might prove dangerous, and throwing a Guinea upon the Table, struck the Bargain at *Alcander*'s Price. The next Day they went to *London*; the News prov'd true, and *Decio* got five hundred Pounds by his Sugars. *Alcander*, whilst he had strove to over-reach the other, was paid in his own Coin, yet all this is called fair dealing; but I am sure neither of them would have desired to be done by, as they did to each other.

(C.) *The Soldiers, that were forced to fight,*
If they survived, got Honour by't.

PAGE 66. LINE 9. So unaccountable is the desire to be thought well of in Men, that tho' they are drag'd into the War against their Will, and some of them for their Crimes, and are compell'd to fight with Threats and often Blows, yet they would be esteem'd for what they would have avoided, if it had been in their Power: Whereas if Reason in Man was of equal weight with his Pride, he could never be pleas'd with Praises, which he is conscious he don't deserve.

By Honour in its proper and genuine Signification we mean nothing else but the good Opinion of others, which is counted more or less substantial, the more or less noise or bustle there is made about the demonstration of it, and when we say the Sovereign is the Fountain of Honour, it signifies that he has the Power by Titles or Ceremonies, or both together to stamp a Mark upon whom he pleases, that shall be as current as his Coin, and procure the Owner the good Opinion of every Body, whether he deserves it or not.

The Reverse of Honour is Dishonour or Ignominy, which consists in the bad Opinion and Contempt of others, and as the first is counted a Reward for good Actions, so this is esteem'd a Punishment for bad ones, and the more or less publick or heinous the manner is in which this Contempt of others is shewn, the more or less the Person so suffering is degraded by it. This Ignominy is likewise called Shame, from the effect it produces; for tho' the Good and Evil of Honour and Dishonour are imaginary, yet there is a reality in Shame, as it signifies a Passion that has its proper Symptoms, over-rules our Reason, and requires as much Labour and Self denial to be subdued, as any of the rest; and since the most important Actions of Life often are regulated according to the Influence this Passion has upon us, a thorough understanding of it must help to illustrate the Notions the World has of Honour and Ignominy. I shall therefore describe it at large.

First to define the Passion of Shame I think it may be call'd *a sorrowful Reflection on our own unworthiness proceeding from an Apprehension that others either do or might, if they knew all, deservedly despise us.* The only Objection of weight that can be rais'd against this Definition is, that innocent Virgins are often asham'd, and blush when they are guilty of no Crime, and can give no manner of Reason for this Frailty : And that Men are often asham'd for others, for, or with whom, they have neither Friendship or Affinity, and consequently that there may be a thousand Instances of Shame given, to which the Words of the Definition are not applicable. To answer this, I would have it first consider'd, that the Modesty of Women is the Result of Custom and Education, by which all unfashionable Denudations and filthy Expressions are render'd frightful and abominable to them, and that notwithstanding this the most Vertuous young Woman alive will often, in spight of her Teeth, have Thoughts and confused Ideas of Things arise in her Imagination, which she would not reveal to some People for a thousand Worlds. Then I say, that when obscene Words are spoken in the presence of an unexperienc'd Virgin, she is afraid that some Body will reckon her to understand what they mean, and consequently that she understands this, and that, and several things which she desires to be thought ignorant of. The reflecting on this, and that Thoughts are forming to her Disadvantage, brings upon her that Passion which we call Shame; and whatever can fling her, tho' never so remote from Lewdness, upon that Set of Thoughts I hinted, and which she thinks Criminal, will have the same effect, especially before Men, as long as her Modesty lasts.

Remark (C)

To try the Truth of this, let them talk as much Bawdy as they please in the Room next to the same Vertuous young Woman, where she is sure that she is undiscover'd, and she will hear, if not hearken to it without blushing at all, because then she looks upon her self as no Party concern'd; and if the Discourse should stain her Cheeks with red, whatever her Innocence may imagine, it is certain that what occasions her Colour is a Passion not half so mortifying as that of Shame; but if in the same Place she hears something said of herself that must tend to her Disgrace, or any thing is named, of which she is secretly guilty, then 'tis Ten to One but she'll be asham'd and blush, tho' no Body sees her; because she has room to fear, that she is, or, if all was known, should be thought of Contemptibly.

That we are often asham'd, and blush for others, which was the second part of the Objection, is nothing else, but that sometimes we make the Case of others too nearly our own; so People shriek out when they see others in danger: Whilst we are reflecting with too much earnest on the effect which such a blameable Action, if it was ours, would produce in us, the Spirits and consequently the Blood, are insensibly moved after the same manner, as if the Action was our own, and so the same Symptoms must appear.

The Shame that raw, ignorant and ill bred People, tho' seemingly without a Cause, discover before their Betters, is always accompanied with, and proceeds from a Consciousness of their Weakness and Inabilities, and the most modest Man, how Vertuous, Knowing and Accomplish'd soever he might be, was never yet asham'd without some Guilt or Diffidence. Such as out of Rusticity, and want of Education are unreasonably subject to, and at every turn overcome by this Passion, we call bashful; and those who out of disrespect to others, and a false Opinion of their own Sufficiency, have learn'd not to be affected with it, when they should be, are call'd Impudent or Shameless. What strange Contradictions

Man is made of! The Reverse of Shame is Pride, (*see Remark M.*) yet no Body can be touch'd with the first, that never felt any thing of the latter; for that we have such an extraordinary Concern in what others think of us, can proceed from nothing but the vast Esteem we have for our selves.

That these two Passions, in which the Seeds of most Vertues are contained, are reallities in our frame and not imaginary Qualities, is demonstrable from the plain and different effects, that in spight of our Reason are produced in us as soon as we are affected with either.

When a Man is overwhelm'd with Shame, he observes a sinking of the Spirits, the Heart feels cold and condensed, and the Blood flies from it to the Circumference of the Body; the Face glows, the Neck and part of the Breast partake of the Fire: He is heavy as Lead; the Head is hung down; and the Eyes through a Mist of Confusion, are fix'd on the Ground: No Injuries can move him; he is weary of his Being, and heartily wishes he could make himself invisible: But when, gratifying his Vanity, he exults in his Pride he discovers quite contrary Symptoms: His Spirits swell and fan the Arterial Blood, a more than ordinary warmth strengthens and dilates the Heart; the Extremities are cool; he feels light to himself, and imagines he could tread on Air; his Head is held up, his Eyes rowl'd about with Sprightliness; he rejoyces at his Being, is prone to Anger, and would be glad that all the World could take Notice of him.[12]

It is incredible how necessary an Ingredient Shame is to make us sociable; it is a Frailty in our Nature, all the World, whenever it affects them, submit to it with Regret, and would prevent it if they could; yet the Happiness of Conversation depends upon it, and no Society could be polish'd, if the Generality of Mankind were not subject to it.

12. The remainder of Remark *C* was added in 1723. – Ed.

Remark (C)

As therefore the Sense of Shame is troublesome, and all Creatures are ever labouring for their own Defence, it is probable, that Man striving to avoid this Uneasiness would in a great Measure conquer his Shame by that he was grown up; but this would be detrimental to the Society, and therefore from his Infancy throughout his Education, we endeavour to increase instead of lessening or destroying this Sense of Shame; and the only Remedy prescrib'd, is a strict Observance of certain Rules to avoid those Things that might bring this troublesome Sense of Shame upon him. But as to rid or cure him of it, the Politician would sooner take away his Life.

The Rules I speak of consist in a dextrous Management of ourselves, a stifling of our Appetites, and hiding the real Sentiments of our Hearts before others. Those who are not instructed in these Rules long before they come to Years of Maturity, seldom make any Progress in them afterwards. To acquire and bring to Perfection the Accomplishment I hint at, nothing is more assisting than Pride and good Sense. The Greediness we have after the Esteem of others, and the Raptures we enjoy in the Thoughts of being liked, and perhaps admired, are Equivalents that over-pay the Conquest of the strongest Passions, and consequently keep us at a great Distance from all such Words or Actions that can bring shame upon us. The Passions we chiefly ought to hide for the Happiness and Embellishment of the Society are Lust, Pride, and Selfishness; therefore the Word Modesty has three different Acceptations, that vary with the Passions it conceals.

As to the first, I mean that Branch of Modesty, that has a general Pretension to Chastity for its Object, it consists in a sincere and painful Endeavour with all our Faculties to stifle and conceal before others, that Inclination which Nature has given us to propagate our Species. The Lessons of it, like those of *Grammar*, are taught us long before we have occasion for, or understand the Usefulness of them; for this Reason Children often are ashamed, and blush out of Modesty, before the Impulse of Nature I hint at makes any Impression upon them. A Girl who is modestly educated, may, before she is two Years old, begin to observe how careful the Women, she converses with, are of covering themselves before Men; and the same Caution being inculcated to her by Precept, as well as Example, it is very probable that at Six she'll be asham'd of shewing her Leg, without knowing any Reason why such an Act is blameable, or what the Tendency of it is.

To be modest, we ought in the first place to avoid all unfashionable Denudations: A Woman is not to be found fault with for going with her Neck bare, if the Custom of the Country allows of it, and when the Mode orders the Stays to be cut very low, a blooming Virgin may, without Fear of rational Censure, shew all the World

How firm her pouting Breasts that white as Snow,
On th' ample Chest at mighty distance grow.

But to suffer her Ancle to be seen, where it is the Fashion for Women to hide their very Feet, is a Breach of Modesty, and she is impudent, who shews half her Face in a Country where Decency bids her to be veil'd. In the second, our Language must be chaste, and not only free, but remote from Obscenities, that is, whatever belongs to the Multiplication of our Species is not to be spoke of, and the least Word or Expression, that tho' at a great Distance has any relation to that Performance, ought never to come from our Lips. Thirdly, all Postures and Motions that can any ways sully the Imagination, that is, put us in mind of what I have call'd Obscenities, are to be forebore with great Caution.

A young Woman moreover, that would be thought wellbred, ought to be circumspect before Men in all her

Behaviour, and never known to receive from, much less to bestow Favours upon them, unless the great Age of the Man, near Consanguinity, or a vast Superiority on either Side plead her Excuse. A young Lady of refin'd Education keeps a strict Guard over her Looks, as well as Actions, and in her Eyes we may read a Consciousness that she has a Treasure about her, not out of Danger of being lost, and which yet she is resolv'd not to part with at any Terms. Thousand Satyrs have been made against Prudes, and as many Encomiums to extol the careless Graces, and negligent Air of virtuous Beauty. But the wiser Sort of Mankind are well assured, that the free and open Countenance of the Smiling Fair, is more inviting, and yields greater Hopes to the Seducer, than the ever-watchful Look of a forbidding Eye.

This strict Reservedness is to be comply'd with by all young Women, especially Virgins, if they value the Esteem of the Polite and knowing World; Men may take greater Liberty, because in them the Appetite is more violent and ungovernable. Had equal Harshness of Discipline been imposed upon both, neither of them could have made the first Advances, and Propagation must have stood still among all the Fashionable People: which being far from the Politician's Aim, it was advisable to ease and indulge the Sex that suffer'd most by the Severity, and make the Rules abate of their Rigour, where the Passion was the strongest, and the Burthen of a strict Restraint would have been the most intollerable.

For this Reason, the Man is allow'd openly to profess the Veneration and great Esteem he has for Women, and shew greater Satisfaction, more Mirth and Gaiety in their Company, than he is used to do out of it. He may not only be complaisant and serviceable to them on all Occasions, but it is reckon'd his Duty to protect and defend them. He may praise the good Qualities they are possess'd of, and extol their Merit with as many Exaggerations as his Invention will let him, and are consistent with good Sense. He may talk of Love, he may sigh and complain of the Rigours of the Fair, and what his Tongue must not utter he has the Privilege to speak with his Eyes, and in that Language to say what he pleases; so it be done with Decency, and short abrupted Glances: But too closely to pursue a Woman, and fasten upon her with one's Eyes, is counted very unmannerly; the Reason is plain, it makes her uneasy, and, if she be not sufficiently fortify'd by Art and Dissimulation, often throws her into visible Disorders. As the Eyes are the Windows of the Soul, so this staring Impudence flings a raw, unexperienc'd Woman into panick Fears, that she may be seen through; and that the Man will discover, or has already betray'd, what passes within her: It keeps her on a perpetual Rack, that commands her to reveal her secret Wishes, and seems design'd to extort from her the grand Truth, which Modesty bids her with all her Faculties to deny.

The Multitude will hardly believe the excessive Force of Education, and in the Difference of Modesty between Men and Women, ascribe that to Nature, which is altogether owing to early Instruction: *Miss* is scarce three Years old, but she's spoke to every Day to hide her Leg, and rebuk'd in good Earnest if she shews it; whilst *Little Master* at the same Age is bid to take up his Coats, and piss like a Man. It is Shame and Education that contain the Seeds of all Politeness, and he that has neither, and offers to speak the Truth of his Heart, and what he feels within, is the most contemptible Creature upon Earth, tho' he committed no other Fault. If a Man should tell a Woman, that he could like no body so well to propagate his Species upon, as her self, and that he found a violent Desire that Moment to go about it, and accordingly offer'd to lay hold of her for that Purpose; the Consequence would be, that he would be call'd a Brute, the

Woman would run away, and himself never be admitted in any civil Company. There is no body that has any Sense of Shame, but would conquer the strongest Passion rather than be so serv'd. But a Man need not conquer his Passions, it is sufficient that he conceals them. Virtue bids us subdue, but good Breeding only requires we should hide our Appetites. A fashionable Gentleman may have as violent an Inclination to a Woman as the brutish Fellow; but then he behaves himself quite otherwise; he first addresses the Lady's Father, and demonstrates his Ability splendidly to maintain his Daughter; upon this he is admitted into her Company, where, by Flattery, Submission, Presents, and Assiduity, he endeavours to procure her Liking to his Person, which, if he can compass, the Lady in a little while resigns her self to him before Witnesses in a most solemn manner; at Night they go to bed together, where the most reserv'd Virgin very tamely suffers him to do what he pleases, and the upshot is, that he obtains what he wanted without having ever ask'd for it.

The next Day they receive Visits, and no body laughs at them, or speaks a Word of what they have been doing. As to the young Couple themselves, they take no more Notice of one another, I speak of well-bred People, than they did the Day before, they eat and drink, divert themselves as usually, and having done nothing to be asham'd of, are look'd upon as, what in reality they may be, the most modest People upon Earth. What I mean by this, is to demonstrate, that by being well bred, we suffer no Abridgment in our sensual Pleasures, but only labour for our mutual Happiness, and assist each other in the luxurious Enjoyment of all worldly Comforts. The fine Gentleman I spoke of, need not practise any greater Self-Denial than the Savage, and the latter acted more according to the Laws of Nature and Sincerity than the first. The Man that gratifies his Appetites after the manner the Custom of the Country allows of, has no censure to Fear. If he is hotter than Goats or Bulls, as soon as the Ceremony is over let him sate and fatigue himself with Joy and Extasies of Pleasure, raise and indulge his Appetites by turns as extravagantly as his Strength and Manhood will give him leave, he may with safety Laugh at the Wise Men that should reprove him: all the Women, and above Nine in Ten of the Men are on his side; nay, he has the Liberty of valuing himself upon the Fury of his unbridled Passion, and the more he wallows in Lust and strains every faculty to be abandonly voluptuous, the sooner he shall have the Good Will and gain the Affection of the Women, not the Young, Vain and Lascivious only, but the Prudent, Grave and most Sober Matrons.

Because Impudence is a Vice, it does not follow that Modesty is a Virtue; it is built upon Shame, a Passion in our Nature, and may be either Good or Bad according to the Actions perform'd from that Motive. Shame may hinder a Prostitute from yielding to a Man before Company, and the same Shame may cause a Bashful good natur'd Creature, that has been overcome by frailty, to make away with her Infant. Passions may do Good by chance, but there can be no merit but in the conquest of them.

Was there Virtue in Modesty, it would be of the same force in the Dark as it is in the Light, which it is not. This the Men of Pleasure know very well, who never trouble their Heads with a Woman's Virtue so they can but conquer her Modesty; Seducers therefore don't make their Attacks at Noonday, but cut their Trenches at Night.

> *Illa verecundis lux est praebenda puellis,*
> *Qua timidus latebras sperat habere pudor.*[13]

People of Substance may Sin without being expos'd for

13. 'A light should be given to bashful maidens in which coy modesty may hope to have concealment.' Ovid, *Amores*, v. 7–8. – Ed.

their stolen Pleasure; but Servants and the Poorer sort of Women have seldom an Opportunity of concealing a Big Belly, or at least the Consequences of it. It is possible that an unfortunate Girl of Good Parentage may be left destitute, and know no other Shift for a Livelihood than to become a Nursery, or a Chambermaid: She may be Diligent, Faithful and Obliging, have abundance of Modesty, and, if you will, be Religious: She may resist Temptations, and preserve her Chastity for Years together, and yet at last meet with an unhappy Moment in which she gives up her Honour to a Powerful Deceiver, who afterwards neglects her. If she proves with Child, her Sorrows are unspeakable, and she can't be reconcil'd with the Wretchedness of her Condition, the fear of shame Attacks her so lively, that every Thought distracts her. All the Family she lives in have a great opinion of her Virtue, and her last Mistress took her for a Saint. How will her Enemies, that envyed her Character, rejoyce, how will her Relations detest her! The more modest she is now, and the more violently the dread of coming to Shame hurries her away, the more Wicked and more Cruel her Resolutions will be, either against her self or what she bears.

It is commonly imagined, that she who can destroy her Child, her own Flesh and Blood, must have a vast stock of Barbarity, and be a Savage Monster, different from other Women; but this is likewise a mistake which we commit for want of understanding Nature and the force of Passions. The same Woman that Murders her Bastard in the most execrable manner, if she is Married afterwards, may take care of, cherish and feel all the tenderness for her Infant that the fondest Mother can be capable of. All Mothers naturally love their Children: but as this is a Passion, and all Passions center in Self-Love, so it may be subdued by any Superiour Passion, to sooth that same Self-Love, which if nothing had interven'd, would have bid her fondle her Offspring. Common Whores, whom all the World knows to be such, hardly ever destroy their Children, nay even those who assist in Robberies and Murders seldom are Guilty of this Crime; not because they are less Cruel or more Virtuous, but because they have lost their Modesty to a greater degree, and the fear of shame makes hardly any impression upon them.

Our Love to what never was within the reach of our Senses is but poor and inconsiderable, and therefore Women have no Natural Love to what they bear; their Affection begins after the Birth: what they feel before is the result of Reason, Education, and the Thoughts of Duty. Even when Children first are Born the Mother's Love is but weak, and encreases with the sensibility of the Child, and grows up to a prodigious height, when by signs it begins to express his Sorrows and Joys, makes his wants known, and discovers his Love to novelty and the Multiplicity of his desires. What Labours and Hazards have not Women undergone to maintain and save their Children, what force and fortitude beyond their Sex have they not shewn in their Behalf! but the vilest Women have exerted themselves on this head as violently as the best. All are prompted to it by a natural Drift and Inclination, without any consideration of the Injury or Benefit the Society receives from it. There is no merit in pleasing our selves, and the very Offspring is often irreparably ruin'd by the excessive Fondness of Parents: for tho' Infants for Two or Three Years may be the better for this indulging Care of Mothers, yet afterwards, if not moderated, it may totally Spoil them, and many it has brought to the Gallows.

If the Reader thinks I have been too tedious on that Branch of Modesty by the help of which we endeavour to appear Chaste, I shall make him amends in the Brevity with which I design to treat of the remaining part, by which we would make others believe, that the esteem we have for them exceeds the value we have for our selves, and that we have no disregard so great to any Interest as we have to our own. This laudable quality is commonly known by the name of Manners and good Breeding, and consists in a Fashionable Habit, acquired by Precept and Example, of flattering the Pride and Selfishness of others, and concealing our own with Judgment and Dexterity. This must be only understood of our Commerce with our Equals and Superiors, and whilst we are in Peace and Amity with them, for our Complaisance must never interfere with the Rules of Honour, nor the Homage that is due to us from Servants and others that depend upon us.

With this Caution, I believe, that the Definition will quadrate with every thing that can be alledg'd as a piece or an example of either Good Breeding or Ill Manners; and it will be very difficult throughout the various Accidents of Human Life and Conversation to find out an instance of Modesty or Impudence that is not comprehended in, and illustrated by it in all Countries and in all Ages. A Man that asks considerable Favours of one who is a Stranger to him, without consideration, is call'd Impudent, because he shews openly his Selfishness without having any regard to the Selfishness of the other. We may see in it likewise the reason why a Man ought to speak of his Wife and Children, and every thing that is dear to him, as sparingly as is possible, and hardly ever of himself, especially in Commendation of them. A well Bred Man may be desirous, and even greedy after Praise and the Esteem of others, but to be prais'd to his Face offends his Modesty, the reason is this; all Human Creatures, before they are yet polish'd, receive an extraordinary Pleasure in hearing themselves prais'd: this we are all conscious of, and therefore when we see a Man openly enjoy and feast on this Delight, in which we have no share, it rouses our Selfishness, and immediately we begin to Envy and Hate him. For this reason the well Bred Man conceals his Joy, and utterly denies that he feels any, and by this means consulting and soothing our Selfishness, he averts that Envy and Hatred, which otherwise he would have justly to Fear. When from our Childhood we observe how those are ridicul'd who calmly can hear their own Praises, it is possible that we may so strenuously endeavour to avoid that Pleasure, that in tract of time we grow uneasy at the approach of it: but this is not following the Dictates of Nature; but warping her by Education and Custom, for if the generality of Mankind took no delight in being prais'd, there could be no Modesty in refusing to hear it.

The Man of Manners picks not the best but rather takes the worst out of the Dish, and gets of every thing, unless it be forc'd upon him, always the most indifferent Share. By this Civility the Best remains for others, which being a Compliment to all that are present, every Body is pleas'd with it: the more they love themselves the more they are forc'd to approve of his Behaviour, and Gratitude stepping in, they are obliged almost whether they will or not, to think favourably of him. After this manner it is that the well Bred Man insinuates himself in the esteem of all the Companies he comes in, and if he gets nothing else by it, the Pleasure he receives in reflecting on the Applause which he knows is secretly given him, is to a Proud Man more than an Equivalent for his former Self-denial, and over-pays to Self-love with Interest, the loss it sustain'd in his Complaisance to others.

If there are Seven or Eight Apples or Peaches among Six People of Ceremony, that are pretty near equal, he who is prevail'd upon to chuse first, will take that, which, if there be any considerable difference, a Child would know to be the worst: this he does to insinuate, that he looks upon those he is with to be of Superior Merit, and that there is not one whom he wishes not better to than he does to himself. 'Tis Custom and a general Practice that makes this Modish Deceit familiar to us, without being shock'd at the

Absurdity of it; for if People had been used to speak from the Sincerity of their Hearts, and Act according to the Natural Sentiments they felt within, till they were Three or Four and Twenty, it would be impossible for them to assist at this Comedy of Manners without either lowd Laughter or Indignation; and yet it is certain, that such a Behaviour makes us more tollerable to one another than we could be otherwise.

It is very Advantageous to the Knowledge of our selves, to be able well to distinguish between good Qualities and Virtues. The Bond of Society exacts from every Member a certain Regard for others, which the Highest is not exempt from in the presence of the meanest even in an Empire: But when we are by our selves, and so far remov'd from Company as to be beyond the reach of their Senses, the Words Modesty and Impudence lose their meaning; a Person may be Wicked, but he cannot be Immodest whilst he is alone, and no Thought can be Impudent that never was communicated to another. A Man of Exalted Pride may so hide it, that no Body shall be able to discover that he has any; and yet receive greater Satisfaction from that Passion than another, who indulges himself in the Declaration of it before all the World. Good Manners have nothing to do with Virtue or Religion; instead of extinguishing, they rather inflame the Passions. The Man of Sense and Education never exults more in his Pride than when he hides it with the greatest dexterity, and in feasting on the Applause which he is sure all good Judges will pay to his Behaviour; he enjoys a Pleasure altogether unknown to the Short-Sighted, surly Alderman, that shews his Haughtiness glaringly in his Face, pulls off his Hat to no Body, and hardly deigns to speak to an Inferior.

A Man may carefully avoid every thing that in the Eye of the World is esteem'd to be the result of Pride, without mortifying himself, or making the least conquest of his

Passion. It is possible that he only sacrifices the insipid out-
ward part of his Pride, which none but silly Ignorant People
take delight in, to that part we all feel within, and which
the Men of the Highest Spirit and most Exalted Genius feed
on with so much extasy in silence. The Pride of Great and
Polite Men is no where more conspicuous than in the De-
bates about Ceremony and Precedency, where they have
an Opportunity of giving their Vices the appearance of
Virtues, and can make the World believe that it is their care,
their Tenderness for the Dignity of their Office, or the
Honour of their Masters, what is the result of their own
personal Pride and Vanity. This is most manifest in all
Negotiations of Ambassadors and Plenipotentiaries, and
must be known by all that observe what is transacted at
publick Treaties, and it will ever be true, that Men of the
best Taste have no Relish in their Pride as long as any
Mortal can find out that they are Proud.

> (D.) *For there was not a Bee, but would*
> *Get more, I won't say, than he should;*
> *But than,* &c.

PAGE 66. LINE 33. The vast Esteem we have of our selves,
and the small value we have for others, make us all very
unfair Judges in our own Cases. Few Men can be perswaded
that they get too much by those they sell to, how extra-
ordinary soever their Gains are, when at the same time there
is hardly a Profit so inconsiderable, but they'll grudge it to
those they buy from; for this Reason the smallness of the
Seller's Advantage being the greatest Perswasive to the
Buyer, Tradesmen are generally forc'd to tell Lyes in their
own Defence, and invent a thousand improbable Stories,
rather than discover what they really get by their Com-
modities. Some old Standers indeed that pretend to more

Honesty, (or what is more likely, have more Pride) than their Neighbours, are used to make but few Words with their Customers, and refuse to sell at a lower Price than what they ask'd at first. But these are commonly cunning Foxes that are above the World, and know that those who have Money, get often more by being surly, than others by being obliging. The Vulgar imagine they can find more Sincerity in the sowr Looks of a grave old Fellow, than there appears in the submissive Air and inviting Complacency of a young Beginner. But this is a grand Mistake; and if they are Mercers, Drapers, or others, that have many sorts of the same Commodity, you may soon be satisfied; look upon their Goods and you'll find each of them have their private Marks, which is a certain Sign that both are equally careful in concealing the prime Cost of what they sell.

(E.) — *As your Gamesters do,*
That, tho' at fair Play, ne'er will own
Before the Losers what they've won.

PAGE 67. LINE 3. This being a general Practice which no Body can be ignorant of that has ever seen any Play, there must be something in the Make of Man that is the occasion of it: But as the searching into this will seem very trifling to many, I desire the Reader to skip this Remark, unless he be in perfect good Humour, and has nothing at all to do.

That Gamesters generally endeavour to conceal their Gains before the Losers, seems to me to proceed from a mixture of Gratitude, Pity and Self-Preservation. All Men are naturally grateful whilst they receive a Benefit, and what they say or do, whilst it affects and feels warm about them, is real, and comes from the Heart; but when that is over, the returns we make generally proceed from Virtue, good Manners, Reason, and the thoughts of Duty, but not from Gratitude, which is a Motive of the Inclination. If we consider, how tyrannically the Immoderate Love we bear to our selves, obliges us to esteem every body that with or without design acts in our favour, and how often we extend our Affection to things inanimate, when we imagine them to contribute to our present Advantage: If, I say, we consider this, it will not be difficult to find out which way our being pleased with those whose Money we win, is owing to a Principle of Gratitude. The next Motive is our Pity, which proceeds from our consciousness of the Vexation there is in losing; and as we love the Esteem of every body, we are afraid of forfeiting theirs by being the cause of their Loss. Lastly, we apprehend their Envy, and so Self-Preservation makes that we strive to extenuate first the Obligation, then the Reason why we ought to Pity, in hopes that we shall have less of their ill Will and Envy. When the Passions shew themselves in their full Strength, they are known by every body. When a Man in Power gives a great Place to one that did him a small kindness in his Youth, we call it Gratitude. When a Woman howls and wrings her Hands at the loss of her Child, the prevalent Passion is Grief; and the uneasiness we feel at the sight of great Misfortunes, as a Man's breaking his Leg, or dashing his Brains out, is every where call'd Pity. But the gentle stroaks, the slight touches of the Passions are generally over-look'd or mistaken.

To prove my Assertion we have but to observe, what generally passes between the *Winner* and the *Loser*. The first is always Complaisant, and if the other will but keep his Temper more than ordinarily obliging, he is ever ready to humour the *Loser*, and willing to rectify his Mistakes with Precaution, and the height of good Manners. The Loser is uneasy, captious, morose, and perhaps Swears and Storms; yet as long as he says or does nothing designedly affronting, the Winner takes all in good part, without offending, disturbing, or contradicting him. *Losers*, says the Proverb, *must have leave to rail*: All which shews, that the Loser is thought in the right to complain, and for that very Reason pity'd. That we are afraid of the Loser's ill Will is plain from our being conscious that we are displeased with those we lose to, and Envy we always dread when we think our selves happier than others: from whence it follows, that when the *Winner* endeavours to conceal his Gains, his design is to avert the Mischiefs he apprehends, and this is Self-Preservation; the Cares of which continue to affect us as long as the Motives that first produced them remain.

But a Month, a Week, or perhaps a much shorter time after, when the Thoughts of the Obligation, and consequently the Winner's Gratitude are worn off, when the Loser has recover'd his Temper, laughs at his Loss, and the Reason of the Winner's Pity ceases; when the Winner's apprehension of drawing upon him the ill Will and Envy of the *Loser* is gone; that is to say, as soon as all the Passions are over, and the Cares of Self-Preservation employ the Winner's Thoughts no longer, he'll not only make no scruple in owning what he has won, but will, if his Vanity steps in, likewise, with Pleasure, brag of, if not exaggerate his Gains.

It is possible, that when People play together who are at Enmity, and perhaps desirous of picking a Quarrel, or where Men playing for Trifles contend for Superiority of Skill, and aim chiefly at the Glory of Conquest, nothing shall happen of what I have been talking of. Different Passions oblige us to take different Measures; what I have said I would have understood of ordinary Play for Money, at which Men endeavour to get, and venture to lose what they value: And even here I know it will be objected by many, that tho' they have been guilty of concealing their

Gains, yet they never observ'd those Passions which I alledge as the Causes of that Frailty; which is no wonder, because few Men will give themselves leisure, and fewer yet take the right Method of examining themselves as they should do. It is with the Passions in Men as it is with Colours in Cloth: It is easy to know a Red, a Green, a Blue, a Yellow, a Black, &c. in as manny different Pieces; but it must be an Artist that can unravel all the various Colours and their Proportions, that make up the Compound of a well mix'd Cloth. In the same manner may the Passions be discover'd by every body whilst they are distinct, and a single one employs the whole Man; but it is very difficult to trace every Motive of those Actions that are the Result of a mixture of Passions.

> (F.) *And Vertue, who from Politicks*
> *Had learn'd a Thousand cunning Tricks,*
> *Was, by their happy Influence,*
> *Made Friends with Vice.—*

PAGE 68. LINE 6. It may be said, that Virtue is made Friends with Vice, when industrious good People, who maintain their Families and bring up their Children handsomely, pay Taxes, and are several ways useful Members of the Society, get a livelyhood by something that chiefly depends on, or is very much influenc'd by the Vices of others, without being themselves guilty of, or accessary to them any otherwise than by way of Trade, as a Druggist may be to Poysoning, or a Sword-Cutler to Bloodshed.

Thus the Merchant, that sends Corn or Cloth into Foreign Parts to purchase Wines and Brandies, encourages the Growth or Manufactury of his own Country; he is a Benefactor to Navigation, encreases the Customs, and is many ways beneficial to the Publick; yet it is not to be denied but that his greatest dependance is *Lavishness* and *Drunkenness*: For if none were to drink Wine but such only as stand in need of it, nor any body more than his Health required, that multitude of Wine-Merchants, Vintners, Coopers, &c. that make such a considerable Shew in this flourishing City, would be in a miserable Condition. The same may be said not only of Card and Dice-makers, that are the immediate Ministers to a Legion of Vices; but of Mercers, Upholsterers, Taylors, and many others that would be starv'd in half a Years time, if *Pride* and *Luxury* were at once to be banish'd the Nation.

> ### (G.) *The Worst of all the Multitude Did something for the common Good.*

PAGE 68. LINE 10. This I know will seem to be a strange Paradox to many; and I shall be ask'd what Benefit the Publick receives from Thieves and House-breakers. They are, I own, very pernicious to Human Society, and every Government ought to take all imaginable Care to root out and destroy them; yet if all People were strictly honest, and no body would meddle with or pry into any thing but his own, half the Smiths of the Nation would want Employment; and abundance of Workmanship (which now serves for Ornament as well as Defence) is to be seen every where both in Town and Country, that would never have been thought of, but to secure us against the Attempts of Pilferers and Robbers.[14]

If what I have said be thought far fetch'd, and my Assertion seems still a Parodox, I desire the Reader to look upon the Consumption of things, and he'll find that the lazyest and most unactive, the profligate and most mischievous are all forc'd to do something for the common

14. The remainder of Remark *G* was added in 1723. – Ed.

good, and whilst their Mouths are not sow'd up, and they continue to wear and otherwise destroy what the Industrious are daily employ'd about to make, fetch and procure, in spight of their Teeth oblig'd to help maintain the Poor and the publick Charges. The Labour of Millions would soon be at an end if there were not other Millions as I say in the Fable

> ————*Employ'd,*
> *To see their Handy-works destroy'd.*

But Men are not to be Judg'd by the Consequences that may succeed their Actions, but the Facts themselves, and the Motives which it shall appear they acted from. If an Ill-natur'd Miser, who is almost a Plumb,[15] and spends but Fifty Pounds a Year, tho' he has no Relation to inherit his Wealth, should be Robb'd of Five Hundred or a Thousand Guineas, it is certain that as soon as this Money should come to Circulate, the Nation would be the better for the Robbery, and receive the same and as real a Benefit from it, as if an Archbishop had left the same Sum to the Publick, yet Justice and the peace of the Society require that he or they who robb'd the Miser should be Hang'd, tho' there were Half a Dozen of 'em concern'd.

Thieves and Pick-pockets steal for a Livelihood, and either what they can get Honestly is not sufficient to keep them, or else they have an aversion to constant Working: they want to gratify their Senses, have Victuals, Strong Drink, Lewd Women, and to be Idle when they please. The Victualler, who Entertains them and takes their Money, knowing which way they come at it, is very near as great a Villain as his Guests. But if he Fleeces them well, minds his Business and is a prudent Man, he may get

15. A man worth £100,000. – Ed.

Money and be punctual with them he deals with: The Trusty Out-Clerk, whose chief aim is his Master's Profit, sends him in what Beer he wants, and takes care not to lose his Custom; whilst thc Man's Money is good he thinks it no Business of his to examine whom he gets it by. In the mean time the Wealthy Brewer, who leaves all the Management to his Servants, knows nothing of the matter, but keeps his Coach, treats his Friends and enjoys his Pleasure with ease and a good Conscience, he gets an Estate, Builds Houses and Educates his Children in Plenty, without ever thinking on the Labour which Wretches perform, the shifts Fools make, and the Tricks Knaves play to come at the Commodity by the vast Sale of which he amasses his great Riches.

A Highwayman having met with a considerable Booty, gives a poor common Harlot, he fancys, Ten Pounds to New Rig her from Top to Toe; is there a Spruce Mercer so Conscientious that he will refuse to sell her a Thread Sattin, tho' he knew who she was? She must have Shoes and Stockings, Gloves, the Stay and Manto-maker, the Sempstress, the Linnen-draper, all must get something by her, and a hundred different Tradesmen dependent on those she laid her Money out with, may touch part of it before a Month is at an end. The Generous Gentleman, in the mean time, his Money being near spent, ventur'd again on the Road, but the Second Day having committed a Robbery near *Highgate*, he was taken with one of his Accomplices, and the next Sessions both were Condemn'd, and suffer'd the Law. The Money due on their Conviction fell to three Country Fellows, on whom it was admirably well bestow'd. One was an Honest Farmer, a Sober Pains-taking Man but reduced by Misfortunes: The Summer before by the Mortality among the Cattle he had lost Six Cows out of Ten, and now his Landlord, to whom he ow'd Thirty Pounds had seiz'd on all his Stock. The other was a Day

Labourer, who struggl'd hard with the World, had a Sick
Wife at Home and several small Children to provide for.
The Third was a Gentleman's Gardiner, who maintain'd
his Father in Prison, where being Bound for a Neighbour
he had lain for Twelve Pounds almost a Year and a Half;
this Act of Filial Duty was the more meritorious, because
he had for some time been engaged to a Young Woman
whose Parents lived in good Circumstances, but would not
give their Consent before our Gardiner had Fifty Guineas
of his own to shew. They receiv'd above Fourscore Pounds
each, which extricated every one of them out of the difficul-
ties they labour'd under, and made them in their Opinion
the happiest People in the World.

Nothing is more destructive, either in regard to the
Health or the Vigilance and Industry of the Poor than the
infamous Liquor, the name of which deriv'd from Juniper
in Dutch, is now, by frequent use and the Laconick Spirit
of the Nation, from a word of midling length shrunk into
a Monosyllable, Intoxicating Gin, that charms the Unactive,
the desperate and crasy of either Sex, and makes the starv-
ing Sot behold his Rags and Nakedness with stupid In-
dolence, or banter both in Senseless Laughter, and more
insipid Jests; It is a Fiery Lake that sets the Brain in Flame,
Burns up the Entrails, and scorches every part within;
and at the same time a Lethe of Oblivion, in which the
Wretch immers'd drowns his most pinching Cares, and
with his Reason all anxious reflection on Brats that cry for
Food, hard Winters Frosts, and horrid Empty Home.

In hot and adust Tempers it makes Men Quarrelsome,
renders 'em Brutes and Savages, sets 'em on to Fight for
nothing, and has often been the cause of Murder. It has
broke and destroy'd the strongest Constitutions, thrown
'em into Consumptions, and been the fatal and immediate
occasion of Apoplexies, Phrensies and Sudden Death. But
as these latter Mischiefs happen but seldom, they might be

overlook'd and conniv'd at, but this cannot be said of the many Diseases that are familiar to the Liquor, and which are daily and hourly produced by it; such as Loss of Appetite, Fevers, Black and Yellow Jaundice, Convulsions, Stone and Gravel, Dropsies, and Leucophlegmacies.

Among the doating Admirers of this Liquid Poyson, many of the meanest Rank, from a sincere Affection to the Commodity it self, become Dealers in it, and take delight to help others to what they love themselves, as Whores commence Bawds to make the profits of one Trade subservient to the Pleasures of the other. But as these Starvlings commonly drink more than their Gains, they seldom by selling mend the wretchedness of Condition they labour'd under whilst they were only Buyers. In the Fagend and Out-skirts of the Town, and all places of the vilest Resort, it's Sold in some part or other of almost every House, frequently in Cellars, and sometimes in the Garret. The petty Traders in this Stygian Comfort are supply'd by others in somewhat higher Station, that keep profess'd Brandy Shops, and are as little to be envied as the former; and among the midling People, I know not a more miserable Shift for a Livelihood than their calling; whoever would thrive in it must in the first place be of a Watchful and Suspicious, as well as a bold and resolute Temper, that he may not be imposed upon by Cheats and Sharpers, nor out-bully'd by the Oaths and Imprecations of Hackney Coachmen and Foot Soldiers; in the second he ought to be a dabster at gross Jokes and loud Laughter, and have all the Winning Ways to allure Customers and draw out their Money, and be well vers'd in the low Jests and Ralleries the Mob make use of to Banter Prudence and Frugality. He must be affable and obsequious to the most despicable; always ready and officious to help a Porter down with his Load, shake Hands with a Basket-Woman, pull off his Hat to an Oyster Wench, and be familiar with a Beggar; with

Patience and good Humour he must be able to endure the filthy Actions and viler Language of Nasty Drabs, and the lewdest Rakehells, and without a frown or the least aversion bear with all the Stench and Squallor, Noise and Impertinence that the utmost Indigence, Laziness and Ebriety, can produce in the most shameless and abandon'd Vulgar.

The vast Number of the Shops I speak of throughout the City and Suburbs, are an astonishing Evidence of the many Seducers, that in a Lawful Occupation are accessary to the Introduction and Increase of all the Sloth, Sottishness, Want and Misery, which the Abuse of Strong Waters is the immediate Cause of, to lift above Mediocrity, perhaps half a score Men that deal in the same Commodity by wholesale, whilst among the Retailers, tho' qualify'd as I required, a much greater Number are broke and ruin'd, for not abstaining from the *Circean* Cup they hold out to others, and the more fortunate are their whole Life-time obliged to take the uncommon Pains, endure the Hardships, and swallow all the ungrateful and shocking Things I named, for little or nothing beyond a bare Sustenance, and their daily Bread.

The short-sighted Vulgar in the Chain of Causes seldom can see further than one Link; but those who can enlarge their View, and will give themselves the Leisure of gazing on the Prospect of concatenated Events, may, in a hundred Places see *Good* spring up, and pullulate from *Evil*, as naturally as Chickens do from Eggs. The Money that arises from the Duties upon Malt, is a considerable Part of the National Revenue, and should no Spirits be distill'd from it, the *Publick* Treasure would prodigiously suffer on that Head. But, if we would set in a true Light the many Advantages, and large Catalogue of solid Blessings that accrue from, and are owing to the Evil I treat of, we are to consider the Rents that are received, the Ground that is till'd, the Tools that are made, the Cattle that are employ'd, and above all, the Multitude of Poor that are maintain'd, by the Variety of Labour, required in Husbandry, in Malting, in Carriage and Distillation, before we can have that Product of Malt, which we call *Low Wines*, and is but the Beginning from which the various Spirits are afterwards to be made.

Besides this, a sharp-sighted good-humour'd Man might pick up abundance of Good from the Rubbish, which I have all flung away for Evil. He would tell me, that whatever Sloth and Sottishness might be occasion'd by the Abuse of Malt-Spirits, the moderate Use of it was of inestimable Benefit to the Poor, who could purchase no Cordials of higher Prices, that it was an universal Comfort, not only in Cold and Weariness, but most of the Afflictions that are peculiar to the Necessitous, and had often to the most destitute supply'd the Places of Meat, Drink, Cloaths, and Lodging. That the stupid Indolence in the most wretched Condition occasion'd by those composing Draughts, which I complain'd of, was a Blessing to Thousands, for that certainly those were the happiest, who felt the least Pain. As to Diseases, he would say, that, as it caused some, so it cured others, and that if the Excess in those Liquors had been sudden Death to some few, the Habit of drinking them daily prolong'd the Lives of many, whom once it agreed with; that for the Loss sustain'd from the insignificant Quarrels it created at home, we were overpaid in the Advantage we receiv'd from it abroad, by upholding the Courage of Soldiers, and animating the Sailors to the Combat; and that in the two last Wars no considerable Victory had been obtain'd without.

To the dismal Account I have given of the Retailers, and what they are forc'd to submit to, he would answer, that not many acquired more than middling Riches in any Trade, and that what I had counted so offensive and intollerable in the Calling, was trifling to those who were used to it; that what seem'd irksome and calamitous to some, was delightful and often ravishing to others; as Men differ'd in Circumstances and Education. He would put me in mind, that the Profit of an Employment ever made amends for the Toil and Labour that belong'd to it, nor forget, *Dulcis odor lucri e re qualibet*[16]; or to tell me, that the Smell of Gain was fragrant even to Night-Workers.

If I should ever urge to him, that to have here and there one great and eminent Distiller was a poor Equivalent for the vile Means, the certain Want, and lasting Misery of so many thousand Wretches, as were necessary to raise them, he would answer, that of this I could be no Judge, because I don't know what vast Benefit they might afterwards be of to the Commonwealth. Perhaps would he say, the Man thus rais'd will exert himself in the Commission of the Peace, or other Station, with Vigilance and Zeal against the Dissolute and Disaffected, and retaining his stirring Temper, be as industrious in spreading Loyalty, and the Reformation of Manners throughout every cranny of the wide populous Town, as once he was in filling it with Spirits; till he becomes at last the Scourge of Whores, of Vagabonds and Beggars, the Terrour of Rioters and discontented Rabbles, and constant Plague to Sabbath-breaking Butchers. Here my good humour'd Antagonist would Exult and Triumph over me, especially if he could instance to me such a bright Example. What an uncommon Blessing would he cry out, is this Man to his Country, how shining and illustrious his Virtue!

To justify his Exclamation he would demonstrate to me, that it was impossible to give a fuller Evidence of Self-denial in a grateful mind, than to see him, at the Expence of his

16. 'The smell of money is sweet from any source whatever.' Mandeville is probably giving an inexact paraphrase of Juvenal, *Satires*, xiv, 204–5. – Ed.

quiet and hazzard of his Life and Limbs, be always haraz-
zing, and even for Trifles persecuting that very Class of
Men, to whom he owes his Fortune, from no other Motive
than his Aversion to Idleness, and great concern for Re-
ligion and the Publick Welfare.

(H.) *Parties directly opposite*
Assist each oth'r, as 'twere for Spight.

PAGE 68. LINE 16. Nothing was more instrumental in for-
warding the Reformation, than the Sloth and Stupidity of
the *Roman* Clergy; yet the same Reformation has rous'd
'em from the Laziness and Ignorance they then labour'd
under, and the followers of *Luther*, *Calvin*, and others, may
be said to have reform'd not only those whom they drew
in to their Sentiments, but likewise those who remain'd
their greatest Opposers. The Clergy of *England* by being
severe upon the Schismaticks, and upbraiding them with
want of Learning, have raised themselves such formidable
Enemies as are not easily answer'd; and again, the Dissenters
by prying into the Lives, and diligently watching all the
Actions of their powerful Antagonists, render those of the
Establish'd Church more cautious of giving Offence, than
in all probability they would, if they had no malicious over-
lookers to fear. It is very much owing to the great number
of *Hugonots* that have always been in *France*, since the late
utter Extirpation of them, that that Kingdom has a less
dissolute and more learned Clergy to boast of than any other
Roman Catholick Country. The Clergy of that Church are
no where more Sovereign than in *Italy*, and therefore no
where more debauch'd; nor any where more Ignorant than
they are in *Spain*, because their Doctrine is no where less
oppos'd.

Who would imagine, that Virtuous Women, unknow-

ingly should be instrumental in promoting the Advantage
of Prostitutes? Or (what still seems the greater Paradox)
that Incontinence should be made serviceable to the Pre-
servation of Chastity? And yet nothing is more true. A
Vicious young Fellow, after having been an Hour or two
at Church, a Ball, or any other Assembly, where there is a
great parcel of handsome Women dress'd to the best Ad-
vantage, will have his Imagination more fired than if he
had the same time been Poling at *Guildhall*, or walking in
the Country among a Flock of Sheep. The consequence of
this is, that he'll strive to satisfy the Appetite that is raised
in him; and when he finds honest Women obstinate and
uncomatable, 'tis very natural to think, that he'll hasten to
others that are more compliable. Who wou'd so much as
surmise, that this is the fault of the Virtuous Women? They
have no Thoughts of Men in dressing themselves, Poor
Souls, and endeavour only to appear clean and decent, every
one according to her Quality.

I am far from encouraging Vice, and think it would be
an unspeakable Felicity to a State, if the Sin of Uncleanness
could be utterly banish'd from it; but I am afraid it is im-
possible. The Passions of some People are too violent to be
curb'd by any Law or Precept; and it is Wisdom in all
Governments to bear with lesser Inconveniencies to prevent
greater. If Courtezans and Strumpets were to be prosecuted
with as much Rigour as some silly People would have it,
what Locks or Bars would be sufficient to preserve the
Honour of our Wives and Daughters? For 'tis not only that
the Women in general would meet with far greater Tempt-
ations, and the Attempts to ensnare the Innocence of
Virgins would seem more excusable even to the sober part
of Mankind than they do now: But some Men would grow
outragious, and ravishing would become a common Crime.
Where Six or Seven Thousand Sailors arrive at once, as it
often happens at *Amsterdam*, that have seen none but their

own Sex for many Months together, how is it to be suppos'd that honest Women should walk the Streets unmolested, if there were no Harlots to be had at reasonable Prices? For which Reason the Wise Rulers of that well order'd City always tolerate an uncertain number of Houses, in which Women are hir'd as publickly as Horses at a Livery Stable; and there being in this Toleration a great deal of Prudence and Oeconomy to be seen, a short account of it will be no tiresome digression.

In the first place the Houses I speak of are allow'd to be no where but in the most slovenly and unpolished part of the Town, where Seamen and Strangers of no Repute chiefly lodge and resort. The Street in which most of them stand is counted scandalous, and the Infamy is extended to all the Neighbourhood round it. In the second, they are only Places to meet and bargain in to make Appointments, in order to promote Interviews of greater Secrecy, and no manner of Lewdness is ever suffer'd to be transacted in them; which order is so strictly observ'd, that bar the ill Manners and Noise of the Company that frequent them, you'll meet with no more Indecency, and generally less Lasciviousness there, than with us are to be seen at a Playhouse. Thirdly, the Female Traders that come to these Evening Exchanges are always the Scum of the People, and generally such as in the Day time carry Fruit and other Eatables about in Wheel barrows. The Habits indeed they appear in at Night are very different from their ordinary ones; yet they are commonly so ridiculously Gay, that they look more like the *Roman* Dresses of stroling Actresses than Gentlewomen's Cloaths: If to this you add the awkwardness, the hard Hands, and course breeding of the Damsels that wear them, there is no great Reason to fear, that many of the better sort of People will be tempted by them.

The Musick in these Temples of *Venus* is perform'd by Organs, not out of Respect to the Deity that is worship'd in them, but the frugality of the Owners, whose Business it is to procure as much sound for as little Money as they can, and the Policy of the Government, who endeavour as little as is possible, to encourage the Breed of Pipers and Scrapers. All Sea-faring Men, especially the *Dutch*, are like the Element they belong to, much given to loudness and roaring, and the Noise of half a dozen of them, when they call themselves Merry, is sufficient to drown twice the number of Flutes or Violins; whereas with one pair of Organs they can make the whole House ring, and are at no other Charge than the keeping of one scurvy Musician which can cost them but little; yet notwithstanding the good Rules and strict Discipline that are observ'd in these Markets of Love, the *Schout*[17] and his Officers are always vexing, mulcting, and upon the least Complaint removing the miserable Keepers of them: Which Policy is of two great uses; first it gives an opportunity to a large parcel of Officers, the Magistrates make use of on many Occasions, and which they could not be without, to squeeze a Living out of the immoderate Gains accruing from the worst of Employments, and at the same time punish those necessary Profligates, the Bawds and Panders, which, tho' they abominate, they desire yet not wholly to destroy. Secondly, as on several accounts it might be dangerous to let the Multitude into the Secret, that those Houses and the Trade that is drove in them are conniv'd at, so by this means appearing unblameable, the wary Magistrates preserve themselves in the good Opinion of the weaker sort of People, who imagine that the Government is always endeavouring, tho' unable, to suppress what it actually tolerates: Whereas if they had a mind to rout them out, their Power in the Administration of Justice is so sovereign and extensive, and they know so well how to have it executed, that one Week, nay one Night, might send them all a packing.

17. A bailiff. – Ed.

Remark (H)

In *Italy* the Toleration of Strumpets is yet more barefac'd, as is evident from their publick Stews. At *Venice* and *Naples* Impurity is a kind of Merchandize and Traffick; the *Courtezans* at *Rome*, and the *Cantoneras* in *Spain*, compose a Body in the State, and are under a Legal Tax and Impost. 'Tis well known, that the Reason why so many good Politicians as these tollerate lewd Houses, is not their Irreligion, but to prevent a worse Evil, an Impurity of a more execrable kind, and to provide for the Safety of Women of Honour. *About Two hundred and fifty Years ago*, says Monsieur *de St Didier*, Venice *being in want of Courtezans, the Republick was obliged to procure a great number from Foreign Parts. Doglioni*, who has written the memorable Affairs of *Venice*, highly extols the Wisdom of the Republick in this Point, which secured the Chastity of Women of Honour daily exposed to publick Violences, the Churches and consecrated Places not being a sufficient Azylum for their Chastity.

Our Universities in *England* are much bely'd if in some Colleges there was not a Monthly Allowance *ad expurgandos Renes*; and time was when the Monks and Priests in *Germany* were allow'd Concubines on paying a certain yearly Duty to their Prelate. *'Tis generally believ'd*, says Monsieur *Bayle*, (to whom I owe the last Paragraph) *that Avarice was the Cause of this shameful Indulgence; but it is more probable their design was to prevent their tempting modest Women, and to quiet the uneasiness of Husbands, whose Resentments the Clergy do well to avoid.* From what has been said it is manifest, that there is a Necessity of sacrifising one part of Womankind to preserve the other, and prevent a Filthinyss of a more heinous Nature. From whence I think I may justly conclude (what was the seeming Paradox I went about to prove) that Chastity may be supported by Incontinence, and the best of Virtues want the Assistance of the worst of Vices.

(I.) The Root of evil Avarice,
That damn'd ill-natur'd baneful Vice,
Was Slave to Prodigality.

PAGE 68. LINE 20. I have joyn'd so many odious Epithets to
the Word Avarice, in compliance to the Vogue of Mankind,
who generally bestow more ill Language upon this than
upon any other Vice; and indeed not undeservedly; for there
is hardly a Mischief to be named which it has not produc'd
at one time or other: But the true Reason why every Body
exclaims so much against it, is, that almost every Body
suffers by it; for the more the Money is hoarded up by some,
the scarcer it must grow among the rest, and therefore when
Men rail very much at Misers, there is generally self Interest
at bottom.

As there is no living without Money, so those that are un-
provided, and have no Body to give them any, are oblig'd
to do some Service or other to the Society, before they can
come at it; but every Body esteeming his Labour as he does
himself, which is generally not under the Value, most People
that want Money only to spend it again presently, imagine
they do more for it than it is worth. Men can't forbear look-
ing upon the Necessaries of Life as their due, whether they
work or not, because they find that Nature, without con-
sulting whether they have Victuals or not, bids them eat
whenever they are hungry; for which Reason every Body
endeavours to get what he wants with as much Ease as he
can; and therefore when Men find that the trouble they are
put to in getting Money is either more or less, according as
those they would have it from are more or less tenacious, it
is very natural for them to be angry at Covetousness in
general; for it obliges them either to go without what they
have occasion for or else to take greater Pains for it than
they are willing.

Avarice, notwithstanding it is the occasion of so many

Evils, is yet very necessary to the Society to glean and gather what has been dropt and scatter'd by the contrary Vice. Was it not for Avarice, Spendthrifts would soon want Materials; and if none would lay up and get faster than they spend, very few could spend faster than they get. That it is a Slave to Prodigality, as I have call'd it, is evident from so many Misers as we daily see toil and labour, pinch and starve themselves to enrich a lavish Heir. Tho' these two Vices appear very opposite, yet they often assist each other. *Florio* is an extravagant young Blade, of a very profuse Temper; as he is the only Son of a very rich Father, he wants to live high, keep Horses and Dogs, and throw his Money about, as he sees some of his Companions do; but the old Hunks will part with no Money, and hardly allows him Necessaries. *Florio* would have borrow'd Money upon his own Credit long ago; but as all would be lost, if he died before his Father, no prudent Man would lend him any. At last he has met with the greedy *Cornaro*, who lets him have Money at Thirty *per Cent.* and now *Florio* thinks himself happy, and spends a Thousand a Year. Where would *Cornaro* ever have got such a prodigious Interest, if it was not for such a Fool as *Florio*, who will give so great a price for Money to fling it away? And how would *Florio* get it to spend, if he had not lit of such a greedy Usurer as *Cornaro*, whose excessive Covetousness makes him over-look the great Risque he runs in venturing such great Sums upon the Life of a wild Debauchee.

Avarice is no longer the Reverse of Profuseness, than whilst it signifies that sordid love of Money, and narrow-ness of Soul that hinders Misers from parting with what they have, and makes them covet it only to hoard up. But there is a sort of Avarice which consists in a greedy desire of Riches, in order to spend them, and this often meets with Prodigality in the same Persons, as is evident in most Courtiers and great Officers, both Civil and Military. In their Buildings and Furniture, Equipages and Entertainments, their Gallantry is display'd with the greatest Profusion, whilst the base Actions they submit to for Lucre, and the many Frauds and Impositions they are guilty of, discover the utmost Avarice. This mixture of contrary Vices comes up exactly to the Character of *Catiline*, of whom it is said, that he was *appetens alieni & sui profusus* greedy after the Goods of others and lavish of his own.[18]

(K.) *That Noble Sin*——

PAGE 68. LINE 23. The Prodigality, I call a noble Sin, is not that which has Avarice for its Companion, and makes Men unreasonably profuse to some of what they unjustly extort from others, but that agreeable good natur'd Vice that makes the Chimney smoak and all the Tradesmen smile, I mean the unmix'd Prodigality of heedless and Voluptuous Men, that being educated in Plenty, abhor the vile Thoughts of Lucre, and lavish away only what others took Pains to scrape together; such as indulge their Inclinations at their own Expence, that have the continual Satisfaction of bartering old Gold for new Pleasures, and from the excessive largeness of a diffusive Soul, are made guilty of despising too much what most People over-value.

When I speak thus honourably of this Vice, and treat it with so much Tenderness and good Manners as I do, I have the same thing at Heart that made me give so many ill Names to the Reverse of it, *viz.* The Interest of the Publick; for as the Avaricious does no Good to himself, and is injurious to all the World besides, except his Heir, so the Prodigal is a Blessing to the whole Society, and injures no body but himself: It is true, that as most of the first are Knaves, so the latter are all Fools; yet they are delicious

18. Sallust, *Bellum Catilinae*, v, 4. – Ed.

Morsels for the Publick to feast on, and may with as much Justice as the *French* call the Monks the Partridges of the Women, be stiled the Woodcocks of the Society. Was it not for Prodigality, nothing could make us amends for the Rapine and Extortion of Avarice in Power. When a Covetous Statesman is gone, who spent his whole Life in fat'ning himself with the spoils of the Nation, and had by pinching and plundering heap'd up an immense Treasure, it ought to fill every good Member of the Society with Joy, to behold the uncommon Profuseness of his Son. This is refunding to the Publick what was robb'd from it. Resuming of Grants is a barbarous way of stripping, and it is ignoble to ruin a Man faster than he does it himself, when he sets about it in such good earnest. Does he not feed an infinite number of Dogs of all sorts and sizes, tho' he never Hunts; keep more Horses than any Nobleman in the Kingdom, tho' he never rides 'em, and give as large an allowance to an ill favour'd Whore as would keep a Dutchess, tho' he never lies with her? Is he not still more extravagant in those things he makes use of? Therefore let him alone or praise him, call him Publick-spirited Lord, nobly Bountiful and magnificently Generous, and in a few Years he'll suffer himself to be stript his own way. As long as the Nation has its own back again, we ought not to quarrel with the manner in which the Plunder is repaid.

Abundance of moderate Men I know that are Enemies to Extreams, will tell me that Frugality might happily supply the Place of the two Vices I speak of, that, if Men had not so many profuse ways of spending Wealth, they would not be tempted to so many evil Practices to scrape it supply the Place of the two Vices I speak of, that, if Men by equally avoiding both Extreams, might render themselves more happy, and be less vicious without than they could with them. Whoever argues thus shews himself a better Man than he is a Politician. Frugality is like Honesty, a mean starving Virtue, that is only fit for small Societies of good peaceable Men, who are contented to be poor so they may be easy; but in a large stirring Nation you may have soon enough of it. 'Tis an idle dreaming Virtue that employs no Hands, and therefore very useless in a trading Country, where there are vast numbers that one way or other must be all set to Work. Prodigality has a thousand Inventions to keep People from sitting still, that Frugality would never think of; and as this must consume a prodigious Wealth, so Avarice again knows innumerable Tricks to rake it together, which Frugality would scorn to make use of.

Authors are always allow'd to compare small things to great ones, especially if they ask leave first. *Si licet exemplis*, &c. but to compare great things to mean trivial ones is insufferable, unless it be in Burlesque; otherwise I would compare the Body Politick (I confess the Simile is very low) to a Bowl of Punch. Avarice should be the sow'ring, and Prodigality the sweetning of it. The Water I would call the Ignorance, Folly and Credulity of the floating insipid Multitude; whilst Wisdom, Honour, Fortitude, and the rest of the sublime Qualities of Men, which separated by Art from the dregs of Nature, the fire of Glory has exalted and refin'd into a Spiritual Essence, should be an equivalent to Brandy. I don't doubt but a *Westphalian*, *Laplander*, or any other dull Stranger that is unacquainted with the wholesome Composition, if he was to taste the several Ingredients apart, would think it impossible they should make any tolerable Liquor. The Lemons would be too sower, the Sugar too luscious, the Brandy he'll say is too strong ever to be drank in any quantity, and the Water he'll call a tasteless Liquor only fit for Cows and Horses: Yet Experience teaches us, that the Ingredients I named judiciously mixt, will make an excellent Liquor, lik'd of and admir'd by Men of exquisite Palates.

As to our two Vices in particular, I could compare Avarice,

that causes so much Mischief, and is complain'd of by every body who is not a Miser, to a griping Acid that sets our Teeth on edge, and is unpleasant to every Palate that is not debauch'd: I could compare the gaudy Trimming and splendid Equipage of a profuse Beau, to the glistning brightness of the finest Loaf Sugar; for as the one by correcting the sharpness prevents the injuries which a gnawing Sower might do to the Bowels, so the other is a pleasing Balsam that heals and makes amends for the smart, which the Multitude always suffers from the Gripes of the Avaricious; whilst the substances of both melt away alike, and they consume themselves by being beneficial to the several Compositions they belong to. I could carry on the Simile as to proportions, and the exact nicety to be observ'd in them, which would make it appear how little any of the Ingredients could be spared in either of the Mixtures: But I will not tire my Reader by pursuing too far a ludicrous Comparison, when I have other Matters to entertain him with of greater Importance; and to sum up what I have said in this and the foregoing Remark, shall only add, that I look upon Avarice and Prodigality in the Society as I do upon two contrary Poysons in Physick, of which it is certain that the noxious qualities being by mutual mischief corrected in both, they may assist each other, and often make a good Medicine between them.

(L.) ———— *Whilst Luxury*
Employ'd a Million of the Poor, &c.

PAGE 68. LINE 23. If every thing is to be Luxury (as in strictness it ought) that is not immediately necessary to make Man subsist as he is a living Creature, there is nothing else to be found in the World, no not even among the naked Savages; of which it is not probable that there are any but

what by this time have made some Improvements upon their
former manner of Living; and either in the preparation of
their Eatables, the ordering of their Huts, or otherwise
added something to what once sufficed them. This definition
every body will say is too rigorous; I am of the same
Opinion, but if we are to abate one Inch of this Severity,
I am afraid we shan't know where to stop. When People
tell us they only desire to keep themselves sweet and clean,
there is no understanding what they would be at, if they
made use of these Words in their genuine, proper, litteral
Sense, they might soon be satisfy'd without much cost or
trouble, if they did not want Water: But these two little ad-
jectives are so comprehensive, especially in the Dialect of
some Ladies, that no body can guess how far they may be
stretcht. The Comforts of Life are likewise so various and
extensive, that no body can tell what People mean by them,
except he knows what sort of Life they lead. The same
obscurity I observe in the words Decency and Conveniency,
and I never understand them unless I am acquainted with
the quality of the Persons that make use of them. People
may go to Church together, and be all of one Mind as
much as they please, I am apt to believe that when
they Pray for their daily Bread, the Bishop includes several
things in that Petition which the Sexton does not think
on.

By what I have said hitherto I would only shew, that if
once we depart from calling every thing Luxury that is not
absolutely necessary to keep a Man alive, that then there is
no Luxury at all; for if the wants of Men are innumerable,
then what ought to supply them has no bounds; what is
call'd superfluous to some degree of People will be thought
requisite to those of higher Quality; and neither the World
nor the Skill of Man can produce any thing so curious or
extravagant, but some most Gracious Sovereign or other,
if it either eases or diverts him, will reckon it among the

Necessaries of Life; not meaning every Body's Life, but that of his Sacred Person.

It is a receiv'd Notion, that Luxury is as destructive to the Wealth of the whole Body Politick, as it is to that of every individual Person who is guilty of it, and that a National Frugality enriches a Country in the same manner as that which is less general increases the Estates of Private Families. I confess, that tho' I have found Men of much better Understanding than my self of this Opinion, I cannot help dissenting from them in this Point. They argue thus: We send, say they, for Example to *Turkey* of Woollen Manufactury, and other things of our own Growth, a Millions worth every Year; for this we bring back Silk, Mohair, Drugs, &c. to the value of Twelve Hundred Thousand Pounds, that are all spent in our own Country. By this, say they, we get nothing; but if most of us would be content with our own Growth, and so consume but half the quantity of those Foreign Commodities, then those in *Turkey*, who would still want the same quantity of our Manufactures, would be forc'd to pay ready Money for the rest, and so by the Ballance of that Trade only, the Nation should get Six Hundred Thousand Pounds *per Annum*.

To examine the force of this Argument, we'll suppose (what they would have) that but half the Silk, &c. shall be consumed in *England* of what there is now; we'll suppose likewise, that those in *Turkey*, tho' we refuse to buy above half as much of their Commodities as we used to do, either can or will not be without the same quantity of our Manufactures they had before, and that they'll pay the Balance in Money; that is to say, that they shall give us as much Gold or Silver as the value of what they buy from us exceeds the value of what we buy from them. Tho' what we suppose might perhaps be done for one Year, it is impossible it should last: Buying is Bartering, and no Nation can buy Goods of others that has none of her own to purchase them with. *Spain* and *Portugal*, that are yearly supply'd with new Gold and Silver from their Mines, may for ever buy for ready Money as long as their yearly encrease of Gold or Silver continues, but then Money is their Growth and the Commodity of the Country. We know that we could not continue long to purchase the Goods of other Nations, if they would not take our Manufactures in Payment for them; and why should we judge otherwise of other Nations? If those in *Turkey* then had no more Money fall from the Skies than we, let us see what would be the consequence of what we supposed. The Six Hundred Thousand Pounds in Silk, Mohair, &c. that are left upon their Hands the first Year, must make those Commodities fall considerably: Of this the *Dutch* and *French* will reap the Benefit as much as our selves; and if we continue to refuse taking their Commodities in Payment for our Manufactures, they can Trade no longer with us, but must content themselves with buying what they want of such Nations as are willing to take what we refuse, tho' their Goods are much worse than ours, and thus our Commerce with *Turkey* must in few Years be infallibly lost.

But they'll say, perhaps, that to prevent the ill consequence I have shew'd, we shall take the *Turkish* Merchandizes as formerly, and only be so frugal as to consume but half the quantity of them our selves, and send the rest Abroad to be sold to others. Let us see what this will do, and whether it will enrich the Nation by the Balance of that Trade with Six Hundred Thousand Pounds. In the first Place, I'll grant them that our People at Home making use of so much more of our own Manufactures, those who were employ'd in Silk, Mohair, &c. will get a living by the various Preparations of Woollen Goods. But in the second, I cannot allow that the Goods can be sold as formerly; for suppose the half that is wore at Home to be sold at the same rate as before, certainly the other half that is sent Abroad will want very much of it:

For we must send those Goods to Markets already supply'd; and besides that, there must be Freight, Insurance, Provision, and all other Charges deducted, and the Merchants in general must lose much more by this half that is re-shipp'd, than they got by the half that is consumed here. For tho' the Woollen Manufactures are our own Product, yet they stand the Merchant that Ships them off to Foreign Countries, in as much as they do the Shopkeeper here that retails them; so that if the Returns for what he sends Abroad repay him not what his Goods cost him here, with all other Charges, till he has the Money and a good Interest for it in Cash, the Merchant must run out, and the upshot would be, that the Merchants in general finding they lost by the *Turkish* Commodities they sent Abroad, would Ship no more of our Manufactures than what would pay for as much Silk, Mohair, &c. as would be consumed here. Other Nations would soon find ways to supply them with as much as we should send short, and some where or other to dispose of the Goods we should refuse: So that all we should get by this Frugality would be, that those in *Turkey* would take but half the quantity of our Manufactures of what they do now, whilst we encourage and wear their Merchandizes, without which they are not able to purchase ours.

As I have had the Mortification for several Years to meet with abundance of sensible People against this Opinion, and who always thought me wrong in this Calculation, so I had the Pleasure at last to see the Wisdom of the Nation fall into the same Sentiments, as is so manifest from an Act of Parliament made in the Year 1721, where the Legislature disobliges a powerful and valuable Company, and overlooks very weighty Inconveniencies at Home to promote the Interest of the *Turkey* Trade, and not only encourages the Consumption of Silk and Mohair, but forces the Subjects on Penalties to make use of them whether they will or not.[19]

19. This paragraph was added in 1723. – Ed.

What is laid to the charge of Luxury besides, is, that it encreases Avarice and Rapine; and where they are reigning Vices, Offices of the greatest Trust are bought and sold; the Ministers that should serve the Publick, both great and small, corrupted, and the Countries every Moment in danger of being betray'd to the highest Bidders: And lastly, that it effeminates and enervates the People, by which the Nations become an easy Prey to the first Invaders. These are indeed terrible things; but what is put to the account of Luxury belongs to Male-Administration, and is the fault of bad Politicks. Every Government ought to be thoroughly acquainted with, and stedfastly to pursue the Interest of the Country. Good Politicians, by dextrous Management, laying heavy Impositions on some Goods, or totally prohibiting them, and lowering the Duties on others, may always turn and divert the course of Trade which way they please; and as they'll ever prefer, if it be equally considerable, the Commerce with such Countries as can pay with Money as well as Goods to those that can make no Returns for what they buy, but in the Commodities of their own Growth and Manufacture, so they will always carefully prevent the Traffick with such Nations as refuse the Goods of others, and will take nothing but Money for their own. But above all, they'll keep a watchful Eye over the Ballance of Trade in general, and never suffer that all the Foreign Commodities together that are imported in one Year, shall exceed in value what of their own Growth or Manufacture is in the same exported to others. Note, that I speak now of the Interest of those Nations that have no Gold or Silver of their own Growth, otherwise this Maxim need not to be so much insisted on.

If what I urg'd last be but diligently look'd after, and the Imports are never allow'd to be superior to the Exports, no Nation can ever be impoverish'd by Foreign Luxury; and they may improve it as much as they please, if they can but in proportion raise the Fund of their own that is to purchase it.

Trade is the Principal, but not the only Requisite to aggrandize a Nation; there are other Things to be taken Care of besides. The *Meum* and *Tuum* must be secur'd, Crimes punish'd, and all other Laws concerning the Administration of Justice, wisely contriv'd, and strictly executed. Foreign Affairs must be likewise prudently manag'd, and the Ministry of every Nation ought to have a good Intelligence Abroad, and be well acquainted with the Publick Transactions of all those Countries, that either by their Neighbourhood, Strength or Interest, may be hurtful or beneficial to them, to take the necessary Measures accordingly, of crossing some and assisting others, as Policy and the Balance of Power direct. The Multitude must be aw'd, no Man's Conscience forc'd, and the Clergy allow'd no greater Share in State Affairs than our Saviour has bequeathed them in his Testament. These are the Arts that lead to worldly Greatness; what Sovereign Power soever makes a good use of them, that has any considerable Nation to govern, whether it be a Monarchy, a Commonwealth, or a mixture of both, can never fail of making it flourish in spight of all the other Powers upon Earth, and no Luxury or other Vice is ever able to shake their Constitution.—— But here I expect a full mouth'd Cry against me. What! has God never punish'd and destroy'd great Nations for their Sins? Yes, but not without means; by infatuating their Governors, and suffering them to depart from either all or some of those general Maxims I have mention'd; and of all the famous States and Empires the World has had to boast of hitherto, none ever came to Ruin whose Destruction was not principally owing to the bad Politicks, Neglects, or Mismanagements of the Rulers.

There is no doubt but more Health and Vigour is to be expected among a People, and their Offspring, from Temperance and Sobriety, than there is from Gluttony and Drunkenness; yet I confess, that as to Luxury's effeminating and enervating a Nation, I have not such frightful Notions now as I have had formerly. When we hear or read of things which we are altogether Strangers to, they commonly bring to our Imagination such Ideas of what we have seen, as (according to our apprehension) must come the nearest to them: And I remember, that when I have read of the Luxury of *Persia*, *Ægypt*, and other Countries where it has been a reigning Vice, and that were effeminated and enervated by it, it has sometimes put me in mind of the cramming and swilling of ordinary Tradesmen at a City Feast, and the beastliness their over-gorging themselves is often attended with; at other times it has made me think on the Distraction of dissolute Sailors, as I had seen them in Company of half a dozen lewd Women roaring along with Fiddles before them; and was I to have been carried into any of their great Cities, I would have expected to have found one third of the People Sick a Bed with Surfeits; another laid up with the Gout, or crippled by a more ignominious Distemper, and the rest, that could go without leading, walk along the Streets in Petticoats.

It is happy for us to have Fear for a Keeper, as long as our Reason is not strong enough to govern our Appetites; and I believe that the great Dread I had more particularly against the Word, *to enervate*, and some consequent Thoughts on the Etymology of it did me abundance of good when I was a School-boy: But since I have seen something of the World, the Consequences of Luxury to a Nation seem not so dreadful to me as they did. As long as Men have the same Appetites, the same Vices will remain. In all large Societies, some will love Whoring and others Drinking. The Lustful that can get no handsome clean Women, will content themselves with dirty Drabs; and those that cannot purchase true *Hermitage* or *Pontack*, will be glad of more ordinary

French Claret. Those that can't reach Wine, take up with worse Liquors, and a Foot Soldier or a Beggar may make himself as drunk with Stale-Beer or Malt-Spirits, as a Lord with *Burgundy, Champaign* or *Tockay*. The cheapest and most slovenly way of indulging our Passions, does as much Mischief to a Man's Constitution, as the most elegant and expensive.

The greatest Excesses of Luxury are shewn in Buildings, Furniture, Equipages and Cloaths; clean Linnen weakens a Man no more than Flannel, Tapistry, fine Painting or good Wainscot are no more unwholesome than bare Walls; and a rich Couch, or a gilt Charriot are no more enervating than the cold Floor or a Country Cart. The refin'd Pleasures of Men of Sence are seldom injurious to their Constitution, and there are many great Epicures that will refuse to eat or drink more than their Heads or Stomachs can bear. Sensual People may take as great Care of themselves as any; and the Errors of the most viciously Luxurious, don't so much consist in the frequent Repetitions of their Lewdness, and their eating and drinking too much, (which are the things which would most enervate them) as they do in the operose Contrivances, the Profuseness and Nicety they are serv'd with, and the vast Expence they are at in their Tables and Amours.

But let us once suppose that the Ease and Pleasure the Grandees and the rich People of every great Nation live in, render them unfit to endure Hardships, and undergo the Toils of War. I'll allow that most of the Common Council of the City would make but very indifferent Foot Soldiers; and I believe heartily, that if your Horse was to be compos'd of Aldermen, and such as most of them are, a small Artillery of Squibs would be sufficient to rout them; But what have the Aldermen, the Common Council, or indeed all People of any Substance to do with the War, but to pay Taxes. The Hardships and Fatigues of War that are Personally suffer'd, fall upon them that bear the Brunt of every thing, the meanest indigent Part of the Nation, the working slaving People: For how excessive soever the Plenty and Luxury of a Nation may be, some Body must do the work. Houses and Ships must be built, Merchandizes must be remov'd, and the Ground till'd. Such a variety of Labours in every great Nation requires a vast multitude, in which there are always loose, idle, extravagant Fellows enough to spare for an Army, and those that are Robust enough to Hedge and Ditch, Plow and Thrash, or else not too much enervated to be Smiths, Carpenters, Sawyers, Clothworkers, Porters or Carmen, will always be strong and hardy enough in a Campaign or two to make good Soldiers, who, where good Orders are kept, have seldom so much Plenty and Superfluity come to their Share as to do them any hurt.

The Mischief then to be fear'd from Luxury among the People of War, cannot extend itself beyond the Officers. The greatest of them are either Men of a very high Birth and Princely Education, or else extraordinary Parts and no less Experience, and whoever is made choice of by a wise Government to command an Army *en chef*, should have a consummate Knowledge in Martial Affairs, Intrepidity to keep him calm in the midst of danger, and many other Qualifications that must be the work of Time and Application, on Men of a quick Penetration, a distinguish'd Genius, and a world of Honour. Strong Sinews and supple Joints are trifling Advantages not regarded in Persons of their Reach and Grandeur, that can destroy Cities o'Bed, and ruin whole Countries whilst they are at Dinner. As they are most commonly Men of great Age, it would be ridiculous to expect a hail Constitution and Agility of Limbs from them: So their Heads be but Active and well furnish'd, 'tis no great Matter what the rest of their Bodies are. If they cannot bear the Fatigue of being on Horseback, they may ride in Coaches, or be carried in Litters. Men's

Conduct and Sagacity are never the less for their being
Cripples, and the best General the King of *France* has now,
can hardly crawl along.[20] Those that are immediately under
the chief Commanders must be very nigh of the same Abili-
ties, and are generally Men that have rais'd themselves to
those Posts by their Merit. The other Officers are all of them
in their several Stations oblig'd to lay out so large a share
of their Pay in fine Cloaths, Accoutrements, and other
Things by the luxury of the Times call'd necessary, that they
can spare but little Money for Debauches, for as they are
advanced and their Sallaries rais'd, so they are likewise
forc'd to increase their Expences and their Equipages, which
as well as every thing else, must still be proportionable to
their Quality. By which means the greatest part of them are
in a manner hindred from those Excesses that might be de-
structive to Health, whilst their Luxury thus turn'd another
way serves moreover to heighten their Pride and Vanity,
the greatest Motives to make them behave themselves like
what they would be thought to be. (*See Remark (R.)*.)

There is nothing refines Mankind more than Love and
Honour. Those two Passions are equivalent to many
Virtues, and therefore the greatest Schools of Breeding and
good Manners are Courts and Armies; the first to accom-
plish the Women, the other to polish the Men. What the
generality of Officers among civiliz'd Nations affect is a
perfect Knowledge of the World and the Rules of Honour,
an Air of Frankness, and Humanity peculiar to Military
Men of Experience, and such a Mixture of Modesty and
Undauntedness, as may bespeak them both Courteous and
Valiant. Where good Sense is fashionable, and a genteel
Behaviour is in esteem, Gluttony and Drunkenness can be
no reigning Vices. What Officers of Distinction chiefly aim
at, is not a Beastly, but a Splendid way of Living, and the
Wishes of the most Luxurious in their several degrees of

20. The Duc de Villars (1653–1734). – Ed.

Quality, are to appear handsomely, and excel each other in Finery of Equipage, Politeness of Entertainments, and the Reputation of a judicious Fancy in every thing about them.

But if there should be more dissolute Reprobates among Officers than there are among Men of other Professions, which is not true, yet the most debauch'd of them may be very serviceable, if they have but a great share of Honour. It is this that covers and makes up for a multitude of Defects in them, and it is this that none (how abandon'd soever they are to Pleasure) dare pretend to be without. But as there is no Argument so convincing as Matter of Fact, let us look back on what so lately happen'd in our two last Wars with *France*.[21] How many puny young Striplings have we had in our Armies tenderly Educated, nice in their Dress, and curious in their Dyet, that underwent all manner of Duties with Gallantry and Chearfulness?

Those that have such dismal Apprehensions of Luxury's enervating and effeminating People, might in *Flanders* and *Spain*, have seen embroider'd Beaux with fine lac'd Shirts and powder'd Wigs, stand as much Fire and lead up to the Mouth of a Cannon, with as little Concern as it was possible for the most stinking Slovens to have done in their own Hair, tho' it had not been comb'd in a Month; and met with abundance of wild Rakes, who had actually impair'd their Healths, and broke their Constitutions with Excesses of Wine and Women, that yet behav'd themselves with Conduct and Bravery against their Enemies. Robustness is the least thing requir'd in an Officer, and if sometimes Strength is of use, a firm Resolution of Mind, which the hopes of Preferment, Emulation, and the Love of Glory inspire them with, will at a push supply the Place of Bodily Force.

Those that understand their Business, and have a sufficient sense of Honour, as soon as they are used to Danger will

21. The war of the Grand Alliance (1689–97) and the War of the Spanish Succession (1701–13). – Ed.

always be capable Officers: and their Luxury, as long as they spend no Body's Money but their own, will never be prejudicial to a Nation.

By all which I think I have proved what I design'd in this Remark on Luxury. First, that in one sense every thing may be call'd so, and in another there is no such thing. Secondly, that with a wise Administration all People may swim in as much foreign Luxury as their Product can purchase, without being impoverish'd by it; and lastly, that where Military Affairs are taken care of as they ought, and the Soldiers well paid and kept in good Discipline, a wealthy Nation may live in all the Ease and Plenty imaginable, and in many Parts of it shew as much Pomp and Delicacy, as Humane Wit can invent, and at the same time be formidable to their Neighbours, and come up to the Character of the Bees in the Fable, of which I said, That

> *Flatter'd in Peace, and fear'd in Wars*
> *They were th' Esteem of Foreigners,*
> *And lavish of their Wealth and Lives,*
> *The Ballance of all other Hives.*

(See what is further said concerning Luxury in *Remarks* (*M.*) and (*Q.*)

(M.) *And odious Pride a Million more.*

PAGE 68. LINE 25. Pride is that Natural Faculty by which every Mortal that has any Understanding over values, and imagines better things of himself than any impartial Judge, thoroughly acquainted with all his Qualities and Circumstances could allow him. We are possess'd of no other Quality so beneficial to Society, and so necessary to render it wealthy and flourishing as this, yet it is that which is most generally detested. What is very peculiar to this faculty of ours, is, that those who are the fullest of it are the least willing to connive at it in others; whereas the heineousness of other Vices is the most extenuated by those who are guilty of 'em themselves. The Chaste Man hates Fornication, and Drunkenness is most abhorr'd by the Temperate; but none are so much offended at their Neighbour's Pride, as the proudest of all, and if any one can pardon it, it is the most humble: From which I think we may justly infer, that its being odious to all the World is a certain sign that all the World is troubled with it. This all Men of Sense are ready to confess, and no body denies but that he has Pride in general. But if you come to Particulars, you'll meet with few that will own any Action you can name of theirs to have proceeded from that Principle. There are likewise many who will allow that among the sinful Nations of the Times, Pride and Luxury, are the great Promoters of Trade, but they refuse to own the necessity there is, that in a more Virtuous Age, (such a one as should be free from Pride) Trade would in a great measure decay.

The Almighty, say they, has endow'd us with the Dominion over all Things which the Earth and Sea produce or contain; there is nothing to be found in either, but what was made for the use of Man; and his Skill and Industry above other Animals were given him, that he might render both them and every thing else within the reach of his Senses, more serviceable to him. Upon this Consideration they think it impious to imagine, that Humility, Temperance, and other Virtues, should debar People from the Enjoyment of those Comforts of Life, which are not denied to the most wicked Nations; and so conclude, that without Pride or Luxury, the same things might be eat, wore, and consumed, the same number of Handicrafts and Artificers employ'd, and a Nation be every way as flourishing as where those Vices are the most predominant.

As to wearing Apparel in particular, they'll tell you, that

Pride, which sticks much nearer to us than our Cloaths, is only lodg'd in the Heart, and that Rags often conceal a greater Portion of it than the most pompous Attire; and that as it cannot be denied but that there have always been Virtuous Princes, who with humble Hearts have wore their splendid Diadems and sway'd their envied Scepters, void of Ambition for the good of others; so it is very probable, that Silver and Gold Brocades, and the richest Embroideries, may, without a thought of Pride, be wore by many whose Quality and Fortune are suitable to them. May not (say they) a good Man of extraordinary Revenues, make every Year a greater variety of Suits than it is possible he should wear out, and yet have no other Ends than to set the Poor at work to encourage Trade, and by employing many to promote the Welfare of his Country? And considering Food and Rayment to be Necessaries, and the two chief Articles to which all our worldly Cares are extended, why may not all Mankind set aside a considerable Part of their Income for the one as well as the other, without the least Tincture of Pride? Nay, is not every Member of the Society in a manner obliged, according to his Ability, to contribute toward the Maintenance of that Branch of Trade on which the whole has so great a dependance? Besides that, to appear decently is a Civility, and often a Duty, which, without any Regard to our selves, we owe to those we converse with.

These are the Objections generally made use of by haughty Moralists, who cannot endure to hear the Dignity of their Species arrain'd; but if we look narrowly into them they may soon be answer'd.

If we had no Vices, I cannot see why any Man should ever make more Suits than he has occasion for, tho' he were never so desirous of promoting the good of the Nation: For tho' in the wearing of a well wrought Silk, rather than a slight Stuff, and the preferring curious fine Cloth to course, he had no other view but the setting of more People to work, and consequently, the Publick Welfare, yet he could consider Cloaths no otherwise than Lovers of their Country do Taxes now; they may pay 'em with Alacrity, but no body gives more than his due; especially where all are justly rated according to their Abilities, as it could no otherwise be expected in a very Virtuous Age. Besides that, in such Golden Times no body would dress above his Condition, no body pinch his Family, cheat or overreach his Neighbour to purchase Finery, and consequently there would not be half the Consumption, nor a third part of the People employ'd as now there are. But to make this more plain and demonstrate, that for the support of Trade there can be nothing equivalent to Pride, I shall examine the several views Men have in outward Apparel, and set forth what daily Experience may teach every body as to Dress.

Cloaths were originally made for two Ends, to hide our Nakedness, and to fence our Bodies against the Weather, and other outward Injuries: To these our boundless Pride has added a third, which is Ornament; for what else but an excess of stupid Vanity, could have prevail'd upon our Reason to fancy that Ornamental, which must continually put us in mind of our Wants and Misery, beyond all other Animals that are ready cloathed by Nature herself? It is indeed to be admired how so sensible a Creature as Man, that pretends to so many fine Qualities of his own, should condescend to value himself upon what is robb'd from so innocent and defenceless an Animal as a Sheep, or what he is beholden for to the most insignificant thing upon Earth, a dying Worm; yet whilst he is Proud of such trifling Depredations, he has the folly to laugh at the Hottentots on the furthest Promontory of *Africk*, who adorn themselves with the Guts of their dead Enemies, without considering that they are the Ensigns of their Valour those Barbarians are fine with, the true *Spolia opima*,[22] and that if their Pride be

22. Rich spoils. – Ed.

more Savage than ours, it is certainly less ridiculous, because they wear the Spoils of the more noble Animal.

But whatever Reflections may be made on this head, the World has long since decided the Matter; handsome Apparel is a main Point, fine Feathers make fine Birds, and People where they are not known, are generally honour'd according to their Cloaths and other Accoutrements they have about them; from the richness of them we judge of their Wealth, and by their ordering of them we guess at their Understanding. It is this which encourages every body, who is conscious of his little Merit, if he is any ways able to wear Cloaths above his Rank, especially in large and Populous Cities, where obscure Men may hourly meet with fifty Strangers to one Acquaintance, and consequently have the Pleasure of being esteem'd by a vast Majority, not as what they are, but what they appear to be; which is a greater Temptation than most People want to be Vain.

Whoever takes delight in viewing the various Scenes of low Life, may on *Easter*, *Whitsun*, and other great Holydays, meet with scores of People, especially Women, of almost the lowest Rank, that wear good and fashionable Cloaths. If coming to talk with them, you treat them more courteously and with greater Respect than what they are conscious they deserve, they'll commonly be ashamed of owning what they are; and often you may, if you are a little Inquisitive, discover in them a most anxious Care to conceal the Business they follow, and the Places they live in. The Reason is plain; whilst they receive those Civilities that are not usually paid them, and which they think only due to their Betters, they have the Satisfaction to imagine, that they appear what they would be, which to weak Minds is a Pleasure almost as substantial as they could reap from the very Accomplishments of their Wishes : This Golden Dream they are unwilling to be disturbed in, and being sure that the meanness of their Condition, if it is known, must sink 'em very low in your Opinion, they hug themselves in their disguize, and take all imaginable Precaution not to forfeit by a useless discovery the Esteem which they flatter themselves that their good Cloaths have drawn from you.

Tho' every body allows, that as to Apparel and manner of living, we ought to behave our selves suitable to our Conditions, and follow the Examples of the most sensible and prudent among our Equals in Rank and Fortune: Yet how few, that are not either miserably Covetous, or else Proud of singularity, have this Discretion to boast of? We all look above our selves, and, as fast as we can, strive to imitate those, that some way or other are superior to us.

The poorest Labourer's Wife in the Parish, who scorns to wear a strong wholesome Frize, as she might, will half starve herself and her Husband to purchase a second hand Gown and Petticoat, that cannot do her half the Service, because, forsooth, it is more genteel. The Weaver, the Shoemaker, the Taylor, the Barber, and every mean working Fellow, that can set up with little, has the Impudence with the first Money he gets, to Dress himself like a Tradesman of Substance. The ordinary Retailer in the cloathing of his Wife, takes Pattern from his Neighbour, that deals in the same Commodity by Wholesale, and the Reason he gives for it, is, that Twelve Years ago the other had not a bigger Shop than himself. The Druggist, Mercer, Draper and other creditable Shopkeepers can find no difference between themselves and Merchants, and therefore dress and live like them. The Merchant's Lady, who cannot bear the Assurance of those Mechanicks, flies for refuge to the other End of the Town, and scorns to follow any Fashion but what she takes from thence. This haughtiness alarms the Court, the Women of Quality are frighten'd to see Merchant's Wives and Daughters dress'd like themselves; this Impudence of the City, they cry, is intollerable; Mantua-makers are sent for, and the contrivance of Fashions becomes all their Study, that they may have always new Modes ready to take up, as soon as those sawcy Cits shall begin to imitate those in being. The same Emulation is continued through the several degrees of Quality to an incredible Expence, till at last the Prince's great Favourites and those of the first Rank of all, having nothing else left to outstrip some of their Inferiors, are forc'd to lay out vast Estates in pompous Equipages, magnificent Furniture, sumptuous Gardens and princely Palaces.

To this Emulation and continual striving to outdo one another, it is owing, that after so many various Shiftings and Changings of Modes, in trumping up new ones and renewing of old ones, there is still a *plus ultra* left for the Ingenious; it is this, or at least the consequence of it, that sets the Poor to Work, adds Spurs to Industry, and incourages the skilful Artificer to search after further Improvements.

It may be objected, that many People of good Fashion, who have been us'd to be well Dress'd, out of Custom wear rich Cloaths with all the indifferency imaginable, and that the benefit to Trade accruing from them cannot be ascrib'd to Emulation or Pride. To this I answer, that it is impossible, that those who trouble their Heads so little with their Dress, could ever have wore those rich Cloaths, if both the Stuffs and Fashions had not been first invented to gratify the Vanity of others, who took greater delight in fine Apparel, than they. Besides that every Body is not without Pride that appears to be so, all the symptoms of that Vice are not easily discover'd; they are manifold and vary according to the Age, Humour, Circumstances, and often Constitution, of the People.

The cholerick City Captain seems impatient to come to Action, and expressing his Warlike Genius by the firmness of his Steps, makes his Pike, for want of Enemies, tremble at the Valour of his Arm. His Martial Finery, as he Marches along, inspires him with an unusual Elevation of Mind, by which endeavouring to forget his Shop as well as himself, he looks up at the Balconies with the fierceness of a *Sarazen* Conqueror. Whilst the phlegmatick Alderman, now become venerable both for his Age and his Authority, contents himself with being thought a considerable Man; and knowing no easier way to express his Vanity, looks big in his Coach, where being known by his paultry Livery, he receives, in sullen State, the Homage that is paid him by the meaner sort of People.

The beardless Ensign counterfeits a Gravity above his Years, and with ridiculous Assurance strives to imitate the stern Countenance of his Collonel, flattering himself all the while, that by his daring Mien you'll judge of his Prowess. The youthful Fair, in a vast concern of being overlook'd, by the continual changing of her Posture betrays a violent desire of being observ'd, and catching, as it were at every Body's eyes, Courts, with obliging Looks, the admiration of her Beholders. The conceited Coxcomb, on the contrary, displaying an Air of Sufficiency, is wholly taken up with the Contemplation of his own Perfections, and in Publick Places discovers such a disregard to others, that the Ignorant must imagine, he thinks himself to be alone.

These and such like are all manifest tho' different Tokens of Pride, that are obvious to all the World, but Man's Vanity is not always so soon found out. When we perceive an Air of Humanity, and Men seem not to be employ'd in admiring themselves, nor altogether unmindful of others, we are apt to pronounce 'em void of Pride, when perhaps they are only fatigu'd with gratifying their Vanity, and become languid from a satiety of Enjoyments. That outward show of Peace within, and drowsy composure of careless Negligence, with which a Great Man is often seen in his plain Chariot to loll at ease, are not always so free from Art, as they may seem to be. *Nothing is more ravishing to the Proud than to be thought happy*.

The well bred Gentleman places his greatest Pride in the

Skill he has of covering it with Dexterity, and some are so expert in concealing this Frailty, that when they are the most guilty of it, the Vulgar think them the most exempt from it. Thus the dissembling Courtier, when he appears in State, assumes an Air of Modesty and good Humour, and whilst he is ready to burst with Vanity, seems to be wholly ignorant of his Greatness, well knowing, that those lovely Qualities must heighten him in the Esteem of others, and be an addition to that Grandeur, which the Coronets about his Coach and Harnesses, with the rest of his Equipage, cannot fail to proclaim without his Assistance.

And as in these, Pride is overlook'd, because industriously conceal'd, so in others again it is denied that they have any, when they shew (or at least seem to shew) it in the most Publick manner. The wealthy Parson, being as well as the rest of his Profession, debar'd from the Gaiety of Laymen, makes it his business to look out for an admirable Black and the finest Cloath that Money can purchase, and distinguishes himself by the fulness of his noble and spotless Garment; his Wigs are as fashionable as that Form he is forced to comply with will admit of; but as he is only stinted in their shape, so he takes care that for goodness of Hair and Colour, few Noblemen shall be able to match 'em; his Body is ever clean, as well as his Cloaths, his sleek Face is kept constantly shav'd, and his handsome Nails are diligently pared, his smooth white Hand and a Brilliant of the first Water, mutually becoming, honour each other with double graces; what Linnen he discovers is transparently curious, and he scorns ever to be seen abroad with a worse Beaver than what a rich Banker would be proud of on his Wedding Day; to all these niceties in Dress he adds a Majestick Gate, and expresses a commanding loftiness in his Carriage; yet common Civility, notwithstanding the evidence of so many concurring Symptoms, won't allow us to suspect any of his Actions to be the result of Pride; considering the Dignity of his Office, it is only Decency in him what would be Vanity in others; and in good Manners to his Calling we ought to believe, that the worthy Gentleman, without any regard to his reverend Person, puts himself to all this trouble and expence meerly out of a respect which is due to the Divine Order he belongs to, and a Religious Zeal to preserve his Holy Function from the Contempt of Scoffers. With all my Heart; nothing of all this shall be call'd Pride, let me only be allow'd to say, that to our Human Capacities it looks very like it.

But if at last I should grant, that there are Men who enjoy all the Fineries of Equipage and Furniture, as well as Cloaths, and yet have no Pride in them, it is certain, that if all should be such, that Emulation I spoke of before must cease, and consequently Trade, which has so great a dependance upon it, suffer in every branch. For to say, that if all Men were truly Vertuous, they might, without any regard to themselves, consume as much out of Zeal to serve their Neighbours and promote the Publick Good, as they do now out of Self love and Emulation, is a miserable shift and an unreasonable supposition. As there have been good People in all Ages, so, without doubt, we are not destitute of them in this; but let us enquire of the Perriwig makers and Taylors, in what Gentlemen, even of the greatest Wealth and highest Quality, they ever could discover such publick spirited Views. Ask the Lacemen, the Mercers and the Linnen drapers, whether the richest, and if you will, the most vertuous Ladies, if they buy with ready Moncy, or intend to pay in any reasonable time, will not drive from Shop to Shop to try the Market, make as many Words, and stand as hard with them to save a Groat or Six Pence in a Yard, as the most necessitous Jilts in Town. If it be urg'd, that if there are not, it is possible there might be such People, I answer, that it is as possible that Cats, instead of killing Rats and Mice, should feed them, and go about the House to suckle and nurse their young ones, or that a Kite should call the

Hens to their Meat, as the Cock does, and sit brooding over
their Chickens instead of devouring 'em; but if they should
all do so, they would cease to be Cats and Kites; it is incon-
sistent with their Natures, and the Species of Creatures
which now we mean, when we name Cats and Kites, would
be extinct as soon as that could come to pass.

(N.)[23] *Envy it self, and Vanity Were Ministers of Industry.*

PAGE 68. LINE 26. Envy is that Baseness in our Nature,
which makes us grieve and pine at what we conceive to be
a Happiness in others. I don't believe there is a Human
Creature in his Senses arrived to Maturity, that at one time
or other has not been carried away by this Passion in good
Earnest; and yet I never met with any one that dared own
he was guilty of it, but in Jest. That we are so generally
ashamed of this Vice, is owing to that strong Habit of
Hypocrisy, by the Help of which, we have learned from our
Cradle to hide even from ourselves the vast Extent of Self-
Love, and all its different Branches. It is impossible Man
should wish better for another than he does for himself, un-
less where he supposes an Impossibility that himself should
attain to those Wishes; and from hence we may easily learn
after what manner this Passion is raised in us. In order to it,
we are to consider First, That as well as we think of our
selves, so ill we often think of our Neighbour with equal
Injustice; and when we apprehend, that others do or will
enjoy what we think they don't deserve, it afflicts and makes
us angry with the Cause of that Disturbance. Secondly, That
we are ever employ'd in wishing well for our selves, every
one according to his Judgment and Inclinations, and when
we observe something we like, and yet are destitute of, in

23. Remark N was added in 1723. – Ed.

the Possession of others; it occasions first Sorrow in us for not having the Thing we like. This Sorrow is incurable, whilst we continue our Esteem for the Thing we want: But as Self-Defence is restless, and never suffers us to leave any Means untried how to remove Evil from us, as far and as well as we are able; Experience teaches us, that nothing in Nature more alleviates this Sorrow than our Anger against those who are possess'd of what we esteem and want. This latter Passion therefore, we cherish and cultivate to save or relieve our selves, at least in part, from the Uneasiness we felt from the first.

Envy then is a Compound of Grief and Anger; the Degrees of this Passion depend chiefly on the Nearness or Remoteness of the Objects as to Circumstances. If one, who is forc'd to walk on Foot envies a great Man for keeping a Coach and Six, it will never be with that Violence, or give him that Disturbance which it may to a Man, who keeps a Coach himself; but can only afford to drive with four Horses. The Symptoms of Envy are as various, and as hard to describe, as those of the Plague; at some time it appears in one Shape, at others in another quite different. Among the Fair the Disease is very common, and the Signs of it very conspicuous in their Opinions and Censures of one another. In beautiful young Women you may often discover this Faculty to a high Degree; they frequently will hate one another mortally at first Sight, from no other Principle than Envy; and you may read this Scorn, and unreasonable Aversion in their very Countenances, if they have not a great deal of Art, and well learn'd to dissemble.

In the rude and unpolish'd Multitude this Passion is very bare-faced; especially when they envy others for the Goods of Fortune: They rail at their Betters, rip up their Faults, and take Pains to misconstrue their most commendable Actions: They murmur at Providence, and loudly complain, that the good Things of this World are chiefly enjoy'd by those who do not deserve them. The grosser Sort of them it often affects so violently, that if they were not with-held by the Fear of the Laws, they would go directly and beat those their Envy is levell'd at, from no other Provocation than what that Passion suggests to them.

The Men of Letters labouring under this Distemper discover quite different Symptoms. When they envy a Person for his Parts and Erudition, their chief Care is industriously to conceal their Frailty, which generally is attempted by denying and depreciating the good Qualities they envy: They carefully peruse his Works, and are displeas'd at every fine Passage they meet with; they look for nothing but his Errors, and wish for no greater Feast than a gross Mistake: In their Censures they are captious as well as severe, make Mountains of Molehills, and will not pardon the least Shadow of a Fault, but exaggerate the most trifling Omission into a Capital Blunder.

Envy is visible in Brute Beasts; Horses shew it in their Endeavours of out-stripping one another; and the best spirited will run themselves to Death before they'll suffer another before them. In Dogs this Passion is likewise plainly to be seen, those who are used to be caress'd will never tamely bear that Felicity in others. I have seen a Lap-Dog that would choak himself with Victuals rather than leave any thing for a Competitor of his own Kind, and we may often observe the same Behaviour in those Creatures which we daily see in Infants that are froward, and by being overfondl'd made humoursome. If out of Caprice they at any time refuse to eat what they have ask'd for, and we can but make them believe that some body else, nay, even the Cat or the Dog is going to take it from them, they will make an end of their Oughts with Pleasure, and feed even against their Appetite.

If Envy was not rivetted in Human Nature, it would not be so common in Children, and Youth would not be so generally spurr'd on by Emulation. Those who would derive every Thing that is beneficial to the Society from a good Principle, ascribe the Effects of Emulation in School-Boys to a Virtue of the Mind; as it requires Labour and Pains; so it is evident, that they commit a Self-Denial, who act from that Disposition; but if we look narrowly into it, we shall find that this Sacrifice of Ease and Pleasure is only made to Envy, and the Love of Glory. If there was not something very like this Passion mix'd with that pretended Virtue, it would be impossible to raise and increase it by the same Means that create Envy. The Boy, who receives a Reward for the Superiority of his Performance, is conscious of the Vexation it would have been to him, if he should have fall'n short of it: This Reflection makes him exert himself, not to be out-done by those whom now he looks upon as his Inferiors, and the greater his Pride is, the more Self-Denial he'll practise to maintain his Conquest. The other, who, in spight of the Pains he took to do well, has miss'd of the Prize, is sorry, and consequently angry with him whom he must look upon as the Cause of his Grief: But to shew this Anger, would be ridiculous, and of no Service to him; so that he must either be contented to be less esteemed than the other Boy; or by renewing his Endeavours become a greater Proficient; and it is ten to one, but the disinterested, good-humour'd, and peaceable Lad will chuse the first, and so become indolent and unactive, whilst the covetous, peevish, and quarrelsome Rascal shall take incredible Pains, and make himself a Conqueror in his Turn.

Envy, as it is very common among Painters, so it is of great Use for their Improvement: I don't mean, that little Dawbers envy great Masters, but most of them are tainted with this Vice against those immediately above them. If the Pupil of a famous Artist is of a bright Genius, and uncommon Application, he first adores his Master; but as his own Skill increases, he begins insensibly to envy what he admired before. To learn the nature of this Passion, and that it consists in what I have named, we are but to observe that, if a Painter by exerting himself comes not only to equal but to exceed the Man he envied, his Sorrow is gone and all his Anger disarm'd; and if he hated him before, he is now glad to be Friends with him, if the other will condescend to it.

Married Women, who are Guilty of this Vice which few are not, are always endeavouring to raise the same Passion in their Spouses; and where they have prevail'd, Envy and Emulation have kept more Men in Bounds, and reform'd more Ill Husbands from sloth, from drinking and other evil courses than all the Sermons that have been preach'd since the time of the Apostles.

As every Body would be happy, enjoy Pleasure and avoid Pain if he could, so Self-love bids us look on every Creature that seems satisfied, as a Rival in Happiness; and the Satisfaction we have in seeing that Felicity disturb'd, without any advantage to our selves but what springs from the Pleasure we have in beholding it, is call'd loving mischief for mischiefs sake; and the Motive of which that frailty is the result, Malice, another Offspring derived from the same Original; for if there was no Envy there could be no Malice. When the Passions lye dormant we have no apprehension of them, and often People think they have not such a Frailty in their Nature, because that Moment they are not affected with it.

A Gentleman well dress'd, who happens to be dirty'd all over by a Coach or a Cart, is laugh'd at, and by his Inferiors much more than his Equals, because they envy him more : they know he is vex'd at it, and imagining him to be happier than themselves they are glad to see him meet with displeasures in his turn : But a Young Lady, if she be in a serious Mood, instead of laughing at, pities him, because a clean Man is a sight she takes delight in, and there is no room for Envy. At Disasters, we either laugh, or pity those that befall them, according to the Stock we are possess'd of either of Malice or Compassion. If a Man falls or hurts himself so slightly that it moves not the latter, we laugh, and here our Pity and Malice shake us alternately: Indeed, Sir, I am very sorry for it, I beg your Pardon for laughing, I am the silliest Creature in the World, then laugh again and again; I am indeed very sorry, and so on. Some are so Malicious they would laugh if a Man broke his Leg, and others are so Compassionate that they can heartily pity a Man for the least Spot in his Cloaths; but no Body is so Savage that no Compassion can touch him, nor any Man so good natured as never to be affected with any Malicious Pleasure. How strangely our Passions Govern us! we envy a Man for being Rich, and then perfectly hate him: but if we come to be his Equals, we are calm, and the least Condescention in him makes us Friends; but if we become visibly Superior to him we can pity his Misfortunes. The Reason why Men of true good Sense Envy less than others, is because they admire themselves with less hesitation than Fools and silly People; for tho' they do not shew this to others, yet the Solidity of their thinking gives them an Assurance of their real Worth, which Men of weak understanding can never feel within, tho' they often Counterfeit it.

The Ostracism of the *Greeks* was a Sacrifice of valuable Men made to Epidemick Envy, and often applied as an infallible Remedy to Cure and prevent the Mischiefs of Popular Spleen and Rancour. A Victim of State often appeases the Murmurs of a whole Nation, and after Ages frequently wonder at Barbarities of this Nature, which under the same Circumstances they would have committed themselves. They are Compliments to the Peoples Malice, which is never better gratify'd, than when they can see a great Man humbled. We believe that we love Justice, and to see Merit rewarded; but if Men continue long in the first Posts of Honour, half of us grow weary of them, look for their Faults, and if we can find none, we suppose they hide them, and 'tis much if the greatest part of us don't wish them discarded. This foul play the best of Men ought ever to apprehend from all who are not their immediate Friends or Acquaintance, because nothing is more tiresome to us than the repetition of Praises we have no manner of share in.

The more a Passion is a Compound of many others, the more difficult it is to define it; and the more it is tormenting to those that labour under it, the greater Cruelty it is capable of inspiring them with against others: Therefore nothing is more whimsical or mischievous than Jealousy, which is made up of Love, Hope, Fear, and a great deal of Envy: The last has been sufficiently treated of already, and what I have to say of Fear the Reader will find under *Remark* (*R.*) So that the better to explain and illustrate this odd Mixture, the Ingredients I shall further speak of in this Place are Hope and Love.

Hoping is wishing with some Degree of Confidence, that the Thing wish'd for will come to pass. The Firmness and Imbecillity of our Hope depend entirely on the greater or lesser Degree of our Confidence, and all Hope includes Doubt; for when our Confidence is arriv'd to that Height, as to exclude all Doubts, it becomes a Certainty, and we take for granted what we only hoped for before. A silver Inkhorn may pass in Speech, because every body knows what we mean by it, but a certain Hope cannot: For a Man who makes use of an Epithet that destroys the Essence of the Substantive he joins it to, can have no Meaning at all; and the more clearly we understand the Force of the Epithet, and the Nature of the Substantive, the more palpable is the Nonsense of the heterogeneous Compound. The Reason therefore why it is not so shocking to some, to hear a Man speak of certain Hope, as if he should talk of hot Ice, or liquid Oak, is not because there is less Nonsense contain'd in the first than there is in either of the latter; but because the Word Hope, I mean the Essence of it, is not so clearly understood by the Generality of the People, as the Words and Essences of Ice and Oak are.

Love in the first place signifies Affection, such as Parents and Nurses bear to Children, and Friends to one another; it consists in a Liking, and Well-wishing to the Person beloved. We give an easy Construction to his Words and Actions, and feel a Proneness to excuse, and forgive his Faults, if we see any; his Interest we make on all Accounts our own, even to our Prejudice, and receive an inward Satisfaction for sympathizing with him in his Sorrows, as well as Joys. What I said last is not impossible, whatever it may seem to be; for when we are sincere in sharing with another in his Misfortunes, Self-Love makes us believe, that the Sufferings we feel must alleviate and lessen those of our Friend, and whilst this fond Reflection is soothing our Pain, a secret Pleasure arises from our grieving for the Person we love.

Secondly, By Love we understand a strong Inclination in its Nature distinct from all other Affections of Friendship, Gratitude, and Consanguinity, that Persons of different Sexes, after liking, bear to one another: It is in this Signification that Love enters into the Compound of *Jealousy*, and is the Effect as well as happy Disguise of that Passion that prompts us to labour for the Preservation of our Species. This latter Appetite is innate both in Men and Women, who are not defective in their Formation, as much as Hunger or Thirst, tho' they are seldom affected with it before the Years of Puberty. Could we undress Nature, and pry into her deepest Recesses, we should discover the Seeds of this Passion, before it exerts it self, as plainly as we see the Teeth in an Embrio, before the Gums are form'd. There are few healthy People of either Sex, whom it has made no Impression upon before Twenty: Yet, as the Peace and Happiness of the Civil Society require that this should be kept a Secret, never to be talk'd of in Publick; so among well-bred People it is counted highly Criminal to mention before Company any thing in plain Words, that is relating to this Mystery of Succession: By which Means the very Name of the Appetite, tho' the most necessary for the Continuance of Mankind, is become odious, and the proper Epithets commonly join'd to Lust are *Filthy* and *Abominable*.

This Impulse of Nature in People of strict Morals, and rigid Modesty, often disturbs the Body for a considerable Time before it is understood or known to be what it is, and it is remarkable that the most polish'd and best instructed are generally the most ignorant as to this Affair; and here I can but observe the Difference between Man in the wild State of Nature, and the same Creature in the Civil Society. In the first, Men and Women, if left rude and untaught in the Sciences of Modes and Manners, would quickly find out the Cause of that Disturbance, and be at a loss no more than other Animals for a present Remedy: Besides, that it is not probable they would want either Precept or Example from the more experienc'd. But in the second, where the Rules of Religion, Law, and Decency are to be follow'd, and obey'd before any Dictates of Nature, the Youth of both Sexes are to be arm'd and fortify'd against this Impulse, and from their Infancy artfully frighten'd from the most remote Approaches of it. The Appetite it self, and all the Symptoms of it, tho' they are plainly felt and understood, are to be stifled with Care and Severity, and in Women flatly disown'd; and, if there be Occasion, with Obstinacy deny'd, even when themselves are visibly affected by them. If it throws them into Distempers, they must be cured by Physick, or else patiently bear them in Silence; and it is the Interest of the Society to preserve Decency and Politeness; that Women should linger, waste, and die, rather than relieve themselves in an unlawful Manner; and among the fashionable Part of Mankind, the People of Birth and Fortune, it is expected, that Matrimony should never be enter'd upon without a curious Regard to Family, Estate, and Reputation, and in the making of Matches the Call of Nature be the very last Consideration.

Those then who would make Love and Lust Synonimous confound the Effect with the Cause of it: yet such is the force of Education, and a Habit of thinking as we are taught, that sometimes Persons of either Sex are actually in Love without feeling any Carnal Desires, or penetrating into the Intentions of Nature, the end proposed by her, without which they could never have been affected with that sort of Passion. That there are such is certain, but many more whose pretences to those refin'd notions are only upheld by Art and Dissimulation. Those, who are really such Platonick Lovers are commonly the pale faced weakly People of cold and phlegmatick Constitutions in either Sex; the hail and robust of bilious Temperament and a sanguine Complexion never entertain any Love so Spiritual as to exclude all thoughts and wishes that relate to the Body. But if the most Seraphick Lovers would know the original of their Inclination, let them but suppose that another should have the Corporal Enjoyment of the Person beloved, and by the Tortures they'll suffer from that Reflection they will soon discover the nature of their Passions: Whereas on the contrary, Parents and Friends receive a Satisfaction in reflecting on the Joys and Comforts of a Happy Marriage, to be tasted by those they wish well to.

The curious, that are skill'd in anatomizing the invisible part of Man will observe, that the more sublime and exempt this Love is from all thoughts of Sensuality, the more spurious it is, and the more it degenerates from its honest original and primitive Simplicity. The Power and Sagacity as well as Labour and Care of the Politician in civilising the Society, has been no where more conspicuous, than in the Happy Contrivance of playing our Passions against one another. By flattering our Pride and still encreasing the good Opinion we have of our selves on the one hand; and inspiring us on the other with a superlative Dread and mortal Aversion against Shame, the Artful Moralists have taught us chearfully to encounter ourselves, and if not subdue, at least so to conceal and disguise our darling Passion Lust, that we scarce know it when we meet with it in our own Breasts; Oh! the mighty Prize we have in view for all our Self-denial! can any Man be so serious as to abstain from Laughter, when he considers that for so much deceit and insincerity practis'd upon our selves as well as others, we have no other recompence than the vain Satisfaction of making our Species appear more exalted and remote from that of other Animals, than it really is; and we in our Consciences know it to be? Yet this is Fact, and in it we plainly perceive the reason why it was necessary to render odious every Word or Action by which we might discover the innate Desire we feel to perpetuate our Kind; and why tamely to submit to the violence of a Furious Appetite (which it is painful to resist) and innocently to obey, the most pressing demand of Nature without Guile or Hypocrisy, like other Creatures should be branded with the Ignominious Name of Brutality.

What we call Love then is not a Genuine, but an Adulterated Appetite, or rather a Compound, a heap of several contradictory Passions blended in one. As it is a product of Nature warp'd by Custom and Education, so the true origin and first motive of it, as I have hinted already, is stifled in well bred People, and almost conceal'd from themselves: all which is the reason that as those affected with it vary in Age, Strength, Resolution, Temper, Circumstances and Manners, the effects of it are so different, whimsical, surprizing and unaccountable.

It is this Passion that makes Jealousy so troublesome, and the envy of it often so Fatal: those who imagine that there may be Jealousy without Love, do not understand that Passion. Men may not have the least Affection for their Wives, and yet be angry with them for their Conduct, and suspicious of them either with or without a Cause: but what in such cases affects them is their Pride, the concern for their Reputation. They feel a hatred against them without remorse; when they are Outrageous, they can beat them and go to sleep contentedly: Such Husbands may watch their Dames themselves, and have them observed by others; but their Vigilance is not so intense; they are not so inquisitive or industrious in their Searches, neither do they feel that anxiety of Heart at the fear of a discovery, as when Love is mix'd with the Passions.

What confirms me in this Opinion is, that we never observe this Behaviour between a Man and his Mistress; for when his Love is gone and he suspects her to be false, he leaves her and troubles his Head no more about her: whereas it is the greatest difficulty imaginable, even to a Man of sense to part with a Mistress as long as he loves her, whatever Faults she may be guilty of. If in his anger he strikes her he is uneasy after it; his Love makes him reflect on the hurt he has done her, and he wants to be reconcil'd to her again. He may talk of hating her, and many times from his Heart wish her hang'd, but if he cannot get entirely rid of his Frailty, he can never disintangle himself from her; tho' she is represented in the most monstrous guilt to his Imagination, and he has resolved and swore a thousand times never to come near her again, there is no trusting him; even when he is fully convinced of her infidelity, if his Love continues, his Despair is never so lasting, but between the blackest fits of it, he relents and finds lucid Intervals of Hope; he forms excuses for her, thinks of pardoning, and in order to it racks his invention for possibilities that may make her appear less Criminal.

Remark (O)

(O.) Real Pleasures, Comforts, Ease

PAGE 69. LINE 10. That the highest Good consisted in Pleasure, was the Doctrine of *Epicurus*, who yet lead a life Exemplary for Continence, Sobriety and other Vertues, which made People of the succeeding Ages quarrel about the signification of Pleasure. Those who argued from the Temperance of the Philosopher, said, that the Delight *Epicurus* meant, was being Virtuous; so *Erasmus* in his Colloquies tells us, that there are no greater *Epicures* than pious Christians. Others that reflected on the dissolute Manners of the greatest part of his Followers, would have it, that by Pleasures he could have understood nothing but sensual Ones, and the Gratification of our Passions. I shall not decide their Quarrel, but am of Opinion, that whether Men be good or bad, what they take delight in is their Pleasure, and not to look out for any further Etymology from the learned Languages, I believe an *Englishman* may justily call every thing a Pleasure that pleases him, and according to this Definition, we ought to dispute no more about Men's Pleasures than their Tastes : *Trahit sua quemque Voluptas.*[24]

The worldly minded, voluptuous and ambitious Man, notwithstanding he is void of Merit, covets Precedence every where, and desires to be dignify'd above his Betters : He aims at spacious Palaces and delicious Gardens; his chief Delight is in excelling others in stately Horses, magnificent Coaches, a numerous Attendance, and dear-bought Furniture. To gratify his Lust, he wishes for genteel, young, beautiful Women of different Charms and Complexions that shall adore his Greatness, and be really in love with his Person : His Cellars he would have stored with the Flower of every Country that produces excellent Wines : His Table he desires may be serv'd with many Courses, and each of them

24. 'Its sweetest pleasure leads each creature on.' Virgil, *Eclogues*, ii, 65. – Ed.

contain a choice variety of Dainties not easily purchas'd, and ample evidences of elaborate and judicious Cookery; whilst harmonious Musick and well-couch'd Flattery entertain his Hearing by turns. He employs, even in the meanest Trifles, none but the ablest and most ingenious Workmen, that his Judgment and Fancy may as evidently appear in the least things that belong to him, as his Wealth and Quality are manifested in those of greater Value. He desires to have several Sets of witty, facetious and polite People to converse with, and among them he would have some famous for Learning and universal Knowledge: For his serious Affairs, he wishes to find Men of Parts and Experience that should be diligent and faithful. Those that are to wait on him he would have handy, mannerly and discreet, of comely Aspect and a graceful Mein: What he requires in them besides, is a respectful Care of every thing that is *His*, Nimbleness without Hurry, Dispatch without Noise, and an unlimited Obedience to his Orders: Nothing he thinks more troublesome than speaking to Servants; wherefore he will only be attended by such, as by observing his Looks have learn'd to interpret his Will from his slightest Motions. He loves to see an elegant Nicety in every thing that approaches him, and in what is to be employ'd about his Person he desires a superlative Cleanliness to be religiously observ'd. The chief Officers of his Houshold he would have to be Men of Birth, Honour and Distinction, as well as Order, Contrivance and Oeconomy; for tho' he loves to be honour'd by every Body, and receives the Respects of the Common People with Joy, yet the Homage that is paid him by Persons of Quality is ravishing to him in a more transcendent manner.

Whilst thus wallowing in a Sea of Lust and Vanity, he is wholly employ'd in provoking and indulging his Appetites, he desires the World should think him altogether free from Pride and Sensuality, and put a favourable Construction

upon his most glaring Vices: Nay, if his Authority can pur-
chase it, he covets to be thought Wise, Brave, Generous,
Good-natur'd, and endu'd with all the Virtues he thinks
worth having. He would have us believe that the Pomp and
Luxury he is serv'd with are as many tiresome Plagues to
him; and all the Grandeur he appears in is an ungrateful
Burden, which, to his Sorrow, is inseparable from the high
Sphere he moves in, that his noble Mind so much exalted
above vulgar Capacities, aims at higher ends, and can
not relish such worthless Enjoyments; that the highest of
his Ambition is to promote the Publick Welfare, and his
greatest Pleasure to see his Country flourish and every Body
in it made happy. These are call'd real Pleasures by the
Vicious, and Earthly minded, and whoever is able, either by
his Skill or Fortune after this refin'd manner at once to
enjoy the World, and the good Opinion of it, is counted
extremely happy by all the most fashionable part of the
People.

But on the other side most of the ancient Philosophers and
grave Moralists, especially the Stoicks, would not allow any
thing to be a real Good that was liable to be taken from
them by others. They wisely consider'd the Instability of
Fortune and the Favour of Princes, the Vanity of Honour
and Popular Applause; the Precariousness of Riches and
all Earthly Possessions, and therefore placed true Happiness
in the calm Serenity of a contented Mind free from Guilt
and Ambition; a Mind, that, having subdued every sensual
Appetite, despises the Smiles as well as Frowns of Fortune,
and taking no delight but in Contemplation, desires nothing
but what every Body is able to give to himself: A Mind,
that arm'd with Fortitude and Resolution has learn'd to
sustain the greatest Losses without Concern, to endure Pain
without Affliction, and to bear Injuries without Resentment.
Many have own'd themselves arriv'd to this height of Self-
denial, and then, if we may believe them, they were rais'd

above Common Mortals, and their Strength extended vastly beyond the pitch of their first Nature: They could behold the Anger of Threatning Tyrants and the most imminent Dangers without Terror, and preserv'd their Tranquility in the midst of Torments: Death itself they could meet with Intrepidity and left the World with no greater Reluctancy than they had shew'd Fondness at their entrance into it.

These among the Ancients have always bore the greatest Sway; yet others that were no Fools neither, have exploded those Precepts as impracticable, call'd their Notions Romantick, and endeavour'd to prove, that what these Stoicks asserted of themselves exceeded all human Force and Possibility, and that therefore the Virtues they boasted of could be nothing but haughty Pretences full of Arrogance and Hypocrisy; yet notwithstanding these Censures, the Serious part of the World, and the generality of wise Men that have liv'd ever since to this Day agree with the Stoicks in the most material Points; as that there can be no true Felicity in what depends on things perishable; that Peace within is the greatest Blessing, and no Conquest like that of our Passions, that Knowledge, Temperance, Fortitude, Humility, and other Embellishments of the Mind are the most valuable Acquisitions; that no Man can be happy but he that is good; and that the Virtuous are only capable of enjoying *real Pleasures*.

I expect to be ask'd why in the Fable I have call'd those Pleasures real that are directly opposite to those which I own the wise Men of all Ages have extoll'd as the most valuable. My Answer is, because I don't call things Pleasures which Men say are best, but such as they seem to be most pleased with; how can I believe that a Man's chief delight is in the Embellishments of the Mind, when I see him ever employ'd about and daily pursue the Pleasures that are contrary to them? *John* never cuts any Pudding, but just enough that you can't say he took none; this little Bit, after much chomping and chewing you see goes down with him like chop'd Hay, after that he falls upon the Beef with a voracious Appetite, and crams himself up to his Throat. Is it not provoking to hear *John* cry every Day that Pudding is all his delight, and that he don't value the Beef of a Farthing?

I could swagger about Fortitude and the Contempt of Riches as much as *Seneca* himself, and would undertake to write twice as much in behalf of Poverty as ever he did, for the tenth part of his Estate. I could teach the way to his *Summum Bonum* as exactly as I know my way home: I could tell People, that to extricate themselves from all worldly Engagements, and to purify the Mind, they must divest themselves of their Passions, as Men take out the Furniture when they would clean a Room thoroughly, and I am clearly of the Opinion, that the Malice and most severe Strokes of Fortune can do no more injury to a Mind thus stript of all Fears, Wishes and Inclinations, than a blind Horse can do in an empty Barn. In the Theory of all this I am very perfect, but the Practice is very difficult; and if you went about picking my Pocket, offer'd to take the Victuals from before me when I am hungry, or made but the least motion of spitting in my Face, I dare not promise how Philosophically I should behave my self. But that I am forced to submit to every caprice of my unruly Nature, you'll say is no Argument that others are as little Masters of theirs, and therefore I am willing to pay Adoration to Virtue wherever I can meet with it, with a Proviso, that I shall not be oblig'd to admit any as such where I can see no Self-denial, or to judge of Mens Sentiments from their Words, where I have their Lives before me.

I have search'd through every Degree and Station of Men, and confess, that I have found no where more Austerity of Manners, or greater Contempt of Earthly Pleasures, than in some Religious Houses, where People freely resigning and retiring from the World to combat themselves, have no other Business but to subdue their Appetites. What can be a greater Evidence of perfect Chastity, and a superlative Love to immaculate Purity in Men and Women, than that in the Prime of their Age, when Lust is most raging, they should actually seclude themselves from each others Company, and by a voluntary Renunciation debar themselves for Life, not only from Uncleanness, but even the most lawful Embraces? Those that abstain from Flesh, and often all manner of Food, one wou'd think in the right way to conquer all Carnal Desires; and I could almost swear, that he don't consult his Ease, who daily mawls his bare Back and Shoulders with unconscionable Stripes, and constantly roused at Midnight from his Sleep, leaves his Bed for his Devotion. Who can despise Riches more, or shew himself less Avaricious than he, who won't so much as touch Gold or Silver, no not with his Feet? Or can any Mortal shew himself less Luxurious or more humble than the Man, that making Poverty his choice, contents himself with Scraps and Fragments, and refuses to eat any Bread but what is bestow'd upon him by the Charity of others?

Such fair Instances of Self-denial would make me bow down to Virtue, if I was not deter'd and warn'd from it by so many Persons of Eminence and Learning, who unanimously tell me that I am mistaken, and all I have seen is Farce and Hypocrisy; that what Seraphick Love they may pretend to, there is nothing but Discord among them, and that how Penitential the Nuns and Fryars may appear in their several Convents, they none of them sacrifise their darling Lusts. That among the Women they are not all Virgins that pass for such, and that if I was to be let into their Secrets, and examine some of their Subterraneous Privacies, I should soon be convinced by Scenes of Horror, that some of them must have been Mothers. That among the Men, I should find Calumny, Envy and Ill Nature in the highest degree, or else Gluttony, Drunkenness, and Impurities of a more execrable kind than Adultery itself: And as for the Mendicant Orders, that they differ in nothing but their Habits from other sturdy Beggars, who deceive People with a pitiful Tone and an outward shew of Misery, and as soon as they are out of sight, lay by their Cant, indulge their Appetites, and enjoy one another.

If the strict Rules, and so many outward signs of Devotion observ'd among those religious Orders, deserve such harsh Censures, we may well despair of meeting with Virtue any where else; for if we look into the Actions of the Antagonists, and greatest Accusers of those Votaries, we shall not find so much as the appearance of self denial. The Reverend Divines of all Sects, even of the most Reform'd Churches in all Countries, take care with the *Cyclops Evangeliophorus* first; *ut ventri bene sit*, and afterwards, *ne quid desit iis quœ sub ventre sunt*:[25] To these they'll desire you to add, convenient Houses, handsome Furniture, good Fires in Winter, pleasant Gardens in Summer, neat Cloaths, and Money enough to bring up their Children: Precedency in all Companies, Respect from every body, and then as much Religion as you please. The things I have named are the necessary Comforts of Life, which the most Modest are not asham'd to claim, and which they are very uneasie without. They are, 'tis true, made of the same Mould, and have the same corrupt Nature with other Men, born with the same Infirmities, subject to the same Passions, and liable to the same Temptations, and therefore if they are diligent in their Calling, and can but abstain from Murder, Adultery, Swearing, Drunkenness, and other heinous Vices, their Lives are call'd unblemish'd, and their Reputations unspotted; their Function renders them holy, and the Gratification of so

25. 'That there be full bellies and plenty of work for the organs below the belly.' Erasmus, 'Cyclops sive Evangeliophorus,' *Colloquies*. – Ed.

many Carnal Appetites, and the Enjoyment of so much luxurious Ease notwithstanding, they may set upon themselves what value their Pride and Parts will allow them.

All this I have nothing against, but I see no Self denial, without which there can be no Virtue. Is it such a Mortification not to desire a greater Share of worldly Blessings, than what every reasonable Man ought to be satisfy'd with? Or is there any mighty Merit in not being flagitious, and forbearing Indecencies that are repugnant to good Manners, and which no prudent Man would be guilty of, tho' he had no Religion at all?

I know I shall be told, that the reason why the Clergy are so violent in their Resentments, when at any time they are but in the least affronted, and shew themselves so void of all Patience when their Rights are invaded, is their great care to preserve their Calling, their Profession from Contempt, not for their own sakes, but to be more serviceable to others. 'Tis the same reason that makes 'em sollictious about the Comforts and Conveniencies of Life; for should they suffer themselves to be insulted over, be content with a courser Diet, and wear more ordinary Cloaths than other People, the Multitude, who judge from outward Appearances, would be apt to think that the Clergy was no more the immediate Care of Providence than other Folks, and so not only undervalue their Persons but despise likewise all the Reproofs and Instructions that came from 'em. This is an admirable Plea, and as it is much made use of I'll try the worth of it.

I am not of the Learned Dr *Eachard's* Opinion,[26] that Poverty is one of those things that bring the Clergy into Contempt, any further than as it may be an occasion of discovering their blind-side: For when Men are always struggling with their low Condition, and are unable to bear

26. John Eachard, author of *Grounds and Occasions of the Contempt of the Clergy and Religion* (1670). – Ed.

the Burden of it without Reluctancy, it is then they shew how uneasy their Poverty sits upon them, how glad they would be to have their Circumstances meliorated, and what a real value they have for the good things of this World. He that harangues on the Contempt of Riches, and the Vanity of Earthly Enjoyments, in a rusty threadbare Gown, because he has no other, and would wear his old greasy Hat no longer, if any body would give him a better; that drinks Small-beer at Home with a heavy Countenance, but leaps at a Glass of Wine if he can catch it Abroad; that with little Appetite feeds upon his own course Mess, but falls to greedily where he can please his Palate, and expresses an uncommon Joy at an Invitation to a splendid Dinner: 'Tis he that is despised, not because he is Poor, but because he knows not how to be so with that Content and Resignation which he preaches to others, and so discovers his Inclinations to be contrary to his Doctrine. But when a Man from the greatness of his Soul (or an obstinate Vanity, which will do as well) resolving to subdue his Appetites in good earnest, refuses all the offers of Ease and Luxury that can be made to him, and embracing a voluntary Poverty with chearfulness, rejects whatever may gratify the Senses, and actually sacrifises all his Passions to his Pride in acting this Part, the Vulgar far from contemning will be ready to Deify and adore him. How famous have the *Cynick* Philosophers made themselves, only by refusing to dissimulate and make use of Superfluities? Did not the most Ambitious Monarch the World ever bore, condescend to visit *Diogenes* in his Tub, and return to a study'd Incivility, the highest Compliment a Man of his Pride was able to make?

Mankind are very willing to take one anothers Word, when they see some Circumstances that corroborate what is told them; but when our Actions directly contradict what we say, it is counted Impudence to desire Belief. If a jolly hail Fellow with glowing Cheecks and warm Hands, newly return'd from some smart Exercise, or else the Cold Bath, tells us in frosty Weather, that he cares not for the Fire, we are easily induced to believe him, especially if he actually turns from it, and we know by his Circumstances that he wants neither Fuel nor Cloaths: But if we should hear the same from the Mouth of a poor starv'd Wretch, with swell'd Hands, and a livid Countenance, in a thin ragged Garment, we should not believe a word of what he said, especially if we saw him shaking and shivering, creep toward the Suny Bank, and we would conclude, let him say what he could, that warm Cloaths and a good Fire would be very accept-able to him. The Application is easy, and therefore if there be any Clergy upon Earth that would be thought not to care for the World, and to value the Soul above the Body, let them only forbear shewing a greater concern for their Sensual Pleasures than they generally do for their Spiritual ones, and they may rest satisfy'd, that no Poverty, whilst they bear it with Fortitude, will ever bring them into Con-tempt, how mean soever their Circumstances may be.

Let us suppose a Pastor that has a little Flock entrusted to him, of which he is very careful: He preaches, visits, ex-horts, reproves among his People with Zeal and Prudence, and does them all the kind Offices that lie in his Power to make them happy. There is no doubt but those under his care must be very much oblig'd to him. Now we'll suppose once more, that this good Man by the help of a little Self-denial, is contented to live upon half his Income, accepting only of Twenty Pounds a Year instead of Forty, which he could claim; and moreover, that he loves his Parishioners so well, that he will never leave them for any Preferment whatever, no not a Bishoprick, tho' it be offer'd. I can't see but all this might be an easy task to a Man who professes Mortification, and has no value for worldly Pleasures; yet such a disinterested Divine I dare promise, notwithstanding the great degeneracy of Mankind, will be lov'd, esteem'd, and have every body's good Word; nay I would swear, that tho' he should yet further exert himself, give above half of his small Revenue to the Poor, live upon nothing but Oatmeal and Water, lie upon Straw, and wear the coursest Cloth that could be made, his mean way of Living would never be reflected on, or be a Disparagement either to himself or the Order he belong'd to; but that on the contrary his Poverty would never be mention'd but to his Glory, as long as his Memory should last.

But (says a charitable young Gentlewoman) tho' you have the Heart to starve your Parson, have you no Bowels of Compassion for his Wife and Children? Pray what must remain of Forty Pounds a Year after it has been twice so unmercifully split? Or would you have the Poor Woman and the innocent Babes likewse live upon Oatmeal and Water, and lie upon Straw, you unconscionable Wretch, with all your Suppositions and Self denials? Nay, is it possible, tho' they should all live at your own murdering rate, that less than Ten Pounds a Year could maintain a Family?— Don't be in a Passion good Mrs. *Abigail*,[27] I have greater regard for your Sex than to prescribe such a lean Diet to married Men; but I confess I forgot the Wives and Children: The main reason was, because I thought poor Priests could have no occasion for them; who could imagine that the Parson, who is to teach others by Example as well as Precept, was not able to withstand those Desires which the wicked World itself calls unreasonable? What is the reason when a 'Prentice marries before he is out of his Time, that unless he meets with a good Fortune, all his Relations are angry with him, and every body blames him? Nothing else but because at that time he has no Money at his disposal, and

27. The parson's wife in *Mrs Abigail; or an Account of a Female Skirmish between the Wife of a Country Squire, and the Wife of a Doctor in Divinity* (1702). – Ed.

being bound to his Master's Service, has no leisure and perhaps little Capacity to provide for a Family. What must we say to a Parson that has Twenty, or if you will Forty Pounds a Year, that being bound more strictly to all the Services a Parish and his Duty require, has little time and generally much less Ability to get any more? Is it not very unreasonable he should Marry? But why should a sober young Man, who is guilty of no Vice, be debarr'd from lawful Enjoyments? Right; Marriage is lawful, and so is a Coach; but what is that to People that have not Money enough to keep one: If he must have a Wife, let him look out for one with Money, or wait for a greater Benefice, or something else to maintain her handsomely, and bear all incident Charges. But no body that has any thing herself will have him, and he can't stay: He has a very good Stomach and all the Symptoms of Health, 'tis not every body that can live without a Woman; tis better to Marry than burn. – What a World of Self-denial is here? The sober young Man is very willing to be Virtuous, but you must not cross his Inclinations; he promises never to be a Deer-stealer, upon Condition that he shall have Venison of his own, and no body must doubt but that if it came to the Push, he is qualify'd to suffer Martyrdom, tho' he owns that he has not Strength enough, patiently to bear a scratch'd Finger.

When we see so many of the Clergy, to indulge their Lust, a brutish Appetite, run themselves after this manner upon an inevitable Poverty, which unless they could bear it with greater Fortitude than they discover in all their Actions, must of necessity make them contemptible to all the World, what Credit must we give them, when they pretend that they conform themselves to the World, not because they take delight in the several Decencies, Conveniencies, and Ornaments of it, but only to preserve their Function from Contempt, in order to be more useful to others? Have we not reason to believe, that what they say is full of Hypocrisy and Falshood, and that concupiscence is not the only Appetite they want to gratify; that the haughty Airs and quick Sense of Injuries, the curious Elegance in Dress, and niceness of Palate, to be observ'd in most of them that are able to shew them, are the Results of Pride and Luxury in them as they are in other People, and that the Clergy are not possess'd of more Intrinsick Virtue than any other Profession?

I am afraid that by this time I have given many of my Readers a real displeasure, by dwelling so long upon the reality of Pleasure; but I can't help it, there is one thing comes into my Head to corroborate what I have urg'd already, which I can't forbear mentioning: It is this: Those who govern others throughout the World, are at least as wise as the People that are govern'd by them, generally speaking: If for this reason we would take Pattern from our Superiors, we have but to cast our Eyes on all the Courts and Governments in the Universe, and we shall soon perceive from the Actions of the Great ones, which Opinion they side with, and what Pleasures those in the highest Stations of all seem to be most fond of: For if it be allowable at all to judge of People's Inclinations from their manner of Living, none can be less injur'd by it than those who are the most at Liberty to do as they please.

If the great ones of the Clergy as well as the Laity of any Country whatever, had no value for Earthly Pleasures, and did not endeavour to gratify their Appetites, why are Envy and Revenge so raging among them, and all the other Passions improv'd and refin'd upon in Courts of Princes more than any where else, and why are their Repasts, their Recreations, and whole manner of Living always such as are approv'd of, coveted, and imitated by the most sensual People of that same Country? If despising all visible Decorations they were only in Love with the Embellishments of the Mind, why should they borrow so many of the Implements, and make use of the most darling Toys of the Luxurious? Why should a Lord-Treasurer, or a Bishop, or even the Grand Signior or the Pope of *Rome*, to be good and Virtuous, and endeavour the Conquest of his Passions, have occasion for greater Revenues, richer Furniture, or a more numerous Attendance, as to Personal Service, than a Private Man? What Virtue is it the Exercise of which requires so much Pomp and Superfluity, as are to be seen by all Men in Power? A Man has as much opportunity to practise Temperance, that has but one Dish at a Meal, as he that is constantly serv'd with three Courses and a dozen Dishes in each: One may exercise as much Patience, and be as full of Self denial on a few Flocks, without Curtains or Tester, as in a Velvet Bed that is Sixteen Foot high. The Virtuous Possessions of the Mind are neither Charge nor Burden: A Man may bear Misfortunes with Fortitude in a Garret, forgive Injuries a foot, and be Chaste, tho' he has not a Shirt to his Back; and therefore I shall never believe, but that an indifferent Skuller, if he was entrusted with it, might carry all the Learning and Religion that one Man can contain, as well as a Barge with six Oars, especially if it was but to cross from *Lambeth* to *Westminster*; or that Humility it so ponderous a Virtue, that it requires six Horses to draw it.

To say, that Men not being so easily govern'd by their Equals as by their Superiors, it is necessary that to keep the multitude in awe, those who rule over us should excel others in outward Appearance, and consequently that all in high Stations should have Badges of Honour, and Ensigns of Power to be distinguish'd from the Vulgar, is a frivolous Objection. This in the first Place can only be of use to poor Princes, and weak and precarious Governments, that being actually unable to maintain the publick Peace, are obliged with a Pageant Shew to make up what they want in real Power: So the Governor of *Batavia* in the *East-Indies* is forced to keep up a Grandeur, and live in a Magnificence above his Quality to strike a Terror in the Natives of *Java*, who, if they had Skill and Conduct, are strong enough to destroy ten times the number of their Masters; but great Princes and States that keep large Fleets at Sea and numerous Armies in the Field, have no occasion for such Stratagems; for what makes 'em formidable Abroad, will never fail to be their Security at Home. Secondly, what must protect the Lives and Wealth of People from the Attempts of wicked Men in all Societies, is the Severity of the Laws, and diligent Administration of impartial Justice. Theft, House-breaking and Murther are not to be prevented by the Scarlet Gowns of the Aldermen, the Gold Chains of the Sheriffs, the fine Trappings of their Horses, or any gawdy Shew whatever: Those pageant Ornaments are beneficial another way; they are eloquent Lectures to 'Prentices, and the use of them is to animate, not to deter: but Men of abandon'd Principles must be aw'd by rugged Officers, strong Prisons, watchful Jaylors, the Hangman and the Gallows. If *London* was to be one Week destitute of Constables and Watchmen to guard the Houses a Nights, half the Bankers would be ruin'd in that time, and if my Lord Mayor had nothing to defend himself but his great two handed Sword, the huge Cap of Maintenance, and his guilded Mace, he would soon be strip'd in the very Streets of the City of all his finery in his stately Coach.

But let us grant, that the Eyes of the Mobility are to be dazled with a gawdy outside; if Virtue was the chief delight of great Men, why should their Extravagance be extended to Things not understood by the Mob, and wholly removed from publick View, I mean their private Diversions, the Pomp and Luxury of the Dining-Room and the Bed-Chamber, and the Curiosities of the Closet? Few of the Vulgar know that there is Wine of a Guinea the Bottle, that Birds no bigger than Larks are often sold for half a Guinea apiece, or that a single Picture may be worth several thou-

sand Pounds: Besides, is it to be imagin'd, that unless it was
to please their own Appetites Men should put themselves to
such vast Expences for a Political Shew, and be so sollicitous
to gain the Esteem of those whom they so much despise in
every thing else? If we allow that the Splendor and all the
Elegancy of a Court are insipid, and only tiresome to the
Prince himself, and are altogether made use of to preserve
Royal Majesty from Contempt: Can we say the same of half
a dozen illegitimate Children, most of them the Offspring of
Adultery by the same Majesty, got, educated and made
Princes at the Expence of the Nation? Therefore it is evi-
dent, that this awing of the Multitude by a distinguish'd
manner of living, is only a Cloak and Pretence, under which
great Men would shelter their Vanity, and indulge every
Appetite about them without Reproach.

A Burgomaster of *Amsterdam* in his plain, black Suit,
follow'd perhaps by one Footman, is fully as much respected
and better obey'd than a Lord Mayor of *London* with all his
splendid Equipage and great Train of Attendance. Where
there is a real Power it is ridiculous to think that any Tem-
perance or Austerity of Life should ever render the Person
in whom that Power is lodg'd contemptible in his Office,
from an Emperor to the Beadle of a Parish. *Cato* in his
Government of *Spain*, in which he acquitted himself with
so much Glory, had only three Servants to attend him; do
we hear that any of his Orders were ever slighted for this,
notwithstanding that he lov'd his Bottle? And when that
great Man march'd on Foot thro' the scorching Sands of
Lybia, and parch'd up with Thirst, refus'd to touch the
Water that was brought him, before all his Soldiers had
drank, do we ever read that this Heroick Forbearance
weakned his Authority, or lessen'd him in the Esteem of his
Army? But what need we go so far off: There has not
these many Ages been a Prince less inclin'd to Pomp and

Luxury than the present* King of *Sweden*,[29] who enamour'd with the Title of *Hero*, has not only sacrifis'd the Lives of his Subjects, and Welfare of his Dominions, but (what is more uncommon in Soveciigns) his own Ease, and all the Comforts of Life, to an implacable Spirit of Revenge; yet he is obey'd to the Ruine of his People, in obstinately maintaining a War that has almost utterly destroy'd his Kingdom.

Thus I have prov'd, that the Real Pleasures of all Men in Nature are worldly and sensual, if we judge from their Practice. I say, all Men *in Nature,* because Devout Christians, who alone are to be excepted here, being regenerated, and preternaturally assisted by the Divine Grace, cannot be said to be in Nature. How strange it is, that they should all so unanimously deny it! Ask not only the Divines and Moralists of every Nation, but likewise all that are rich and powerful, about real Pleasure, and they'll tell you, with the *Stoicks,* that there can be no true Felicity in Things Mundane and Corruptible; but then look upon their Lives, and you will find they take delight in no other.

What must we do in this Dilemma? Shall we be so uncharitable, as judging from Men's Actions to say, That all the World prevaricates, and that this is not their Opinion, let them talk what they will? Or shall we be so silly, as relying on what they say, to think them sincere in their Sentiments, and so not believe our own Eyes? Or shall we rather endeavour to believe our selves and them too, and say with *Montagne*, that they imagine, and are fully perswaded, that they believe what yet they do not believe? These are his Words; *Some impose on the World, and would be thought to believe what they really don't; but much the greater number impose upon themselves, not considering nor thoroughly apprehending what it is to believe.* But this is

* This was wrote in 1714.[28]

28. This note was added in 1723. – Ed.

29. Charles XII, who reigned from 1697 to 1718. – Ed.

making all Mankind either Fools or Impostors, which to avoid, there is nothing left us, but to say what Mr. *Bayle* has endeavour'd to prove at large in his Reflections on Comets; That Man is so unaccountable a Creature as to act most commonly against his Principle; and this is so far from being injurious, that it is a Compliment to Human Nature, for we must say either this or worse.

This Contradiction in the Frame of Man is the Reason that the Theory of Virtue is so well understood, and the Practice of it so rarely to be met with. If you ask me where to look for those beautiful shining Qualities of Prime Ministers, and the great Favourites of Princes that are so finely painted in Dedications, Addresses, Epitaphs, Funeral Sermons and Inscriptions, I answer *There*, and no where else. Where would you look for the Excellency of a Statue, but in that part which you see of it? 'Tis the Polish'd outside only that has the Skill and Labour of the Sculptor to boast of; what's out of sight is untouch'd. Would you break the Head, or cut open the Breast to look for the Brains or the Heart, you'd only shew your Ignorance and destroy the Workmanship. This has often made me compare the Virtues of great Men to your large *China* Jars; they make a fine Shew, and are Ornamental even to a Chimney; one would by the Bulk they appear in, and the Value that is set upon 'em, think they might be very useful, but look into a thousand of them, and you'll find nothing in them but Dust and Cobwebs.

(P.) —— The very Poor
Lived better than the Rich before.

PAGE 69. LINE 11. If we trace the most flourishing Nations in their Origin, we shall find that in the remote Beginnings of every Society, the richest and most considerable Men among them were a great while destitute of a great many Comforts of Life that are now enjoy'd by the meanest and most humble Wretches: So that many things, which were once look'd upon as the invention of Luxury, are now allow'd even to those that are so miserably poor as to become the Objects of publick Charity, nay counted so necessary, that we think no Human Creature ought to want them.

In the first Ages Man, without doubt, fed on the Fruits of the Earth, without any previous Preparation, and reposed himself naked like other Animals on the Lap of their common Parent: Whatever has contributed since to make Life more Comfortable, as it must have been the Result of Thought, Experience, and some Labour, so it more or less deserves the Name of Luxury, the more or less trouble it required and deviated from the primitive Simplicity. Our Admiration is extended no farther than to what is new to us, and we all overlook the Excellency of Things we are used to, be they never so curious. A Man would be laugh'd at, that should discover Luxury in the plain Dress of a poor Creature that walks along in a thick Parish Gown and a course Shirt underneath it; and yet what a number of People, how many different Trades, and what a variety of Skill and Tools must be employ'd to have the most ordinary *Yorkshire* Cloth? What depth of Thought and Ingenuity, what Toil and Labour, and what length of Time must it have cost, before Man could learn from a Seed to raise and prepare so useful a Product as Linnen?

Must that Society not be vainly curious, among whom this admirable Commodity, after it is made, shall not be thought fit to be used even by the poorest of all, before it is brought to a perfect whiteness, which is not to be procur'd but by the assistance of all the Elements joyn'd to a world of Industry and Patience? I have not done yet; Can we reflect not only on the Cost laid out upon this Luxurious Invention, but likewise on the little time the Whiteness of it continues, in which part of its Beauty consists, that every six or seven Days at furthest it wants cleaning, and whilst it lasts is a continual Charge to the wearer; can we, I say, reflect on all this, and not think it an extravagant Piece of Nicety, that even those who receive Alms of the Parish, should not only have whole Garments made of this operose Manufacture, but likewise that as soon as they are soil'd, to restore them to their pristine Purity, they should make use of one of the most Judicious as well as difficult Compositions that Chymistry can boast of; with which dissolv'd in Water by the help of Fire, the most detersive, and yet innocent *Lixivium*[30] is prepar'd that Human Industry has hitherto been able to invent?

It is certain, Time was that the Things I speak of would have bore those lofty Expressions, and in which every Body would have reason'd after the same manner; but the Age we live in would call a Man Fool who should talk of Extravagance and Nicety, if he saw a poor Woman, after having wore her Crown Cloath Smock a whole Week, wash it with a bit of stinking Soap of a Groat a Pound.

The Arts of Brewing and making Bread, have by slow degrees been brought to the Perfection they now are in, but to have invented them at once, and *a priori* would have required more Knowledge and a deeper Insight into the Nature of Fermentation, than the greatest Philosopher has hitherto been endowed with; yet the Fruits of both are now enjoy'd by the meanest of our Species, and a starving Wretch knows not how to make a more humble, or a more

30. Lye. – Ed.

modest Petition than by asking for a Bit of Bread or a Draught of Small Beer.

Man has learn'd by Experience, that nothing was softer than the small Plumes and Down of Birds, and found, that heap'd together they would by their Elasticity gently resist any incumbent Weight, and heave up again of themselves as soon as the Pressure is over. To make use of them to sleep upon was, no doubt, first invented to Compliment the Vanity as well as Ease of the Wealthy and Potent, but they are long since become so common, that almost every Body lies upon Featherbeds, and to substitute Flocks in the room of them, is counted a miserable shift of the most Necessitous. What a vast height must Luxury have been arriv'd to before it cou'd be reckon'd a Hardship to repose upon the soft Wool of Animals!

From Caves, Huts, Hovels, Tents and Barracks, with which Mankind took up at first, we are come to warm and well wrought Houses, and the meanest Habitations to be seen in Cities, are regular Buildings contriv'd by Persons skill'd in Proportions and Architecture. If the ancient *Britons* and *Gauls* should come out of their Graves, with what Amazement wou'd they gaze on the mighty Structures every where rais'd for the Poor! Should they behold the Magnificence of a *Chelsea College*,[31] a *Greenwich Hospital*, or what surpasses all them, a *Des Invalides* at *Paris*, and see the Care, the Plenty, the Superfluities and Pomp which People that have no Possessions at all are treated with in those stately Palaces, those who were once the greatest and richest of the Land would have Reason to envy the most reduced of our Species now.

Another piece of Luxury the Poor enjoy, that is not look'd upon as such, and which there is no doubt but the Wealthiest in a Golden Age would abstain from, is their making use

31. Chelsea Hospital, by Sir Christopher Wren. – Ed.

of the Flesh of Animals to eat. In what concerns the
Fashions and Manners of the Ages Men live in they never
examine into the real Worth or Merit of the Cause, and
generally judge of Things not as their Reason, but Custom
directs them. Time was when the Funeral Rites in the dis-
posing of the Dead were perform'd by Fire, and the
Cadavers of the greatest Emperors were burnt to Ashes.
Then burying the Corpse in the Ground was a Funeral for
Slaves, or made a Punishment for the worst of Malfactors.
Now nothing is decent or honourable but interring, and
burning the Body is reserv'd for Crimes of the blackest dye.
At some times we look upon Trifles with Horror, at other
times we can behold Enormities without Concern. If we see
a Man walk with his Hat on in a Church, though out of
Service time it shocks us, but if on a Sunday night we meet
half a dozen Fellows Drunk in the Street, the Sight makes
little or no Impression upon us. If a Woman at a Merry-
making dresses in Man's Cloaths, it is reckon'd a Frolick
among Friends, and he that finds too much Fault with it is
counted censorious: Upon the Stage it is done without
Reproach, and the most Vertuous Ladies will dispense with
it in an Actress, tho' every Body has a full view of her Legs
and Thighs; but if the same Woman, as soon as she has
Petticoats on again, should show her Leg to a Man as high
as her Knee, it would be a very immodest Action, and every
Body will call her impudent for it.

I have often thought, if it was not for this Tyranny which
Custom usurps over us, that Men of any tollerable good
Nature could never be reconcil'd to the killing of so many
Animals for their daily Food, as long as the bountiful
Earth so plentifully provides them with varieties of vege-
table Dainties. I know that Reason excites our Compassion
but faintly, and therefore I would not wonder how Men
should so little commiserate such imperfect Creatures as

Cray fish, Oysters, Cockles, and indeed all Fish in general:
As they are mute, and their inward Formation, as well as
outward Figure, vastly different from ours, they express
themselves unintelligibly to us, and therefore 'tis not strange
that their Grief should not affect our Understanding, which
it cannot reach; for nothing stirs us to Pity so effectually,
as when the Symptoms of Misery strike immediately upon
our Senses, and I have seen People mov'd at the Noise a
live Lobster makes upon the Spit, that could have kill'd half
a dozen Fowls with Pleasure. But in such perfect Animals
as Sheep and Oxen, in whom the Heart, the Brain and
Nerves differ so little from ours, and in whom the Separa-
tion of the Spirits from the Blood, the Organs of Sense, and
consequently Feeling itself, are the same as they are in
Human Creatures, I can't imagine how a Man not hardned
in Blood and Massacre, is able to see a violent Death, and
the Pangs of it, without Concern.

In answer to this, most People will think it sufficient to
say, that all Things being allow'd to be made for the Service
of Man, there can be no Cruelty in putting Creatures to
the use they were design'd for; but I have heard Men make
this Reply, whilst their Nature within them has reproach'd
them with the Falshood of the Assertion. There is of all the
Multitude not one Man in ten but what will own, (if he was
not brought up in a Slaughter-house) that of all Trades he
could never have been a *Butcher*; and I question whether
ever any body so much as kill'd a Chicken without Reluct-
ancy the first time. Some People are not to be perswaded to
taste of any Creatures they have daily seen and been ac-
quainted with, whilst they were alive; others extend their
scruple no further than to their own Poultry, and refuse to
eat what they fed and took care of themselves, yet all of
them will feed heartily and without Remorse on Beef, Mut-
ton and Fowls, when they are bought in the Market. In
this behaviour, methinks, there appears something like a

consciousness of Guilt, it looks as if they endeavour'd to save themselves from the Imputation of a Crime (which they know sticks somewhere) by removing the cause of it as far as they can from themselves; and I can discover in it some strong remains of Primitive Pity and Innocence, which all the arbitrary Power of Custom, and the violence of Luxury, have not yet been able to conquer.

What I build upon I shall be told is a Folly that Wise Men are not guilty of: I own it; but whilst it proceeds from a real Passion inherent in our Nature, it is sufficient to demonstrate that we are born with a Repugnancy to the killing, and consequently the eating of Animals; for it is impossible that a natural Appetite should ever prompt us to act, or desire others to do, what we have an aversion to, be it as foolish as it will.

Every body knows, that Surgeons in the Cure of dangerous Wounds and Fractures, the extirpation of Limbs, and other dreadful Operations, are often compell'd to put their Patients to extraordinary Torments, and that the more desperate and calamitous Cases occur to them, the more the outcries and bodily Sufferings of others must become familiar to them; for this Reason our *English* Law, out of a most affectionate Regard to the Lives of the Subject, allows them not to be of any Jury upon Life and Death, as supposing that their Practice it self is sufficient to harden and extinguish in them that Tenderness, without which no Man is capable of setting a true value upon the Lives of his fellow Creatures. Now if we ought to have no Concern for what we do to Brute Beasts, and there was not imagin'd to be any cruelty in killing them, why should of all Callings *Butchers*, and only they jointly with *Surgeons*, be excluded from being Jury men by the same Law?

I shall urge nothing of what *Pythagoras* and many other Wise Men have said concerning this Barbarity of eating Flesh; I have gone too much out of my way already, and shall therefore beg the Reader, if he would have any more of this, to run over the following Fable, or else, if he be tired, to let it alone, with an assurance that in doing of either he shall equally oblige me.

A *Roman* Merchant in one of the *Carthaginian* Wars was cast away upon the Coast of *Africk*: Himself and his Slave with great difficulty got safe ashoar; but going in quest of Relief, were met by a Lyon of a mighty size. It happened to be one of the Breed that ranged in *Æsop*'s Days, and one that could not only speak several Languages, but seem'd moreover very well acquainted with Human Affairs. The Slave got upon a Tree, but his Master not thinking himself safe there, and having heard much of the generosity of Lyons, fell down prostrate before him, with all the signs of Fear and Submission. The Lyon, who had lately fill'd his Belly, bids him rise and for a while lay by his Fears, assuring him withal, that he should not be touch'd, if he could give him any tollerable Reasons why he should not be devour'd. The Merchant obey'd, and having now receiv'd some glimmering hopes of safety, gave a dismal account of the Shipwrack he had suffer'd, and endeavouring from thence to raise the Lyon's Pity pleaded his Cause with abundance of good Rhethorick; but observing by the countenance of the Beast that Flattery and fine Words made very little Impression, he betook himself to Arguments of greater Solidity, and reasoning from the excellency of Man's Nature and Abilities, remonstrated how improbable it was that the Gods should not have design'd him for a better use than to be eat by Savage Beasts. Upon this the Lyon became more attentive, and vouchsaved now and then a reply, till at last the following Dialogue ensued between them.

Oh Vain and Covetous Animal, (*said the Lyon*) whose Pride and Avarice can make him leave his Native Soil, where his natural Wants might be plentifully supply'd, and try rough Seas and dangerous Mountains to find out Superfluities, why should you esteem your Species above ours? And if the Gods have given you a Superiority over all Creatures, then why beg you of an Inferior? *Our Superiority* (answer'd the Merchant) *consists not in bodily force but strength of Understanding; the Gods have endued us with a Rational Soul, which, tho' invisible, is much the better part of us.* I desire to touch nothing of you but what is good to eat, but why do you value your self so much upon that part which is invisible? *Because it is Immortal, and shall meet with Rewards after Death for the Actions of this Life, and the Just shall enjoy eternal Bliss and Tranquility with the Heroes and Demi-Gods in the Elysian Fields.* What Life have you led? *I have honoured the Gods, and study'd to be beneficial to Man.* Then why do you fear Death, if you think the Gods as just as you have been? *I have a Wife and five small Children that must come to want if they lose me.* I have two Whelps that are not big enough to shift for themselves, that are in want now, and must actually be starv'd if I can provide nothing for them: Your Children will be provided for one way or other, at least as well when I have eat you as if you had been drown'd.

As to the Excellency of either Species, the value of things among you has ever encreas'd with the scarcity of them, and to a Million of Men there is hardly one Lyon; besides that, in the great Veneration Man pretends to have for his kind, there is little Sincerity farther than it concerns the share which every ones Pride has in it for himself; 'tis a folly to boast of the Tenderness shewn and Attendance given to your young ones, or the excessive and lasting trouble bestow'd in the Education of 'em: Man being born the most necessitous and most helpless Animal, this is only an instinct of Nature, which in all Creatures has ever proportion'd the care of the Parents to the Wants and Imbecilities of the Offspring. But if Man had a real value for his kind, how is it possible that often Ten Thousand of them, and sometimes Ten times as many, should be destroy'd in few hours for the Caprice of two. All degrees of Men despise those that are inferior to them, and if you could enter into the Hearts of Kings and Princes, you would hardly find any but what have less value for the greatest part of the Multitudes they rule over, than those have for the Cattle that belong to them. Why should so many pretend to derive their Race, tho' but spuriously, from the immortal Gods; why should all of them suffer others to kneel down before them, and more or less take delight in having Divine Honours pay'd them, but to insinuate that themselves are of a more exalted Nature, and a Species superior to that of their Subjects?

Savage I am, but no Creature can be call'd cruel but what either by Malice or Insensibility extinguishes his natural Pity: The Lyon was born without Compassion; we follow the instinct of our Nature; the Gods have appointed us to live upon the waste and spoil of other Animals, and as long as we can meet with dead ones, we never hunt after the Living. 'Tis only Man, mischievous Man, that can make Death a sport, Nature taught your Stomach to crave nothing but Vegetables; but your violent fondness to change, and greater eagerness after Novelties, have prompted you to the Destruction of Animals without Justice or necessity, perverted your Nature and warp'd your Appetites which way soever your Pride or Luxury have call'd them. The Lyon has a ferment within him that consumes the toughest Skin and hardest Bones as well as the Flesh of all Animals without exception: Your squeamish Stomach, in which the Digestive heat is weak and inconsiderable, won't so much as admit of the most tender Parts of them, unless above half the Concoction has been perform'd by artificial Fire before hand; and yet what Animal have you spared to satisfy the Caprices of a languid Appetite? Languid I say; for what is Man's Hunger if compair'd to the Lyon's: Yours, when it is at the worst, makes you Faint, mine makes me Mad: Oft have I tried with Roots and Herbs to allay the violence of it, but in vain; nothing but large quantities of Flesh can any ways appease it.

Yet the fierceness of our Hunger, notwithstanding Lyons have often requited Benefits received; but ungrateful and perfidious Man feeds on the Sheep that Cloaths him, and spares not her innocent young ones, whom he has taken into his care and custody. If you tell me the Gods made Man Master over all other Creatures, what Tyranny was it then to destroy them out of wantonness? No, fickle timerous Animal, the Gods have made you for Society, and design'd that Millions of you, when well joyn'd together, should compose the strong *Leviathan*. A single Lyon bears some sway in the Creation, but what is single Man? A small and inconsiderable part, a trifling Atom of one great Beast. What Nature designs she executes, and 'tis not safe to judge of what she purpos'd, but from the effects she shews: If she had intended that Man, as Man from a superiority of Species, should lord it over all other Animals, the Tiger, nay the Whale and Eagle, would have obey'd his Voice.

But if your Wit and Understanding exceeds ours, ought not the Lyon in deference to that Superiority to follow the Maxims of Men, with whom nothing is more sacred than that the Reason of the strongest is ever the most prevalent? Whole Multitudes of you have conspired and compass'd the Destruction of one, after they had own'd the Gods had made him their Superior, and one has often ruin'd and cut off whole Multitudes, whom by the same Gods he had sworn to defend and maintain. Man never acknowledg'd Superiority without Power, and why should I? The Excellence I boast of is visible, all Animals tremble at the sight of the Lyon, not out of Panick Fear. The Gods have given me Swiftness to overtake, and Strength to conquer what ever comes near me. Where is there a Creature that has Teeth and Claws like mine; behold the thickness of these massy Jaw bones; consider the width of them, and feel the firmness of this brawny Neck. The nimblest Deer, the wildest Boar, the stoutest Horse, and strongest Bull are my Prey wherever I meet them. Thus spoke the Lyon, and the Merchant fainted away.

The Lyon, in my Opinion, has stretch'd the Point too far; yet when to soften the Flesh of Male Animals, we have by Castration prevented the firmness their Tendons and every Fibre would have come to without it, I confess I think it ought to move a human Creature when he reflects upon the cruel care with which they are fatned for Destruction. When a large and gentle Bullock, after having resisted a ten times greater force of Blows than would have kill'd his Murderer, falls stun'd at last, and his arm'd Head is fasten'd to the Ground with Cords; as soon as the wide Wound is made, and the Jugulars are cut asunder, what Mortal can without Compassion hear the painful Bellowings intercepted by his Blood, the bitter Sighs that speak the sharpness of his Anguish, and the deep sounding Groans with loud anxiety fetch'd from the bottom of his strong and palpitating Heart? Look on the trembling and violent Convulsions of his Limbs; see, whilst his reeking Gore streams from him, his Eyes become dim and languid, and behold his Struglings, Gasps and last efforts for Life, the certain Signs of his approaching Fate? When a Creature has given such convincing and undeniable Proofs of the Terrors upon him, and the Pains and Agonies he feels, is there a follower of *Descartes* so inur'd to Blood, as not to refute, by his Commiseration, the Philosophy of that vain Reasoner?

(*Q.*) —— *For frugally*
They now lived on their Salary.

PAGE 72. LINE 22. When People have small comings in, and are honest withal, it is then that the generality of them begin to be frugal, and not before. Frugality in *Ethick*s is call'd that Virtue from the Principle of which Men abstain from Superfluities, and despising the operose contrivances of Art to procure either Ease or Pleasure, content themselves with the natural Simplicity of Things, and are carefully Temperate in the Enjoyment of them without any Tincture of Covetousness. Frugality thus limited, is perhaps scarcer than many may imagine; but what is generally understood by it is a Quality more often to be met with, and consists in a *Medium* between Profuseness and Avarice, rather leaning to the latter. As this prudent Oeconomy, which some People call *Saving*, is in Private Families the most certain Method to encrease an Estate, so some imagine, that whether a Country be barren or fruitful, the same Method, if generally pursued (which they think practicable) will have the same effect upon a whole Nation, and that, for Example, the *English* might be much richer than they are, if they would be as frugal as some of their Neighbours. This, I think, is an Error, which to prove I shall first refer the Reader to what has been said upon this head in Remark (*L*) and then go on thus.

Experience teaches us first, that as People differ in their Views and Perceptions of Things, so they vary in their Inclinations; one Man is given to Covetousness, another to Prodigality, and a third is only *Saving*. Secondly, that Men are never, or at least very seldom, reclaimed from their darling Passions, either by Reason or Precept, and that if any thing ever draws 'em from what they are naturally propense to, it must be a change in their Circumstances or their Fortunes. If we reflect upon these Observations, we shall find that to render the generality of a Nation lavish, the Product of the Country must be considerable in proportion to the Inhabitants, and what they are profuse of cheap; that on the contrary, to make a Nation generally frugal, the Necessaries of Life must be scarce, and consequently dear; and that therefore let the best Politician do what he can, the Profuseness or Frugality of a People in general, must always depend upon, and will in spight of his Teeth, be ever proportion'd to the Fruitfulness and Product of the Country, the number of Inhabitants, and the Taxes they are to bear. If any body would refute what I have said, let them only prove from History, that there ever was in any Country a National Frugality without a National Necessity.

Let us examine then what things are requisite to aggrandize and enrich a Nation. The first desirable Blessings for any Society of Men are a fertile Soil and a happy Climate, a mild Government, and more Land than People. These Things will render Man easy, loving, honest and sincere. In this Condition they may be as Virtuous as they can, without the least injury to the Publick, and consequently as happy as they please themselves. But they shall have no Arts or Sciences, or be quiet longer than their Neighbours will let them; they must be poor, ignorant, and almost wholly destitute of what we call the Comforts of Life, and all the Cardinal Virtues together won't so much as procure a tolerable Coat or a Porridge Pot among 'em: For in this State of slothful Ease and stupid Innocence, as you need not fear great Vices, so you must not expect any considerable Virtues. Man never exerts himself but when he is rous'd by his Desires: Whilst they lie dormant, and there is nothing to raise them, his Excellence and Abilities will be for ever undiscover'd, and the lumpish Machine, without the Influence of his Passions, may be justly compar'd to a huge Wind-mill without a breath of Air.

Would you render a Society of Men strong and powerful,

you must touch their Passions. Divide the Land, tho' there be never so much to spare, and their Possessions will make them Covetous: Rouse them, tho' but in Jest, from their Idleness with Praises, and Pride will set them to work in earnest: Teach them Trades and Handicrafts, and you'll bring Envy and Emulation among them: To encrease their Numbers, set up a variety of Manufactures, and leave no Ground uncultivated: Let Property be inviolably secured, and Priviledges equal to all Men: Suffer no body to act but what is lawful, and every body to think what he pleases; for a Country where every body may be maintained that will be employ'd, and the other Maxims are observ'd, must always be throng'd and can never want People, as long as there is any in the World. Would you have them Bold and Warlike, turn to Military Discipline, make good use of their Fear, and flatter their Vanity with Art and Assiduity: But would you moreover render them an opulent, knowing and polite Nation, teach 'em Commerce with Foreign Countries, and if possible get into the Sea, which to compass spare no Labour nor Industry, and let no difficulty deter you from it: Then promote Navigation, cherish the Merchant, and encourage Trade in every Branch of it; this will bring Riches, and where they are, Arts and Sciences will soon follow, and by the help of what I have named and good Management, it is that Politicians can make a People potent, renown'd and flourishing.

But would you have a frugal and honest Society, the best Policy is to preserve Men in their Native Simplicity, strive not to encrease their Numbers; let them never be acquainted with Strangers or Superfluities, but remove and keep from them every thing that might raise their Desires, or improve their Understanding.

Great Wealth and Foreign Treasure will ever scorn to come among Men, unless you'll admit their inseparable Companions, Avarice and Luxury. Where Trade is considerable Fraud will intrude. To be at once well-bred and sincere, is no less than a Contradiction; and therefore whilst Man advances in Knowledge, and his Manners are polish'd, we must expect to see at the same time his Desires enlarg'd, his Appetites refin'd, and his Vices encreas'd.

The *Dutch* may ascribe their present Grandeur to the Virtue and Frugality of their Ancestors as they please; but what made that contemptible spot of Ground so considerable among the principal Powers of *Europe*, has been their Political Wisdom in postponing every thing to Merchandize and Navigation, the unlimited Liberty of Conscience that is enjoy'd among them, and the unwearied Application with which they have always made use of the most effectual means to encourage and increase Trade in general.

They never were noted for Frugality before *Philip* II. of *Spain* began to rage over them with that unheard of Tyranny. Their Laws were trampled upon, their Rights and large Immunities taken from them, and their Constitution torn to pieces. Several of their Chief Nobles were condemn'd and executed without legal Form of Process. Complaints and Remonstrances were punish'd as severely as Resistance, and those that escaped being massacred, were plunder'd by ravenous Soldiers. As this was intollerable to a People that had always been used to the mildest of Governments, and enjoy'd greater Privileges than any of the Neighbouring Nations, so they chose rather to dye in Arms than perish by cruel Executioners. If we consider the Strength *Spain* had then, and the low Circumstances those Distress'd States were in, there never was heard of a more unequal Strife; yet such was their Fortitude and Resolution, that only seven of those Provinces uniting themselves together, maintain'd against the greatest and best disciplin'd Nation in *Europe*, the most tedious and bloody War, that is to be met with in ancient or modern History.

Rather than to become a Victim to the *Spanish* Fury, they

were contented to live upon a third part of their Revenues, and lay out far the greatest part of their Income in defending themselves against their merciless Enemies. These Hardships and Calamities of a War within their Bowels, first put them upon that extraordinary Frugality, and the Continuance under the same difficulties for above Fourscore Years, could not but render it Customary and Habitual to them. But all their Arts of Saving, and Penurious way of Living, could never have enabled them to make head against so Potent an Enemy, if their Industry in promoting their Fishery and Navigation in general, had not help'd to supply the Natural Wants and Disadvantages they labour'd under.

The Country is so small and so populous, that there is not Land enough, (though hardly an Inch of it is unimprov'd) to feed the Tenth part of the Inhabitants. *Holland* it self is full of large Rivers, and lies lower than the Sea, which would run over it every Tide, and wash it away in one Winter, if it was not kept out by vast Banks and huge Walls: The Repairs of those, as well as their Sluices, Keys, Mills, and other Necessaries they are forc'd to make use of to keep themselves from being drown'd are a greater Expence to them one Year with another, than could be rais'd by a general Land Tax of Four Shillings in the Pound, if to be deducted from the neat Produce of the Landlord's Revenue.

Is it a wonder that People under such Circumstances, and loaden with greater Taxes besides than any other Nation, should be oblig'd to be saving? But why must they be a Pattern to others, who besides that they are more happily situated, are much richer within themselves, and have, to the same number of People, above ten times the Extent of Ground? The *Dutch* and we often buy and sell at the same Markets, and so far our Views may be said to be the same: Otherwise the Interests and Political Reasons of the two Nations as to the private Oeconomy of either, are very different. It is their Interest to be Frugal and spend little; because they must have every thing from Abroad, except Butter, Cheese and Fish, and therefore of them, especially the latter, they consume three times the quantity, which the same number of People do here. It is our Interest to eat plenty of Beef and Mutton to maintain the Farmer, and further improve our Land, of which we have enough to feed our selves, and as many more, if it was better cultivated: The *Dutch* perhaps have more Shipping, and more ready Money than we, but then those are only to be considered as the Tools they work with. So a Carrier may have more Horses than a Man of ten times his worth, and a Banker that has not above fifteen or sixteen Hundred Pounds in the World, may have generally more ready Cash by him than a Gentleman of two Thousand a Year. He that keeps three or four Stage-Coaches to get his Bread, is to a Gentleman that keeps a Coach for his Pleasure, what the *Dutch* are in comparison to us; having nothing of their own but Fish, they are Carriers and Freighters to the rest of the World, whilst the Basis of our Trade chiefly depends upon our own Product.

Another Instance, that what makes the Bulk of the People saving, are heavy Taxes, scarcity of Land, and such Things that occasion a Dearth of Provisions, may be given from what is observable among the *Dutch* themselves. In the Province of *Holland* there is a vast Trade, and an unconceiveable Treasure of Money. The Land is almost as rich as Dung itself, and (as I have said once already) not an Inch of it unimprov'd. In *Gelderland* and *Overyssel* there's hardly any Trade, and very little Money: The Soil is very indifferent, and abundance of Ground lies waste. Then what is the Reason that the same *Dutch* in the two latter Provinces, tho' Poorer than the first, are yet less stingy and more hospitable? Nothing but that their Taxes in most Things are less Extravagant, and in proportion to the Number of

People, they have a great deal more Ground. What they save in *Holland*, they save out of their Bellies; 'tis Eatables, Drinkables and Fewel that their heaviest Taxes are upon, but they wear better Cloaths, and have richer Furniture, than you'll find in the other Provinces.

Those that are frugal by Principle, are so in every Thing, but in *Holland* the People are only sparing in such Things as are daily wanted, and soon consumed; in what is lasting they are quite otherwise: In Pictures and Marble they are Profuse; in their Buildings and Gardens they are extravagant to Folly. In other Countries you may meet with stately Courts and Palaces of great Extent that belong to Princes, which no Body can expect in a Commonwealth, where so much equality is observ'd as there is in this; but in all *Europe* you shall find no private Buildings so sumptuously Magnificent, as a great many of the Merchant's and other Gentlemen's Houses are in *Amsterdam*, and some other great Cities of that small Province; and the generality of those that build there, lay out a greater proportion of their Estates on the Houses they dwell in than any People upon the Earth.

The Nation I speak of was never in greater streights, nor their Affairs in a more dismal Posture since they were a Republick than in the Year 1671, and the beginning of 1672.[32] What we know of their Oeconomy and Constitution with any certainty has been chiefly owing to Sir *William Temple*, whose Observations upon their Manners and Government, it is evident from several Passages in his Memoirs were made about that time. The *Dutch* indeed were then very frugal; but since those Days, and that their Calamities have not been so pressing, (tho' the Common People, on whom the principal Burthen of all Excises and Impositions lies, are perhaps much as they were) a great

32. The crisis was occasioned by a war with France and England. – Ed.

Alteration has been made among the better sort of People in their Equipages, Entertainments, and whole manner of Living.

Those who would have it that the Frugality of that Nation flows not so much from Necessity, as a general Aversion to Vice and Luxury, will put us in mind of their publick Administration and Smallness of Sallaries, their Prudence in bargaining for and buying Stores and other Necessaries, the great Care they take not to be imposed upon by those that serve them, and their Severity against them that break their Contracts. But what they would ascribe to the Virtue and Honesty of Ministers, is wholly due to their strict Regulations, concerning the management of the publick Treasure, from which their admirable Form of Government will not suffer them to depart; and indeed one good Man may take anothers Word, if they so agree, but a whole Nation ought never to trust to any Honesty, but what is built upon Necessity; for unhappy is the People, and their Constitution will be ever precarious, whose Welfare must depend upon the Virtues and Consciences of Ministers and Politicians.

The *Dutch* generally endeavour to promote as much Frugality among their Subjects as 'tis possible, not because it is a Virtue, but because it is, generally speaking, their Interest, as I have shew'd before; for as this latter changes, so they alter their Maxims, as will be plain in the following Instance.

As soon as their *East India* Ships come home, the Company pays off the Men, and many of them receive the greatest part of what they have been earning in seven or eight, and some fifteen or sixteen Years time. These poor Fellows are encourag'd to spend their Money with all Profuseness imaginable, and considering that most of them, when they set out at first were Reprobates, that under the Tuition of a strict Discipline, and a miserable Dyet, have been so long kept at hard Labour, without Money, in the midst of Danger, it cannot be difficult to make them Lavish as soon as they have Plenty.

They squander away in Wine, Women and Musick, as much as People of their Taste and Education are well capable of, and are suffer'd, (so they but abstain from doing of Mischief) to revel and riot with greater Licentiousness than is Customary to be allow'd to others. You may in some Cities see them accompanied with three or four Lewd Women, few of them Sober, run roaring through the Streets by broad Daylight with a Fidler before them: And if the Money, to their thinking, goes not fast enough these ways, they'll find out others, and sometimes fling it among the Mob by handfuls. This Madness continues in most of them whilst they have any thing left, which never lasts long, and for this reason, by a Nick-name, they are call'd, *Lords of six Weeks*, that being generally the time by which the Company has other Ships ready to depart; where these infatuated Wretches (their Money being gone) are forc'd to enter themselves again, and may have leisure to repent their Folly.

In this Stratagem there is a double Policy: First, if these Saylors that have been inured to the hot Climates and unwholsome Air and Dyet, should be frugal and stay in their own Country, the Company would be continually oblig'd to employ fresh Men, of which (besides that they are not so fit for their Business) hardly one in two ever lives in some Places of the *East Indies*, which would often prove a great Charge as well as Disappointment to them. The second is, that the large Sums so often distributed among those Saylors, are by this means made immediately to circulate throughout the Country, from whence, by heavy Excises and other Impositions, the greatest part of it is soon drawn back into the publick Treasure.

To convince the Champions for National Frugality by another Argument, that what they urge is impracticable, we'll suppose that I am mistaken in every thing, which in

Remark (L) I have said in behalf of Luxury and the Necessity of it to maintain Trade; after that let us examine what a general Frugality, if it was by Art and Management to be forc'd upon People, whether they have occasion for it or not, would produce in such a Nation as ours. We'll grant then that all the People in *Great Britain* shall consume but four Fifths of what they do now, and so lay by one Fifth part of their Income: I shall not speak of what Influence this would have upon almost every Trade, as well as the Farmer, the Grazier and the Landlord, but favourably suppose (what is yet impossible) that the same Work shall be done, and consequently the same Handicrafts be employ'd as there are now. The Consequence would be, that unless Money should all at once fall prodigiously in Value, and every thing else, contrary to Reason, grow very dear, at the five Years end all the working People, and the poorest of Labourers, (for I won't meddle with any of the rest) would be worth in ready Cash as much as they now spend in a whole Year; which, by the by, would be more Money than ever the Nation had at once.

Let us now, overjoy'd with this encrease of Wealth, take a view of the Condition the working People would be in, and reasoning from Experience, and what we daily observe of them, judge what their Behaviour would be in such a Case. Every body knows that there is a vast number of Journymen Weavers, Taylors, Clothworkers, and twenty other Handicrafts; who, if by four Days Labour in a Week they can maintain themselves, will hardly be perswaded to work the fifth; and that there are Thousands of Labouring Men of all sorts, who will, tho' they can hardly subsist, put themselves to fifty Inconveniencies, disoblige their Masters, pinch their Bellies, and run in Debt, to make Holidays. When Men shew such an extraordinary proclivity to Idleness and Pleasure, what reason have we to think that they would ever work, unless they were oblig'd to it by immediate Necessity? When we see an Artificer that cannot be drove to his Work before *Tuesday*, because the *Monday* Morning he has two Shillings left of his last Week's Pay; why should we imagine he would go to it at all, if he had fifteen or twenty Pounds in his Pocket?

What would, at this rate, become of our Manufactures? If the Merchant would send Cloth Abroad, he must make it himself, for the Clothier cannot get one Man out of twelve that used to work for him. If what I speak of was only to befal the Journeymen Shoemakers, and no body else, in less than a Twelvemonth half of us would go barefoot. The chief and most pressing use there is for Money in a Nation, is to pay the Labour of the Poor, and when there is a real Scarcity of it, those who have a great many Workmen to pay, will always feel it first; yet notwithstanding this great necessity of Coin, it would be easier, where Property was well secured, to live without Money than without Poor; for who would do the Work? For this reason the quantity of circulating Coin in a Country ought always to be propor-tion'd to the number of Hands that are employ'd; and the Wages of Labourers to the price of Provisions.[33] From whence it is demonstrable, that whatever procures Plenty makes Labourers cheap, where the Poor are well managed; who as they ought to be kept from starving, so they should receive nothing worth saving. If here and there one of the lowest class by uncommon industry, and pinching his Belly, lifts himself above the Condition he was brought up in, no body ought to hinder him; Nay it is undeniably the wisest course for every Person in the Society, and for every private Family to be frugal; but it is the Intrest of all Rich Nations, that the greatest part of the Poor should almost never be Idle, and yet continually spend what they get.

All Men, as Sir *William Temple* observes very well, are

33. The remainder of this paragraph was added in 1723. – Ed.

more prone to Ease and Pleasure, than they are to Labour, when they are not prompted to it by Pride or Avarice, and those that get their Living by their daily Labour, are seldom powerfully influenc'd by either: So that they have nothing to stir them up to be serviceable but their Wants, which it is Prudence to relieve, but Folly to cure. The only thing then that can render the labouring Man industrious, is a moderate quantity of Money; for as too little will, according as his Temper is, either dispirit or make him Desperate, so too much will make him Insolent and Lazy.

A Man would be laugh'd at by most People, who should maintain that too much Money could undo a Nation: Yet this has been the Fate of *Spain*; to this the learned Don *Diego Savedra* ascribes the Ruin of his Country. The Fruits of the Earth in former Ages had made *Spain* so rich, that King *Lewis* XI[34] of *France* being come to the Court of *Toledo*, was astonish'd at its Splendour, and said, that he had never seen any thing to be compar'd to it, either in *Europe* or *Asia*; he that in his Travels to the *Holy Land* had run through every Province of them. In the Kingdom of *Castille* alone, (if we may believe some Writers) there were for the *Holy War* from all Parts of the World got together one hundred Thousand Foot, ten thousand Horse and sixty thousand Carriages for Baggage, which *Alonso* III maintain'd at his own Charge, and paid every Day as well Soldiers as Officers and Princes, every one according to his Rank and Dignity: Nay, down to the Reign of *Ferdinand* and *Isabella*, (who equip'd *Columbus*) and some time after, *Spain* was a fertile Country, where Trade and Manufactures flourish'd and had a knowing industrious People to boast of. But as soon as that mighty Treasure, that was obtain'd with more Hazard and Cruelty than the World till then had known, and which to come at, by the *Spaniard*'s own Confession, had cost the Lives of twenty Millions of *Indians*; as

34. A mistake for Louis VI or possibly Louis VII. – Ed.

soon, I say, as that Ocean of Treasure came rowling in upon them, it took away their Senses, and their Industry forsook them. The Farmer left his Plough, the Mechanick his Tools, the Merchant his Compting-house, and every body scorning to work, took his Pleasure and turn'd Gentleman. They thought they had reason to value themselves above all their Neighbours, and now nothing but the Conquest of the World would serve them.

The Consequence of this has been, that other Nations have supply'd what their own Sloth and Pride deny'd them; and when every body saw, that notwithstanding all the Prohibitions the Government could make against the Exportation of Bullion, the *Spaniard* would part with his Money, and bring it you aboard himself at the hazard of his Neck, all the World endeavour'd to work for *Spain*. Gold and Silver being by this means yearly divided and shared among all the Trading Countries, have made all Things dear, and most Nations of *Europe* Industrious, except their Owners, who ever since their mighty Acquisitions, sit with their Arms across, and wait every Year with impatience and anxiety, the arrival of their Revenues from Abroad, to pay others for what they have spent already: And thus by *too much Money*, the making of Colonies and other Mismanagements, of which it was the occasion *Spain* is from a fruitful and well peopled Country, with all its mighty Titles and Possessions, made a Barren and empty Thorough fair, thro' which Gold and Silver pass from *America* to the rest of the World, and the Nation, from a rich, acute, diligent and laborious, become a slow, idle, proud and beggarly People; so much for *Spain*: The next Country where Money may be call'd the Product is *Portugal*, and the Figure which that Kingdom with all its Gold makes in *Europe*, I think is not much to be envyed.

The great Art then to make a Nation happy, and what we call flourishing, consists in giving every body an Opportunity of being employ'd; which to compass, let a Government's first care be to promote as great a variety of Manufactures, Arts and Handicrafts, as Human Wit can invent; and the second to encourage Agriculture and Fishery in all their Branches, that the whole Earth may be forc'd to exert itself as well as Man; for as the one is an infallible Maxim to draw vast multitudes of People into a Nation, so the other is the only Method to maintain them.

It is from this Policy, and not the trifling Regulations of Lavishness and Frugality, (which will ever take their own Course, according to the Circumstances of the People) that the Greatness and Felicity of Nations must be expected; for let the Value of Gold and Silver either rise or fall, the Enjoyment of all Societies will ever depend upon the Fruits of the Earth, and the Labour of the People; both which joyn'd together are a more certain, a more inexhaustible and a more real Treasure than the Gold of *Brazil*, or the Silver of *Potosi*.[35]

(R.) *No Honour now, &c.*

PAGE 73. LINE 4. Honour in its Figurative Sense is a Chimera without Truth or Being, an Invention of Moralists and Politicians, and signifies a certain Principle of Vertue not related to Religion, found in some Men that keeps 'em close to their Duty and Engagements whatever they be; as for Example, a Man of Honour enters into a Conspiracy with others to murder a King; he is obliged to go thorough Stitch with it, and if overcome by Remorse or good Nature, he startles at the Enormity of his Purpose, discovers the Plot, and turns a Witness against his Accomplices, he then forfeits his Honour, at least among the Party he belong'd to. The Excellency of this Principle is, that the Vulgar are

35. The great mining centre of eighteenth-century Peru. – Ed.

destitute of it, and it is only to be met with in People of the better sort, as some Oranges have Kernels, and others not, tho' the outside be the same. In great Families it is like the Gout, generally counted Hereditary, and all Lords Children are born with it. In some that never felt any thing of it, it is acquired by Conversation and Reading, (especially of Romances) in others by Preferment; but there is nothing that encourages the Growth of it more than a Sword, and upon the first wearing of one, some People have felt considerable Shutes of it in Four and twenty Hours.

The chief and most important Care a Man of Honour ought to have, is the Preservation of this Principle, and rather than forfeit it, he must lose his Employments and Estate, nay, Life itself; for which reason, whatever Humility he may shew by way of good Breeding, he is allow'd to put an inestimable Value upon himself, as a Possessor of this invisible Ornament. The only Method to preserve this Principle, is to live up to the Rules of Honour, which are Laws he is to walk by: Himself is oblig'd always to be faithful to his Trust, to prefer the publick Interest to his own, not to tell Lies, nor defraud or wrong any Body, and from others to suffer no Affront, which is a Term of Art for every Action designedly done to undervalue him.

The Men of ancient Honour, of which I reckon *Don Quixot* to have been the last upon Record, were very nice Observers of all these Laws, and a great many more than I have named; but the Moderns seem to be more remiss; they have a profound Veneration for the last of 'em, but they pay not an equal Obedience to any of the other, and whoever will but strictly comply with that I hint at, shall have abundance of Trespasses against all the rest conniv'd at.

A Man of Honour is always counted impartial, and a Man of Sense of course; for no body ever heard of a Man of Honour that was a Fool: For this reason, he has nothing to do with the Law, and is always allow'd to be a Judge in his own Case; and if the least Injury be done either to himself or his Friend, his Relation, his Servant, his Dog, or any thing which he is pleased to take under his Honourable Protection, Satisfaction must be forthwith demanded, and if it proves an Affront, and he that gave it likewise a Man of Honour, a Battle must ensue. From all this it is evident, that a Man of Honour must be possessed of Courage, and that without it his other Principle would be no more than a Sword without a Point. Let us therefore examine what Courage consists in, and whether it be, as most People will have it, a real Something that valiant Men have in their Nature distinct from all their other Qualities or not.

There is nothing so universally sincere upon Earth, as the Love which all Creatures, that are capable of any, bear to themselves; and as there is no Love but what implies a Care to preserve the Thing beloved, so there is nothing more sincere in any Creature than his Will, Wishes and Endeavours to preserve himself. This is the Law of Nature, by which no Creature is endued with any Appetite or Passion but what either directly or indirectly tends to the Preservation either of himself or his Species.

The means by which Nature obliges every Creature continually to stir in this Business of Self-Preservation, are grafted in him, and (in Man) call'd Desires, which either compel him to crave what he thinks will sustain or please him, or command him to avoid what he imagines might displease, hurt or destroy him. These Desires or Passions have all their different Symptoms by which they manifest themselves to those they disturb, and from that variety of Disturbances they make within us, their various Denominations have been given them, as has been shewn already in Pride and Shame.

The Passion that is rais'd in us when we apprehend that Mischief is approaching us, is call'd Fear: The Disturbance it makes within us is always more or less violent in proportion, not of the Danger, but our Apprehension of the Mischief dreaded, whether real or imaginary. Our Fear then being always proportion'd to the Apprehension we have of the Danger, it follows, that whilst that Apprehension lasts, a Man can no more shake off his Fear than he can a Leg or an Arm. In a Fright it is true, the Apprehension of Danger is so sudden, and attacks us so lively, (as sometimes to take away Reason and Senses) that when 'tis over we often don't remember that we had any Apprehension at all; but from the Event, 'tis plain we had it, for how could we have been frighten'd if we had not apprehended that some Evil or other was coming upon us?

Most People are of Opinion, that this apprehension is to be conquer'd by Reason, but I confess I am not: Those that have been frighten'd will tell you, that as soon as they could recollect themselves, that is, make use of their Reason, their apprehension was conquer'd. But this is no Conquest at all, for in a fright the Danger was either altogether imaginary, or else it is past by that time they can make use of their Reason, and therefore if they find there is no Danger, it is no wonder that they should not apprehend any: But when the Danger is permanent, let them then make use of their Reason, and they'll find that it may serve them to examine the greatness and reality of the Danger, and that if they find it less than they imagin'd, their apprehension will be lessen'd accordingly; but if the Danger proves real, and the same in every circumstance as they took it to be at first, then their Reason instead of diminishing will rather encrease their apprehension. Whilst this Fear lasts, no Creature can fight offensively, and yet we see Brutes daily fight obstinately, and worry one another to Death; so that some other Passion must be able to overcome this Fear, and the most contrary to it is Anger; which to trace to the bottom I must beg leave to make another Digression.

No Creature can subsist without Food, nor any Species of them (I speak of the more perfect Animals) continue long unless young ones are continually born as fast as the old ones die. Therefore the first and fiercest Appetite that Nature has given them is Hunger, the next is Lust; the one prompting them to procreate as the other bids them eat. Now if we observe that Anger is that Passion which is rais'd in us when we are cross'd or disturb'd in our Desires, and that as it sums up all the strength in Creatures, so it was given them that by it they might exert themselves more vigorously in endeavouring to remove, overcome, or destroy whatever obstructs them in the pursuit of Self-Preservation; we shall find that Brutes, unless themselves or what they love, or the Liberty of either are threatned or attack'd, have nothing worth notice that can move them to Anger but *Hunger* or *Lust*. 'Tis they that make them more fierce, for we must observe, that the Appetites of Creatures are as actually cross'd, whilst they want and cannot meet with what they desire (tho' perhaps with less violence) as when hindred from enjoying what they have in view. What I have said will appear more plainly, if we but mind what no body can be ignorant of, which is this: All Creatures upon Earth live either upon the Fruits and Product of it, or else the Flesh of other Animals, their fellow Creatures. The latter, which we call Beasts of Prey, Nature has arm'd accordingly, and given them Weapons and Strength to overcome and tear asunder those whom she has design'd for their Food, and likewise a much keener Appetite than to other Animals that live upon Herbs, &c. For as to the first, if a Cow lov'd Mutton as well as she does Grass, being made as she is, and having no Claws or Talons, and but one Row of Teeth before that are all of an equal length, she would be starv'd even among a Flock of Sheep. Secondly, as to their voraciousness, if Experience did not teach it us, our Reason might: In the first place it is highly probable that the

Hunger, which can make a Creature fatigue, harrass and expose himself to danger for every bit he eats, is more piercing than that which only bids him eat what stands before him, and which he may have for stooping down. In the second, it is to be considered, that as Beasts of Prey have an instinct by which they learn to crave, trace, and discover those Creatures that are good Food for them, so the others have likewise an instinct that teaches them to shun, conceal themselves, and run away from those that hunt after them: From hence it must follow, that Beasts of Prey, tho' they could almost eat for ever, go yet more often with empty Bellies than other Creatures, whose Victuals neither fly from nor oppose them. This must perpetuate as well as encrease their Hunger, which hereby becomes a constant Fuel to their Anger.

If you ask me what stirs up this Anger in Bulls and Cocks that will fight to Death, and yet are neither Animals of Prey nor very voracious, I answer, *Lust*. Those Creatures, whose Rage proceeds from Hunger, both Male and Female attack every thing they can master, and fight obstinately against all: But the Animals, whose Fury is provok'd by a Venereal ferment, being generally Males, exert themselves chiefly against other Males of the same Species. They may do mischief by chance to other Creatures, but the main objects of their hatred are their Rivals, and it is against them only that their Prowess and Fortitude are shewn. We see likewise in all those Creatures of which the Male is able to satisfy a great number of Females, a more considerable superiority in the Male express'd by Nature in his Make and Features as well as fierceness, than is observ'd in other Creatures where the Male is contented with one or two Females. Dogs, tho' become Domestick Animals, are ravenous to a Proverb, and those of them that will fight being Carnivorous, would soon become Beasts of Prey, if not fed by us; what we may observe in them is an ample proof of what I have hitherto advanc'd. Those of a true fighting Breed, being voracious Creatures, both Male and Female, will fasten upon any thing, and suffer themselves to be kill'd before they give over. As the Female is rather more salacious than the Male, so there is no difference in their make at all, what distinguishes the Sexes excepted, and the Female is rather the fiercest of the two. A Bull is a terrible Creature when he is kept up, but where he has twenty or more Cows to range among, in a little time he'll become as tame as any of them, and a dozen Hens will spoil the best game Cock in *England*; Harts and Deer are counted chaste and timorous Creatures, and so indeed they are almost all the Year long, except in Rutting time, and then on a sudden they become bold to admiration, and often make at the Keepers themselves.

That the influence of those two principal Appetites, Hunger and Lust, upon the temper of Animals, is not so whimsical as some may imagine, may be partly demonstrated from what is observable in our selves; for though our Hunger is infinitely less violent than that of Wolves and other ravenous Creatures, yet we see that People who are in Health and have a tolerable Stomach, are more fretful, and sooner put out of Humour for Trifles when they stay for their Victuals beyond their usual Hours, than at any other time. And again, tho' Lust in Man is not so raging as it is in Bulls and other salacious Creatures, yet nothing provokes Men and Women both sooner and more violently to Anger, than what crosses their Amours, when they are heartily in Love; and the most fearful and tenderly educated of either Sex, have slighted the greatest dangers, and set aside all other considerations to compass the destruction of a Rival.

Hitherto I have endeavour'd to demonstrate, that no Creature can fight offensively as long as his Fear lasts; that Fear cannot be conquer'd but by another Passion; that the most contrary to it, and most effectual to overcome it is

Anger; that the two principal Appetites which disappointed can stir up this last named Passion are *Hunger* and *Lust*, and that in all Brute Beasts the proness to Anger and Obstinacy in fighting generally depend upon the violence of either or both those Appetites together: From whence it must follow, that what we call Prowess or natural Courage in Creatures, is nothing but the effect of Anger, and that all fierce Animals must be either very Ravenous or very Lustful, if not both.

Let us now examine what by this Rule we ought to judge of our own Species. From the tenderness of Man's Skin, and the great care that is required for Years together to rear him; from the Make of his Jaws, the evenness of his Teeth, the breadth of his Nails, and the slightness of both, it is not probable that Nature should have design'd him for Rapine; for this Reason his Hunger is not voracious as it is in Beasts of Prey; neither is he so salacious as other Animals that are call'd so, and being besides very industrious to supply his wants, he can have no reigning Appetite to perpetuate his Anger, and must consequently be a timorous Animal.

What I have said last must only be understood of Man in his Savage State; for if we examine him as a Member of a Society and a taught Animal, we shall find him quite another Creature: As soon as his Pride has room to Play, and Envy, Avarice and Ambition begin to catch hold of him, he is rous'd from his natural Innocence and Stupidity. As his Knowledge encreases, his Desires are enlarg'd, and consequently his Wants and Appetites are multiply'd: Hence it must follow, that he will be often cross'd in the pursuit of them, and meet with abundance more disappointment to stir up his Anger in this than his former Condition, and Man would in a little time become the most hurtful and noxious Creature in the World, if let alone, whenever he could over power his Adversary, if he had no Mischief to fear but from the Person that anger'd him.

The first care therefore of all Governments is by severe Punishments to curb his Anger when it does hurt, and so by encreasing his Fears prevent the mischief it might produce. When various Laws to restrain him from using Force are strictly executed, Self Preservation must teach him to be peaceable; and as it is every body's business to be as little disturb'd as is possible, his Fears will be continually augmented and enlarg'd as he advances in Experience, Understanding and Foresight. The consequence of this must be, that as the Provocations he will receive to Anger will be infinite in the civiliz'd State, so his Fears to damp it will be the same, and thus in a little time he'll be taught by his Fears to destroy his Anger, and by Art to consult in an opposite Method the same Self Preservation for which Nature before had furnished him with Anger, as well as the rest of his Passions.

The only useful Passion then that Man is possess'd of toward the peace and quiet of a Society, is his Fear, and the more you work upon it the more orderly and governable he'll be; for how useful soever Anger may be to Man, as he is a single Creature by himself, yet the Society has no manner of occasion for it: But Nature being always the same in the Formation of Animals, produces all Creatures as like to those that beget and bear them as the place she forms them in, and the various influences from without will give her leave, and consequently all Men, whether they are born in Courts or Forests, are susceptible of Anger. When this Passion overcomes (as among all degrees of People it sometimes does) the whole Set of Fears Man has, he has true Courage, and will fight as boldly as a Lyon or a Tyger, and at no other time; and I shall endeavour to prove, that whatever is call'd Courage in Man, when he is not Angry, is spurious and artificial.

It is possible by good Government to keep a Society always quiet in itself, but no body can ensure Peace from without for ever. The Society may have occasion to extend their limits further, and enlarge their Territories, or others may invade theirs, or some thing else will happen that Man must be brought to fight; for how civiliz'd soever Men may be, they never forget that Force goes beyond Reason: The Politician now must alter his Measures, and take off some of Man's Fears; he must strive to perswade him, that all what was told him before of the Barbarity of killing Men ceases as soon as these Men are Enemies to the Publick, and that their Adversaries are neither so good nor so strong as themselves. These Things well manag'd will seldom fail of drawing the hardiest, the most quarrelsome, and the most mischievous in to Combat; but unless they are better qualify'd, I won't answer for their behaviour there. If once you can make them undervalue their Enemies, you may soon stir them up to Anger, and while that lasts they'll fight with greater Obstinacy than any disciplin'd Troops: But if any thing happens that was unforeseen, and a sudden great Noise, a Tempest, or any strange or uncommon Accident, that seems to threaten 'em, intervenes, Fear seizes 'em, disarms their Anger, and makes 'em run away to a Man.

This natural Courage therefore, as soon as People begin to have more Wit, must be soon exploded. In the first place those that have felt the smart of the Enemy's Blows, won't always believe what is said to undervalue him, and are often not easily provok'd to Anger. Secondly, Anger consisting in an Ebullition of the Spirits, is a Passion of no long continuance (*Ira furor brevis est*)[36] and the Enemies, if they withstand the first Shock of these Angry People, have commonly the better of it. Thirdly, as long as People are angry, all Counsel and Discipline are lost upon them, and they can never be brought to use Art or Conduct in their Battels. Anger then, without which no Creature has natural

36. Horace, *Epistles*, I, ii, 62. – Ed.

Courage, being altogether useless in a War to be manag'd by Stratagem, and brought into a regular Art, the Government must find out an equivalent for Courage that will make men fight.

Whoever would civilize Men, and establish them into a Body Politick, must be thoroughly acquainted with all the Passions and Appetites, Strength and Weaknesses of their Frame, and understand how to turn their greatest Frailties to the advantage of the Publick. In the Enquiry into the Origin of Moral Virtue, I have shewn how easily Men were induc'd to believe any thing that is said in their Praise. If therefore a Law giver or Politician, whom they have a great Veneration for, should tell them, that the generality of Men had within them a Principle of Valour distinct from Anger, or any other Passion, that made them to despise Danger and face Death itself with Intrepidity, and that they who had the most of it were the most valuable of their kind, it is very likely, considering what has been said, that most of them, tho' they felt nothing of this Principle, would swallow it for Truth, and that the Proudest feeling themselves mov'd at this piece of Flattery, and not well vers'd in distinguishing the Passions, might imagine that they felt it heaving in their Breasts, by mistaking Pride for Courage. If but One in Ten can be perswaded openly to declare, that he is possess'd of this Principle, and maintain it against all Gainsayers, there will soon be half a dozen that shall assert the same. Whoever has once own'd it is engaged, the Politician has nothing to do but to take all imaginable Care to flatter the Pride of those that brag of, and are willing to stand by it, a thousand different ways: The same Pride that drew him in first will ever after oblige him to defend the Assertion, till at last the fear of discovering the reality of his Heart, comes to be so great that it out-does the fear of Death itself. Do but encrease Man's Pride, and his fear of Shame will ever be proportion'd to it; for the greater value a Man sets upon himself, the more Pains he'll take and the greater Hardships he'll undergo to avoid Shame.

The great Art then to make Man Courageous, is first to make him own this Principle of Valour within, and afterwards to inspire him with as much horror against Shame, as Nature has given him against Death; and that there are things to which Man has, or may have, a stronger aversion than he has to Death, is evident from *Suicide*. He that makes Death his choice, must look upon it as less terrible than what he shuns by it; for whether the Evil dreaded be present or to come, real or imaginary, no body would kill himself wilfully but to avoid something. *Lucretia* held out bravely against all the attacks of the Ravisher, even when he threaten'd her Life; which shews that she valued her Virtue beyond it: But when he threaten'd her Reputation with eternal Infamy, she fairly surrender'd, and then slew herself; a certain sign that she valued her Virtue less than her Glory, and her Life less than either. The fear of Death did not make her yield, for she resolv'd to die before she did it, and her complyance must only be consider'd as a Bribe to make *Tarquin* forbear sullying her Reputation; so that Life had neither the first nor second place in the esteem of *Lucretia*. The courage then which is only useful to the Body Politick, and what is generally call'd true Valour, is artificial, and consists *in a Superlative Horror against Shame, by* Flattery *infused into Men of exalted* Pride.

As soon as the Notions of Honour and Shame are received among a Society, it is not difficult to make Men fight. First, take care they are perswaded of the Justice of their Cause, for no Man fights heartily that thinks himself in the wrong; then shew them that their Altars, their Possessions, Wives, Children, and every thing that is near and dear to them is concerned in the present Quarrel, or at least may be influenced by it hereafter; then put Feathers in their Caps, and distinguish them from others, talk of Publick-Spiritedness, the Love of their Country, facing an Enemy with Intrepidity, despising Death, the Bed of Honour, and such like high sounding Words, and every Proud Man will take up Arms and fight himself to Death before he'll turn tail, if it be by Day light. One Man in an Army is a check upon another, and a hundred of them that single and without witness would be all Cowards, are for fear of incurring one another's Contempt made Valiant by being together. To continue and heighten this artificial Courage, all that run away ought to be punish'd with Ignominy; those that fought well, whether they did beat or were beaten, must be flatter'd and solemnly commended; those that lost their Limbs rewarded, and those that were kill'd ought, above all, to be taken notice of, artfully lamented, and to have extraordinary Encomiums bestow'd upon them; for to pay Honours to the Dead, will ever be a sure Method to make Bubbles of the Living.

When I say that the Courage made use of in the Wars is artificial, I don't imagine that by the same Art all Men may be made equally Valiant: As Men have not an equal share of Pride, and differ from one another in Shape and inward Structure, it is impossible they should be all equally fit for the same uses. Some Men will never be able to learn Musick, and yet make good Mathematicians; others will play excellently well upon the Violin, and yet be Coxcombs as long as they live, let them converse with whom they please. But to shew that this is no evasion I shall prove, that, setting aside what I said of artificial Courage already, what the greatest Heroe differs in from the rankest Coward, is altogether Corporeal, and depends upon the inward make of Man. What I mean is call'd Constitution; by which is understood the orderly or disorderly mixture of the *Fluids* in our Body: That Constitution which favours Courage, consists in the natural Strength, Elasticity, and due Contexture of the finer Spirits, and upon them wholly depends what we call Stedfastness, Resolution and Obstinacy. It is the only Ingredient that is common to natural and artificial Bravery, and is to either what Size is to white Walls, which hinders them from coming off, and makes them lasting. That some People are very much, others very little frighten'd at things that are strange and sudden to them, is likewise altogether owing to the firmness or imbecility in the Tone of the Spirits. Pride is of no use in a Fright, because whilst it lasts we can't think, which, being counted a disgrace, is the reason People are always angry with any thing that frightens them as soon as the surprize is over; and when at the turn of a Battle the Conquerors give no Quarter, and are very cruel, it is a sign their Enemies fought well, and had put them first into great Fears.

That Resolution depends upon this Tone of the Spirits, appears likewise from the effects of strong Liquors, the fiery Particles whereof crowding into the Brain, strengthen the Spirits; their Operation imitates that of Anger, which I said before was an Ebullition of the Spirits. It is for this reason that most People when they are in Drink, are sooner touch'd and more prone to Anger than at other times, and some raving Mad without any Provocation at all. It is likewise observ'd, that Brandy makes Men more Quarrelsome at the same pitch of Drunkenness than Wine; because the Spirits of distill'd Waters have abundance of fiery Particles mixt with them, which the other has not. The Contexture of Spirits is so weak in some, that tho' they have Pride enough, no Art can ever make them fight or overcome their Fears; but this is a Defect in the Principle of the *Fluids*, as other Deformities are faults of the *Solids*. These pusilanimous People are never thoroughly provok'd to Anger, where there is any Danger, and drinking ever makes 'em bolder, but seldom so resolute as to attack any, unless they be Women or Children, or such who they know dare not resist. This Constitution is often influenced by Health and

Sickness, and impair'd by great losses of Blood; sometimes it is corrected by Diet; and it is this which the Duke *de la Rochefocault* means when he says; *Vanity, Shame, and above all* Constitution, *make up very often the Courage of Men and Virtue of Women*.

There is nothing that more improves the useful Martial Courage I treat of, and at the same time shews it to be artificial, than Practice; for when Men are disciplin'd, come to be acquainted with all the Tools of Death and Engines of Destruction, when the Shouts, the Outcries, the Fire and Smoak, the Groans of Wounded, and ghastly Looks of dying Men, with all the various Scenes of mangled Carcasses and bloody Limbs tore off, begin to be familiar to them, their Fears abate apace; not that they are now less afraid to die than before, but being used so often to see the same Dangers, they apprehend the reality of them less than they did: As they are deservedly valued for every Siege they are at, and every Battle they are in, it is impossible but the several Actions they share in must continually become as many solid Steps by which their Pride mounts up, and thus their Fear of Shame, which, as I said before, will always be proportion'd to their Pride, encreasing as the apprehension of the Danger decreases, it is no wonder that most of them learn to discover little or no Fear; and some great Generals are able to preserve a Presence of Mind, and counterfeit a calm Serenity within the midst of all the Noise, Horror and Confusion that attend a Battle.

So silly a Creature is Man, as that, intoxicated with the fumes of Vanity, he can feast on the thoughts of the Praises that shall be paid his Memory in future Ages with so much extasy, as to neglect his present Life, nay court and covet Death, if he but imagines that it will add to the Glory he had acquir'd before. There is no pitch of Self-denial that a Man of Pride and Constitution cannot reach, nor any Passion so violent but he'll sacrifise it to another which is superior to it; and here I cannot but admire at the Simplicity of some good Men, who when they hear of the Joy and Alacrity with which holy Men in Persecutions have suffer'd for their Faith, imagine that such Constancy must exceed all human Force, unless it was supported by some miraculous Assistance from Heaven. As most People are unwilling to acknowledge all the frailties of their Species, so they are unacquainted with the Strength of our Nature, and know not that some Men of firm Constitution may work themselves up into Enthusiasm by no other help than the violence of their Passions; yet it is certain, that there have been Men who only assisted with Pride and Constitution to maintain the worst of Causes, have undergone Death and Torments with as much chearfulness as the best of Men, animated with Piety and Devotion, ever did for the true Religion.

To prove this assertion I could produce many Instances; but one or two will be sufficient. *Jordanus Bruno* of *Nola*, who wrote that silly piece of Blasphemy call'd *Spaccio della Bestia triumfante*, and the infamous *Vannini* were both executed for openly professing and teaching of *Atheism*: The latter might have been pardon'd the Moment before the Execution, if he would have retracted his Doctrine; but rather than recant, he chose to be burnt to Ashes. As he went to the Stake, he was so far from shewing any concern, that he held his Hand out to a Physician whom he happen'd to know, desiring him to judge of the calmness of his Mind by the regularity of his Pulse, and from thence taking an opportunity of making an impious Comparison, utter'd a Sentence too execrable to be mention'd. To these we may joyn one *Mahomet Effendi*, who, as Sir *Paul Ricaut* tells us, was put to Death at *Constantinople*, for having advanc'd some Notions against the Existence of a God. He likewise might have sav'd his Life by confessing his Error, and renouncing it for the future; but chose rather to persist in his

Blasphemies, saying, *Tho' he had no Reward to expect, the
Love of Truth constrain'd him to suffer Martyrdom in its
defence.*

I have made this Digression chiefly to shew the Strength
of Humane Nature, and what meer Man may perform by
Pride and Constitution alone. Man may certainly be as
violently rous'd by his Vanity as a Lyon is by his Anger, and
not only this, Avarice, Revenge, Ambition, and almost
every Passion, Pity not excepted, when they are extraordin-
ary, may, by overcoming Fear, serve him instead of Valour,
and be mistaken for it even by himself; as daily Experience
must teach every body that will examine and look into the
Motives from which some Men act. But that we may more
clearly perceive what this pretended Principle is really built
upon, let us look into the management of Military Affairs,
and we shall find that Pride is no where so openly encour-
aged as there. As for Cloaths, the very lowest of the Com-
mission Officers have them richer, or at least more gay and
splendid, than are generally wore by other People of four or
five times their Income. Most of them, and especially those
that have Families, and can hardly subsist, would be very
glad, all *Europe* over, to be less Expensive that way; but it is
a Force put upon them to uphold their Pride, which they
don't think on.

But the ways and means to rouse Man's Pride, and catch
him by it, are no where more grossly conspicuous than in
the Treatment which the Common Soldiers receive, whose
Vanity is to be work'd upon, (because there must be so many)
at the cheapest Rate imaginable. Things we are accustom'd
to we don't mind, or else what Mortal that never had seen
a Soldier could look without laughing upon a Man accoutred
with so much paultry Gaudiness and affected Finery? The
coursest Manufacture that can be made of Wool dy'd of a
Brickdust colour, goes down with him, because it is in imi-
tation of Scarlet or Crimson Cloth, and to make him think

himself as like his Officer as 'tis possible with little or no
Cost, instead of Silver or Gold Lace, his Hat is trim'd
with white or yellow Worsted, which in others would
deserve *Bedlam*; yet these fine Allurements, and the noise
made upon a Calf's Skin, have drawn in and been the De-
struction of more Men in reallity, than all the killing Eyes
and bewitching Voices of Women ever slew in Jest. To Day
the Swineherd puts on his red Coat, and believes every body
in earnest that calls him Gentleman, and two Days after
Sergeant *Kite*[37] gives him a swinging wrap with his Cane,
for holding his Musket an Inch higher than he should do.
As to the real Dignity of the Employment, in the two last
Wars Officers, when Recruits were wanted, were allow'd
to list Fellows convicted of Burglary and other Capital
Crimes, which shews, that to be made a Soldier is deem'd
to be a Preferment next to hanging. A Trooper is yet worse
than a Foot Soldier; for when he is most at Ease, he has the
Mortification of being Groom to a Horse that spends more
Money than himself. When a Man reflects on all this, the
Usage they generally receive from their Officers, their Pay,
and the Care that is taken of them, when they are not
wanted, must he not wonder how Wretches can be so silly
as to be proud of being call'd *Gentlemen Soldiers*? Yet if
they were not, no Art, Discipline or Money would be cap-
able of making them so Brave as Thousands of them are.

If we will mind what Effects Man's Bravery without any
other Qualifications to sweeten him, would have out of an
Army, we shall find that it would be very pernicious to the
Civil Society, for if Man could conquer all his Fears, you
would hear of nothing but Rapes, Murthers and Violences of
all sorts, and Valiant Men would be like Gyants in
Romances: Politicks therefore discover'd in Men a mixt
Mettle-Principle, which was a Compound of Justice, Honesty

37. The sergeant in George Farquhar's *The Recruiting Officer*
(1706). – Ed.

and all the Moral Virtues joyn'd to Courage, and all that were possess'd of it turn'd Knights-Errant of course. They did abundance of Good throughout the World, by taming Monsters, delivering the Distress'd, and killing the Opressors. But the Wings of all the Dragons being clipt, the Gyants destroy'd, and the Damsels every where set at liberty, except some few in *Spain* and *Italy*, who remain'd still Captivated by their Monsters, the Order of Chivalry, to whom the Standard of Ancient Honour belong'd, has been laid aside some time. It was like their Armours very massy and heavy; the many Virtues about it made it very troublesome, and as Ages grew wiser and wiser, the Principle of Honour in the beginning of the last Century, was melted over again, and brought to a new Standard; they put in the same weight of Courage, half the quantity of Honesty, and a very little Justice, but not a Scrap of any other Virtue, which has made it very easie and portable to what it was. However, such as it is there would be no living without it in a large Nation; it is the tye of Society, and though we are beholden to our Frailties for the chief Ingredient of it, there is no Virtue at least that I am acquainted with, that has been half so instrumental to the civilizing of Mankind, who in great Societies would soon degenerate into cruel Villains and treacherous Slaves, were Honour to be remov'd from among them.

As to the Duelling Part which belongs to it, I pity the Unfortunate whose Lot it is; but to say, that those who are guilty of it go by false Rules, or mistake the Notions of Honour, is ridiculous; for either there is no Honour at all, or it teaches Men to resent Injuries, and accept of Challenges. You may as well deny that it is the fashion what you see everybody wear, as to say that demanding and giving Satisfaction is against the Laws of true Honour. Those that rail at Duelling, don't consider the Benefit the Society receives from that Fashion: If every ill bred Fellow might use what Language he pleas'd, without being call'd to an

Account for it, all Conversation would be spoil'd. Some grave People tell us, that the *Greeks* and *Romans* were such valiant Men, and yet knew nothing of Duelling but in their Country's Quarrel. This is very true, but for that reason the Kings and Princes in *Homer* gave one another worse Language than our Porters and Hackney Coachmen would be able to bear without Resentment.

Would you hinder Duelling, pardon no body that offends that way, and make the Laws against it as severe as you can, but don't take away the thing itself, the Custom of it. This will not only prevent the Frequency of it, but likewise by rendring the most resolute and most Powerful cautious and circumspect in their Behaviour, polish and brighten Society in general. Nothing civilizes a Man equally as his Fear, and if not all, (as my Lord *Rochester* said) at least most Men would be Cowards if they durst[38]: The dread of being call'd to an Account keeps abundance in awe, and there are thousands of Mannerly and well accomplish'd Gentlemen in *Europe*, who would have been insolent and insupportable Coxcombs without it; besides if it was out of Fashion to ask Satisfaction for Injuries which the Law cannot take hold of, there would be twenty times the Mischief done there is now, or else you must have twenty times the Constables and other Officers to keep the Peace. I confess that though it happens but seldom, it is a Calamity to the People, and generally the Families it falls upon; but there can be no perfect Happiness in this World, and all Felicity has an Allay. The Act itself is uncharitable, but when above Thirty in a Nation destroy themselves in one Year, and not half that number are kill'd by others, I don't think the People can be said to love their Neighbours worse than themselves. It is strange that a Nation should grudge to see perhaps half a dozen Men sacrifis'd in a Twelvemonth to obtain so valuable a Blessing, as the Politeness of Manners, the Pleasure

38. In *A Satyr against Mankind* (1675). – Ed.

of Conversation, and the happiness of Company in general, that is often so willing to expose, and sometimes loses as many thousands in a few Hours without knowing whether it will do any good or not.

I would have no body that reflects on the mean Original of Honour complain of being gull'd and made a Property by cunning Politicians, but desire every body to be satisfied, that the Governors of Societies and those in high Stations are greater Bubbles to Pride than any of the rest. If some great Men had not a superlative Pride and every body understood the Enjoyment of Life, who wou'd be a Lord Chancellor of *England*, a Prime Minister of State in *France*, or what gives more Fatigue, and not a sixth part of the Profit of either, a Grand Pensionary of *Holland*? The reciprocal Services which all Men pay to one another, are the Foundation of the Society. The great ones are not flatter'd with their high Birth for nothing, 'tis to rouse their Pride, and excite them to glorious Actions, that we extol their Race, whether it deserves it or not, and some Men have been complimented with the Greatness of their Family, and the Merit of their Ancestors, when in the whole Generation you cou'd not find two but what were uxorious Fools, silly Bigots, noted Poltroons or debauch'd Whoremasters. The establish'd Pride that is inseparable from those that are possess'd of Titles already, makes them often strive as much not to seem unworthy of them, as the working Ambition of others that are yet without, renders them industrious and indefatigable to deserve them. When a Gentleman is made a Baron or an Earl, it is as great a Check upon him in many respects, as a Gown and Cassock are to a young Student that has been newly taken into Orders.

The only thing of weight that can be said against modern Honour is, that it is directly opposite to Religion. The one bids you bear Injuries with Patience, the other tells you if you don't resent them, you are not fit to live. Religion commands you to leave all Revenge to God, Honour bids you trust your Revenge to no body but your self, even where the Law wou'd do it for you. Religion plainly forbids Murther, Honour openly justifies it. Religion bids you not shed Blood upon any account whatever, Honour bids you fight for the least Trifle. Religion is built on Humility, and Honour upon Pride. How to reconcile them must be left to wiser Heads than mine.

The Reason why there are so few Men of real Virtue, and so many of real Honour, is, because all the Recompence a Man has of a Virtuous Action, is the Pleasure of doing it, which most People reckon but poor Pay; but the Self denial a Man of Honour submits to in one Appetite, is immediately rewarded by the Satisfaction he receives from another, and what he abates of his Avarice, or any other Passion is doubly repaid to his Pride: Besides, Honour gives large Grains of Allowance, and Virtue none. A Man of Honour must not cheat or tell a Lye; he must punctually repay what he borrows at Play, though the Creditor has nothing to shew for it; but he may drink and swear and owe Money to all the Tradesmen in Town, without taking Notice of their dunning. A Man of Honour must be true to his Prince and Country, whilst he is in their Service; but if he thinks himself not well used, he may quit it, and do them all the Mischief he can. A Man of Honour must never change his Religion for Interest, but he may be as Debauch'd as he pleases, and never practise any. He must make no Attempts upon his Friend's Wife, Daughter, Sister, or any body that is trusted to his Care, but he may lye with all the World besides.

(S.) No Limner for his Art is famed;
Stone-cutters, Carvers are not named:

PAGE 74. LINE 6. It is, without doubt, that among the Consequences of a National Honesty and Frugality, it wou'd be one not to build any new Houses, or use new Materials, as long as there were old ones enough to serve. By this three Parts in four of *Masons, Carpenters, Bricklayers, &c.* would want Employment; and the building Trade being once destroy'd, what wou'd become of *Limning, Carving,* and other Arts that are ministring to Luxury, and have been carefully forbid by those Lawgivers that preferr'd a good and honest, to a great and wealthy Society, and endeavour'd to render their Subjects rather Virtuous than Rich. By a Law of *Lycurgus,* it was enacted, That the Ceilings of the *Spartan Houses* should only be wrought by the Ax, and their Gates and Doors only smooth'd by the Saw; and this, says *Plutarch,* was not without Mystery; for if *Epaminondas* could say with so good a Grace, inviting some of his Friends to his Table, *Come, Gentlemen, be secure, Treason would never come to such a poor Dinner as this*: Why might not this great Law giver, in all probability, have thought, that such ill-favour'd Houses would never be capable of receiving Luxury and Superfluity?

It is reported, as the same Author tells us, that King *Leotichidas,* the first of that Name, was so little used to the sight of Carv'd Work, that being entertain'd at *Corinth* in a stately Room, he was much surpriz'd to see the Timber and Ceiling so finely wrought, and ask'd his Host whether the Trees grew so in his Country.

The same want of Employment wou'd reach innumerable Callings, and among the rest, that of the

Weavers that join'd rich Silk with Plate,
And all the Trades subordinate.

234

(As the Fable has it) wou'd be one of the first that shou'd have reason to complain; for the Price of Land and Houses being, by the removal of the vast numbers that had left the Hive, sunk very low on the one side, and every body abhorring all other ways of Gain, but such as were strictly honest on the other, it is not probable that many without Pride or Prodigality shou'd be able to wear Cloath of Gold and Silver, or rich Brocades. The Consequence of which wou'd be, that not only the *Weaver* but likewise the *Silver-spinner*, the *Flatter*, the *Wire-drawer*, the *Bar-man*, and the *Refiner*, wou'd in a little time be affected with this Frugality.

(T.)[39] ———— *To live Great,*
Had made her Husband rob the State.

PAGE 74. LINE 20. What our common Rogues when they are going to be hang'd chiefly complain of, as the Cause of their untimely End, is next to the Neglect of the Sabbath their having kept Company with ill Women, meaning Whores; and I don't question, but that among the lesser Villains many venture their Necks to indulge and satisfy their low Amours. But the Words that have given Occasion to this Remark, may serve to hint to us, that among the great ones Men are often put upon such dangerous Projects, and forc'd into such pernicious Measures by their Wives, as the most subtle Mistriss never could have persuaded them to. I have shewn already that the worst of Women and most profligate of the Sex did contribute to the Consumption of Superfluities, as well as the Necessaries of Life, and consequently were Beneficial to many peaceable Drudges, that work hard to maintain their Families, and have no worse design than an honest Livelyhood. – Let them be banish'd notwithstanding, says a good Man : When every Strumpet

39. Remark *T* was added in 1723. – Ed.

is gone and the Land wholly freed from Lewdness, God Almighty will pour such Blessings upon it as will vastly exceed the profits, that are now got by Harlots. – This perhaps would be true; but I can make it evident, that with or without Prostitutes, nothing could make amends for the detriment Trade would sustain if all those of that Sex, who enjoy the happy State of Matrimony should Act and behave themselves as a Sober Wise Man could wish them.

The variety of Work that is perform'd, and the number of Hands employ'd to gratify the Fickleness and Luxury of Women is prodigious, and if only the married ones should hearken to Reason and Just Remonstrances, think themselves sufficiently answer'd with the first refusal, and never ask a second time, what had been once denied them: If, I say, Married Women would do this, and then lay out no Money but what their Husbands knew and freely allow'd of, the Consumption of a thousand things they now make use of would be lessened by at least a fourth part. Let us go from House to House and observe the way of the World only among the midling People, Creditable Shopkeepers, that spend Two or Three hundred a Year, and we shall find that the Women, when they have half a score Suits of Cloaths, Two or Three of them not the worse for wearing, will think it a sufficient Plea for new Ones, if they can say that they have never a Gown or Petticoat, but what they have been often seen in, and are known by, especially at Church; I don't speak now of profuse extravagant Women, but such as are counted Prudent and Moderate in their Desires.

If by this pattern we should in proportion Judge of the highest Ranks, where the richest Cloaths are but a trifle to their other Expences, and not forget the Furniture of all sorts, Equipages, Jewels and Buildings of Persons of Quality, we would find the fourth part, I speak of a vast Article in Trade, and that the Loss of it would be a greater Calamity to such a Nation as ours, than it is possible to conceive any other, a raging Pestilence not excepted: for the Death of half a Million of People could not cause a tenth part of the disturbance to the Kingdom, that the same number of Poor unemploy'd would certainly create, if at once they were to be added to those, that already one way or other are a Burthen to the Society.

Some few Men have a real Passion for their Wives, and are fond of them without reserve; others that don't care, and have little Occasion for Women, are yet seemingly uxorious, and love out of Vanity; they take delight in a Handsome Wife, as a Coxcomb does in a Fine Horse, not for the use he makes of it, but because it is His: The Pleasure lies in the consciousness of an uncontroulable Possession, and what follows from it, the Reflection on the mighty thoughts he imagines others to have of his Happiness. The Men of either sort may be very lavish to their Wives, and often preventing their wishes crowd New Cloaths and other Finery upon them faster, than they can ask it, but the greatest part are wiser than to indulge the Extravagancies of their Wives so far, as to give them immediately every thing they are pleas'd to Fancy.

It is incredible what vast quantity of Trinkets as well as Apparel are purchas'd and used by Women, which they could never have come at by any other means, than pinching their Families, Marketting, and other ways of cheating and pilfring from their Husbands: Others by ever teazing their Spouses, tire them into Compliance, and conquer even obstinate Churls by perseverance and their assiduity of asking: A Third sort are outragious at a denial, and by downright Noise and Scolding Bully their tame Fools out of any thing they have a mind to; Whilst Thousands by the force of wheedling know how to overcome the best weigh'd Reasons and the most positive reiterated refusals; the Young and Beautiful especially laugh at all remonstrances and denials, and few of them scruple to Employ the most tender Minutes of Wedlock to promote a sordid Interest. Here had I time I could inveigh with warmth against those Base, those Wicked Women, who calmly play their Arts and false deluding Charms against our Strength and Prudence, and act the Harlots with their Husbands! Nay, she is worse than Whore, who impiously prophanes and prostitutes the Sacred Rites of Love to Vile Ignoble Ends; that first excites to Passion and invites to Joys with seeming Ardour, then racks our fondness for no other purpose than to extort a Gift, whilst full of Guile in Counterfeited Transports she watches for the Moment when Men can least deny.

I beg pardon for this start out of my way, and desire the experienc'd Reader duly to weigh what has been said as to the main Purpose, and after that call to mind the temporal Blessings, which Men daily hear not only toasted and wish'd for, when People are merry and doing of nothing; but likewise gravely and solemnly pray'd for in Churches, and other religious Assemblies, by Clergymen of all Sorts and Sizes: And as soon as he shall have laid these Things together, and, from what he has observ'd in the common Affairs of Life, reason'd upon them consequentially without prejudice, I dare flatter my self, that he will be oblig'd to own, that a considerable Portion, of what the Prosperity of *London* and Trade in general, and consequently the Honour, Strength, Safety, and all the worldly Interest of the Nation consist in, depends entirely on the Deceit and vile Stratagems of Women; and that Humility, Content, Meekness, Obedience to reasonable Husbands, Frugality and all the Virtues together, if they were possess'd of them in the most eminent Degree, could not possibly be a thousandth Part so serviceable, to make an Opulent, powerful, and what we call a flourishing Kingdom, than their most hateful Qualities.

I don't question, but many of my Readers will be startled

at this Assertion, when they look on the Consequences that may be drawn from it; and I shall be ask'd, whether People may not as well be virtuous in a populous, rich, wide, extended Kingdom, as in a small, indigent State or Principality, that is poorly inhabited: And if that be impossible, Whether it is not the Duty of all Sovereigns to reduce their Subjects, as to Wealth and Numbers, as much as they can. If I allow they may, I own my self in the wrong; and if I affirm the other, my Tenets will justly be call'd impious, or at least dangerous to all large Societies. As it is not in this Place of the Book only, but a great many others, that such Queries might be made even by a well-meaning Reader, I shall here explain my self, and endeavour to solve those Difficulties, which several Passages might have rais'd in him, in order to demonstrate the Consistency of my Opinion to Reason, and the strictest Morality.

I lay down as a first Principle, that in all Societies great or small, it is the Duty of every Member of it to be good, that Virtue ought to be encourag'd, Vice discountenanc'd, the Laws obey'd, and the Transgressors punish'd. After this I affirm, that if we consult History both Antient and Modern, and take a View of what has past in the World, we shall find that Human Nature since the Fall of *Adam* has always been the same, and that the Strength and Frailties of it have ever been conspicuous in one Part of the Globe or other, without any Regard to Ages, Climates, or Religion. I never said nor imagin'd, that Man could not be virtuous as well in a rich and mighty Kingdom, as in the most pitiful Commonwealth; but I own it is my Sense that no Society can be rais'd into such a rich and mighty Kingdom, or so rais'd, subsist in their Wealth and Power for any considerable Time without the Vices of Man.

This I imagine is sufficiently prov'd throughout the Book; and as Human Nature still continues the same, as it has always been for so many thousand Years, we have no great Reason to suspect a future Change in it, whilst the World endures. Now I cannot see, what Immorality there is in shewing a Man the Origin and Power of those Passions, which so often, even unknowingly to himself, hurry him away from his Reason; or that there is any Impiety in putting him upon his Guard against himself, and the secret Stratagems of Self-Love, and teaching him the difference between such Actions as proceed from a Victory over the Passions, and those that are only the result of a Conquest which one Passion obtains over another; that is, between real, and Counterfeited Virtue. It is an admirable Saying of a worthy Divine,[40] *That tho' many Discoveries have been made in the World of Self-Love, there is yet abundance of* Terra incognita *left behind.* What hurt do I do to Man if I make him more known to himself than he was before? But we are all so desperately in Love with Flattery, that we can never relish a Truth that is mortifying, and I don't believe that the Immortality of the Soul, a Truth broach'd long before Christianity, would have ever found such a general reception in human Capacities as it has, had it not been a pleasing one, that extoll'd and was a Compliment to the whole Species, the Meanest and most Miserable not excepted.

Every one loves to hear the Thing well spoke of, that he has a share in, even Bayliffs, Goal-keepers, and the Hangman himself would have you think well of their Functions; nay Thieves and House-breakers have a greater Regard to those of their Fraternity than they have for Honest People, and I sincerely believe, that it is chiefly Self Love that has gain'd this little Treatise, as it was before the last Impression, so many Enemies; every one looks upon it as an affront done to himself, because it detracts from the Dignity, and lessens the fine notions he had conceiv'd of Mankind, the

40. La Rochefoucauld. – Ed.

most Worshipful Company he belongs to. When I say that Societies cannot be rais'd to Wealth and Power, and the top of Earthly Glory without Vices, I don't think that by so saying I bid Men be Vicious any more, than I bid 'em be Quarrelsome or Covetous, when I affirm that the Profession of the Law could not be maintain'd in such Numbers and Splendour, if there was not abundance of too Selfish and Litigious People.

But as nothing would more clearly demonstrate the falsity of my Notions, than that the generality of the People should fall in with them, so I don't expect the Approbation of the Multitude. I write not to many, nor seek for any Well-wishers, but among the few than can think abstractly, and have their Minds elevated above the Vulgar. If I have shewn the way to worldly Greatness I have always without hesitation preferr'd the Road that leads to Virtue.

Would you banish Fraud and Luxury, prevent Profaneness and Irreligion, and make the generality of the People Charitable, Good and Virtuous, break down the Printing-Presses, melt the Founds and burn all the Books in the Island, except those at the Universities, where they remain unmolested, and suffer no Volume in private hands but a Bible: Knock down Foreign Trade, piohibit all Commerce with Strangers, and permit no Ships to go to Sea, that ever will return, beyond Fisher-Boats. Restore to the Clergy, the King and the Barons their Ancient Privileges, Prerogatives and Possessions: Build New Churches, and convert all the Coin you can come at into Sacred Utensils: Erect Monasteries and Almshouses in abundance, and let no Parish be without a Charity-School. Enact Sumptuary Laws, and let your Youth be inured to hardship: Inspire them with all the nice and most refined notions of Honour and Shame, of Friendship and of Heroism, and introduce among them a great variety of imaginary Rewards: Then let the Clergy Preach Abstinence and Self-denial to others, and take what

Liberty they please for themselves; let them bear the greatest sway in the management of State Affairs, and no Man be made Lord-Treasurer but a Bishop.

By such pious Endeavours, and wholesome Regulations, the Scene would soon be alter'd; the greatest part of the Covetous, the Discontented, the Restless and Ambitious Villains would leave the Land, vast swarms of Cheating Knaves would abandon the City, and be dispers'd throughout the Country: Artificers would learn to hold the Plough, Merchants turn Farmers, and the sinful over-grown *Jerusalem*, without Famine, War, Pestilence, or Compulsion, be emptied in the most easy manner, and ever after cease to be dreadful to her Sovereigns. The happy reform'd Kingdom would by this means be crowded in no part of it, and every thing Necessary for the Sustenance of Man be cheap and abound: On the contrary, the Root of so many Thousand Evils, Money would be very scarce, and as little wanted, where every Man should enjoy the Fruits of his own Labour, and our own dear Manufacture unmix'd be promiscuously wore by the Lord and the Peasant. It is impossible, that such a Change of Circumstances should not Influence the Manners of a Nation, and render them Temperate, Honest, and Sincere, and from the next Generation we might reasonably expect a more healthy and robust Off-spring than the present; an harmless, innocent and well-meaning People, that would never dispute the Doctrine of Passive Obedience, nor any other Orthodox Principles, but be submissive to Superiors, and unanimous in Religious Worship.

Here I fancy my self interrupted by an *Epicure*, who not to want a restorative Diet in case of Necessity, is never without live Ortelans, and I am told, that Goodness and Probity are to be had at a cheaper rate than the Ruin of a Nation, and the Destruction of all the comforts of Life; that Liberty and Property may be maintain'd without Wickedness or Fraud, and Men be Good Subjects without being

Slaves, and religious tho' they refus'd to be Priest-rid: that
to be frugal and saving is a Duty incumbent only on those,
whose Circumstances require it, but that a Man of a good
Estate does his Country a Service by living up to the Income
of it: that as to himself he is so much Master of his
Appetites that he can abstain from any thing upon occasion:
that where true *Hermitage* was not to be had he could con-
tent himself with plain *Bourdeaux*, if it had a good Body;
that many a Morning instead of St. *Lawrence* he has made
a shift with *Fronteniac*, and after Dinner given *Cyprus*
Wine, and even *Madera*, when he has had a large Company,
and thought it Extravagant to treat with *Tockay*; but that
all voluntary Mortifications are Supersticious, only belong-
ing to blind Zealots and Enthusiasts. He'll quote my Lord
Shaftsbury against me, and tell me that People may be
Virtuous and Sociable without Self-denial, that it is an
affront to Virtue to make it inaccessible, that I make a Bug-
bear of it to frighten Men from it as a thing impracticable;
but that for his part he can praise God, and at the same
time enjoy his Creatures with a good Conscience; neither
will he forget any thing to his purpose of what I have said
page 149. He'll ask me at last, whether the Legislature, the
Wisdom of the Nation itself, whilst they endeavour as much
as is possible to discourage Prophaneness and Immorality,
and promote the Glory of God, do not openly profess at the
same time to have nothing more at Heart than the Ease and
Welfare of the Subject, the Wealth, Strength, Honour and
what else is call'd the true Interest of the Country; and
moreover, whether the most Devout and most Learned of
our Prelates in their greatest Concern for our Conversion,
when they beseech the Deity to turn their own as well as
our Hearts from the World and all Carnal Desires, do not
in the same Prayer as loudly sollicit him to pour all Earthly
Blessings and Temporal Felicity on the Kingdom they
belong to.

These are the Apologies, the Excuses and common Pleas, not only of those, who are notoriously vicious, but the generality of Mankind, when you touch the Copy-hold of their Inclinations, and trying the real value they have for Spirituals, would actually strip them of what their Minds are wholly bent upon. Ashamed of the many Frailties they feel within, all Men endeavour to hide themselves, their Ugly Nakedness, from each other, and wrapping up the true motives of their Hearts in the Specious Cloak of Sociableness, and their concern for the publick Good, they are in hopes of concealing their filthy Appetites and the deformity of their Desires; whilst they are conscious within of the fondness for their darling Lusts, and their incapacity, barefac'd to tread the arduous, Ruggid Path of Virtue.

As to the two last Questions, I own they are very puzling: To what the *Epicure* asks I am oblig'd to Answer in the Affirmative; and unless I would (which God forbid!) arrain the Sincerity of Kings, Bishops and the whole Legislative Power, the Objection, stands good against me: All I can say for my self is, that in the connexion of the Facts there is a Mystery past Human Understanding; and to convince the Reader, that this is no Evasion, I shall Illustrate the Incomprehensibility of it in the following Parable.

In Old Heathen Times there was, they say, a Whimsical Country, where the People talk'd much of Religion, and the greatest part as to outward appearance seem'd really Devout: The chief moral Evil among them was Thirst, and to quench it a Damnable Sin; yet they unanimously agreed that every one was born Thirsty more or less: Small Beer in moderation was allow'd to all, and he was counted an Hypocrite, a Cynick, or a Madman, who pretended that one could live altogether without it; yet those, who owned they loved it, and drank it to excess, were counted Wicked. All this while the Beer it self was reckon'd a Blessing from Heaven, and there was no harm in the use of it; all the enormity lay in the abuse, the Motive of the Heart, that made them drink it. He that took the least Drop of it to quench his Thirst, committed a heinous Crime, whilst others drank large Quantities without any Guilt, so they did it indifferently, and for no other Reason than to mend their Complexion.

They Brew'd for other Countries as well as their own, and for the Small Beer they sent abroad, they receiv'd large returns of Westphaly-Hams, Neats-Tongues, Hung-Beef, and Bolonia-Sausages; Red-Herrings, Pickl'd-Sturgeon, Cavear, Anchovis and every thing that was proper to make their Liquor go down with Pleasure. Those, who kept great stores of Small Beer by them without making use of it, were generally envied, and at the same time very odious to the publick, and no body was easy that had not enough of it come to his own Share. The greatest Calamity they thought could befall them, was to keep their Hops and Barley upon their hands, and the more they yearly con-sumed of them, the more they reckon'd the Country to flourish.

The Government had made very wise Regulations con-cerning the returns that were made for their Exports, en-couraged very much the Importation of Salt and Pepper, and laid heavy Duties on every thing that was not well season'd, and might any ways obstruct the Sale of their own Hops and Barley. Those at *Helm* when they acted in publick, shew'd themselves on all Accounts exempt and wholly divested from Thirst, made several Laws to prevent the Growth of it, and punish the Wicked who openly dared to quench it. If you examin'd them in their private Persons, and pry'd narrowly into their Lives and Conversations, they seem'd to be more fond, or at least drank larger Draughts of Small Beer than others, but always under pretence that the mending of Complexions required greater quantities of Liquor in them, than it did in those they Ruled over; and

that, what they had chiefly at Heart, without any regard
to themselves, was to procure great plenty of Small Beer
among the Subjects in general, and a great demand for their
Hops and Barley.

As no body was debarr'd from Small Beer, the Clergy
made use of it as well as the Laity, and some of them very
plentifully; yet all of them desired to be thought less Thirsty
by their Function than others, and never would own that
they drank any but to mend their Complexions. In their
Religious Assemblies they were more sincere; for as soon
as they came there, they all openly confess'd, the Clergy
as well as the Laity, from the highest to the lowest,
that they were Thirsty, that mending their Complexions
was what they minded the least, and that all their Hearts
were set upon small beer and quenching their Thirst, what-
ever they might pretend to the contrary. What was remark-
able is, that to have laid hold of those Truths to any one's
Prejudice, and made use of those Confessions afterwards out
of their Temples, would have been counted very imperti-
nent, and every body thought it an heinous Affront to be
call'd *Thirsty*, tho' you had seen him drink Small-Beer by
whole Gallons. The chief Topicks of their Preachers was the
great Evil of Thirst, and the Folly there was in quenching
it. They exhorted their Hearers to resist the Temptations of
it, enveigh'd against Small-Beer, and often told them it was
Poyson, if they drank it with Pleasure, or any other Design
than to mend their Complexions.

In their Acknowledgments to the Gods they thank'd them
for the Plenty of comfortable Small-Beer they had receiv'd
from them, notwithstanding they had so little deserv'd it,
and continually quench'd their Thirst with it; whereas they
were so thorowly satisfy'd, that it was given them for a
better Use. Having begg'd Pardon for those Offences, they
desired the Gods to lessen their Thirst, and give them
Strength to resist the Importunities of it; yet, in the midst

of their sorest Repentance, and most humble Supplications, they never forgot Small-Beer, and pray'd that they might continue to have it in great Plenty, with a solemn Promise, that how neglectful soever they might hitherto have been in this Point, they would for the future not drink a Drop of it with any other Design than to mend their Complexions.

These were standing Petitions put together to last; and having continued to be made use of without any Alterations for several hundred Years together; it was thought by some, that the Gods, who understood Futurity, and knew that the same Promise they heard in *June* would be made to them the *January* following, did not rely much more on those Vows, than we do on those waggish Inscriptions by which Men offer us their Goods, to day for Money, and to morrow for nothing. They often began their Prayers very mystically, and spoke many things in a spiritual Sense; yet, they never were so abstract from the World in them, as to end one without beseeching the Gods to bless and prosper the Brewing Trade in all its Branches, and, for the Good of the Whole, more and more to increase the Consumption of Hops and Barley.

(V.) *Content the Bane of Industry.*

PAGE 75. LINE 8. I have been told by many, that the Bane of Industry is Laziness, and not Content; therefore to prove my Assertion, which seems a Paradox to some, I shall treat of Laziness and Content separately, and afterwards speak of Industry, that the Reader may judge which it is of the two former that is most opposite to the latter.

Laziness is an Aversion to Business, generally attended with an unreasonable desire of remaining unactive, and every body is lazy, who without being hinder'd by any other warrantable Employment, refuses or puts off any Business which he ought to do for himself or others. We seldom call any body lazy, but such as we reckon inferior to us, and of whom we expect some Service. Children don't think their Parents lazy, nor Servants their Masters, and if a Gentleman indulges his Ease and Sloth so abominably, that he won't put on his own Shoes, though he is young and slender, no body shall call him lazy for it, if he can keep but a Footman or some body else to do it for him.

Mr. *Dryden* has given us a very good Idea of superlative Slothfulness in the Person of a Luxurious King of *Ægypt*.[41] His Majesty having bestow'd some considerable Gifts on several of his Favourites, is attended by some of his chief Ministers with a Parchment which he was to sign to confirm those Grants. First he walks a few Turns to and fro with a heavy uneasiness in his Looks, then sets himself down like a Man that's tired, and at last with abundance of Reluctancy to what he was going about, he takes up the Pen, and falls a complaining very seriously of the length of the Word *Ptolomey*, and expresses a great deal of Concern, that he had not some short Monosyllable for his Name, which he thought wou'd save him a world of Trouble.

We often reproach others with Laziness, because we are guilty of it our selves. Some days ago as two young Women sate knotting together, says one to the other, there comes a wicked Cold through that Door, you are the nearest to it, Sister, pray shut it. The other, who was the youngest, vouchsav'd indeed to cast an Eye towards the Door, but sate still and said nothing; the eldest spoke again two or three times, and at last the other making her no Answer, nor offering to stir, she got up in a Pet and shut the Door herself; coming back to sit down again, she gave the younger a very hard Look, and said, *Lord, Sister* Betty, *I would not be so lazy as you are for all the World*; which she spoke so

41. In *Cleomenes* (1692). – Ed.

earnestly, that it brought a Colour in her Face. The youngest should have risen I own, but if the eldest had not over-valued her Labour, she would have shut the Door herself, as soon as the Cold was offensive to her, without making any words of it. She was not above a Step farther from the Door than her Sister, and as to Age, there was not eleven Months difference between them, and they were both under Twenty. I thought it a hard Matter to determine which was the laziest of the two.

There are a thousand Wretches that are always working the Marrow out of their Bones for next to nothing, because they are unthinking and ignorant of what the Pains they take are worth; whilst others who are cunning and understand the true value of their Work, refuse to be employ'd at under Rates, not because they are of an unactive Temper, but because they won't beat down the Price of their Labour. A Country Gentleman sees at the back side of the *Exchange* a Porter walking to and fro with his Hands in his Pockets. Pray, says he, Friend, will you step for me with this Letter as far as *Bow Church*, and I'll give you a Penny. *I'll go with all my Heart*, says t'other, *but I must have Two-pence, Master*; which the Gentleman refusing to give, the Fellow turn'd his Back, and told him, he'd rather play for nothing than work for nothing. The Gentleman thought it an unaccountable piece of Laziness in a Porter, rather to saunter up and down for nothing, than to be earning a Penny with as little trouble. Some Hours after he happen'd to be with some Friends at a Tavern in *Threadneedlestreet*, where one of them calling to mind that he had forgot to send for a Bill of Exchange that was to go away with the Post that Night, was in great Perplexity, and immediately wanted some body to go for him to *Hackney* with all the Speed imaginable. It was after Ten, in the middle of Winter, a very rainy Night, and all the Porters thereabouts were gone to Bed. The Gentleman grew very uneasy, and said whatever it cost him that some body he must send; at last one of the Drawers seeing him so very pressing, told him that he knew a Porter, who would rise, if it was a Job worth his while. *Worth his while*, said the Gentleman very eagerly, *don't doubt of that, good Lad, if you know of any body, let him make what haste he can, and I'll give him a Crown if he be back by Twelve o'Clock.* Upon this the Drawer took the Errand, left the Room, and in less than a Quarter of an Hour came back with the welcome News that the Message would be dispatch'd with all Expedition. The Company in the mean time diverted themselves as they had done before, but when it began to be towards Twelve, the Watches were pull'd out, and the Porter's return was all the Discourse. Some were of Opinion he might yet come before the Clock had struck; others thought it impossible, and now it wanted but three Minutes of Twelve when in comes the nimble Messenger smoaking hot, with his Cloaths as wet as Dung with the Rain, and his Head all over in a Bath of Sweat. He had nothing dry about him but the inside of his Pocket-Book, out of which he took the Bill he had been for, and by the Drawer's Direction, presented it to the Gentleman it belonged to; who being very well pleas'd with the Dispatch he had made, gave him the Crown he had promis'd, whilst another fill'd him a Bumper, and the whole Company commended his diligencc. As the Fellow came nearer the Light, to take up the Wine, the Country Gentleman I mention'd at first, to his great Admiration, knew him to be the same Porter that had refus'd to earn his Penny, and whom he thought the laziest Mortal Alive.

This Story teaches us, that we ought not to confound those who remain unemploy'd for want of an Opportunity of exerting themselves to the best Advantage, with such as for want of Spirit, hug themselves in their Sloth, and will rather starve than stir. Without this Caution, we must pronounce all the World more or less lazy, according to their Estimation of the Reward they are to purchase with their Labour, and then the most Industrious may be call'd lazy.

Content I call that calm Serenity of the Mind, which Men enjoy whilst they think themselves happy, and rest satisfy'd with the Station they are in: It implies a favourable Construction of our present Circumstances, and a peaceful Tranquillity, which Men are Strangers to as long as they are sollicitous about mending their Condition. This is a Virtue of which the Applause is very precarious and uncertain; for according as Men's Circumstances vary, they'll either be blam'd or commended for being possess'd of it.

A single Man that works hard at a laborious Trade, has a hundred a Year left him by a Relation: This Change of Fortune makes him soon weary of working, and not having Industry enough to put himself forward in the World, he resolves to do nothing at all, and live upon his Income. As long as he lives within Compass, pays for what he has, and offends no body, he shall be call'd an honest, quiet Man. The Victualler, his Landlady, the Taylor and others divide what he has between them, and the Society is every Year the better for his Revenue, whereas, if he should follow his own or any other Trade, he must hinder others, and some body would have the less for what he should get; and therefore, tho' he should be the idlest Fellow in the World, lie a' Bed Fifteen Hours in Four and twenty, and do nothing but sauntring up and down all the rest of the time, no body wou'd discommend him, and his unactive Spirit is honoured with the Name of Content.

But if the same Man marries, gets three or four Children, and still continues of the same easy Temper, rests satisfied with what he has, and without endeavring to get a Penny, indulges his former Sloth: First, his Relations, afterwards all his Acquaintance will be allarm'd at his Negligence: They foresee that his Income will not be sufficient to bring up so many Children handsomely, and are afraid some of them may, if not a Burden, become a Disgrace to them. When these Fears have been for some time whisper'd about from one to another, his Uncle *Gripe* takes him to Task, and accosts him in the following Cant; *What, Nephew, no Business yet! Fie upon't! I can't imagine how you do to spend your Time; if you won't work at your own Trade, there are fifty ways that a Man may pick up a Penny by: You have a Hundred a Year, 'tis true, but your Charges encrease every Year, and what must you do when your Children are grown up? I have a better Estate than you my self and yet you don't see me leave off my Business; nay, I declare it, might I have the World I could not lead the Life you do. 'Tis no Business of mine, I own, but every body crys, 'tis a shame a young Man as you are, that has his Limbs and his Health should not turn his Hand to something or other.* If these Admonitions do not reform him in a little time, and he continues half a Year longer without Employment, he'll become a Discourse to the whole Neighbourhood, and for the same Qualifications that once got him the Name of a quiet contented Man, he shall be call'd the worst of Husbands and the laziest Fellow upon Earth: From whence it is manifest, that when we pronounce Actions good or evil, we only regard the Hurt or Benefit the Society receives from them, and not the Person who commits them. (*See Page* 86).

Diligence and Industry are often used promiscuously, to signify the same thing, but there is a great difference between them. A poor Wretch may want neither Diligence nor Ingenuity, be a saving Pains taking Man, and yet without striving to mend his Circumstances remain contented with the Station he lives in; but Industry implies besides the other qualities a Thirst after Gain, and an Indefatigable desire of meliorating our Condition. When Men think either the Customary Profits of their Calling, or else the share of Business, they have too small, they have two ways to deserve the Name of Industrious, and they must be either Ingenious enough to find out uncommon, and yet warrantable Methods to encrease their Business or their Profit, or else supply that Defect by a multiplicity of Occupations. If a Tradesman takes care to provide his Shop, and gives due Attendance to those that come to it, he is a diligent Man in his Business, but if, besides that, he takes particular Pains to sell to the same Advantage a better Commodity than the rest of his Neighbours, or if by his absequiousness, or some other good quality, getting into a large Acquaintance, he uses all possible Endeavours of drawing Customers to his House, he then may be call'd Industrious. A Cobler, tho' he is not employ'd half of his Time, if he neglects no Business, and makes dispatch when he has any, is a diligent Man; but if he runs of Errants when he has no work, or makes but Shoepins, and serves as a Watchman a Nights, he deserves the Name of Industrious.

If what has been said in this Remark be duely weigh'd, we shall find either that Laziness and Content are very near a'kin, or if there be a great difference between them, that the latter is more contrary to Industry than the former.

(X.) *To make a Great an honest Hive.*

PAGE 76. LINE 2. This perhaps might be done where People are contented to be poor and hardy; but if they would likewise enjoy their Ease and the Comforts of the World, and be at once an opulent, potent, and flourishing as well as a Warlike Nation, it is utterly impossible. I have heard People speak of the mighty Figure the *Spartans* made above all the Common-Wealths of *Greece*, notwithstanding their uncommon Frugality and other exemplary Virtues. But certainly there never was a Nation whose Greatness was more empty than theirs: The Splendor they liv'd in was inferior to that of a Theatre, and the only thing they could be proud of, was, that they enjoy'd nothing. They were indeed both fear'd and esteem'd Abroad: They were so fam'd for Valour and Skill in Martial Affairs, that their Neighbours did not only court their Friendship and Assistance in their Wars, but were satisfy'd and thought themselves sure of the Victory, if they could but get a *Spartan* General to Command their Armies. But then their Discipline was so rigid, and their manner of Living so Austere and void of all Comfort, that the most temperate Man among us would refuse to submit to the Harshness of such uncouth Laws. There was a perfect equality among them: Gold and Silver Coin were cried down; their current Money was made of Iron, to render it of a great Bulk and little worth: To lay up Twenty or Thirty Pounds, requir'd a pretty large Chamber, and to remove it nothing less than a Yoke of Oxen. Another Remedy, they had against Luxury, was, that they were oblig'd to eat in common of the same Meat, and they so little allow'd any body to Dine or Sup by himself at Home, that *Agis*, one of their Kings, having vanquish'd the *Athenians*, and sending for his Commons at his return Home (because he desir'd privately to eat with his Queen) was refus'd by the *Polemarchi*.

In training up their Youth, their chief Care, says *Plutarch*, was to make them good Subjects, to fit them to endure the fatigues of long and tedious Marches, and never to return without Victory from the Field. When they were Twelve Years old, they lodg'd in little Bands, upon Beds made of the Rushes, which grew by the Banks of the River *Eurotas*; and because their Points were sharp, they were to break them off with their Hands without a Knife:

If it were a hard Winter, they mingled some Thistle down with their Rushes to keep them warm (see *Plutarch* in the Life of *Lycurgus*.) From all these Circumstances it is plain, that no Nation on Earth was less effeminate; but being debarr'd from all the Comforts of Life, they could have nothing for their Pains but the Glory of being a Warlike People inur'd to Toils and Hardships, which was a happiness that few People would have car'd for upon the same Terms: And tho' they had been Masters of the World, as long as they enjoy'd no more of it, *Englishmen* would hardly have envy'd them their Greatness. What Men want now adays has sufficiently been shewn in Remark (*O*) where I have treated of real Pleasures.

(Y.) *T' enjoy the World's Conveniencies.*

PAGE 76. LINE 3. That the Words Decency and Conveniency were very ambiguous, and not to be understood, unless we were acquainted with the Quality and Circumstances of the Persons that made use of them, has been hinted already in Remark (*L*). The Goldsmith, Mercer, or any other of the most creditable Shopkeepers, that has Three or Four Thousand Pounds to set up with, must have two Dishes of Meat every Day, and something extraordinary for *Sundays*. His Wife must have a Damask Bed against her lying in, and two or three Rooms very well furnish'd: The following Summer she must have a House, or at least very good Lodgings in the Country. A Man that has a Being out of Town, must have a Horse; his Footman must have another. If he has a tolerable Trade, he expects in Eight or Ten Years time to keep his Coach, which notwithstanding he hopes that after he has slaved (as he calls it) for Two or Three and Twenty Years, he shall be worth at least a Thousand a Year for his Eldest Son to inherit, and

Two or Three Thousand Pounds for each of his other
Children to begin the World with; and when Men of such
Circumstances pray for their daily Bread, and mean nothing
more extravagant by it, they are counted pretty modest
People. Call this Pride, Luxury, Superfluity, or what you
please, it is nothing but what ought to be in the Capital
of a flourishing Nation : Those of inferiour Condition must
content themselves with less costly Conveniencies, as others
of higher Rank will be sure to make theirs more expensive.
Some People call it but Decency to be serv'd in Plate, and
reckon a Coach and Six among the necessary Comforts of
Life; and if a Peer has not above Three or Four Thousand
a Year, his Lordship is counted Poor.[42]

Since the first Edition of this Book, several have attack'd
me with Demonstrations of the certain Ruin, which ex-
cessive Luxury must bring upon all Nations, who yet were
soon answer'd, when I shew'd them the Limits within
which I had confin'd it; and therefore that no Reader for
the Future may misconstrue me on this Head, I shall point
at the Cautions I have given, and the Proviso's I have made
in the former as well as this present Impression, and which
if not overlook'd, must prevent all Rational Censure, and
obviate several Objections that otherwise might be made
against me. I have laid down as Maxims never to be de-
parted from, that the* Poor should be kept strictly to
Work, and that it was Prudence to relieve their Wants, but
Folly to cure them; that Agriculture† and Fishery should
be promoted in all their Branches in order to render Provi-
sions, and consequently Labour cheap. I have named‡
Ignorance as a necessary Ingredient in the Mixture of
Society : From all which it is manifest that I could never

42. The remainder of Remark Y was added in 1723. – Ed.
*p. 209, 210.
†p. 212.
‡p. 135.

have imagined, that Luxury was to be made general through every part of a Kingdom. I have likewise required* that Property should be well secured, Justice impartially administred, and in every thing the Interest of the Nation taken care of: But what I have insisted on the most and repeated more than once is the great Regard that is to be had to the Ballance of Trade, and the care the Legislature ought to take that the Yearly† Imports never exceed the Exports; and where this is observed, and the other things I spoke of are not neglected, I still continue to assert that no Foreign Luxury can undo a Country: The height of it is never seen but in Nations that are vastly populous, and there only in the upper part of it, and the greater that is the larger still in proportion must be the lowest, the Basis that supports all, the multitude of Working Poor.

Those who would too nearly imitate others of Superior Fortune must thank themselves if they are ruin'd. This is nothing against Luxury; for whoever can subsist and lives above his Income is a Fool. Some Persons of Quality may keep three or four Coaches and Six, and at the same time lay up Money for their Children; whilst a young Shop-keeper is undone for keeping one sorry Horse. It is impossible there should be a rich Nation without Prodigals, yet I never knew a City so full of Spendthrifts, but there were Covetous People enough to Answer their Number. As an Old Merchant breaks for having been extravagant or care-less a great while, so a young beginner falling into the same Business gets an Estate by being saving or more industrious before he is Forty Years Old: Besides that the frailties of Men often work by contraries: Some Narrow Souls can never thrive because they are too stingy, whilst longer Heads amass great Wealth by spending their Money freely, and seeming to despise it. But the vicissitudes of Fortune

*142.
†141, 142.

are necessary, and the most lamentable are no more detrimental to Society than the Death of the Individual Members of it. Christnings are a proper Ballance to Burials. Those who immediately lose by the Misfortunes of others are very sorry, complain and make a noise; but the others who get by them, as there always are such, hold their Tongues, because it is odious to be thought the better for the Losses and Calamities of our Neighbour. The various Ups and Downs compose a Wheel that always turning round gives motion to the whole Machine. Philosophers, that dare extend their Thoughts beyond the narrow compass of what is immediately before them, look on the alternate changes in the Civil Society no otherwise than they do on the risings and fallings of the Lungs, the latter of which are as much a Part of Respiration in the more perfect animals as the first; so that the fickle Breath of never Stable Fortune is to the Body Politick, the same as floating Air is to a living Creature.

Avarice then and Prodigality are equally necessary to the Society. That in some Countries Men are more generally lavish than in others proceeds from the difference in Circumstances that dispose to either Vice, and arise from the condition of the Social Body as well as the Temperament of the Natural. I beg pardon of the attentive Reader, if here in behalf of short memories I repeat some things the substance of which they have already seen in Remark (*Q*). More Money than Land, heavy Taxes and scarcity of Provisions, Industry, Laboriousness, an active and stiring Spirit, Ill Nature and a Saturnine Temper; Old Age, Wisdom, Trade, Riches acquired by our own Labour, and Liberty and Property well secured, are all things that dispose to Avarice. On the contrary, Indolence, Content, Good Nature, a Jovial Temper, Youth, Folly, Arbitrary Power, Money easily got, plenty of Provisions and the uncertainty of Possessions are Circumstances that render Men prone to

Prodigality: Where there is the most of the first the pre-
vailing Vice will be Avarice, and Prodigality where the
other turns the Scale; but a National Frugality there never
was nor never will be without a National Necessity.

Sumptuary Laws may be of use to an indigent Country,
after great Calamities of War, Pestilence, or Famine, when
Work has stood still, and the Labour of the Poor been in-
terrupted; but to introduce them into an opulent Kingdom
is the wrong way to consult the Interest of it. I shall end
my Remarks on the Grumbling Hive with assuring the
Champions of National Frugality that it would be impos-
sible for the *Persians* and other Eastern People to purchase
the vast quantities of fine *English* Cloth they consume,
should we load our Women with less Cargo's of *Asiatick*
Silks.

AN

Essay on Charity,

AND

Charity-Schools[43]

43. This essay was added in 1723. – Ed.

Charity is that Virtue by which part of that sincere Love we have for our selves is transferr'd pure and unmix'd to others, not tyed to us by the Bonds of Friendship or Consanguinity, and even meer Strangers, whom we have no Obligation to, nor hope or expect any thing from. If we lessen any ways the Rigour of this Definition, part of the Virtue must be lost. What we do for our Friends and Kindred, we do partly for our selves: When a Man acts in behalf of Nephews or Nieces, and says they are my Brother's Children, I do it out of Charity; he deceives you; for if he is capable, it is expected from him, and he does it partly for his own Sake: If he values the Esteem of the World, and is nice as to Honour and Reputation, he is obliged to have a greater Regard to them than for Strangers, or else he must suffer in his Character.

The Exercise of this Virtue relates either to Opinion, or to Action, and is manifested in what we think of others, or what we do for them. To be charitable then in the first Place, we ought to put the best Construction on all that others do or say, that the Things are capable of. If a Man builds a fine House, tho' he has not one Symptom of Humility, furnishes it richly, and lays out a good Estate in Plate and Pictures, we ought not to think that he does it out of Vanity, but to encourage Artists, employ Hands, and set the Poor to work for the Good of his Country: And if a Man sleeps at Church, so he does not snore, we ought to think he shuts his Eyes to increase his Attention. The Reason is, because in our Turn we desire that our utmost Avarice should pass for Frugality; and that for Religion, which we know to be Hypocrisy. Secondly, That Virtue is conspicuous in us, when we bestow our Time and Labour for nothing, or employ our Credit with others in behalf of those who stand in need of it, and yet could not expect such an Assistance from our Friendship or Nearness of Blood. The last Branch of Charity consists in giving away (whilst we are alive) what we value our selves, to such as I have already named; being contented rather to have and enjoy less, than not relieve those who want, and shall be the Objects of our Choice.

This Virtue is often counterfeited by a Passion of ours call'd *Pity* or *Compassion*, which consists in a Fellow-feeling and Condolance for the Misfortunes and Calamities of others; all Mankind are more or less affected with it; but the weakest Minds generally the most. It is raised in us, when the Sufferings and Misery of other Creatures make so forcible an Impression upon us, as to make us uneasy. It comes in either at the Eye or Ear, or both, and the nearer, and more violently the Object of Compassion strikes those Senses, the greater Disturbance it causes in us, often to such a Degree as to occasion great Pain and Anxiety.

Should any one of us be lock'd up in a Ground-Room, where in a Yard joining to it, there was a thriving good-humour'd Child at play of two or three Years old, so near us that through the Grates of the Window we could almost touch it with our Hand; and if whilst we took delight in the harmless Diversion, and imperfect Prittle-Prattle of the innocent Babe, a nasty over-grown Sow should come in upon the Child, set it a screaming, and frighten it out of its Wits; it is natural to think, that this would make us uneasy, and that with crying out, and making all the menacing Noise we could, we should endeavour to drive the Sow away. But if this should happen to be an half-starv'd Creature, that mad with Hunger went roaming about in quest of Food, and we should behold the ravenous Brute in spite of our Cries, and all the threatning Gestures we could think of, actually lay hold of the helpless Infant, destroy and devour it: To see her widely open her destructive Jaws, and the poor Lamb beat down with greedy Haste; to look on the defenceless Posture of tender Limbs first trampled on, then tore asunder; to see the filthy Snout digging in the yet living Entrails, suck up the smoaking Blood, and now and then to hear the Crackling of the Bones, and the cruel Animal with Savage Pleasure grunt o'er the horrid Banquet; to hear and see all this, what Tortures would it give the Soul beyond Expression! Let me see the most shining Virtue the Moralists have to boast of so manifest either to the Person possess'd of it, or those who behold his Actions: Let me see Courage, or the Love of one's Country so apparent without any Mixture, clear'd and distinct, the first from Pride and Anger, the other from the Love of Glory, and every Shadow of Self-Interest, as this Pity would be clear'd and distinct from all other Passions. There would be no need of Virtue or Self-Denial to be moved at such a Scene, and not only a Man of Humanity of good Morals and Commiseration, but likewise an Highwayman, an House-Breaker, or a Murderer could feel Anxieties on such an Occasion; how calamitous soever a Man's Circumstances might be, he would forget his Misfortunes for the time, and the most troublesome Passion would give way to Pity, and not one of the Species has a Heart so obdurate or engaged, that it would not ake at such a sight, as no Language has an Epithet to fit it.

Many will wonder at what I have said of Pity, that it comes in at the Eye or Ear, but the Truth of this will be known when we consider that the nearer the Object is the more we suffer, and the more remote it is the less we are troubled with it. To see People Executed for Crimes, if it is a great way off, moves us but little, in comparison to what it does when we are near enough to see the Motion of the Soul in their Eyes, observe their Fears and Agonies, and are able to read the Pangs in every Feature of the Face. When the Object is quite removed from our Senses, the Relation of the Calamities or the reading of them can never raise in us the Passion call'd Pity. We may be concern'd at bad News, the Loss and Misfortunes of Friends and those whose Cause we espouse; but this is not Pity, but Grief or Sorrow; the same as we feel for the Death of those we love, or the Destruction of what we value.

When we hear that three or four thousand Men, all Strangers to us, are kill'd with the Sword, or forc'd into some River where they are drown'd, we say and perhaps believe that we pity them. It is Humanity bids us have Compassion with the Sufferings of others, and Reason tells us, that whether a thing be far off or done in our sight our Sentiments concerning it ought to be the same, and we should be asham'd to own that we felt no Commiseration in us when any thing requires it. He is a cruel Man, he has no Bowels of Compassion: all these things are the Effects of Reason and Humanity, but Nature makes no Compliments, when the Object does not strike, the body does not feel it; and when Men talk of pitying People out of sight, they are to be believed in the same manner as when they say, that they are our humble Servants. In paying the usual Civilities at first meeting those who do not see one another every Day, are often very glad and very sorry alternately for five or six times together in less than two Minutes, and yet at parting carry away not a jot more of Grief or Joy than they met with. The same it is with Pity, and it is a thing of choice no more than fear or anger. Those who have a strong and lively Imagination, and can make Representations of things in their Minds, as they would be if they were actually before them, may work themselves up into something that resembles Compassion; but this is done by Art, and often the help of a little Enthusiasm, and is only an imitation of Pity: the Heart feels little of it, and it is as faint as what we suffer at the acting of a Tragedy; where our Judgment leaves part of the mind uninform'd, and to indulge a lazy Wantonness suffers it to be led into an Errour, which is necessary to have a Passion rais'd, the slight strokes of which are not unpleasant to us when the Soul is in an idle unactive Humour.

As Pity is often by our selves and in our own cases mistaken for Charity, so it assumes the shape, and borrows the very name of it; a Beggar asks you to exert that Vertue for Jesus Christ's sake, but all the while his great design is to raise your Pity. He represents to your View the worst side of his Ailments and bodily Infirmities; in chosen words he gives you an Epitome of his Calamities real or fictitious; and whilst he seems to pray God that he will open your Heart, he is actually at work upon your Ears: the greatest Profligate of them flys to Religion for aid, and assists his Cant with a doleful Tone and a study'd dismality of Gestures: But he trusts not to one Passion only, he flatters your Pride with Titles and Names of Honour and Distinction: your Avarice he sooths with often repeating to you the smallness of the Gift he sues for, and conditional promises of future returns with an Interest extravagant beyond the Statute of Usury tho' out of the reach of it. People not used to great Cities, being thus attack'd on all sides, are commonly forc'd to yield, and can't help giving something tho' they can hardly spare it themselves. How oddly are we manag'd by Self-love! It is ever watching in our Defence, and yet, to sooth a predominant Passion, obliges us to Act against our Interest: For when Pity seizes us, if we can but imagine that we contribute to the Relief of him we have Compassion with, and are Instrumental to the lessening of his Sorrows it eases us, and therefore pitiful People often give an Alms when they really feel that they would rather not.

When Sores are very bare or seem otherwise afflicting in an extraordinary manner, and the Beggar can bear to have them expos'd to the Cold Air, it is very shocking to some People; 'tis a shame they cry such Sights should be suffer'd; the main reason is, it touches their Pity feelingly, and at the same time they are resolv'd, either because they are Covetous, or count it an idle Expence, to give nothing, which makes them more uneasy. They turn their Eyes, and where the Cries are dismal, some would willingly stop their Ears if they were not ashamed. What they can do is to mend their Pace, and be very angry in their Hearts that Beggars should be about the Streets. But it is with Pity as it is with Fear, the more we are conversant with Objects that excite either Passion, the less we are disturb'd by them, and those to whom all these scenes and tones are by custom made familiar, they make little Impression upon. The only thing the Industrious Beggar has left to conquer those fortified Hearts, if he can walk either with or without Crutches, is to follow close and with uninterrupted Noise, teaze and importune them, to try if he can make them buy their Peace. Thus thousands give Money to Beggars from the same motive as they pay their Corn-cutter, to walk Easy. And many a Half-penny is given to impudent and designedly persecuting Rascals, whom, if it could be done handsomly, a man would cane with much greater Satisfaction. Yet all this by the courtesy of the Country is call'd Charity.

The Reverse of Pity is Malice: I have spoke of it where I treat of Envy. Those who know what it is to examine themselves, will soon own that it is very difficult to trace the Root and origin of this Passion. It is one of those we are most ashamed of, and therefore the hurtful part of it is easily subdued and corrected by a Judicious Education. When any body near us stumbles, it is natural even before reflection to stretch out our Hands to hinder or at least break the fall, which shews that whilst we are Calm we are rather bent to Pity. But tho' Malice by it self is little to be fear'd, yet assisted with Pride, it is often mischievous, and becomes most terrible when egg'd on and heighten'd by Anger. There is nothing that more readily or more effectually extinguishes Pity than this mixture, which is call'd Cruelty: From whence we may learn that to perform a meritorious Action, it is not sufficient barely to conquer a Passion unless it likewise be done from a laudable Principle, and consequently how necessary that Clause was in the Definition of Vertue, that our Endeavours were to proceed from *a rational Ambition of being Good*.

Pity, as I have said somewhere else, is the most amiable of all our Passions, and there are not many occasions on which we ought to conquer or curb it. A Surgeon may be as compassionate as he pleases so it does not make him omit or forbear to perform what he ought to do. Judges likewise and Juries may be influenc'd with Pity, if they take care that plain Laws and Justice it self are not infringed and do not suffer by it. No Pity does more Mischief in the World than what is excited by the Tenderness of Parents, and hinders them from managing their Children as their rational Love to them would require, and themselves could wish it. The Sway likewise which this Passion bears in the Affections of Women is more considerable than is commonly imagined, and they daily commit Faults that are altogether ascribed to Lust, and yet are in a great measure owing to Pity.

What I named last is not the only Passion that mocks and resembles Charity; Pride and Vanity have built more Hospitals than all the Virtues together. Men are so tenacious of their Possessions, and Selfishness is so rivited in our Nature, that whoever can but any ways conquer it shall have the Applause of the Publick, and all the Encouragement imaginable to conceal his Frailty and sooth any other

Appetite he shall have a mind to indulge. The Man that supplies with his private Fortune, what the whole must otherwise have provided for, obliges every Member of the Society, and therefore all the World are ready to pay him their Acknowledgment, and think themselves in Duty bound to pronounce all such Actions virtuous, without examining or so much as looking into the Motives from which they were perform'd. Nothing is more destructive to Virtue or Religion it self, than to make Men believe that giving Money to the Poor, tho' they should not part with it till after Death, will make a full Atonement in the next World, for the Sins they have committed in this. A Villain who has been guilty of a barbarous Murder may by the help of false Witnesses escape the Punishment he deserv'd: He prospers, we'll say, heaps up great Wealth, and by the Advice of his Father Confessor leaves all his Estate to a Monastery, and his Children Beggars. What fine Amends has this good Christian made for his Crime, and what an honest Man was the Priest who directed his Conscience? He who parts with all he has in his Life-time, whatever Principle he acts from, only gives away what was his own; but the rich Miser who refuses to assist his nearest Relations whilst he is alive, tho' they never designedly disobliged him, and disposes of his Money for what we call Charitable uses after his Death, may imagine of his Goodness what he pleases, but he robbs his Posterity. I am now thinking of a late Instance of Charity, a prodigious Gift, that has made a great Noise in the World: I have a mind to set it in the Light I think it deserves, and beg leave, for once to please Pedants, to treat it somewhat Rhetorically.

That a Man[44] with small Skill in Physick and hardly any Learning, should by vile Arts get into Practice and lay up

44. Dr John Radcliffe (1650–1714), the famous physician, who left his large fortune to the University of Oxford. – Ed.

great Wealth is no mighty wonder; but that he should so deeply work himself into the good Opinion of the World as to gain the general Esteem of a Nation, and establish a Reputation beyond all his contemporaries with no other qualities but a perfect Knowledge of Mankind, and a capacity of making the most of it, is something extra-ordinary. If a Man arrived to such a height of Glory should be almost distracted with Pride, sometimes give his attendance on a Servant or any mean Person for nothing, and at the same time neglect a Nobleman that gives exorbi-tant Fees, at other times refuse to leave his Bottle for his Business without any regard to the quality of the Persons that sent for him, or the Danger they are in: If he should be surly and morose, affect to be an Humorist, treat his patients like Dogs, tho' People of distinction, and value no Man but what would deify him, and never call in question the certainty of his Oracles: If he should insult all the World, affront the first Nobility, and extend his insolence even to the Royal Family: If to maintain as well as to in-crease the Fame of his sufficiency, he should scorn to con-sult with his Betters on what emergency soever, look down with contempt on the most deserving of his Profession, and never confer with any other Physician but what will pay homage to his Superiour Genius, creep to his Humour and never approach him but with all the slavish Obsequious-ness a Court Flaterer can treat a Prince with: If a Man in his life time should discover on the one hand such mani-fest Symptoms of Superlative Pride, and an insatiable greediness after Wealth at the same time, and on the other no regard to Religion or Affection to his Kindred, no Compassion to the Poor, and hardly any Humanity to his Fellow Creatures; if he gave no proofs that he lov'd his Country, had a Publick Spirit or was a lover of Arts, of Books or of Literature, what must we Judge of his motive, the principle he acted from, when after his Death we find that he has left a Trifle among his Relations who stood in need of it, and an immense Treasure to an University that did not want it.

Let a Man be as charitable as it is possible for him to be without forfeiting his Reason or good Sense; can he think otherwise, but that this famous Physician did in the making of his Will, as in every thing else, indulge his darling Passion, entertaining his Vanity with the Happiness of the Contrivance? When he thought on the Monuments and Inscriptions, with all the Sacrifices of Praise that would be made to him, and above all the yearly Tribute of Thanks, of Reverence and Veneration that would be paid to his Memory with so much Pomp and Solemnity; when he consider'd, how in all these Performances Wit and Invention would be rack'd, Art and Eloquence ransack'd to find out Encomiums suitable to the Publick Spirit, the Munificence and the Dignity of the Benefactor, and the artful Gratitude of the Receivers; when he thought on, I say, and consider'd these Things, it must have thrown his ambitious Soul into vast Extasies of Pleasure, especially when he ruminated on the Duration of his Glory, and the Perpetuity he would by this Means procure to his Name. Charitable Opinions are often stupidly false; when Men are dead and gone, we ought to judge of their Actions, as we do of Books, and neither wrong their Understanding nor our own. The *British Esculapius* was undeniably a Man of Sense, and if he had been influenc'd by Charity, a Publick Spirit, or the Love of Learning, and had aim'd at the Good of Mankind in general, or that of his own Profession in particular, and acted from any of these Principles, he could never have made such a Will; because so much Wealth might have been better managed, and a Man of much less Capacity would have found out several better Ways of laying out the Money. But if we consider, that he was as undeniably a Man of vast Pride, as he was a Man of Sense, and give our selves leave only to surmise, that this extraordinary Gift might have proceeded from such a Motive, we shall presently discover the Excellency of his Parts, and his consummate Knowledge of the World; for, if a Man would render himself immortal, be ever prais'd and deify'd after his Death, and have all the Acknowledgment, the Honours, and Compliments paid to his Memory, that Vain-Glory herself could wish for, I don't think it in human Skill to invent a more effectual Method. Had he follow'd Arms, behaved himself in five and twenty Sieges, and as many Battles, with the Bravery of an *Alexander*, and exposed his Life and Limbs to all the Fatigues and Dangers of War for fifty Campaigns together; or devoting himself to the *Muses*, sacrific'd his Pleasure, his Rest, and his Health to Literature, and spent all his Days in a laborious Study, and the Toils of Learning; or else abandoning all worldly Interest, excell'd in Probity, Temperance, and Austerity of Life, and ever trod in the strictest Path of Virtue, he would not so effectually have provided for the Eternity of his Name, as after a voluptuous Life, and the luxurious Gratification of his Passions, he has now done without any Trouble or Self-Denial, only by the Choice in the Disposal of his Money, when he was forc'd to leave it.

A rich Miser, who is thorowly selfish, and would receive the Interest of his Money even after his Death, has nothing else to do than to defraud his Relations, and leave his Estate to some famous University: they are the best Markets to buy Immortality at with little Merit; in them Knowledge, Wit, and Penetration are the Growth, I had almost said, the Manufacture of the Place: There Men are profoundly skill'd in Human Nature, and know what it is their Benefactors want; and there extraordinary Bounties shall always meet with an extraordinary Recompence, and the Measure of the Gift is ever the Standard of their Praises, whether the Donor be a Physician or a Tinker, when once the living Witnesses that might laugh at them are extinct. I can never think on the Anniversary of the Thanksgiving-Day decreed to a great Man, but it puts me in mind of the miraculous Cures, and other surprising Things that will be said of him a hundred Years hence, and I dare prognosticate, that before the End of the present Century, he will have Stories forg'd in his Favour, (for Rhetoricians are never upon Oath) that shall be as fabulous at least as any Legends of the Saints.

Of all this our subtle Benefactor was not ignorant, he understood Universities, their Genius, and their Politicks, and from thence foresaw and knew that the Incense to be offer'd to him would not cease with the present or a few succeeding Generations, and that it would not only last for the trifling Space of three or four hundred Years, but that it would continue to be paid to him through all Changes and Revolutions of Government and Religion, as long as the Nation subsists, and the Island it self remains.

It is deplorable that the Proud should have such Temptations to wrong their Lawful Heirs: For when a Man in ease and affluence, brimfull of Vain Glory and humour'd in his Pride by the greatest of a Polite Nation, has such an infallible Security in Petto for an Everlasting Homage and Adoration to his *Manes* to be paid in such an extraordinary manner, he is like a Hero in Battle, who in feasting on his own Imagination tastes all the Felicity of Enthusiasm. It buoys him up in Sickness, relieves him in Pain, and either Guards him against or keeps from his view all the Terrours of Death, and the most dismal Apprehensions of Futurity.

Should it be said that to be thus Censorious, and look into matters, and Mens Consciences with that nicety will discourage People from laying out their Money this way; and that let the Money and the Motive of the Donour be what they will, he that receives the Benefit is the Gainer, I would not disown the charge, but am of Opinion, that it is no Injury to the Publick, should one prevent Men from crowding too much Treasure into the Dead Stock of the Kingdom. There ought to be a vast disproportion between the Active and Unactive part of the Society to make it Happy, and where this is not regarded the multitude of Gifts and Endowments may soon be excessive and detrimental to a Nation. Charity, where it is too extensive, seldom fails of promoting Sloth and Idleness, and is good for little in the Common Wealth but to breed Drones and destroy Industry. The more Colleges and Alms-houses you Build the more you may. The first Founders and Benafactors may have just and good Intentions, and would perhaps for their own Reputations seem to Labour for the most laudable purposes, but the Executors of those Wills, the Governours that come after them have quite other views, and we seldom see Charities long applied as it was first intended they should be. I have no design that is Cruel, nor the least aim that Savours of Inhumanity. To have sufficient Hospitals for Sick and Wounded I look upon as an indispensible Duty both in Peace and War: Young Children without Parents, Old Age without Support, and all that are disabled from Working ought to be taken care of with Tenderness and Alacrity. But as on the one hand I would have none neglected that are helpless, and really necessitous without being wanting to themselves, so on the other I would not encourage Beggary or Laziness in the Poor: All should be set to Work that are any ways able, and Scrutinies should be made even among the Infirm: Employments might be found out for most of our Lame, and many that are unfit for hard Labour, as well as the Blind, as long as their Health and Strength would allow of it. What I have now under consideration leads me naturally to that kind of Distraction the Nation has labour'd under for some time, the Enthusiastick Passion for Charity-Schools.

The generality are so bewitch'd with the Usefulness and Excellency of them, that whoever dares openly oppose them is in danger of being Stoned by the Rabble. Children that are taught the Principles of Religion and can read the Word of God, have a greater opportunity to improve in Virtue and good Morality, and must certainly be more civilis'd than others, that are suffer'd to run at random and have no body to look after them. How perverse must be the Judgment of those, who would not rather see Children decently dress'd, with clean Linnen at least once a Week, that in an orderly manner follow their Master to Church, than in every open place meet with a Company of Black-Guards without Shirts or any thing whole about them, that insensible of their Misery are continually encreasing it with Oaths and Imprecations! can any one doubt but these are the great nursery of Thieves and Pick-pockets? What Numbers of Felons and other Criminals have we Tried and Convicted every Sessions! This will be prevented by Charity-Schools, and when the Children of the Poor receive a better Education, the Society will in a few Years reap the Benefit of it, and the Nation be clear'd of so many Miscreants as now this great City and all the Country about it are fill'd with.

This is the General Cry, and he that speaks the least Word against it, an Uncharitable, hard Hearted, and Inhuman if not a Wicked, Prophane and Atheistical Wretch. As to the comliness of the sight, no body disputes it, but I would not have a Nation pay too dear for so transient a Pleasure, and if we might set aside the finery of the Shew, every thing that is material in this Popular Oration might soon be answer'd.

As to Religion, the most knowing and polite Part of a Nation have every where the least of it; Craft has a greater

Hand in making Rogues than Stupidity, and Vice in general is no where more predominant than where Arts and Sciences flourish. Ignorance is, to a Proverb, counted to be the Mother of Devotion, and it is certain that we shall find Innocence and Honesty no where more general than among the most illiterate, the poor silly Country People. The next to be consider'd, are the Manners and Civility that by Charity-Schools are to be grafted into the Poor of the Nation. I confess that in my Opinion to be in any degree possess'd of what I named is a frivolous if not a hurtful Quality, at least nothing is less requisite in the Labourious Poor. It is not Compliments we want of them but their Work and Assiduity. But I give up this Article with all my Heart, good manners we'll say are necessary to all People, but which way will they be furnish'd with them in a Charity-School. Boys there may be taught to pull off their Caps promiscuously to all they meet, unless it be a Beggar: But that they should acquire in it any Civility beyond that I can't conceive.

The Master is not greatly qualify'd, as may be guess'd by his Salary, and if he could teach them Manners, he has not time for it: Whilst they are at School they are either learning or saying their Lesson to him, or employ'd in Writing or Arithmetick, and as soon as School is done, they are as much at Liberty as other Poor Peoples Children. It is precept and the example of Parents, and those they Eat, Drink and Converse with, that have an Influence upon the Minds of Children: Reprobate Parents that take Ill Courses and are regardless of their Children, won't have a mannerly civiliz'd Offspring tho' they went to a Charity-School till they were Married. The honest pains-taking People, be they never so poor, if they have any notion of Goodness and Decency themselves, will keep their Children in awe, and never suffer them to rake about the Streets, and lie out a-Nights. Those who will work themselves, and

have any command over their Children, will make them
do something or other that turns to Profit as soon as they
are able, be it never so little; and such as are so Ungovern-
able, that neither Words or Blows can work upon them,
no Charity-School will mend: Nay, Experience teaches us,
that among the Charity-Boys there are abundance of bad
ones that Swear and Curse about, and, bar the Cloaths, are
as much Blackguard as ever *Tower-Hill* or St. *James*'s
produced.

I am now come to the enormous Crimes, and vast Multi-
tude of Malefactors that are all laid upon the want of this
notable Education. That abundance of Thefts and Rob-
beries are daily committed in and about the City, and great
numbers Yearly suffer Death for those Crimes, is un-
deniable: But because this is ever hook'd in when the Use-
fulness of Charity-Schools is call'd in Question, as if there
was no dispute, but they would in a great measure remedy,
and in time prevent those Disorders, I intend to examine
into the real Causes of those Mischiefs so justly complain'd
of, and doubt not but to make it appear that Charity-
Schools, and every thing else that promotes Idleness, and
keeps the Poor from Working, are more Accessary to the
growth of Villainy, than the want of Reading and Writing,
or even the grossest Ignorance and Stupidity.

Here I must interrupt my self to obviate the Clamours of
some impatient People, who upon Reading of what I said
last will cry out that, far from encouraging Idleness, they
bring up their Charity-Children to Handicrafts, as well as
Trades, and all manner of Honest Labour. I promise them
that I shall take notice of that hereafter, and answer it with-
out stifling the least thing that can be said in their Behalf.

In a populous City it is not difficult for a young Rascal,
that has push'd himself into a Crowd, with a small Hand
and nimble Fingers to whip away a Handkerchief or Snuff
Box from a Man who is thinking on Business, and regard-

less of his Pocket. Success in small Crimes seldom fails of ushering in greater, and he, that picks Pockets with impunity at Twelve, is likely to be a House-breaker at Sixteen, and a thorough paced Villain long before he is Twenty. Those, who are Cautious as well as Bold, and no Drunkards, may do a world of Mischief before they are discover'd; and this is one of the greatest Inconveniencies of such vast overgrown Cities as *London* or *Paris*, that they harbour Rogues and Villains as Granaries do Vermin; they afford a perpetual shelter to the worst of People, and are places of Safety to Thousands of Criminals, who daily commit Thefts and Burglaries, and yet by often changing their places of Abode, may conceal themselves for many Years, and will perhaps for ever escape the hands of Justice unless by chance they are apprehended in a Fact. And when they are taken, the Evidences perhaps want clearness or are otherwise insufficient, the Depositions are not strong enough, Juries and often Judges are touch'd with Compassion; Prosecutors tho' vigorous at first often relent before the time of Trial comes on: Few Men prefer the publick Safety to their own Ease; a Man of Good Nature is not easily reconcil'd with the taking away of another Man's Life, tho' he has deserv'd the Gallows. To be the cause of any one's Death, tho' Justice requires it, is what most People are startled at, especially Men of Conscience and Probity, when they want Judgment or Resolution; as this is the reason that Thousands escape that deserve to be Capitally Punish'd, so it is likewise the cause that there are so many Offenders, who boldly venture in hopes, that if they are taken they shall have the same good Fortune of getting off.

But if Men did imagine and were fully persuaded, that as surely as they committed a Fact that deserv'd Hanging, so surely they would be Hang'd, Executions would be very rare, and the most desperate Felon would almost as soon hang himself as he would break open a House. To be Stupid and Ignorant is seldom the Character of a Thief. Robberies on the High-way and other bold Crimes are generally perpetrated by Rogues of Spirit and a Genius, and Villains of any Fame are commonly subtle cunning Fellows, that are well vers'd in the Method of Trials, and acquainted with every Quirk in the Law, that can be of Use to them, that overlook not the smallest Flaw in an Indictment, and know how to make an Advantage of the least slip of an Evidence and every thing else, that can serve their turn to bring 'em off.

It is a mighty Saying, that it is better that Five Hundred Guilty People should escape, than that one Innocent Person should suffer: This Maxim is only true as to Futurity, and in relation to another World; but it is very false in regard to the Temporal Welfare of the Society. It is a terrible thing a Man should be put to Death for a Crime he is not Guilty of; yet so oddly Circumstances may meet in the infinite variety of Accidents, that it is possible it should come to pass, all the Wisdom that Judges, and Conscientiousness that Juries may be possess'd of, notwithstanding. But where Men endeavour to avoid this with all the Care and Precaution human prudence is able to take, should such a Misfortune happen perhaps once or twice in Half a Score Years, on Condition that all that time Justice should be Administred with all the Strictness and Severity, and not one Guilty Person suffer'd to Escape with Impunity; it would be a vast Advantage to a Nation, not only as to the securing of every ones Property and the peace of the Society in General, but it would likewise save the Lives of Hundreds, if not Thousands, of Necessitous Wretches, that are daily hang'd for Trifles, and who would never have attempted any thing against the Law, or at least not have ventured on Capital Crimes, if the hopes of getting off should they be taken, had not been one of the Motives that animated their Resolution. Therefore where the Laws are plain and severe all the remisness in the Execution of them, Lenity of Juries and frequency of Pardons are in the main a much greater Cruelty to a populous State or Kingdom, than the use of Racks and the most exquisite Torments.

Another great Cause of those Evils is to be look'd for in the want of Precaution in those that are robb'd, and the many Temptations that are given. Abundance of Families are very remiss in looking after the Safety of their Houses, some are Robb'd by the carelessness of Servants, others for having grudg'd the price of Bars and Shutters. Brass and Pewter are ready Money, they are every where about the House; Plate perhaps and Money are better secured, but an ordinary Lock is soon open'd, when once a Rogue is got in.

It is manifest then that many different Causes concur, and several scarce avoidable Evils contribute to the misfortune of being pester'd with Pilferers, Thieves, and Robbers, which all Countries ever were and ever will be, more or less, in and near considerable Towns, more especially vast and over-grown Cities. 'Tis Opportunity makes the Thief; careles-ness and neglect in Fastning Doors and Windows, the excessive Tenderness of Juries and Prosecutors, the small difficulty of getting a Reprieve and frequency of Pardons, but above all the many Examples of those, who are known to be Guilty, are destitute both of Friends and Money, and yet by imposing on the Jury, Baffling the Witnesses or other Tricks and Stratagems, find out means to escape the Gallows. These are all strong Temptations that conspire to draw in the Necessitous, who want Principle and Educa-tion.

To these you may add as Auxiliaries to mischief, an habit of Sloth and Idleness and strong aversion to Labour and Assiduity, which all Young People will contract that are not brought up to down right Working, or at least kept employ'd most Days in the Week, and the greatest part of the Day. All Children that are Idle, even the best of either Sex, are bad Company to one another whenever they meet.

It is not then the want of Reading and Writing, but the concurrence and a complication of more Substantial Evils that are the perpetual nursery of abandon'd Profligates in great and opulent Nations; and whoever would accuse Ignorance, Stupidity and Dastardness, as the first, and what Physicians call the Procatartic Cause,[45] let him examine into the Lives, and narrowly inspect the Conversations and Actions of ordinary Rogues and our common Felons, and he will find the reverse to be true, and that the blame ought rather to be laid on the excessive Cunning and Subtlety, and too much Knowledge in general, which the worst of Miscreants and the Scum of the Nation are possess'd of.

Human Nature is every where the same: Genius, Wit and Natural Parts are always sharpen'd by Application, and may be as much improv'd in the practice of the meanest Villainy, as they can in the exercise of Industry or the most Heroic Virtue. There is no Station of Life, where Pride, Emulation and the love of Glory may not be display'd. A Young Pick-pocket that makes a Jest of his Angry Prosecutor, and dextrously wheedles the Old Justice into an Opinion of his Innocence, is envied by his Equals and admired by all the Fraternity. Rogues have the same Passions to gratify as other Men, and value themselves on their Honour and Faithfulness to one another, their Courage, Intrepidity and other Manly Virtues as well as People of better Professions; and in daring Enterprizes the Resolution of a Robber may be as much supported by his Pride, as that of an Honest Soldier, who Fights for his Country.

The Evils then we complain of are owing to quite other Causes than what we assign for them. Men must be very wavering in their Sentiments, if not inconsistent with themselves, that at one time will uphold Knowledge and Learn-

45. The primary cause of a disease. – Ed.

ing to be the most proper means to promote Religion, and defend at another that Ignorance is the Mother of Devotion.

But of the Reasons alledg'd for this general Education are not the true ones, whence comes it that the whole Kingdom both great and small are so Unanimously Fond of it? There is no miraculous conversion to be perceiv'd among us, no Universal Bent to Goodness and Morality that has on a sudden overspread the Island: there is as much Wickedness as ever, Charity is as Cold, and real Virtue as Scarce: The Year Seventeen Hundred and Twenty has been as Prolifick in deep Villainy, and remarkable for Selfish Crimes and premeditated Mischief, as can be pick'd out of any Century whatever; not committed by Poor Ignorant Rogues that could neither Read nor Write, but the better sort of People as to Wealth and Education, that most of them were great Masters in Arithmetick, and lived in Reputation and Splendour.[46] To say that when a thing is once in Vogue, the multitude follows the common cry, that Charity Schools are in Fashion in the same manner as Hoop'd Petticoats, by Caprice, and that no more Reason can be given for the one than the other, I am afraid will not be Satisfactory to the Curious, and at the same time I doubt much, whether it will be thought of great Weight by many of my Readers, what I can advance besides.

The real Source of this present Folly is certainly very abstruse and remote from sight, but he that affords the least light in matters of great obscurity does a kind office to the Enquirers. I am willing to allow, that in the Beginning the first Design of those Schools was Good and Charitable, but to know what encreases them so extravagantly, and who are the chief Promoters of them now, we must make our search another way, and address our selves to the rigid Party-men that are zealous for their Cause, either Episcopacy or Presbytery; but as the latter are but the Poor

46. Mandeville is referring to the South Sea Bubble. – Ed.

Mimicks of the first, tho' equally pernicious, we shall confine our selves to the National Church, and take a turn through a Parish that is not bless'd yet with a Charity School. – But here I think my self obliged in conscience to ask pardon of my Reader for the tiresom Dance I am going to lead him if he intends to follow me, and therefore I desire that he would either throw away the Book and leave me, or else arm himself with the Patience of *Job* to endure all the Impertinencies of Low Life, the Cant and Tittle Tattle he is like to meet with before he can go half a Street's length.

First we must look out among the young Shop-keepers, that have not half the Business they could wish for, and consequently Time to spare. If such a New-beginner has but a little Pride more than ordinary, and loves to be medling, he is soon mortify'd in the Vestry, where Men of Substance and long standing, or else your pert litigious or opinionated Bawlers, that have obtained the Title of Notable Men, commonly bear the sway. His Stock and perhaps Credit are but inconsiderable, and yet he finds within himself a strong Inclination to Govern. A Man thus qualified thinks it a thousand pities there is no Charity-School in the Parish: he communicates his Thoughts to two or three of his Acquaintance first; they do the same to others, and in a Month's time there is nothing else talk'd of in the Parish. Every body invents Discourses and Arguments to the Purpose according to his Abilities. – It is an errant Shame, says one, to see so many Poor that are not able to educate their Children, and no provision made for them where we have so many Rich People. What d'ye talk of Rich, answers another, they are the worst: they must have so many Servants, Coaches and Horses: They can lay out Hundreds, and some of them Thousands of Pounds for Jewels and Furniture, but not spare a Shilling to a poor Creature that wants it: When Modes and Fashions are discours'd of they can hearken with great Attention, but are wilfully deaf to the Cries of the Poor. Indeed Neighbour, replies the first, you are very right, I don't believe there is a worse Parish in *England* for Charity than ours: 'Tis such as you and I that would do good if it was in our power, but of those that are able there's very few that are willing.

Others more violent fall upon particular Persons, and fasten Slander on every Man of Substance they dislike, and a thousand idle Stories in behalf of Charity are rais'd and handed about to defame their Betters. Whilst this is doing throughout the Neighbourhood, he that first broach'd the pious Thought rejoices to hear so many come in to it, and places no small Merit in being the first cause of so much Talk and Bustle: But neither himself nor his Intimates being considerable enough to set such a thing on foot, some body must be found out who has greater Interest: he is to be address'd to, and shew'd the Necessity, the Goodness, the Usefulness and Christianity of such a Design: next he is to be flatter'd. – Indeed Sir, if you would espouse it, no body has a greater Influence over the best of the Parish than your self: One Word of you I am sure would engage such a one: If you once would take it to heart, Sir, I would look upon the thing as done, Sir. – If by this kind of Rhetorick they can draw in some old Fool or conceited Busy-body that is rich, or at least reputed to be such, the thing begins to be feasible, and is discours'd of among the better sort. The Parson, or his Curate, and the Lecturer are every where extolling the Pious Project. The first Promoters mean while are indefatigable: If they were Guilty of any open Vice they either Sacrifice it to the love of Reputation or at least grow more cautious and learn to play the Hypocrite, well knowing that to be flagitious or noted for Enormities is inconsistent with the Zeal which they pretend to for Works of Supererrogation and Excessive Piety.

The number of these diminutive Patriots encreasing, they

form themselves into a Society, and appoint stated Meetings, where every one concealing his Vices has liberty to display his Talents. Religion is the Theme, or else the Misery of the Times occasion'd by Atheism and Prophaneness. Men of Worth, who live in Splendor, and thriving People that have a great deal of Business of their own, are seldom seen among them. Men of Sense and Education likewise, if they have nothing to do, generally look out for better diversion. All those who have a higher aim, shall have their attendance easily excus'd, but contribute they must or else lead a weary Life in the Parish. Two sorts of People come in voluntarily, Stanch Churchmen, who have good reasons for it in Petto, and your sly Sinners that look upon it as meritorious, and hope that it will expiate their Guilt, and Satan be Nonsuited by it at a small Expence. Some come in to it to save their Credit, others to retrieve it, according as they have either lost or are afraid of losing it; others again do it Prudentially to encrease their Trade and get Acquaintance, and many would own to you, if they dared to be sincere and speak the Truth, that they would never have been concern'd in it, but to be better known in the Parish. Men of Sense that see the Folly of it and have no body to Fear, are persuaded into it not to be thought singular or to run Counter to all the World; even those who are resolute at first in denying, it is ten to one but at last they are teaz'd and importun'd into a Compliance. The Charge being calculated for most of the Inhabitants, the Insignificancy of it is another Argument that prevails much, and many are drawn in to be Contributors, who without that would have stood out and strenuously opposed the whole Scheme.

The Governours are made of the midling People, and many inferiour to that Class are made use of, if the forwardness of their Zeal can but over-ballance the meanness of their Condition. If you should ask these Worthy Rulers, why they take upon them so much Trouble to the detriment of their own Affairs and loss of Time, either singly or the whole body of them, they would all Unanimously Answer, that it is the regard they have for Religion and the Church, and the Pleasure they take in Contributing to the Good, and Eternal Welfare of so many Poor Innocents that in all probability would run into Perdition in these Wicked Times of Scoffers and Free-thinkers. They have no Thought of Interest even those who deal in and provide these Children with what they want, have not the least design of getting by what they sell for their Use, and tho' in every thing else their Avarice and Greediness after Lucre be glaringly conspicuous, in this Affair they are wholly divested from Selfishness, and have no Worldly Ends. One Motive above all, which is none of the least with most of them, is to be carefully conceal'd, I mean the Satisfaction there is in Ordering and Directing: There is a Melodious Sound in the word Governour that is charming to mean People: Every Body admires Sway and Superiority, even *Imperium in Belluas*[47] has its Delights, there is a Pleasure in Ruling over any thing, and it is this chiefly that supports Human Nature in the Tedious Slavery of School-masters. But if there be the least Satisfaction in governing the Children, it must be ravishing to govern the School-master himself. What fine things are said and perhaps Wrote to a Governour, when a School-master is to be Chosen! How the Praises tickle, and how Pleasant it is not to find out the Fulsomness of the Flattery, the Stifness of the Expressions, or the Pedantry of the Stile!

Those who can examine Nature will always find, that what these People most pretend to is the least, and what they utterly deny their greatest Motive. No Habit or Quality is more easily acquired than Hypocrisy, nor any thing sooner learn'd than to deny the Sentiments of our Hearts and the Principle we Act from: But the Seeds of every Passion are

47. 'Rule over beasts', Terence, *Eunuchus*, 415. – Ed.

innate to us, and no body comes into the World without them. If we will mind the Pastimes and Recreations of Young Children, we shall observe nothing more general in them, than that all who are suffer'd to do it, take delight in playing with Kittens and little Puppy Dogs. What makes them always lugging and pulling the poor Creatures about the House proceeds from nothing else but that they can do with them what they please, and put them into what posture and shape they list, and the Pleasure they receive from this is originally owing to the love of Dominion and that Usurping Temper all Mankind are Born with.

When this great Work is brought to bear, and actually accomplish'd, Joy and Serenity seem to overspread the Face of every Inhabitant, which likewise to account for I must make a short digression. There are every where slovenly sorry Fellows that are used to be seen always Ragged and Dirty: These People we look upon as miserable Creatures in General, and unless they are very remarkable we take little Notice of them, and yet among these there are handsome and well shaped Men as well as among their Betters. But if one of these turns Soldier, what a vast Alteration is there observ'd in him for the better, as soon as he is put in his Red Coat, and we see him look smart with his Granadiers Cap and a great Ammunition Sword! All who knew him before are struck with other Ideas of his Qualities, and the Judgment which both Men and Women form of him in their Minds is very different from what it was. There is some thing Analogous to this in the Sight of Charity Children; there is a natural Beauty in Uniformity which most People delight in. It is diverting to the Eye to see Children well match'd, either Boys or Girls, march two and two in good Order; and to have them all whole and tight in the same Cloaths and Trimming must add to the Comliness of the Sight; and what makes it still more generally entertaining is the imaginary Share which even Servants and

the meanest in the Parish have in it, to whom it costs noth-
ing: our Parish Church, our Charity Children. In all this
there is a Shadow of property that tickles every Body that
has a Right to make Use of the Words, but more especially
those who actually contribute and had a great Hand in
advancing the pious Work.

It is hardly conceivable that Men should so little know
their own Hearts and be so ignorant of their inward Con-
dition, as to mistake Frailty, Passion and Enthusiasm for
Goodness, Virtue and Charity; yet nothing is more true
than that the Satisfaction, the Joy and Transports they feel
on the accounts I named pass with these miserable Judges
for principles of Piety and Religion. Whoever will con-
sider what I have said for two or three Pages, and suffer
his Imagination to rove a little further on what he has heard
and seen concerning this Subject, will be furnished with
sufficient Reasons abstract from the love of God and true
Christianity, why Charity-Schools are in such uncommon
Vogue, and so unanimously approv'd of and admired among
all sorts and conditions of People. It is a Theme which every
Body can talk of and understands thoroughly, there is not a
more inexhaustible fund for Tittle Tattle, and a variety of
low conversation in Hoy-boats and Stage-coaches. If a Gover-
nour that in Behalf of the School or the Sermon exerted him-
self more than ordinary, happens to be in Company, how
he is commended by the Women, and his Zeal and Charit-
able Disposition extoll'd to the Skies! Upon my word, Sir,
says an Old Lady we are all very much obliged to you, I
don't think any of the other Governours could have made
Interest enough to procure us a Bishop; 'twas on your
Account I am told that his Lordship came, tho' he was not
very well: To which the other replies very gravely, that
it is his Duty, but that he values no Trouble nor Fatigue
so he can be but serviceable to the Children, poor Lambs:
Indeed, says he, I was resolv'd to get a pair of Lawn Sleeves

tho' I rid all Night for it, and I am very glad I was not disappointed.

Sometimes the School it self is discours'd of, and of whom in all the Parish it is most expected he should Build one : The old Room where it is now kept is ready to drop down : Such a one had a vast Estate left him by his Uncle, and a great deal of Money besides; a Thousand Pounds would be nothing in his Pocket.

At others the great Crowds are talk'd of that are seen at some Churches, and the considerable Sums that are gather'd; from whence by an easy transition they go over to the Abilities, the different Talents and Orthodoxy of Clergymen. Dr. — is a Man of great Parts and Learning, and I believe he is very hearty for the Church, but I don't like him for a Charity-Sermon. There is no better Man in the World than —; he forces the Money out of their Pockets. When he Preach'd last for our Children I am sure there was abundance of People that gave more than they intended when they came to Church. I could see it in their Faces and rejoyc'd at it Heartily.

Another Charm that renders Charity-Schools so bewitching to the Multitude is the general Opinion Establish'd among them, that they are not only actually Beneficial to Society as to Temporal Happiness, but likewise that Christianity enjoyns and requires of us, we should erect them for our Future Welfare. They are earnestly and fervently recommended by the whole body of the Clergy, and have more Labour and Eloquence laid out upon them than any other Christian Duty; not by young Parsons or poor Scholars of little Credit, but the most Learned of our Prelates and the most Eminent for Orthodoxy, even those who do not often fatigue themselves on any other Occasion. As to Religion, there is no doubt but they know what is chiefly required of us, and consequently the most necessary to Salvation : and as to the World, who should understand

the Interest of the Kingdom better than the Wisdom of the
Nation, of which the Lords Spiritual are so considerable a
Branch? The consequence of this Sanction is first, that
those, who with their Purses or Power are Instrumental to
the encrease or maintenance of these Schools, are tempted
to place a greater merit in what they do than otherwise
they could suppose it deserv'd. Secondly, that all the rest,
who either cannot or will not any ways contribute towards
them, have still a very good reason why they should speak
well of them; for tho' it be difficult, in things that interfere
with our Passions, to act well, it is always in our power to
wish well, because it is perform'd with little Cost. There is
hardly a Person so Wicked among the Superstitious Vulgar,
but in the liking he has for Charity-Schools, he imagines to
see a Glimmering Hope that it will make an Atonement for
his Sins, from the same Principle as the most Vicious com-
fort themselves with the Love and Veneration they bear to
the Church, and the greatest Profligates find an Opportunity
in it to shew the Rectitude of their Inclinations at no Ex-
pence.

But if all these were not inducements sufficient to make
Men stand up in Defence of the Idol I speak of, there is
another that will infallibly Bribe most People to be Advo-
cates for it. We all naturally love Triumph, and whoever
engages in this Cause is sure of Conquest at least in Nine
Companies out of Ten. Let him dispute with whom he will,
considering the Speciousness of the pretence, and the
Majority he has on his side, it is a Castle, an impregnable
Fortress he can never be beat out of, and was the most Sober,
Virtuous Man alive to produce all the Arguments, to prove
the detriment Charity-Schools, at least the Multiplicity of
them, do to Society, which I shall give hereafter, and such
as are yet stronger, against the greatest Scoundrel in the
World, who should only make use of the common Cant of
Charity and Religion, the Vogue would be against the first,

and himself lose his Cause in the Opinion of the Vulgar.

The Rise then and Original of all the Bustle and Clamour that is made throughout the Kingdom in Behalf of Charity-Schools is chiefly Built on Frailty and Human Passion, at least it is more than possible that a Nation should have the same Fondness and feel the same Zeal for them as are shewn in ours, and yet not be prompted to it by any principle of Virtue or Religion. Encouraged by this Consideration, I shall with the greater Liberty attack this Vulgar Error, and endeavour to make it evident, that far from being Beneficial, this forc'd Education is pernicious to the Publick, the Welfare whereof as it demands of us a regard Superiour to all other Laws and considerations, so it shall be the only Apology I intend to make for differing from the present Sentiments of the Learned and Reverend Body of our Divines, and venturing plainly to deny, what I have just now own'd to be openly asserted by most of our Bishops as well as Inferior Clergy. As our Church pretends to no Infallibility even in Spirituals, her proper Province, so it cannot be an Affront to her to Imagine that she may err in Temporals which are not so much under her immediate care. – But to my Task.

The whole Earth being Curs'd and no Bread to be had but what we eat in the sweat of our Brows, vast Toil must be undergone before Man can provide himself with Necessaries for his Sustenance and the bare support of his corrupt and defective Nature as he is a single Creature; but infinitely more to make Life comfortable in a Civil Society, where Men are become taught Animals and great numbers of them have by mutual compact framed themselves into a Body Politick; and the more Man's Knowledge encreases in this State, the greater will be the variety of Labour required to make him easy. It is impossible that a Society can long subsist and suffer many of its Members to live in Idleness, and enjoy all the Ease and Pleasure they can invent, without having at the same time great multitudes of People that to make good this defect, will condescend to be quite the Reverse, and by use and patience inure their Bodies to Work for others and themselves besides.

The plenty and cheapness of Provisions depends in a great measure on the Price and Value that is set upon this Labour, and consequently the Welfare of all Societies even before they are tainted with Foreign Luxury, requires that it should be perform'd by such of their Members as in the first place are sturdy and robust and never used to Ease or Idleness, and in the second, soon contented as to the necessaries of Life; such as are glad to take up with the coursest Manufacture in every thing they wear, and in their Diet have no other aim than to feed their Bodies when their Stomachs prompt them to Eat, and, with little regard to Taste or Relish, refuse no Wholesome Nourishment that can be swallow'd when Men are Hungry, or ask any thing for their Thirst but to quench it.

As the greatest part of the Drudgery is to be done by Daylight, so it is by this only that they actually measure the time of their Labour, without any thought of the Hours they are employ'd, or the Weariness they feel; and the Hireling in the Country must get up in the Morning, not because he has rested enough, but because the Sun is going to rise. This last Article alone would be an intollerable hardship to Grown People under Thirty, who during nonage had been used to lye a Bed as long as they could sleep; but all three together make up such a Condition of Life as a Man more mildly Educated would hardly chuse; tho' it should deliver him from a Goal or a Shrew.

If such People there must be, as no great Nation can be happy without vast Numbers of them, would not a Wise Legislature cultivate the Breed of them with all imaginable Care, and provide against their Scarcity as he would prevent the Scarcity of Provision it self? No Man would be Poor and Fatigue himself for a Livelihood if he could help it: The absolute necessity all stand in for Victuals and Drink, and in cold Climates for Cloaths and Lodging, makes them submit to any thing that can be bore with. If no body did Want no body would Work; but the greatest Hardships are look'd upon as Solid Pleasures when they keep a Man from Starving.

From what has been said it is manifest, that in a Free Nation where Slaves are not allow'd of, the surest wealth consists in a multitude of Laborious Poor; for besides that they are the never failing Nursery of Fleets and Armies, without them there could be no enjoyment, and no Product of any Country could be valuable. To make the Society Happy and People Easy under the meanest Circumstances, it is requisite that great numbers of them should be Ignorant as well as Poor. Knowledge both enlarges and multiplies our Desires, and the fewer things a Man Wishes for, the more easily his Necessities may be supply'd.

The Welfare and Felicity therefore of every State and Kingdom, require that the Knowledge of the Working Poor should be confin'd within the Verge of their Occupations, and never extended (as to things visible) beyond what relates to their Calling. The more a Shepherd, a Plowman or any other Peasant knows of the World, and the things that are Foreign to his Labour or Employment, the less fit he'll be to go through the Fatigues and Hardships of it with Chearfulness and Content.

Reading, Writing and Arithmetick are very necessary to those, whose Business require such Qualifications, but where Peoples Livelihood has no dependance on these Arts, they are very pernicious to the Poor, who are forc'd to get their Daily Bread by their Daily Labour. Few Children make any progress at School, but at the same time they are capable of being employ'd in some Business or other, so that every Hour those of poor People spend at their Book is so much time lost to the Society. Going to School in comparison to Working is Idleness, and the longer Boys continue in this easy sort of Life. the more unfit they'll be when grown up for downright Labour, both as to Strength and Inclination. Men who are to remain and end their Days in a Labourious, Tiresome and Painful Station of Life, the sooner they are put upon it at first, the more patiently they'll submit to it for ever after. Hard Labour and the coursest Diet are a proper Punishment to several kinds of Malefactors, but to impose either on those that have not been used and brought up to both is the greatest Cruelty, when there is no Crime you can charge them with.

Reading and Writing are not attain'd to without some labour of the Brain and assiduity, and before People are tollerably vers'd in either, they esteem themselves infinitely above those who are wholly Ignorant of them, often with so little Justice and Moderation as if they were of another Species. As all Mortals have naturally an Aversion to trouble and pains-taking, so we are all fond of, and apt to over-value those Qualifications we have purchas'd at the Expence of our ease and quiet for Years together. Those who spent a great part of their Youth in Learning to Read, Write and Cypher, expect and not unjustly to be employ'd where those Qualifications may be of use to them; the generality of them will look upon downright Labour with the utmost con-tempt, I mean labour perform'd in the service of others, in the lowest Station of Life, and for the meanest considera-tion. A Man who has had some Education, may follow Hus-bandry by choice, and be diligent at the dirtiest and most laborious Work; but then the concern must be his own, and Avarice, the care of a Family, or some other pressing Motive must put him upon it, but he wont make a good Hireling and serve a Farmer for a pitiful Reward, at least he is not so fit for it as a Day Labourer that has always been employ'd about the Plow and Dung Cart, and remembers not that ever he has lived otherwise.

When Obsequiousness and mean Services are required, we shall always observe that they are never so chearfully nor so heartily perform'd as from Inferiours to Superiours; I mean Inferiours not only in Riches and Quality, but likewise in Knowledge and Understanding. A Servant can have no unfeign'd Respect for his Master, as soon as he has Sense enough to find out that he serves a Fool. When we are to learn or to obey we shall experience in our selves, that the greater Opinion we have of the Wisdom and Capacity of those that are either to Teach or Command us, the greater deference we pay to their Laws and Instructions. No Creatures submit contentedly to their Equals, and should a Horse know as much as a Man, I should not desire to be his Rider.

Here I am obliged again to make a Digression, tho' I declare I never had a less mind to it than I have at this Minute; but I see a Thousand Rods in Piss,[48] and the whole Posse of diminutive Pedants against me for Assaulting the Christ-cross-row,[49] and opposing the very Elements of Literature.

This is no Panick Fear, and the Reader will not imagine my apprehensions ill Grounded, if he considers what an Army of petty Tyrants I have to Cope with, that all either actually persecute with Birch or else are solliciting for such a Preferment. For if I had no other Adversaries than the starving Wretches of both Sexes, throughout the Kingdom of *Great Britain*, that from a natural antipathy to Working, have a great Dislike to their present Employment, and perceiving within a much stronger Inclination to Command than ever they felt to Obey others, think themselves qualify'd, and wish from their Hearts to be Masters and Mistresses of Charity-Schools, the Number of my Enemies would by the most modest Computation, amount to One Hundred Thousand at Least.

48. Punishments in waiting. – Ed.
49. The alphabet. – Ed.

Methinks I hear them cry out that a more dangerous Doctrine never was broach'd, and Popery's a Fool to it, and ask what Brute of a *Saracen* it is that draws his ugly Weapon for the Destruction of Learning. It is ten to one but they'll indict me for endeavouring by Instigation of the Prince of Darkness, to introduce into these Realms greater Ignorance and Barbarity than ever Nation was plunged into by *Goths* and *Vandals* since the Light of the Gospel first appeared in the World. Whoever labours under the Publick Odium has always Crimes laid to his charge he never was guilty of, and it will be suspected that I have had a hand in obliterating the Holy Scriptures, and perhaps affirm'd that it was at my Request that the small Bibles publish'd by Patent in the Year 1721, and chiefly made use of in Charity Schools, were through badness of Print and Paper render'd illegible : which yet I protest I am as innocent of as the Child unborn. But I am in a thousand Fears; the more I consider my Case the worse I like it, and the greatest Comfort I have is in my sincere Belief, that hardly any body will mind a word of what I say; or else if ever the People suspected that what I write would be of any weight to any considerable part of the Society, I should not have the Courage barely to think on all the Trades I should disoblige; and I cannot but smile when I reflect on the Variety of uncouth Sufferings that would be prepar'd for me, if the Punishment they would differently inflict upon me, was Emblematically to point at my Crime. For if I was not suddenly stuck full of useless Penknives up to the Hilts, the Company of Stationers would certainly take me in hand, and either have me buried alive in their Hall under a great heap of Primers and Spelling-books, they would not be able to sell; or else send me up against Tide to be bruised to Death in a Paper Mill that would be obliged to stand still a Week upon my account. The Inkmakers at the same time would for the Publick Good offer to choak me with Astringents, or drown me in the black Liquor that would be left upon their Hands; which, if they joyn'd stock, might easily be perform'd in less than a Month; and if I should escape the Cruelty of these united Bodies the Resentment of a private Monopolist would be as fatal to me, and I should soon find my self pelted and knock'd o' the head with little squat Bibles clasp'd in Brass and ready arm'd for Mischief, that, Charitable Learning ceasing, would be fit for nothing but unopen'd to fight with, and Exercises truly Polemick.

The Digression I spoke of just now is not the foolish Trifle that ended with the last Paragraph, and which the grave Critick, to whom all Mirth is unseasonable, will think very impertinent; but a serious Apologetical one I am going to make out of hand, to clear my self from having any Design against Arts and Sciences, as some Heads of Colleges and other careful Preservers of Human Learning might have apprehended upon seeing Ignorance recommended as a necessary Ingredient in the mixture of Civil Society.

In the first place I would have near double the number of Professors in every University of what there is now. Theology with us is generally well provided, but the two other Faculties have very little to boast of, especially Physick. Every Branch of that Art ought to have two or three Professors, that would take pains to communicate their Skill and Knowledge to others. In Publick Lectures a vain Man has great Opportunities to set off his Parts, but private Instructions are more useful to Students. Pharmacy and the Knowledge of the Simples are as necessary as Anatomy or the History of Diseases : It is a shame that when Men have taken their Degree, and are by Authority entrusted with the Lives of the Subject, they should be forc'd to come to *London* to be acquainted with the *Materia Medica* and the Composition of Medicines, and receive Instructions from others that never had University Education themselves; it is certain that in the City I named there is ten times more

Opportunity for a Man to improve himself in Anatomy, Botany, Pharmacy and the Practice of Physick than at both our Universities together. What has an Oyl-shop to do with Silks; or who would look for Hams and Pickles at a Mercers? Where things are well managed, Hospitals are made as subservient to the Advancement of Students in the Art of Physick as they are to the Recovery of Health in the Poor.

Good Sense ought to govern Men in Learning as well as in Trade: No Man ever bound his Son Prentice to a Goldsmith to make him a Linnendraper; then why should he have a Divine for his Tutor to become a Lawyer or a Physician? It is true that the Languages, Logick and Philosophy should be the first Studies in all the Learned Professions; but there is so little Help for Physick in our Universities that are so rich, and where so many idle People are well paid for eating and drinking, and being magnificently as well as commodiously lodg'd, that bar Books and what is common to all the Three Faculties, a Man may as well qualify himself at *Oxford* or *Cambridge* to be a Turky-Merchant as he can to be a Physician: Which is in my Humble Opinion a great sign that some part of the great Wealth they are possess'd of is not so well applied as it might be.

Professors should besides their Stipends allow'd them by the Publick, have Gratifications from every Student they Teach, that Self-Interest as well as Emulation and the Love of Glory might spur them on to Labour and Assiduity. When a Man excels in any one study or part of Learning, and is qualify'd to teach others, he ought to be procured if Money will purchase him, without regarding what Party, or indeed what Country or Nation he is of, whether Black or White. Universities should be publick Marts for all manner of Literature, as your Annual Fairs, that are kept at *Leipsich, Francfort,* and other places in *Germany,* are for different Wares and Merchandizes, where no difference is made between Natives and Foreigners, and which Men resort to from all Parts of the World with equal Freedom and equal Privilege.

From paying the Gratifications I spoke of I would excuse all Students design'd for the Ministry of the Gospel. There is no Faculty so immediately necessary to the Government of a Nation as that of Theology, and as we ought to have great numbers of Divines for the Service of this Island, I would not have the meaner People discouraged from bringing up their Children to that Function. For tho' Wealthy Men, if they have many Sons, sometimes make one of them a Clergyman, as we see even Persons of Quality take up Holy Orders, and there are likewise People of good Sense, especially Divines, that from a Principle of Prudence bring up their Children to that Profession, when they are morally assured that they have Friends or Interest enough, and shall be able either by a good Fellowship at the University, Advowsons or other means to procure 'em a Livelihood: But these produce not the large Number of Divines that are Yearly Ordain'd, and for the Bulk of the Clergy we are indebted to another Original.

Among the midling People of all Trades there are Bigots who have a Superstitious Awe for a Gown and Cassock: of these there are Multitudes that feel an ardent Desire of having a Son promoted to the Ministry of the Gospel, without considering what is to become of them afterwards, and many a kind Mother in this Kingdom, without consulting her own Circumstances or her Child's Capacity, transported with this laudable Wish is Daily Feasting on this pleasing Thought, and often before her Son is Twelve Years Old, mixing Maternal Love with Devotion, throws her self into Extasies and Tears of Satisfaction, by reflecting on the Future Enjoyment she is to receive from seeing him stand in a Pulpit, and with her own Ears hearing him Preach the Word of God. It is to this Religous Zeal, or at least the Human Frailties that pass for and represent it, that we owe the great plenty of poor Scholars the Nation enjoys. For considering the inequality of Livings, and the smalness of Benefices up and down the Kingdom, without this happy Disposition in Parents of small Fortune, we could not possibly be furnish'd from any other Quarter with proper Persons for the Ministry, to attend all the Cures of Souls, so pitifully provided for, that no Mortal could Live upon them that had been Educated in any Tolerable Plenty, unless he was possess'd of real Virtue, which it is Foolish and indeed Injurious, we should more expect from the Clergy than we generally find it in the Laity.

The great Care I would take to promote that part of Learning which is more immediately useful to Society, should not make me neglect the more Curious and Polite, but all the Liberal Arts and every Branch of Literature should be encouraged throughout the Kingdom, more than they are, if my wishing could do it. In every County there should be one or more Large Schools Erected at the Publick Charge, for Latin and Greek that should be divided into Six or more Classes, with particular Masters in each of them. The whole should be under the Care and Inspection of some Men of Letters in Authority, who would not only be Titular Governours, but actually take pains at least Twice a Year, in hearing every Class thoroughly examin'd by the Master of it, and not content themselves with Judging of the Progress the Scholars had made from Themes and other Exercises that had been made out of their Sight.

At the same time I would discourage and hinder the multiplicity of those petty Schools, that never would have had any Existence had the Masters of them not been extremely indigent. It is a Vulgar Error that no body can spell or write *English* well without a little smatch of *Latin*. This is upheld by Pedants for their own Interest, and by none more strenuously maintain'd than such of 'em as are poor Scholars in more than one Sense: in the mean time it is

an abominable Falshood. I have known, and am still ac-
quainted with several, and some of the Fair Sex, that never
learn'd any *Latin*, and yet keep to strict Orthography, and
write admirable good Sense; whereas on the other hand every
body may meet with the Scriblings of pretended Scholars
at least, such as went to a Grammar School for several Years,
that have Grammar Faults and are ill-spelt. The understand-
ing of *Latin* thoroughly is highly necessary to all that are
design'd for any of the Learned Professions, and I would
have no Gentleman without Literature; even those who are
to be brought up Attorneys, Surgeons and Apothecaries,
should be much better vers'd in that Language than gener-
ally they are; but to Youth who afterwards are to get a
Livelihood in Trades and Callings, in which *Latin* is not
daily wanted, it is of no Use, and the learning of it an evi-
dent Loss of just so much Time and Money as are bestowed
upon it. When Men come into Business, what was taught
them of it in those petty Schools is either soon forgot, or
only fit to make them impertinent, and often very trouble-
some in Company. Few Men can forbear valuing them-
selves on any Knowledge they had once acquired, even
after they have lost it; and unless they are very modest and
discreet, the undigested scraps, which such People com-
monly remember of *Latin*, seldom fail of rendering them at
one time or other ridiculous to those who understand it.

Reading and Writing I would Treat as we do Musick
and Dancing, I would not hinder them nor force them upon
the Society: As long as there was any thing to be got by
them, there would be Masters enough to Teach them; but
nothing should be taught for nothing but at Church: And
here I would exclude even those who might be design'd
for the Ministry of the Gospel; for if Parents are so miser-
ably Poor that they can't afford their Children these first
Elements of Learning, it is Impudence in them to aspire
any further.

It would Encourage likewise the lower sort of People to give their Children this part of Education, if they could see them preferr'd to those of idle Sots or sorry Rake-hells, that never knew what it was to provide a Rag for their Brats but by Begging. But now when a Boy or a Girl are wanted for any small Service, we reckon it a Duty to employ our Charity Children before any other. The Education of them looks like a Reward for being Vicious and Unactive, a Benefit commonly bestow'd on Parents, who deserve to be punish'd for shamefully neglecting their Families. In one Place you may hear a Rascal Half-drunk, Damning himself, call for th'other Pot, and as a good Reason for it add, that his Boy is provided for in Cloaths and has his Schooling for nothing: In another you shall see a poor Woman in great Necessity, whose Child is to be taken care of, because herself is a Lazy Slut, and never did any thing to remedy her Wants in good earnest, but bewailing them at a Gin-shop.

If every Body's Children are well taught, who by their own Industry can Educate them at our Universities, there will be Men of Learning enough to supply this Nation and such another; and Reading, Writing or Arithmetick would never be wanting in the Business that requires them, tho' none were to learn them but such whose Parents could be at the Charge of it. It is not with Letters as it is with the Gifts of the Holy Ghost, that they may not be purchased with Money; and bought Wit, if we believe the Proverb, is none of the Worst.

I thought it necessary to say thus much of Learning, to obviate the Clamours of the Enemies to Truth and fair Dealing, who had I not so amply explain'd my self on this Head, would have represented me as a Mortal Foe to all Literature and useful Knowledge, and a wicked Advocate for Universal Ignorance and Stupidity. I shall now make good my promise of answering what I knew the Wellwishers to Charity-Schools would object against me, by saying that they brought up the Children under their care to Warrantable and Laborious Trades, and not to Idleness as I did insinuate.

I have sufficiently shew'd already, why going to School was Idleness if compared to Working, and exploded this sort of Education in the Children of the Poor, because it Incapacitates them ever after for down right Labour, which is their proper Province, and in every Civil Society a Portion they ought not to repine or grumble at, if exacted from them with Discretion and Humanity. What remains is that I should speak as to their putting them out to Trades, which I shall endeavour to demonstrate to be destructive to the Harmony of a Nation, and an impertinent Intermedling with what few of these Governours know any thing of.

In order to this let us examine into the Nature of Societies, and what the Compound ought to consist of if we would raise it to as high a degree of Strength, Beauty and Perfection, as the Ground we are to do it upon will let us. The Variety of Services that are required to supply the Luxurious and Wanton Desires as well as real Necessities of Man, with all their subordinate Callings, is in such a Nation as ours prodigious; yet it is certain that, tho' the number of those several Ocupations be excessively great, it is far from being infinite; if you add one more than is required it must be superfluous. If a Man had a good Stock and the best Shop in *Cheapside* to sell Turbands in, he would be ruin'd, and if *Demetrius* or any other Silversmith made nothing but *Diana*'s Shrines he would not get his Bread, now the Worship of that Goddess is out of Fashion. As it is Folly to set up Trades that are not wanted, so what is next to it is to encrease in any one Trade the Numbers beyond what are required. As things are managed with us, it would be preposterous to have as many Brewers as there are Bakers, or as many Woollendrapers as there are Shoemakers. This Proportion as to Numbers in every Trade finds it self, and is never better kept than when no body meddles or interferes with it.

People that have Children to educate that must get their Livelihood, are always consulting and deliberating what Trade or Calling they are to bring them up to, till they are fix'd, and thousands think on this that hardly think at all on any thing else. First they confine themselves to their Circumstances, and he that can give but Ten Pounds with his Son must not look out for a Trade where they ask an Hundred with an Apprentice: but the next they think on is always which will be the most advantageous: if there be a Calling where at that time People are more generally employ'd than they are in any other in the same Reach, there are presently half a score Fathers ready to supply it with their Sons. Therefore the greatest Care most Companies have is about the Regulation of the Number of Prentices. Now when all Trades complain, and perhaps justly, that they are overstock'd, you manifestly injure that Trade, to which you add one Member more than would flow from the Nature of Society. Besides that the Governors of Charity Schools don't deliberate so much what Trade is the best, but what Tradesmen they can get that will take the Boys with such a Sum; and few Men of Substance and Experience will have any thing to do with these Children: they are afraid of a hundred Inconveniencies from the necessitous Parents of them: So that they are bound at least most commonly, either to Sots and neglectful Masters, or else such as are very needy and don't care what becomes of their Prentices, after they have received the Money: by which it seems as if we study'd nothing more than to have a perpetual Nursery for Charity Schools.

When all Trades and Handicrafts are overstock'd, it is a certain sign there is a Fault in the management of the Whole; for it is impossible there should be too many People if the Country is able to Feed them. Are Provisions Dear? whose Fault is that, as long as you have Ground Untill'd and Hands Unemploy'd? But I shall be answer'd, that to encrease Plenty, must at long run undo the Farmer or lessen the Rents all over *England*. To which I reply, that what the Husbandman complains of most is what I would redress: The greatest Grievance of Farmers, Gardiners and others, where hard Labour is required, and dirty Work to be done, is that they can't get Servants for the same Wages they used to have them at. The Day Labourer grumbles at Sixteen Pence to do no other Drudgery than what Thirty Years ago his Grandfather did chearfully for half the Money. As to the Rents, it is impossible they should fall whilst you encrease your Numbers, but the price of Provisions and all Labour in general must fall with them if not before; and a Man of a Hundred and Fifty Pounds a Year, has no reason to complain that his Income is reduced to One Hundred, if he can Buy as much for that One Hundred as before he could have done for Two.

There is no Intrinsick Worth in Money but what is alterable with the Times, and whether a Guinea goes for Twenty Pounds or for a Shilling, it is (as I have already hinted before) the Labour of the Poor and not the high and low value that is set on Gold or Silver, which all the comforts of Life must arise from. It is in our Power to have a much greater Plenty than we enjoy, if Agriculture and Fishery were taken care of, as they might be; but we are so little capable of encreasing our Labour, that we have hardly Poor enough to do what is necessary to make us subsist. The proportion of the Society is spoil'd, and the Bulk of the Nation which should every where consist of Labouring Poor, that are unacquainted with every thing but their Work, is too little for the other parts. In all Business where downright Labour is shun'd or over-paid, there is plenty of People. To One Merchant you have Ten Book-keepers, or at least Pretenders; and every where in the Country the Farmer wants Hands. Ask for a Footman that for some time has been in Gentlemens Families and you'll get a Dozen that are all Butlers. You may have Chamber-maids by the Score, but you can't get a Cook under Extravagant Wages.

No Body will do the Dirty Slavish Work, that can help it. I don't discommend them, but all these things shew that the People of the meanest Rank know too much to be Serviceable to us. Servants require more than Masters and Mistresses can afford, and what madness is it to Encourage them in this, by industriously encreasing at our Cost that Knowledge which they will be sure to make us pay for over again! And it is not only that those who are Educated at our own Expence encroach upon us, but the Raw Ignorant Country Wenches and Boobily Fellows that can do, and are good for, nothing impose upon us likewise. The scarcity of Servants occasion'd by the Education of the first, gives a Handle to the latter of advancing their Price, and demanding what ought only to be given to Servants that understand their Business, and have most of the good Qualities that can be required in them.

There is no place in the World where there are more Clever Fellows to look at or to do an Errand than some of our Footmen; but what are they good for in the main? The greatest part of them are Rogues and not to be trusted; and if they are Honest half of them are Sots, and will get Drunk three or four times a Week. The surly ones are generally Quarrelsome, and valuing their Manhood beyond all other considerations, care not what Cloaths they spoyl, or what Disappointments they may occasion, when their Prowess is in Question. Those who are Good-natured, are generally sad Whoremasters that are ever running after the Wenches, and spoyl all the Maid Servants they come near. Many of them are Guilty of all these Vices, Whoring,

Drinking, Quarrelling, and yet shall have all their Faults
over-look'd and bore with, because they are Men of good
Mien and humble Address that know how to wait on
Gentlemen; which is an unpardonable Folly in Masters,
and generally ends in the Ruin of Servants.

Some few there are that are not addicted to any of these
Failings, and understand their Duty besides; but as these
are Rarities so there is not one in Fifty but what over-rates
himself; his Wages must be extravagant and you can never
have done giving him; every thing in the House is his
Perquisite, and he won't stay with you unless his Vails[50]
are sufficient to maintain a midling Family; and tho' you
had taken him from the Dunghill, out of an Hospital, or a
Prison, you shall never keep him longer than he can make
of his Place what in his high Estimation of himself he shall
think he deserves; Nay, the best and most civilis'd, that
never were Saucy or Impertinent, will leave the most in-
dulgent Master, and, to get handsomely away, frame Fifty
Excuses, and tell downright Lyes as soon as they can mend
themselves. A Man, who keeps an Half-Crown or Twelve-
penny Ordinary, looks not more for Money from his Custo-
mers than a Footman does from every Guest that Dines or
Sups with his Master; and I question whether the one does
not often think a Shilling or Half a Crown, according to
the Quality of the Person, his due as much as the other.

A Housekeeper who cannot afford to make many Enter-
tainments, and does not often invite People to his Table
can have no creditable Man-Servant, and is forc'd to take
up with some Country Booby or other Awkward Fellow,
who will likewise give him the Slip as soon as he imagines
himself fit for any other Service, and is made wiser by his
rascally Companions. All noted Eating Houses and Places
that many Gentlemen resort to for Diversion or Business,
more especially the Precincts of *Westminster-Hall*, are the

50. Gratuities. – Ed.

great Schools for Servants, where the dullest Fellows may have their Understandings improved; and get rid at once of their Stupidity and their Innocence. They are the Accademies for Footmen where Publick Lectures are daily read on all Sciences of low Debauchery by the experienc'd Professors of them, and Students are instructed in above Seven Hundred illiberal Arts, how to Cheat, Impose upon, and find out the blind side of their Masters, with so much Application that in few Years they become Graduates in Iniquity. Young Gentlemen and others that are not thoroughly vers'd in the World, when they get such knowing Sharpers in their Service, are commonly indulging above measure; and for Fear of discovering their want of Experience hardly dare to contradict or deny them any thing, which is often the Reason that by allowing them unreasonable Privileges they expose their Ignorance when they are most endeavouring to conceal it.

Some perhaps will lay the things I complain of to the charge of Luxury, of which I said that it could do no Hurt to a Rich Nation, if the Imports never did exceed the Exports; but I don't think this imputation Just, and nothing ought to be scored on the Account of Luxury, that is downright the Effect of Folly. A Man may be very extravagant in indulging his Ease and his Pleasure, and render the Enjoyment of the World as Operose and Expensive as they can be made, if he can afford it, and at the same time shew his good Sense in every thing about him : This he cannot be said to do if he industriously renders his People incapable of doing him that Service he expects from them. 'Tis too much Money, excessive Wages, and unreasonable Vails that spoil Servants in *England*. A Man may have Five and Twenty Horses in his Stables without being Guilty of Folly, if it suits with the rest of his Circumstances, but if he keeps but one and over feeds it to shew his Wealth he is a Fool for his Pains. Is it not Madness to suffer that Servants should take three and others five *per Cent.* of what they pay to Tradesmen for their Masters, as is so well known to Watchmakers and others that sell Toys, superfluous Nicknacks, and other Curiosities, if they deal with People of Quality, and Fashionable Gentlemen that are above telling their own Money? If they should accept of a present when offer'd, it might be conniv'd at, but it is an unpardonable Impudence that they should claim it as their due, and contend for it if refused. Those who have all the Necessaries of Life provided for, can have no occasion for Money but what does them hurt as Servants, unless they were to hoard it up for Age or Sickness, which among our *Skip-kennels*[51] is not very common, and even then it makes them Saucy and Insupportable.

I am credibly inform'd that a parcel of Footmen are arriv'd to that height of Insolence as to have enter'd into a Society together, and made Laws by which they oblige themselves not to serve for less than such a Sum, nor carry Burdens or any Bundle or Parcel above a certain Weight, not exceeding Two or Three Pounds, with other regulations directly opposite to the Interest of those they Serve, and altogether destructive to the use they were design'd for. If any of them be turn'd away for strictly adhearing to the Orders of this Honourable Corporation, he is taken care of till another Service is provided for him, and there is no Money wanting at any time to commence and maintain a Law-suit against any Master that shall pretend to strike or offer any other Injury to his Gentleman Footman, contrary to the Statutes of their Society. If this be true, as I have reason to believe it is, and they are suffer'd to go on in Consulting and Providing for their own Ease and Conveniency any further, we may expect quickly to see the *French* Comedy *Le Maitre Le Valet*[52] Acted in good earnest

51. Footmen. – Ed.
52. A play by Scarron. – Ed.

in most Families, which if not redress'd in a little time, and those Footmen encrease their Company to the Number it is possible they may, as well as Assemble when they please with Impunity, it will be in their Power to make a Tragedy of it whenever they have a mind to 't.

But suppose those Apprehensions frivolous and groundless, it is undeniable that Servants in general are daily encroaching upon Masters and Mistresses, and endeavouring to be more upon the Level with them. They not only seem sollicitous to abolish the low dignity of their Condition, but have already considerably rais'd it in the common Estimation from the Original meanness which the Publick Welfare requires it should always remain in. I don't say that these things are altogether owing to Charity Schools, there are other Evils they may be partly ascrib'd to. *London* is too big for the Country, and in several Respects we are wanting to our selves. But if a Thousand Faults were to concur before the Inconveniencies could be produced we Labour under, can any Man doubt who will consider what I have said, that Charity Schools are Accessary, or at least that they are more likely, to Create and Encrease than to lessen or redress those Complaints.

The only thing of Weight then that can be said in their behalf is, that so many Thousand Children are Educated by them in the Christian Faith and the Principles of the Church of *England*. To demonstrate that this is not a sufficient Plea for them, I must desire the Reader, as I hate Repetitions, to look back on what I have said before, to which I shall add, that whatever is necessary to Salvation and requisite for Poor Labouring People to know concerning Religion, that Children learn at School, may fully as well either by Preaching or Catechizing, be taught at Church, from which or some other Place of Worship I would not have the meanest of a Parish that is able to walk to it be absent on *Sundays*. It is the Sabbath the most use-

ful Day in Seven that is set apart for Divine Service and
Religious Exercise as well as resting from Bodily Labour,
and it is a Duty incumbent on all Magistrates to take par-
ticular Care of that Day. The Poor more especially and
their Children should be made to go to Church on it both
in the Fore and Afternoon, because they have no Time on
any other. By Precept and Example they ought to be en-
couraged and used to it from their very Infancy; the wilful
Neglect of it ought to be counted Scandalous, and if down-
right Compulsion to what I urge might seem too Harsh and
perhaps impracticable, all Diversions at least ought strictly
to be prohibited, and the Poor hindred from every Amuse-
ment Abroad that might allure or draw them from it.

Where this Care is taken by the Magistrates as far as it
lies in their Power, Ministers of the Gospel may instill into
the smallest Capacities, more Piety and Devotion, and better
Principles of Virtue and Religion than Charity-Schools ever
did or ever will produce, and those who complain, when
they have such Opportunities that they cannot imbue their
Parishioners with sufficient Knowledge of what they stand
in need of as Christians, without the assistance of Reading
and Writing, are either very Lazy or very Ignorant and un-
deserving themselves.

That the most Knowing are not the most Religious, will
be evident if we make a Trial between People of different
Abilities even in this Juncture, where going to Church is
not made such an Obligation on the Poor and Illiterate, as
it might be. Let us pitch upon a Hundred Poor Men the
first we can light on, that are above Forty, and were brought
up to hard Labour from their Infancy, such as never went
to School at all, and always lived remote from Knowledge
and Great Towns: Let us compare to these an equal num-
ber of very good Scholars, that shall all have had Univer-
sity Education; and be, if you will, half of them Divines,
well versed in Philology and Polemick Learning; then let

us impartially examine into the Lives and Conversations of both, and I dare engage that among the first who can neither Read nor Write, we shall meet with more Union and Neighbourly Love, less Wickedness and Attachment to the World, more Content of Mind, more Innocence, Sincerity, and other good Qualities that conduce to the Publick Peace and Real Felicity, than we shall find among the latter, where on the contrary, we may be assured of the height of Pride and Insolence, eternal Quarrels and Dissentions, Irreconcilable Hatreds, Strife, Envy, Calumny and other Vices destructive to mutual Concord which the illiterate labouring Poor are hardly ever tainted with to any considerable Degree.

I am very well persuaded, that what I have said in the last Paragraph will be no News to most of my Readers; but if it be Truth, why should it be stifled, and why must our concern for Religion be eternally made a Cloak to hide our real Drifts and worldly Intentions? Would both Parties agree to pull off the Masque, we should soon discover that whatever they pretend to, they aim at nothing so much in Charity-Schools as to strengthen their Party, and that the great Sticklers for the Church, by Educating Children in the Principles of Religion, mean, inspiring them with a Superlative Veneration for the Clergy of the Church of *England*, and a strong Aversion and immortal Animosity against all that dissent from it. To be assured of this, we are but to mind on the one hand, what Divines are most admired for their Charity Sermons and most fond to Preach them, and on the other; whether of late Years we have had any Riots or Party Scuffles among the Mob, in which the Youth of a Famous Hospital in this City, were not always the most forward Ring-leaders.

The Grand Asserters of Liberty, who are ever guarding themselves and Skirmishing against Arbitrary Power, often when they are in no danger of it, are generally speaking, not very Superstitious, nor seem to lay great stress on any Modern Apostleship: Yet some of these likewise speak up lowdly for Charity-Schools, but what they expect from 'em has no relation to Religion or Morality: They only look upon them as the proper means to destroy and disappoint the power of the Priests over the Laity. Reading and Writing encrease Knowledge, and the more Men know, the better they can Judge for themselves, and they imagine that, if Knowledge could be rendred Universal, People could not be Priest-rid, which is the thing they fear the most.

The First, I confess, it is very probable will get their Aim. But sure Wise Men that are not Red-hot for a Party or Bigots to the Priests, will not think it worth while to suffer so many Inconveniencies, as Charity-Schools may be the Occasion of, only to promote the Ambition and Power of the Clergy. To the other I would answer, that if all those who are Educated at the Charge of their Parents or Relations, will but think for themselves and refuse to have their reason imposed upon by the Priests, we need not be concerned for what the Clergy will work upon the Ignorant that have no Education at all. Let them make the most of them, considering the Schools we have for those who can and do pay for Learning, it is ridiculous to imagine that the abolishing of Charity-Schools would be a step towards any Ignorance that could be prejudicial to the Nation.

I would not be thought Cruel, and am well assured if I know any thing of my self, that I abhor Inhumanity; but to be Compassionate to excess where Reason forbids it, and the general Interest of the Society requires steadiness of Thought and Resolution, is an unpardonable Weakness. I know it will be ever urged against me, that it is Barbarous the Children of the Poor should have no Opportunity of exerting themselves as long as God has not debarr'd them from Natural Parts and Genius more than the Rich. But I cannot think this is harder than it is, that they should not have Money as long as they have the same Inclinations to spend as others. That Great and Useful Men have sprung from Hospitals, I don't deny, but it is likewise very probable, that when they were first employ'd, many as capable as themselves not brought up in Hospitals were neglected, that with the same good Fortune would have done as well as they, if they had been made use of instead of 'em.

There are many examples of Women that have excell'd in Learning, and even in War, but this is no reason we should bring 'em all up to *Latin* and *Greek* or else Military Discipline, instead of Needle-work and Housewifry. But there is no scarcity of Sprightliness or Natural Parts among us, and no Soil or Climate has Human Creatures to boast of, better form'd either inside or outside than this Island generally produces. But it is not Wit, Genius or Docility we want, but Diligence, Application, and Assiduity.

Abundance of hard and dirty Labour is to be done, and course Living is to be complied with: Where shall we find a better Nursery for these Necessities than the Children of the Poor? none certainly are nearer to it or fitter for it. Besides that the things I have call'd Hardships, neither seem nor are such to those, who have been brought up to 'em, and know no better. There is not a more contented People among us, than those who work the hardest and are the least Acquainted with the Pomp and Delicacies of the World.

These are Truths that are undeniable; yet I know few People will be pleas'd to have them divulg'd; what makes them odious is an unreasonable Vein of Petty Reverence for the Poor, that runs through most Multitudes, and more particularly in this Nation, and arises from a mixture of Pity, Folly and Superstition. It is from a lively sense of this Compound that Men cannot endure to hear or see any thing said or acted against the Poor; without considering, how Just the one, or Insolent the other. So a Beggar must not be beat tho' he strikes you first. Journeymen Taylors go to Law with their Masters and are obstinate in a wrong Cause,[53] yet they must be pitied; and Murmuring Weavers must be reliev'd, and have Fifty silly things done to humour them, tho' in the midst of their Poverty they insult their Betters, and on all Occasions appear to be more prone to make Holy Days and Riots than they are to Working or Sobriety.

This puts me in mind of our Wool, which considering the posture of our Affairs, and the Behaviour of the Poor, I sincerely believe ought not upon any Account to be carried abroad: But if we look into the reason, why suffering it to be fetch'd away is so pernicious, our heavy Complaint and Lamentations that it is exported can be no great Credit to us. Considering the mighty and manifold Hazards that must be run before it can be got off the Coast, and safely Landed beyond Sea; it is manifest that the Foreigners, before they can work our Wool, must pay more for it very considerably, than what we can have it for at Home. Yet notwithstanding this great difference in the Prime Cost, they can afford to sell the Manufactures made of it cheaper at Foreign Markets than our selves. This is the Disaster we groan under, the intollerable Mischief, without which the Exportation of that Commodity could be no greater prejudice to us than that of Tin or Lead, as long as our Hands were fully employ'd, and we had still Wool to spare.

There is no People yet come to higher Perfection in the Woollen Manufacture, either as to dispatch or goodness of Work, at least in the most considerable Branches, than our selves, and therefore what we complain of can only depend on the difference in the Management of the Poor, between other Nations and ours. If the Labouring People in one

53. In 1720 seven thousand tailors formed a trade union which was outlawed by an act of Parliament later in the year. – Ed.

Country will Work Twelve Hours in a Day, and Six Days in a Week, and in another they are employ'd but Eight Hours in a Day and not above Four Days in a Week, the one is obliged to have Nine Hands for what the other does with Four. But if moreover the Living, the Food and Raiment, and what is consumed by the Workmen of the Industrious costs but half the Money of what is expended among an equal number of the other, the Consequence must be that the first will have the Work of Eighteen Men for the same Price as the other gives for the Work of Four. I would not insinuate neither do I think, that the difference either in diligence or necessaries of Life between us and any Neighbouring Nation is near so great as what I speak of, yet I would have it considered, that half of that difference and much less is sufficient to over-ballance the Disadvantage they labour under as to the Price of Wool.

Nothing to me is more evident than that no Nation in any Manufactory whatever can undersell their Neighbours with whom they are at best but Equals as to Skill and Dispatch, and the conveniency for Working, more especially when the Prime Cost of the thing to be Manufactured is not in their favour, unless they have Provisions, and whatever is relating to their Sustenance Cheaper, or else Workmen that are either more Assiduous and will remain longer at their Work or be content with a meaner and courser way of Living than those of their Neighbours. This is certain, that where Numbers are Equal, the more Laborious People are, and the fewer Hands the same quantity of Work is perform'd by, the greater Plenty there is in a Country of the Necessaries for Life, the more considerable and the cheaper that Country may render its Exports.

It being granted then, that abundance of Work is to be done, the next thing which I think to be likewise undeniable is, that the more chearfully it is done the better, as well for those that perform it as for the rest of the Society. To be happy is to be pleas'd, and the less Notion a Man has of a better way of Living, the more content he'll be with his own; and on the other hand the greater a Man's Knowledge and Experience is in the World, the more exquisite the Delicacy of his Taste, and the more consummate Judge he is of things in general, certainly the more difficult it will be to please him. I would not advance any thing that is Barbarous or Inhuman: But when a Man enjoys himself, Laughs and Sings, and in his Gesture and Behaviour shews me all the tokens of Content and Satisfaction, I pronounce him happy and have nothing to do with his Wit or Capacity. I never enter into the reasonableness of his Mirth, at least I ought not to judge of it by my own Standard, and Argue from the Effect which the thing that makes him merry would have upon me. At that rate a Man that hates Cheese must call me Fool for loving Blue Mold. *De gustibus non est disputandum*[54] is as true in a Metaphorical as it is in the Literal Sense, and the greater the distance is between People as to their Condition, their Circumstances and manner of Living, the less capable they are of Judging of one anothers Troubles or Pleasures.

Had the meanest and most uncivilis'd Peasant leave *Incognito* to observe the greatest King for a Fortnight: tho' he might pick out several things he would like for himself, yet he would find a great many more, which, if the Monarch and he were to change Conditions, he would wish for his part to have immediately alter'd or redress'd, and which with amazement he sees the King submit to. And again if the Sovereign was to examine the Peasant in the same manner. His Labour would be Insufferable, the Dirt and Squallor, his Diet and Amours, his Pastimes and Recreations would be all abominable; but then what Charms would he find in the other's peace of Mind, the Calmness

54. 'There is no disputing tastes', according to the well-known Latin proverb. – Ed.

and Tranquillity of his Soul. No Necessity for Dissimulation with any of his Family, or feign'd Affection to his Mortal Enemies; no Wife in a Foreign Interest, no Danger to apprehend from his Children; no Plots to unravel, no Poyson to fear; no popular Statesman at Home or cunning Courts Abroad to manage: no seeming Patriots to bribe; no unsatiable Favourite to gratify; no Selfish Ministry to obey, no divided Nation to please, or fickle Mob to humour that would direct and interfere with his Pleasures.

Was impartial reason to be Judge between real Good and real Evil, and a Catalogue made accordingly of the several Delights and Vexations differently to be met with in both Stations, I question whether the Condition of Kings would be at all preferable to that of Peasants, even as Ignorant and Laborious as I seem to require the latter to be. The reason why the generality of People would rather be Kings than Peasants is first owing to Pride and Ambition, that is deeply riveted in Human Nature, and which to gratify we daily see Men undergo and despise the greatest hazards and difficulties. Secondly to the difference there is in the force with which our Affection is wrought upon as the Objects are either Material or Spiritual. Things that immediately strike our outward senses act more violently upon our Passions than what is the result of Thought and the dictates of the most demonstrative Reason, and there is a much stronger Biass to gain our Liking or Aversion in the first than there is in the latter.

Having thus demonstrated that what I urge could be no Injury or the least diminution of Happiness to the Poor, I leave it to the Judicious Reader, whether it is not more probable we should encrease our Exports by the methods I hint at, than by sitting still and Damning and Sinking our Neighbours for beating us at our own Weapons, some of them out selling us in Manufactures made of our own Product which they dearly purchas'd, others growing Rich in spight of Distance and Trouble, by the same Fish which we neglect, tho' it is ready to jump into our Mouths.

As by discouraging Idleness with Art and Steadiness you may compel the Poor to labour without Force, so by bringing them up in Ignorance you may inure them to real Hardships without being ever sensible themselves that they are such. By bringing them up in Ignorance, I mean no more, as I have hinted long ago, than that as to Worldly Affairs their Knowledge should be confin'd within the Verge of their own Occupations, at least that we should not take pains to extend it beyond those Limits. When by these two Engines we shall have made Provisions, and consequently Labour cheap, we must infallibly out-sell our Neighbours; and at the same time encrease our Numbers. This is the Noble and Manly way of encountring the Rivals of our Trade, and by dint of Merit out-doing them at Foreign Markets.

To allure the Poor we make use of policy in some cases with Success. Why should we be neglectful of it in the most important point, when they make their boast that they will not live as the Poor of other Nations? If we cannot alter their Resolution, why should we applaud the Justness of their Sentiments against the Common Interest. I have often wondred formerly how an *English Man* that pretended to have the Honour and Glory as well as the Welfare of his Country at Heart, could take delight in the Evening to hear an Idle Tenant that owed him above a Years Rent ridicule the *French* for wearing Wooden Shoes, when in the Morning he had had the Mortification of hearing the great King *William*, that Ambitious Monarch as well as able Statesman, openly own to the World and with Grief and Anger in his looks complain of the Exorbitant Power of *France*. Yet I don't recommend Wooden Shoes, nor do the maxims I would introduce require Arbitrary Power in one Person. Liberty and Property I hope may remain secured, and yet the Poor be better employ'd than they are, tho' their Children should wear out their Cloaths by useful Labour, and blacken them with Country Dirt for something, instead of tearing them off their Backs at play, and dawbing 'em with Ink for nothing.

There is above Three or Four Hundred Years Work, for a Hundred Thousand Poor more than we have in this Island. To make every part of it Useful, and the whole thoroughly Inhabited, many Rivers are to be made Navigable, Canals to be cut in Hundreds of Places. Some Lands are to be drain'd and secured from Inundations for the future: Abundance of barren Soil is to be made fertile, and Thousands of Acres rendred more beneficial by being made more accessible. *Dii Laboribus omnia vendunt.*[55] There is no difficulty of this Nature, that Labour and Patience cannot Surmount. The highest Mountains may be thrown into their Valleys that stand ready to receive them, and Bridges might be laid where now we would not dare to think of it. Let us look back on the Stupendious Works of the *Romans*, more especially their Highways and Aqueducts. Let us consider in one view the vast extent of several of their Roads, how substantial they made them, and what duration they have been of, and in another a poor Traveller that at every Ten Miles end is stop'd by a Turnpike, and dunn'd for a Penny for mending the Roads in the Summer, with what every Body knows will be Dirt before the Winter that succeeds it is expired.

The Conveniency of the Publick ought ever to be the Publick Care, and no Private Interest of a Town or a whole County should ever hinder the Execution of a Project or Contrivance that would manifestly tend to the Improvement of the whole; and every Member of the Legislature, who knows his Duty and would chuse, rather to act like a wise Man, than curry Favour with his Neighbours, will

55. 'The gods sell everything for labour.' Latin proverb. – Ed.

prefer the least Benefit accruing to the whole Kingdom to the most visible Advantage of the Place he serves for.

We have Materials of our own, and want neither Stone nor Timber to do any thing, and was the Money that People give uncompell'd to Beggars who don't deserve it, and what every Housekeeper is obliged to pay to the Poor of his Parish that is otherwise employ'd or ill applied, to be put together every Year, it would make a sufficient Fund to keep a great many Thousands at work. I don't say this because I think it practicable, but only to shew that we have Money enough to spare to employ vast multitudes of Labourers: neither should we want so much for it as we perhaps might imagine. When it is taken for granted that a Soldier, whose Strength and Vigour is to be kept up at least as much as any Body's, can Live upon Six Pence a Day, I can't conceive the Necessity of giving the greatest part of the Year Sixteen and Eighteen Pence to a Day Labourer.

The Fearful and Cautious People that are ever Jealous of their Liberty, I know will cry out, that where the Multitudes I speak of should be kept in constant Pay, Property and Privileges would be precarious. But they might be answer'd, that sure means might be found out, and such Regulations made, as to the Hands in which to trust the management and direction of these Labourers; that it would be impossible for the Prince or any Body else to make an ill Use of their numbers.

What I have said in the Four or Five last Paragraphs, I foresee will with abundance of Scorn be Laugh'd at by many of my Readers, and at best be call'd Building Castles in the Air; but whether that is my Fault or theirs is a Question. When the Publick Spirit has left a Nation, they not only lose their Patience with it, and all thoughts of Perseverance, but become likewise so narrow-soul'd, that it is a pain for them even to think of things that are of uncommon extent or require great length of Time; and whatever is Noble or Sublime in such Conjunctures is counted Chimerical. Where deep Ignorance is entirely routed and expell'd, and low Learning promiscuously scatter'd on all the People, Self-Love turns Knowledge into Cunning, and the more this last Qualification prevails in any Country the more the People will fix all their Cares, Concern and Application on the Time present, without regard of what is to come after them, or hardly ever thinking beyond the next Generation.

But as Cunning, according to my Lord *Verulam*, is but Lefthanded Wisdom, so a prudent Legislature ought to provide against this Disorder of the Society as soon as the Symptoms of it appear, among which the following are the most obvious. Imaginary Rewards are generally despised: every body is for turning the Penny and short Bargains: he that is diffident of every thing and believes nothing but what he sees with his own Eyes is counted the most prudent, and in all their Dealings Men seem to Act from no other Principle than that of the Devil take the hindmost. Instead of planting Oaks, that will require a Hundred and Fifty Years before they are fit to be cut down, they Build Houses with a design that they shall not stand above Twelve or Fourteen Years. All Heads run upon the uncertainty of things, and the vicissitudes of human Affairs. The Mathematicks become the only valuable Study, and are made use of in every thing even where it is ridiculous, and Men seem to repose no greater Trust in Providence than they would in a Broken Merchant.

It is the Business of the publick to supply the Defects of the Society, and take that in hand first which is most neglected by private Persons. Contraries are best cured by Contraries, and therefore as Example is of greater efficacy than Precept in the amendment of National Failings, the Legislature ought to resolve upon some great undertakings that must be the Work of Ages as well as vast Labour, and convince the World that they did nothing without an anxious regard to their latest Posterity. This will fix or at least help to settle the volatile Genius and fickle Spirit of the Kingdom, put us in mind that we are not born for our selves only, and be a means of rendring Men less distrustful, and inspiring them with a true love for their Country, and a tender Affection for the Ground it self, than which nothing is more necessary to aggrandize a Nation. Forms of Government may alter, Religions and even Languages may change, but *Great Britain* or at least (if that likewise might lose its Name) the Island it self will remain and in all human probability last as long as any part of the Globe. All Ages have ever paid their kind Acknowledgments to their Ancestors for the Benefits derived from them, and a Christian who enjoys the multitude of Fountains and vast Plenty of Water to be met with in the City of St. *Peter*, is an ungrateful Wretch if he never casts a thankful Remembrance on Old *Pagan Rome*, that took such prodigious Pains to procure it.

When this Island shall be cultivated and every Inch of it made Habitable and Useful, and the whole the most convenient and agreeable Spot upon Earth, all the Cost and Labour laid out upon it, will be gloriously Repaid by the Incense of them that shall come after us; and those who burn with the Noble Zeal and desire after Immortality, and took such Care to improve their Country may rest satisfy'd, that a Thousand and Two Thousand Years hence they shall live in the Memory and everlasting Praises of the future Ages that shall then enjoy it.

Here I should have concluded this Rhapsody of Thoughts, but something comes in my Head concerning the main Scope and Design of this Essay, which is to prove the Necessity there is for a certain Portion of Ignorance in a Well-order'd Society, that I must not omit, because by mentioning it I shall make an Argument on my side of what if I had not spoke of it, might easily have appear'd as a strong Objection against me. It is the Opinion of most People, and mine among the rest, that the most commendable Quality of the present Czar of *Muscovy*[56] is his unwearied Application in raising his Subjects from their native Stupidity and Civilizing his Nation: but then we must consider it is what they stood in need of, and that not long ago the greatest part of them were next to Brute Beasts. In proportion to the Extent of his Dominions and the Multitudes he Commands, he had not that Number or Variety of Tradesmen and Artificers which the true Improvement of the Country required, and therefore was in the right in leaving no Stone unturn'd to procure them. But what is that to us who labour under a contrary Disease? Sound Politicks are to the Social Body what the Art of Medicine is to the Natural, and no Physician would treat a Man in a Lethargy as if he was sick for want of Rest, or prescribe in a Dropsy what should be administred in a Diabetes. In short, *Russia* has too few Knowing Men, and *Great Britain* too many.

56. Peter the Great, who reigned from 1682 to 1725. – Ed.

A

Search into the Nature of Society[57]

57. This essay was added in 1723. – Ed.

The Generality of Moralists and Philosophers have hitherto agreed that there could be no Virtue without Self-denial, but a late Author, who is now much Read by Men of Sense is of a contrary Opinion, and imagines that Men without any trouble or violence upon themselves may be Naturally Virtuous. He seems to require and expect Goodness in his Species, as we do a sweet taste in Grapes and China Oranges, of which, if any of them are Sower, we boldly pronounce that they are not come to that Perfection their nature is capable of. This Noble Writer (for it is the Lord *Shaftsbury* I mean in his Characteristicks) Fancies, that as Man is made for Society, so he ought to be born with a kind Affection to the whole, of which he is a part, and a propensity to seek the Welfare of it. In pursuance of this supposition, he calls every Action perform'd with Regard to the publick Good, Virtuous; and all Selfishness, wholly excluding such a Regard, Vice. In respect to our Species he looks upon Virtue and Vice as permanent Realities that must ever be the same in all Countries and all Ages, and imagines that a Man of sound Understanding, by following the rules of Good Sense may not only find out that *Pulchrum & honestum* both in Morality and the Works of Art and Nature, but likewise Govern himself by his Reason with as much ease and readiness as a good Rider manages a well taught Horse by the Bridle.

The attentive Reader, who perused the foregoing part of this Book, will soon perceive that two Systems cannot be more opposite than his Lordship's and mine. His Notions I confess are generous and refined: They are a High

Compliment to Human-Kind, and capable by the help of a little Enthusiasm of Inspiring us with the most Noble Sentiments concerning the Dignity of our exalted Nature : What pity it is that they are not true! I would not advance thus much if I had not already demonstrated in almost every Page of this Treatise, that the Solidity of them is inconsistent with our Daily Experience. But to leave not the least shadow of an Objection that might be made un-answer'd, I design to exspatiate on some things which hitherto I have but slightly touch'd upon, in order to con-vince the Reader, not only that the good and amiable quali-ties of Man are not those that make him beyond other Animals a Sociable Creature; but moreover that it would be utterly impossible, either to raise any Multitudes into a Populous Rich and Flourishing Nation, or when so rais'd, to keep and maintain them in that condition without the assistance of what we call Evil both Natural and Moral.

The better to perform what I have undertaken, I shall previously examine into the Reality of the *pulchrum & honestum,* the το κάλον that the Ancients have talk'd of so much : The meaning of this is to discuss, whether there be a real Worth and Excellency in things, a preeminence of one above another, which every body will always agree to that well understands them; or that there are few things if any, that have the same esteem paid them, and which the same Judgment is past upon in all Countries and all Ages. When we first set out in quest of this Intrinsick Worth, and find one thing better than another and a third better than that, and so on, we begin to entertain great hopes of Suc-cess; but when we meet with several things that are all very good or all very bad, we are puzled and agree not always with our selves, much less with others. There are different Faults as well as Beauties, that as Modes and Fashions alter and Men vary in their Tastes and Humours, will be differ-ently admired or disapproved of.

Judges of Painting will never disagree in Opinion, when a Fine Picture is compared to the dawbing of a Novice; but how strangely have they differ'd as to the Works of Eminent Masters! There are Parties among Connoisseurs, and few of them agree in their esteem as to Ages and Countries, and the best Pictures bear not always the best Prices: A Noted Original will be ever worth more than any Copy that can be made of it by an unknown hand, tho' it should be better. The Value that is set on Paintings depends not only on the Name of the Master and the time of his Age he drew them in, but likewise in a great measure on the scarcity of his Works, and what is still more unreasonable, the Quality of the Persons in whose possession they are, as well as the length of time they have been in Great Families; and if the *Cartons* now at *Hampton-Court* were done by a less Famous Hand than that of *Raphael*, and had a private Person for their owner, who would be forc'd to sell them, they would never yield the tenth part of the Money which with all their Gross Faults they are now esteem'd to be Worth.

Notwithstanding all this, I will readily own, that the Judgment to be made of Painting might become of universal certainty, or at least less alterable and precarious than almost any thing else: The Reason is plain, there is a Standard to go by that always remains the same. Painting is an imitation of Nature, a Copying of things which Men have every where before them. My good humour'd Reader I hope will forgive me, if thinking on this Glorious Invention I make a Reflection a little out of Season, tho' very much conducive to my main design; which is, that Valuable as the Art is I speak of, we are beholden to an imperfection in the chief of our Senses for all the Pleasures and ravishing Delight we receive from this Happy Deceit. I shall explain my self. Air and Space are no Objects of Sight, but as soon as we can see with the least Attention, we observe that the Bulk of the things we see is lessen'd by degrees, as they are further remote from us, and nothing but Experience gain'd from these Observations can teach us to make any tollerable Guesses at the distance of things. If one Born Blind should remain so till Twenty, and then be suddenly bless'd with Sight, he would be strangely puzled as to the difference of distances, and hardly able immediately by his Eyes alone, to determine which was nearest to him, a Post almost within the reach of his Stick, or a Steeple that should be Half a Mile off. Let us look as narrowly as we can upon a Hole in a Wall, that has nothing but the open Air behind it, and we shall not be able to see otherwise, but that the Sky fills up the Vacuity, and is as near us as the back part of the Stones that circumscribe the space where they are wanting. This Circumstance, not to call it a Defect, in our Sence of Seeing, makes us liable to be imposed upon, and every thing, but Motion, may by Art be represented to us on a Flat in the same manner as we see them in Life and Nature. If a Man had never seen this Art put into practice, a Looking Glass might soon convince him that such a thing was possible, and I can't help thinking but that the Reflections from very smooth and well polish'd Bodies made upon our Eyes, must have given the first handle to the inventions of Drawings and Painting.

In the Works of Nature, Worth and Excellency are as uncertain: and even in Human Creatures what is Beautiful in one Country is not so in another. How Whimsical is the Florist in his Choice! Sometimes the Tulip, sometimes the Auricula, and at other times the Carnation shall engross his Esteem, and every Year a new Flower in his Judgment beats all the old ones, tho' it is much inferior to them both in Colour and Shape. Three Hundred Years ago Men were Shaved as closely as they are now: Since that they have wore Beards, and cut them in a vast variety of Forms, that were all as becoming when Fashionable as now they would be Ridiculous. How mean and comically a Man looks that is otherwise Well Dress'd in a Narrow Brim'd Hat when every Body wears Broad ones, and again, how monstrous is a very Great Hat, when the other extreem has been in Fashion for a considerable time. Experience has taught us, that these Modes seldom last above Ten or Twelve Years, and a Man of Threescore must have observ'd five or six Revolutions of 'em at least, yet the beginnings of these Changes, tho' we have seen several, seem always uncouth and are offensive afresh whenever they return. What Mortal can decide which is the Handsomest Abstract from the Mode in being, to wear great Buttons or small ones? The many ways of laying out a Garden Judiciously are almost Innumerable, and what is call'd Beautiful in them varies according to the different Tastes of Nations and Ages. In Grass Plats, Knots and Parterr's a great diversity of Forms is generally agreeable; but a Round may be as pleasing to the Eye as a Square: An Oval cannot be more suitable to one place than it is possible for a Triangle to be to another; and the preeminence an Octogon has over an Hexagon is no greater in Figures, than at Hazard Eight has above Six among the Chances.

Churches, ever since Christians have been able to Build them, resemble the Form of a Cross, with the upper end pointing toward the *East*, and an Architect, where there is room, and it can be conveniently done, who should neglect it, would be thought to have committed an unpardonable Fault: But it would be foolish to expect this of a Turkish Mosque or a Pagan Temple. Among the many Beneficial Laws that have been made these Hundred Years, it is not easy to name one of greater Utility, and at the same time more exempt from all Inconveniencies, than that which has regulated the Dresses of the Dead. Those who were old enough to take notice of things when that Act was made, and are yet alive, must remember the general Clamour that was made against it. At first nothing could be more shocking to Thousands of People than that they were to be Buried in Woollen, and the only thing that made that Law supportable was, that there was room left for People of some Fashion to indulge their Weakness without Extravagancy, considering the other Expences of Funerals where Mourning is given to several, and Rings to a great many. The Benefit that accrues to the Nation from it is so visible that nothing ever could be said in reason to condemn it, which in few Years made the Horrour conceiv'd against it lessen every Day. I observ'd then that Young People who had seen but few in their Coffins did the soonest strike in with the Innovation; but that those who, when the Act was made, had Buried many Friends and Relations remain'd averse to it the longest, and I remember many that never could be reconcil'd to it to their dying Day. By this time Burying in Linnen being almost forgot, it is the general Opinion that nothing could be more decent than Woollen, and the present manner of Dressing a Corps: which shews that our Liking or Disliking of things chiefly depends on Mode and Custom, and the Precept and Example of our Betters and such whom one way or other we think to be Superiour to us.

In Morals there is no greater certainty. Plurality of Wives is odious among Christians, and all the Wit and Learning of a Great Genius in defence of it has been rejected with contempt: But Polygamy is not shocking to a Mahometan. What Men have learn'd from their Infancy Enslaves them, and the Force of Custom warps Nature, and at the same time imitates her in such a manner that it is often difficult to know which of the two we are influenc'd by. In the *East* formerly Sisters Married Brothers, and it was meritorious for a Man to Marry his Mother. Such Alliances are abominable, but it is certain that, whatever Horrour we conceive at the thoughts of them, there is nothing in Nature repugnant against them, but what is built upon Mode and Custom. A Religious Mahometan that has never tasted any Spirituous Liquor, and has often seen People Drunk, may receive as great an aversion against Wine as another with us of the least Morality and Education may have against lying with his Sister, and both imagine that their Antipathy proceeds from Nature. Which is the best Religion? is a Question that has caused more Mischief than all other Questions together. Ask it at *Peking*, at *Constantinople* and at *Rome*, and you'll receive three distinct Answers extremely different from one another, yet all of them equally possitive and peremptory. Christians are well assured of the falsity of the Pagan and Mahometan Superstitions: as to this point there is a perfect Union and Concord among them, but enquire of the several Sects they are divided into; which is the true Church of Christ? And all of them will tell you it is theirs, and to convince you, go together by the Ears.

It is manifest then that the Hunting after this *Pulchrum & Honestum* is not much better than a Wild-Goose-Chace that is but little to be depended upon: But this is not the greatest Fault I find with it. The imaginary Notions that Men may be Virtuous without Self-denial are a vast inlet to Hypocrisy, which being once made habitual, we must not only deceive others, but likewise become altogether unknown to our selves, and in an instance I am going to give, it will appear, how for want of duely examining himself this might happen to a Person of Quality of Parts and Erudition, one every way resembling the Author of the Characteristicks himself.

A Man that has been brought up in Ease and Affluence, if he is of a Quiet Indolent Nature, learns to shun every thing that is troublesome, and chuses to curb his Passions, more because of the inconveniencies that arise from the eager pursuit after Pleasure, and the yeilding to all the demands of our Inclinations, than any dislike he has to sensual Enjoyments; and it is possible, that a Person Educated under a great Philosopher,[58] who was a Mild and good Natur'd as well as able Tutor, may in such happy Circumstances have a better Opinion of his inward State than it really deserves, and believe himself Virtuous, because his Passions lye dormant. He may form fine Notions of the Social Virtues, and the contempt of Death, write well of them in his Closet, and talk Eloquently of them in Company, but you shall never catch him Fighting for his Country, or Labouring to retrieve any National Losses. A Man that deals in Metaphysicks may easily throw himself into an Enthusiasm, and really believe that he does not fear Death whilst it remains out of Sight. But should he be ask'd, why having this Intrepidity either from Nature or acquired by Philosophy, he did not follow Arms when his Country was involv'd in War; or when he saw the Nation daily robb'd by those at the Helm, and the Affairs of the *Exchequer* perplex'd, why he did not go to Court and make use of all his Friends and Interest to be a Lord Treasurer, that by his Integrity and Wise Management he might restore the Publick Credit; It is probable he would answer that he lov'd Retirement, had no other Ambition than to be a Good Man, and never aspired to have any share in the Government, or that he hated all Flatery and Slavish Attendance, the Insincerity of Courts and Bustle of the World. I am willing to believe him, but may not a Man of an Indolent Temper and Unactive Spirit say, and be sincere in, all this, and at the same time indulge his Appetites without being able to subdue them, tho' his Duty Summons him to it. Virtue consists in Action, and whoever is possest of this Social Love and kind Affection to his Species, and by his Birth or Quality can claim any Post in the Publick Management, ought not to sit still when he can be Serviceable, but exert

58. John Locke, who was Shaftesbury's tutor. – Ed.

himself to the utmost for the good of his Fellow Subjects. Had this Noble Person been of a Warlike Genius or a Boysterous Temper, he would have chose another Part in the Drama of Life, and Preach'd a quite contrary Doctrine: For we are ever pushing our Reason which way soever we feel Passion to draw it, and Self-Love pleads to all Human Creatures for their different Views, still furnishing every individual with Arguments to justify their Inclinations.

That boasted middle way, and the calm Virtues recommended in the Characteristicks are good for nothing but to breed Drones, and might qualify a Man for the stupid Enjoyments of a Monastick Life, or at best a Country Justice of Peace, but they would never fit him for Labour and Assiduity, or stir him up to great Atchievements and perilous Undertakings. Man's natural Love of Ease and Idleness and Proneness to indulge his sensual Pleasures, are not to be cured by Precept: His strong Habits and Inclinations can only be subdued by Passions of greater Violence. Preach and Demonstrate to a Coward the unreasonableness of his Fears and you'll not make him Valiant, more than you can make him Taller by bidding him to be Ten Foot high, whereas the secret to raise Courage, as I have made it Publick in *Remark R,* is almost infallible.

The Fear of Death is the strongest when we are in our greatest Vigour, and our Appetite is keen; when we are sharp Sighted, Quick of Hearing, and every part performs its Office. The reason is plain, because then Life is most delicious and our Selves most capable of enjoying it. How comes it then that a Man of Honour should so easily accept of a Challenge tho' at Thirty and in perfect Health? It is his Pride that conquers his Fear: For when his Pride is not concern'd this Fear will appear most glaringly. If he is not used to the Sea let him but be in a Storm, or, if he never was Ill before, have but a sore Throat or a slight Fever and he'll shew a Thousand anxiety's, and in them the inestimable value he sets on Life. Had Man been naturally humble and proof against Flattery the Politician could never have had his Ends, or known what to have made of him. Without Vices the excellency of the Species would have ever remain'd undiscover'd, and every worthy that has made himself Famous in the World is a strong Evidence against this amiable System.

If the Courage of the great *Macedonian* came up to Distraction when he Fought alone against a whole Garrison, his Madness was not less when he fancy'd himself to be a God, or at least doubted whether he was or not; and as soon as we make this Reflection, we discover both the Passion, and the Extravagancy of it, that boy'd up his Spirits in the most imminent dangers, and carried him through all the Difficulties and Fatigues he underwent.

There never was in the World a brighter example of an able and compleat Magistrate than *Cicero*: When I think on his Care and Vigilance, the real Hazards he slighted and the Pains he took for the Safety of *Rome*; his Wisdom and Sagacity in detecting and disappointing the Stratagems of the boldest and most subtle Conspirators, and at the same time on his Love to Litterature, Arts, and Sciences, his capacity in Metaphysicks, the justness of his Reasonings, the force of his Eloquence, the politeness of his Stile, and the genteel Spirit that runs through his Writings; when I think I say on all these things together, I am struck with amazement, and the least I can say of him is that he was a Prodigious Man. But when I have set the many good qualities he had in the best Light, it is as evident to me on the other side, that had his Vanity been inferior to his greatest Excellency, the good Sense and Knowledge of the World he was so eminently possess'd of could never have let him be such a fulsome as well as noisy Trumpeter as he was of his own Praises, or suffer'd him rather than not proclaim his own Merit, to make a Verse that a School-

Boy would have been laugh'd at for. O! *Fortunatum*, &c.[59]

How strict and severe was the Morality of rigid *Cato*, how steady and unaffected the Virtue of that grand Asserter of Roman Liberty! but tho' the Equivalent this Stoick enjoy'd, for all the Self-denial and Austerity he practis'd, remain'd long conceal'd, and his peculiar Modesty hid from the World, and perhaps himself, a vast while the Frailty of his Heart that forc'd him into Heroism, yet it was brought to light in the last Scene of his Life, and by his Suicide it plainly appear'd, that he was govern'd by a Tyrannical Power superior to the Love of his Country, and that the implacable Hatred and superlative Envy he bore to the Glory, the real Greatness and Personal Merit of *Cæsar* had for a long time sway'd all his Actions under the most noble Pretences. Had not this violent Motive over-rul'd his consummate Prudence he might not only have saved himself, but likewise most of his Friends that were ruin'd by the Loss of him, and would in all probability, if he could have stoop'd to it, been the Second Man in *Rome*. But he knew the boundless Mind and unlimited Generosity of the Victor: it was his Clemency he fear'd, and therefore chose Death because it was less terrible to his Pride than the Thought of giving his mortal Foe so tempting an Opportunity of shewing the Magnanimity of his Soul, as *Cæsar* would have found in forgiving such an inveterate Enemy as *Cato*, and offering him his Friendship; and which, it is thought by the Judicious, that Penetrating as well as Ambitious Conqueror would not have slipt if the other had dar'd to live.

Another Argument to prove the kind Disposition and real Affection we naturally have for our Species, is our Love

59. 'O fortunate Roman state, born in my consulate!' This verse from Cicero's *De Consulatu Suo*, of which Mandeville gives only the opening words, was often ridiculed. Juvenal quotes it in his *Satires*, x, 122. – Ed.

of Company and the Aversion, Men that are in their Sences generally have to Solitude beyond other Creatures. This bears a fine gloss in the *Characteristicks*, and is set off in very good Language to the best Advantage: the next Day after I read it first, I heard abundance of People cry Fresh Herrings, which with the Reflection on the vast Shoals of that and other Fish that are caught together, made me very merry, tho' I was alone: but as I was entertaining my self with this Contemplation, came an impertinent idle Fellow, whom I had the Misfortune to be known by, and ask'd me how I did, tho' I was and dare say look'd as healthy and as well as ever I was or did in my Life. What I answer'd him I forgot, but remember that I could not get rid of him in a good while, and felt all the uneasiness my friend *Horace* complains of from a Persecution of the like nature.

I would have no sagacious Critick pronounce me a Man-hater from this short Story; whoever does is very much mistaken. I am a great Lover of Company, and if the Reader is not quite tired with mine, before I shew the Weakness and Ridicule of that piece of Flattery made to our Species, and which I was just now speaking of, I will give him a Description of the Man I would chuse for Conversation, with a Promise that before he has finish'd what at first he might only take for a Digression foreign to my purpose, he shall find the Use of it.

By Early and Artful Instruction he should be thoroughly imbued with the notions of Honour and Shame, and have contracted an habitual aversion to every thing that has the least tendency to Impudence, Rudeness or Inhumanity. He should be well vers'd in the Latin Tongue and not ignorant of the Greek, and moreover understand one or two of the Modern Languages besides his own. He should be acquainted with the Fashions and Customs of the Ancients, but thoroughly skill'd in the History of his own Country and the Manners of the Age he lives in. He should besides

Litterature have study'd some useful Science or other, seen some Foreign Courts and Universities, and made the true use of Travelling. He should at times take delight in Dancing, Fencing, Riding the Great Horse, and know something of Hunting and other Country Sports, without being attach'd to any, and he should treat them all as either Exercises for Health, or Diversions that should never interfere with Business, or the attaining to more valuable Qualifications. He should have a smatch of Geometry and Astronomy as well as Anatomy and the Oeconomy of Human Bodies. To understand Musick so as to perform, is an Accomplishment, but there is abundance to be said against it, and instead of it I would have him know so much of Drawing as is required to take a Landskip, or explain ones meaning of any Form or Model we would describe, but never to touch a Pencil. He should be very early used to the Company of Modest Women, and never be a Fortnight without Conversing with the Ladies.

Gross Vices, as Irreligion, Whoring, Gaming, Drinking and Quarreling I won't mention; even the meanest Education guards us against them; I would always recommend to him the Practice of Virtue, but I am for no Voluntary Ignorance, in a Gentleman, of any thing that is done in Court or City. It is impossible a Man should be perfect, and therefore there are Faults I would connive at, if I could not prevent them, and if between the Years of Nineteen and Three and Twenty, Youthful Heat should sometimes get the better of his Chastity, so it was done with caution; should he on some Extraordinary Occasion overcome by the pressing Solicitations of Jovial Friends, drink more than was consistent with strict Sobriety, so he did it very seldom and found it not to interfere with his Health or Temper, or if by the height of his Mettle and great Provocation in a Just Cause, he had been drawn into a Quarrel, which true Wisdom and a less strict adherence to the Rules of Honour might have declined or prevented, so it never befel him above once; If I say he should have happen'd to be Guilty of these things, and he would never speak, much less Brag of them himself, they might be pardon'd or at least over-look'd at the Age I named, if he left off then and continued discreet for ever after. The very Disasters of Youth have sometimes frighten'd Gentlemen into a more steady Prudence than in all probability they would ever have been Masters of without them. To keep him from Turpitude and things that are openly Scandalous, there is nothing better than to procure him free access in one or two Noble Families where his frequent Attendance is counted a Duty : And whilst by that means you preserve his Pride, he is kept in a continual dread of Shame.

A Man of a tollerable Fortune, pretty near accomplish'd, as I have required him to be that still improves himself and sees the World till he is Thirty, cannot be disagreeable to converse with at least whilst he continues in Health and Prosperity, and has nothing to spoil his Temper. When such a one either by chance or appointment, meets with Three or Four of his Equals, and all agree to pass away a few Hours together, the whole is what I call Good Company. There is nothing said in it that is not either instructive or diverting to a Man of Sense. It is possible they may not always be of the same Opinion, but there can be no contest between any but who shall yield first to the other he differs from. One only speaks at a time, and no louder than to be plainly understood by him who sits the farthest off. The greatest Pleasure aim'd at by every one of them is to have the Satisfaction of Pleasing others, which they all practically know may as effectually be done by hearkning with Attention and an approving Countenance, as if we said very good things our selves.

Most People of any Taste would like such a Conversation, and justly prefer it to being alone, when they knew not how to spend their time; but if they could employ themselves in something from which they expected either a more solid or a more lasting Satisfaction, they would deny themselves this Pleasure, and follow what was of greater consequence to 'em. But would not a Man, tho' he had seen no Mortal in a Fortnight, remain alone as much longer, rather than get into Company of Noisy Fellows that take delight in Contradiction, and place a Glory in picking a Quarrel? Would not one that has Books, Read for ever, or set himself to Write upon some Subject or other, rather than be every Night with Partymen who count the Island to be good for nothing whilst their Adversaries are suffer'd to live upon it? Would not a Man be by himself a Month, and go to Bed before Seven a Clock rather than mix with Fox Hunters, who having all Day long tried in vain to break their Necks, joyn at Night in a second Attempt upon their Lives by Drinking, and to express their Mirth, are louder in senseless Sounds within doors, than their Barking, and less Troublesome Companions are only without? I have no great value for a Man who would not rather tire himself with Walking, or if he was shut up, scatter Pins about the Room in order to pick them up again, than keep Company for six Hours with Half a Score Common Sailers the Day their Ship was paid off.

I will grant nevertheless that the greatest part of Mankind rather than be alone any considerable time, would submit to the things I named: But I cannot see, why this love of Company, this strong desire after Society should be construed so much in our Favour, and alledged as a mark of some Intrinsick Worth in Man not to be found in other Animals. For to prove from it the Goodness of our Nature and a generous Love in Man, extended beyond himself on the rest of his Species, by virtue of which he was a Sociable Creature, this eagerness after Company, and aversion of being alone ought to have been most conspicuous and most violent in the best of their kind, the Men of the greatest Genius, Parts and Accomplishments, and those, who are the least subject to Vice; the contrary of which is true. The weakest Minds, who can the least govern their Passions, Guilty Consciences that abhor Reflection, and the worthless, who are incapable of producing any thing of their own that's useful, are the greatest Enemies to Solitude, and will take up with any Company rather than be without; whereas the Men of Sense and of Knowledge, that can think and contemplate on things, and such as are but little disturb'd by their Passions, can bear to be by themselves the longest without reluctancy; and, to avoid Noise, Folly, and Impertinence will run away from Twenty Companies; and, rather than meet with any thing disagreeable to their good Taste, will prefer their Closet or a Garden, nay a Common or a Desart to the Society of some Men.

But let us suppose the love of Company so inseparable from our Species, that no Man could endure to be alone one Moment, what conclusions could be drawn from this? does not Man love Company as he does every thing else for his own sake? No Friendships or Civilities are lasting that are not Reciprocal. In all your Weekly and Daily Meetings for Diversion as well as Annual Feasts, and the most Solemn Carouzals, every Member that assists at them has his own Ends, and some frequent a Club which they would never go to unless they were the Top of it. I have known a Man who was the Oracle of the Company, be very constant, and as uneasy at any thing that hindred him from coming at the Hour, leave his Society altogether, as soon as another was added that could match, and disputed Superiority with him. There are People who are incapable of holding an Argument, and yet malicious enough to take delight in hearing others Wrangle, and tho' they never concern themselves in the Controversy, would think a Company Insipid where they could not have that Diversion. A Good House, Rich

Furniture, a Fine Garden, Horses, Dogs, Ancestors, Rela-
tions, Beauty, Strength, Excellency in any thing whatever,
Vices as well as Virtues may all be Accessary to make Men
long for Society, in hopes that what they value themselves
upon will at one time or other become the Theme of the
Discourse, and give an inward Satisfaction to them. Even
the most polite People in the World, and such as I spoke
of at first, give no Pleasure to others that is not repaid to
their Self-Love, and does not at last Center in themselves,
let them wind it and turn it as they will. But the plainest
demonstration that in all Clubs and Societies of Conversable
People every body has the greatest consideration for himself
is, that the disinterested, who rather over-pays than
Wrangles; the good Humour'd, that is never waspish nor
soon offended; the Easy and Indolent, that hates Disputes
and never talks for Triumph, is every where the darling of
the Company: Whereas the Man of Sense and Knowledge,
that will not be imposed upon or talk'd out of his reason,
the Man of Genius and Spirit, that can say sharp and witty
things, tho' he never Lashes but what deserves it, the Man
of Honour, who neither gives nor takes an Affront, may be
esteem'd, but is seldom so well beloved as a Weaker Man
less Accomplish'd.

As in these Instances the Friendly Qualities arise from
our contriving perpetually our own Satisfaction, so on other
occasions they proceed from the natural timidity of Man, and
the Sollicitous Care he takes of himself. Two *Londoners*,
whose Business oblige them not, to have any Commerce
together, may know, see and pass by one another every Day
upon the *Exchange*, with not much greater Civility than
Bulls would: Let them meet at *Bristol* they'll pull off their
Hats, and on the least opportunity enter into Conversation,
and be glad of one anothers Company. When *French,
English* and *Dutch* meet in *China* or any other Pagan Coun-
try; being all *Europeans*, they look upon one another as

Countrymen, and if no Passion interferes, will feel a Natural Propensity to love one another. Nay Two Men that are at Enmity, if they are forc'd to Travel together, will often lay by their Animosities, be affable and converse in a Friendly manner, especially if the Road be unsafe, and they are both Strangers in the Place they are to go to. These things by Superficial Judges are attributed to Man's Sociableness, his natural propensity to Friendship and love of Company, but whoever will duely examine things and look into Man more narrowly, will find that on all these Occasions we only endeavour to strengthen our Interest, and are moved by the Causes already alledg'd.

What I have endeavour'd hitherto, has been to prove, that the *pulchrum & honestum*, excellency, and real worth of things are most commonly precarious and alterable as Modes and Customs vary; that consequently the inferences drawn from their certainty are Insignificant, and that the generous Notions concerning the natural Goodness of Man are hurtful as they tend to mislead and are merely Chimerical : The truth of this latter I have Illustrated by the most obvious Examples in History. I have spoke of our Love of Company and Aversion to Solitude, examin'd thoroughly the various Motives of them, and made it appear that they all center in Self-Love. I intend now to investigate into the nature of Society, and diving into the very rise of it, make it evident, that not the Good and Amiable, but the Bad and Hateful Qualities of Man, his Imperfections and the want of Excellencies which other Creatures are endued with, are the first causes that made Man sociable beyond other Animals the Moment after he lost Paradise; and that if he had remain'd in his primitive Innocence, and continued to enjoy the Blessings that attended it, there is no Shadow of Probability that he ever would have become that sociable Creature he is now.

How necessary our Appetites and Passions are for the

welfare of all Trades and Handicrafts has been sufficiently prov'd throughout the Book, and that they are our bad Qualities, or at least produce them, no Body denies. It remains then that I should set forth the variety of Obstacles that hinder and perplex Man in the Labour he is constantly employ'd in, the procuring of what he wants; and which in other Words is call'd the Business of Self-Preservation: Whilst at the same time I demonstrate that the Sociableness of Man arises only from these Two things, *viz*. The multiplicity of his Desires, and the continual Opposition he meets with in his Endeavours to gratify them.

The Obstacles I speak of relate either to our own Frame, or the Globe we Inhabit, I mean the Condition of it, since it has been curs'd. I have often endeavour'd to contemplate separately on the Two things I named last, but could never keep them asunder; they always interfere and mix with one another; and at last make up together a frightful Chaos of Evil. All the Elements are our Enemies, Water Drowns and Fire consumes those who unskilfully Approach them. The Earth in a Thousand Places produces Plants and other Vegetables that are hurtful to Man, whilst she Feeds and Cherishes a variety of Creatures that are noxious to him; and suffers a Legion of Poysons to dwell within her: But the most unkind of all the Elements is, that which we cannot Live one Moment without: It is impossible to repeat all the Injuries we receive from the Wind and Weather, and tho' the greatest part of Mankind have ever been employed in defending their Species from the inclemency of the Air, yet no Art or Labour have hitherto been able to find a Security against the Wild Rage of some Meteors.

Hurricanes it is true happen but seldom, and few Men are swallowed up by Earthquakes, or devour'd by Lions, but whilst we escape those Gigantick Mischiefs we are persecuted by Trifles. What a vast variety of Insects are tormenting to us; what multitudes of them insult and make

Game of us with Impunity! The most despicable Scruple not
to Trample and Graze upon us as Cattle do upon a Field:
which yet is often bore with, if moderately they use their
Fortune, but here again our Clemency becomes a Vice, and
so Encroaching are their Cruelty and Contempt of us on our
Pity, that they make laystals of our Heads, and devour our
Young ones if we are not daily Vigilant in Pursuing and
Destroying them.

There is nothing Good in all the Universe to the best
designing Man, if either through Mistake or Ignorance he
commits the least Failing in the Use of it; There is no
Innocence or Integrity that can protect a Man from a Thou-
sand Mischiefs that surround him: On the contrary every
thing is Evil, which Art and Experience have not taught us to
turn into a Blessing. Therefore how diligent in Harvest time
is the Husband-Man in getting in his Crop and sheltering it
from Rain, without which he could never have enjoy'd
it! As Seasons differ with the Climates Experience has
taught us differently to make use of them, and in one part
of the Globe we may see the Farmer Sow whilst he is Reap-
ing in the other, from all which we may learn how vastly this
Earth must have been alter'd since the Fall of our first
Parents. For should we Trace Man from his Beautiful, his
Divine Original, not proud of Wisdom acquired by haughty
Precept or tedious Experience, but endued with consum-
mate Knowledge the moment he was form'd; I mean the
State of Innocence, in which no Animal or Vegetable upon
Earth, nor Mineral under Ground was noxious to him, and
himself secure from the Injuries of the Air as well as all
other Harms, was contented with the necessaries of Life,
which the Globe he inhabited furnish'd him with, without
his assistance. When yet not conscious of Guilt, he found
himself in every Place to be the well obey'd Unrival'd Lord
of all, and unaffected with his Greatness was wholly wrapt
up in sublime Meditations on the Infinity of his Creator,

who daily did vouchsafe Intelligibly to speak to him, and Visit without Mischief.

In such a Golden Age no Reason or Probability can be alledged why Mankind ever should have rais'd themselves into such large Societies as there have been in the World, as long as we can give any tollerable Account of it. Where a Man has every thing he desires, and nothing to Vex or Disturb him; there is nothing can be added to his Happiness, and it is impossible to name a Trade, Art, Science, Dignity or Employment that would not be Superfluous in such a Blessed State. If we pursue this Thought we shall easily perceive that no Societies could have sprung from the Amiable Virtues and Loving Qualities of Man, but on the contrary that all of them must have had their Origin from his Wants, his Imperfections and the variety of his Appetites: We shall find likewise that the more their Pride and Vanity are display'd, and all their Desires enlarg'd, the more capable they must be of being rais'd into large and vastly numerous Societies.

Was the Air always as inoffensive to our Naked Bodies, and as Pleasant as to our thinking it is to the generality of Birds in Fair Weather, and Man had not been affected with Pride, Luxury and Hypocrisy as well as Lust, I cannot see what could have put us upon the invention of Cloaths and Houses. I shall say nothing of Jewels, of Plate, Painting, Sculpture, Fine Furniture, and all that rigid Moralists have call'd Unnecessary and Superfluous: But if we were not soon tired with Walking a Foot, and were as nimble as some other Animals; if Men were naturally laborious, and none unreasonable in seeking and indulging their Ease, and likewise free from other Vices, and the Ground was every where even Solid and Clean, who would have thought of Coaches or ventur'd on a Horse's Back? What occasion has the Dolphin for a Ship, or what Carriage would an Eagle ask to Travel in?

I hope the Reader knows that by Society I understand a Body Politick, in which Man either subdued by Superiour Force or by Persuasion drawn from his Savage State, is become a Disciplin'd Creature, that can find his own Ends in Labouring for others, and where under one Head or other Form of Government each Member is render'd Subservient to the Whole, and all of them by cunning Management are made to Act as one. For if by Society we only mean a Number of People, that without Rule or Government should keep together out of a Natural Affection to their Species or Love of Company, as a Herd of Cows or a Flock of Sheep, then there is not in the World a more unfit Creature for Society than Man; an Hundred of them that should be all Equals, under no Subjection, or Fear of any Superiour upon Earth, could never Live together awake Two Hours without Quarrelling, and the more Knowledge, Strength, Wit, Courage and Resolution there was among them, the worse it would be.

It is probable that in the Wild State of Nature Parents would keep a Superiority over their Children, at least while they were in Strength, and that even afterwards the Remembrance of what the others had experienc'd might produce in them something between Love and Fear, which we call Reverence: It is probable likewise that the second Generation following the Example of the first, a Man with a little cunning would always be able, as long as he lived and had his Senses, to maintain a Superior Sway over all his own Offspring and Descendants how numerous soever they might grow. But the old Stock once dead, the Sons would Quarrel, and there could be no Peace long, before there had been War. Eldership in Brothers is of no great Force, and the Preeminence that is given to it only invented as a shift to live in Peace. Man as he is a fearful Animal, naturally not rapacious, loves Peace and Quiet, and he would never Fight if no body offended him, and he could have

what he fights for without it. To this fearful Disposition
and the Aversion he has to his being disturb'd, are owing
all the various Projects and forms of Government. Mon-
archy without doubt was the first. Aristocracy and
Democracy were two different Methods of mending the In-
conveniencies of the first, and a mixture of these three an
Improvement on all the rest.

But be we Savages or Politicians it is impossible that Man,
mere fallen Man should act with any other View but to
please himself whilst he has the Use of his Organs, and the
greatest Extravagancy either of Love or Despair can have
no other Center. There is no difference between Will and
Pleasure in one sense, and every Motion made in spight of
them must be unnatural and convulsive. Since then Action is
so confin'd, and we are always forc'd to do what we please,
and at the same time our Thoughts are free and uncon-
troul'd, it is impossible we could be sociable Creatures with-
out Hypocrisy. The Proof of this is plain, since we cannot
prevent the Idea's that are continuayly arising within us, all
Civil Commerce would be lost, if by Art and Prudent Dis-
simulation we had not learn'd to hide and stifle them; and
if all, we think, was to be laid open to others in the same
manner as it is to our selves, it is impossible that endued
with Speech we could be sufferable to one another. I am
persuaded that every Reader feels the truth of what I say;
and I tell my Antagonist that his Conscience flys in his
Face, whilst his Tongue is preparing to refute me. In all
Civil Societies Men are taught insensibly to be Hypocrites
from their Cradle, no body dares to own that he gets by Pub-
lick Calamities, or even by the loss of Private Persons. The
Sexton would be Stoned should he wish openly for the
Death of the Parishioners, tho' every body knew that he had
nothing else to live upon.

To me it is a great Pleasure, when I look on the Affairs
of Human Life, to behold into what various, and often

strangely opposite Forms the hope of Gain and thoughts of Lucre shape Men according to the different Employments they are of, and Stations they are in. How Gay and Merry does every Face appear at a well-ordered Ball, and what a Solemn Sadness is observ'd at the Masquerade of a Funeral! But the Undertaker is as much pleas'd with his Gains as the Dancing Master: Both are equally tired in their Occupations, and the Mirth of the one is as much forc'd as the Gravity of the other is affected. Those who have never minded the Conversation of a Spruce Mercer, and a Young Lady his Customer that comes to his Shop, have neglected a Scene of Life that is very Entertaining. I beg of my Serious Reader that he would for a while abate a little of his Gravity, and suffer me to examine these People separately, as to their Inside and the different Motives they Act from.

His Business is to sell as much Silk as he can at a Price by which he shall get what he proposes, to be reasonable according to the Customary Profits of the Trade. As to the Lady, what she would be at is to please her Fancy, and buy cheaper by a Groat or Six Pence *per* Yard than the things she wants are commonly Sold at. From the Impression the Gallantry of our Sex has made upon her, she imagines, (if she be not very deform'd,) that she has a fine Mien and easy Behaviour, and a peculiar Sweetness of Voice; that she is Handsome, and if not Beautiful at least more agreeable than most Young Women she knows. As she has no pretensions to purchase the same things with less Money than other People, but what are built on her good qualities, so she sets her self off to the best advantage her Wit and Discretion will let her. The thoughts of Love are here out of the Case; so on the one hand she has no room for playing the Tyrant, and giving her self Angry and Peevish Airs, and on the other more liberty of speaking kindly, and being affable than she can have almost on any other occasion. She knows that abundance of Well-bred People come to his

Shop, and endeavours to render her self as Amiable as Virtue and the Rules of Decency allow of. Coming with such a resolution of Behaviour she cannot meet with any thing to ruffle her Temper.

Before her Coach is yet quite stopp'd, she is approach'd by a Gentleman-like-man, that has every thing Clean and Fashionable about him, who in low obeisance pays her Homage, and as soon as her Pleasure is known that she has a mind to come in, hands her into the Shop, where immediately he slips from her and through a by-way, that remains visible only for half a Moment, with great address entrenches himself behind the Counter: Here facing her, with a profound Reverence and modish Phrase he begs the favour of knowing her Commands. Let her say and dislike what she pleases, she can never be directly contradicted: She deals with a Man in whom consummate Patience is one of the Mysteries of his Trade, and what ever Trouble she creates, she is sure to hear nothing but the most obliging Language, and has always before her a chearful Countenance, where Joy and Respect seem to be blended with good Humour, and altogether make up an Artificial Serenity more ingaging than untaught Nature is able to produce.

When two Persons are so well met, the Conversation must be very agreeable, as well as extremely mannerly, tho' they talk about trifles. Whilst she remains irresolute what to take he seems to be the same in advising her, and is very cautious how to direct her Choice; but when once she has made it and is fix'd, he immediately becomes positive, that it is the best of the sort, extols her Fancy, and the more he looks upon it, the more he wonders he should not before have discovered the preeminence of it over any thing he has in his Shop. By Precept, Example and great Application he has learn'd unobserv'd to slide into the inmost recesses of the Soul, sound the Capacity of his Customers, and find out their Blind Side unknown to them:

By all which he is instructed in Fifty other Stratagems to make her over-value her own Judgment as well as the Commodity she would purchase. The greatest Advantage he has over her, lies in the most material part of the Commerce between them, the debate about the Price, which he knows to a Farthing, and she is wholly Ignorant of: Therefore he no where more egregiously imposes on her Understanding; and tho' here he has the liberty of telling what Lies he pleases, as to the Prime Cost and the Money he has refus'd, yet he trusts not to them only; but attacking her Vanity makes her believe the most incredible things in the World, concerning his own Weakness and her Superior Abilities: He had taken a Resolution, he says, never to part with that Piece under such a Price, but she has the power of talking him out of his Goods beyond any body he ever Sold to: He protests that he loses by his Silk, but seeing that she has a Fancy for it, and is resolv'd to give no more, rather than disoblige a Lady he has such an uncommon value for, he'll let her have it, and only begs that another time she will not stand so hard with him. In the mean time the Buyer, who knows that she is no Fool and has a voluble Tongue, is easily persuaded that she has a very winning way of Talking, and thinking it sufficient for the sake of Good Breeding to disown her Merit, and in some witty repartee retort the Compliment, he makes her swallow very contentedly the substance of every thing he tells her. The upshot is, that with the satisfaction of having saved Nine-pence *per* Yard, she has bought her Silk exactly at the same Price as any body else might have done, and often gives Six-pence more, than rather than not have Sold it, he would have taken.

It is possible that this Lady for want of being sufficiently flatter'd, for a Fault she is pleased to find in his Behaviour, or perhaps the tying of his Neckcloth, or some other Dislike as Substantial may be lost, and her Custom bestow'd on some other of the Fraternity. But where many of them live

in a cluster, it is not always easily determin'd which Shop
to go to, and the reasons some of the Fair Sex have for their
choice are often very Whimsical and kept as a great Secret.
We never follow our Inclinations with more freedom, than
where they cannot be traced, and it is unreasonable for
others to suspect them. A Virtuous Woman has prefer'd one
House to all the rest, because she had seen a Handsome
Fellow in it, and another of no bad Character for having
receiv'd greater Civility before it, than had been paid her
any where else, when she had no thoughts of buying and
was going to *Paul's* Church: for among the Fashionable
Mercers the Fair Dealer must keep before his own Door,
and to draw in Random Customers make use of no other
freedom or importunities than an obsequious Air, with a
submissive Posture, and perhaps a Bow to every well dress'd
Female that offers to look towards his Shop.

What I have said last makes me think on another way
of inviting Customers the most distant in the World from
what I have been speaking of, I mean that which is prac-
tis'd by the Watermen, especially on those, whom by their
Mien and Garb they know to be Peasants. It is not un-
pleasant to see half a dozen People surround a Man, they
never saw in their lives before, and two of them that can
get the nearest, clapping each an Arm over his Neck, hug
him in as loving and familiar a manner as if he was their
Brother newly come home from an *East-India* Voyage; a
third lays hold of his Hand, another of his Sleeve, his Coat,
the Buttons of it, or any thing he can come at, whilst a fifth
or a sixth, who has scampered twice round him already
without being able to get at him, plants himself directly
before the Man in hold and within three Inches of his Nose,
contradicting his Rivals with an open mouthed cry, shews
him a dreadful set of large Teeth and a small remainder of
chew'd Bread and Cheese, which the Country Man's
Arrival had hindred from being swallow'd.

At all this no offence is taken, and the Peasant justly thinks they are making much of him; therefore far from opposing them he patiently suffers himself to be push'd or pull'd which way the strength that surrounds him shall direct. He has not the delicacy to find Fault with a Man's Breath, who has just blown out his Pipe, or a Greasy Head of Hair that is rubbing against his Chops: Dirt and Sweat he has been used to from his Cradle, and it is no disturbance to him to hear half a Score People, some of them at his Ear and the furthest not five Foot from him bawl out as if he was a Hundred Yards off: He is conscious that he makes no less Noise when he is Merry himself, and is secretly pleas'd with their boysterous Usages. The hawling and pulling him about he construes the way it is intended; it is a Courtship he can feel and understand: He can't help wishing them well for the esteem they seem to have for him: He loves to be taken notice of, and admires the *Londoners* for being so pressing in the offers of their Service to him, for the value of Three-pence or less; whereas in the Country at the Shop he uses, he can have nothing but he must first tell them what he wants, and, tho' he lays out Three or Four Shillings at a time, has hardly a word spoke to him unless it be in Answer to a Question himself is forc'd to ask first. This alacrity in his behalf moves his gratitude, and unwilling to disoblige any, from his Heart he knows not whom to chuse. I have seen a Man think all this, or some thing like it, as plainly as I could see the Nose in his Face; and at the same time move along very contentedly under a load of Watermen, and with a Smiling Countenance carry seven or eight Stone more than his own Weight, to the Water-side.

If the little Mirth I have shewn in the drawing of these two Images from low Life, misbecomes me I am sorry for it, but I promise not to be guilty of that Fault any more, and will now without loss of time proceed with my Argument

in artless dull Simplicity, and demonstrate the gross Error
of those, who imagine that the Social Virtues and the
amiable Qualities that are praise worthy in us, are equally
Beneficial to the Publick as they are to the Individual Per-
sons that are possess'd of them, and that the means of
thriving and whatever conduces to the Welfare and Real
Happiness of private Families must have the same effect
upon the whole Society. This I confess I have labour'd for
all along, and I flatter my self not unsuccessfully: But I
hope no Body will like a Problem the worse for seeing the
truth of it proved more ways than one.

It is certain that the fewer desires a Man has and the less
he Covets, the more easy he is to himself; the more active
he is to supply his own Wants and the less he requires to
be waited upon, the more he will be beloved and the less
trouble he is in a Family; the more he loves Peace and Con-
cord the more Charity he has for his Neighbour, and the
more he shines in real Virtue, there is no doubt, but that in
proportion he is acceptable to God and Man. But let us be
Just, what Benefit can these things be of, or what Earthly
Good can they do, to promote the Wealth, the Glory and
Worldly Greatness of Nations? It is the Sensual Courtier
that sets no limits to his Luxury; the Fickle Strumpet that
invents New Fashions every Week; the Haughty Dutchess
that in Equipage, Entertainments and all her Behaviour
would imitate a Princess; the profuse Rake and lavish Heir,
that scatter about their Money without Wit or Judgment,
buy every thing they see, and either destroy or give it away
the next day; the Covetous and perjur'd Villain that
squeez'd an Immense Treasure from the Tears of Widows
and Orphans and left the Prodigals the Money to Spend. It
is these that are the Prey and proper Food of a full grown
Leviathan; or in other words, such is the Calamitous Con-
dition of Human Affairs that we stand in need of the
Plagues and Monsters I named to have all the variety of

Labour perform'd, which the Skill of Men is capable of inventing in order to procure an Honest Livelihood to the vast Multitudes of Working Poor, that are required to make a large Society: And it is folly to imagine that Great and Wealthy Nations can subsist, and be at once Powerful and Polite without.

I protest against Popery as much as ever *Luther* or *Calvin* did, or Queen *Elizabeth* herself, but I believe from my Heart, that the Reformation has scarce been more Instrumental in rendring the Kingdoms and States that have embraced it, flourishing beyond other Nations than the silly and capricious Invention of Hoop'd and Quilted Petticoats. But if this should be denied me by the Enemies of Priestly Power, at least I am sure that, bar the great Men who have Fought for and against that Lay-Mans Blessing, it has from its first beginning to this Day not employ'd so many Hands, honest industrious labouring hands, as the abominable improvement on Female Luxury I named has done in Few Years. Religion is one thing and Trade is another. He that gives most Trouble to Thousands of his Neighbours, and invents the most operose Manufactures is right or wrong the greatest Friend to the Society.

What a Bustle is there to be made in several Parts of the World, before a Fine Scarlet or Crimson Cloth can be produced, what multiplicity of Trades and Artificers must be employ'd! Not only such as are Obvious, as Woolcombers, Spinners, the Weaver, the Clothworker, the Scowrer, the Dier, the Setter, the Drawer and the Packer; but others that are more remote and might seem Foreign to it; as the Millwright, the Pewterer and the Chymist, which yet are all necessary as well as a great Number of other Handicrafts to have the Tools, Utensils and other Implements belonging to the Trades already Named: But all these things are done at Home, and may be perform'd without extraordinary Fatigue or Danger; the most frightful Prospect is left behind, when we reflect on the Toil and Hazard that are to be undergone Abroad, the vast Seas we are to go over, the different Climates we are to endure, and the several Nations we must be obliged to for their Assistance. *Spain* alone it is true might furnish us with Wool to make the finest Cloth; but what Skill and Pains, what Experience and Ingenuity are required to Dye it of those Beautiful Colours! How widely are the Drugs and other Ingredients dispers'd through the Universe that are to meet in one Kettle. Allom indeed we have of our own; Argol we might have from the *Rhine*, and Vitriol from *Hungary*; all this is in *Europe*; but then for Saltpeter in quantity we are forc'd to go as far as the *East-Indies*. Cochenille, unknown to the Ancients, is not much nearer to us, tho' in a quite different part of the Earth: we buy it, 'tis true from the *Spaniards*; but not being their Product they are forc'd to fetch it for us from the remotest Corner of the New World in the *West-Indies*. Whilst so many Sailors are broiling in the Sun and swelter'd with Heat in the *East* and *West* of us, another set of them are freezing in the *North* to fetch Potashes from *Russia*.

When we are thoroughly acquainted with all the Variety of Toil and Labour, the Hardships and Calamities that must be undergone to compass the End I speak of, and we consider the vast Risques and Perils that are run in those Voyages, and that few of them are ever made but at the Expence, not only of the Health and Welfare, but even the Lives of many: When we are acquainted with, I say, and duly consider the things I named, it is scarce possible to conceive a Tyrant so inhuman and void of Shame, that beholding things in the same View, he should exact such terrible Services from his Innocent Slaves; and at the same Time dare to own, that he did it for no other Reason, than the Satisfaction a Man receives from having a Garment made of Scarlet or Crimson Cloth. But to what Height of

Luxury must a Nation be arriv'd, where not only the King's Officers, but likewise his Guards, even the Private Soldiers should have such impudent Desires!

But if we turn the Prospect, and look on all those Labours as so many voluntary Actions, belonging to different Callings and Occupations, that Men are brought up to for a Livelyhood, and in which every one Works for himself, how much soever he may seem to Labour for others: If we consider, that even the Saylors who undergo the greatest Hardships, as soon as one Voyage is ended, even after Ship-wreck, are looking out and solliciting for employment in another: If we consider, I say, and look on these things in another View, we shall find that the Labour of the Poor, is so far from being a Burthen and an Imposition upon them; that to have Employment is a Blessing, which in their Addresses to Heaven they Pray for, and to procure it for the generality of them is the greatest Care of every Legislature.

As Children and even Infants are the Apes of others, so all Youth have an ardent desire of being Men and Women, and become often ridiculous by their impatient Endeavours to appear what every Body sees they are not; all large Societies are not a little indebted to this Folly for the Perpetuity or at least long Continuance of Trades once Establish'd. What Pains will Young People take, and what Violence will they not commit upon themselves to attain to insignificant and often blameable Qualifications, which for want of Judgment and Experience they admire in others, that are Superiour to them in Age! This fondness of Imitation makes them Accustom themselves by degrees to the Use of things that were Irksome, if not Intollerable to them at first; till they know not how to leave them, and are often very Sorry for having inconsiderately encreas'd the Necessaries of Life without any Necessity. What Estates have been got by Tea and Coffee! What a vast Traffick is drove, what a variety of Labour is perform'd in the World to the

Maintenance of Thousands of Families that altogether depend on two silly if not odious Customs; the taking of Snuff and smoaking of Tobacco; both which it is certain do infinitely more hurt than good to those that are addicted to them! I shall go further and demonstrate the usefulness of private losses and misfortunes to the Publick, and the folly of our Wishes, when we pretend to be most Wise and Serious. The Fire of *London* was a great Calamity, but if the Carpenters, Bricklayers, Smiths and all, not only that are employ'd in Building but likewise those that made and dealt in the same Manufactures and other Merchandizes that were Burnt, and other Trades again that got by them when they were in full Employ, were to Vote against those who lost by the Fire; the Rejoycings would equal if not exceed the Complaints. In recruiting what is lost and destroy'd by Fire, Storms, Sea-fights, Seiges, Battles a considerable part of Trade consists; the truth of which and whatever I have said of the Nature of Society will plainly appear from what follows.

It would be a difficult Task to enumerate all the Advantages and different Benefits, that accrue to a Nation on account of Shipping and Navigation; but if we only take into Consideration the Ships themselves and every Vessel great and small, that is made Use of for Water Carriage, from the least Wherry to a First Rate Man of War; the Timber and Hands, that are employ'd in the Building of them, and consider the Pitch, Tar, Rosin, Grease, the Masts, Yards, Sails and Rigging; the variety of Smiths Work, the Cables, Oars and every thing else belonging to them, we shall find, that to furnish only such a Nation as ours with all these Necessaries makes up a considerable part of the Traffick of *Europe*, without speaking of the Stores and Ammunition of all sorts, that are consumed in them, or the Mariners, Watermen and others with their Families, that are maintain'd by them.

But should we on the other Hand take a View of the manifold Mischiefs and variety of Evils, moral as well as natural, that befal Nations on the Score of Seafaring and their Commerce with Strangers, the Prospect would be very frightful; and could we suppose a large Populous Island, that should be wholly unacquainted with Ships and Sea Affairs, but otherwise a Wise and Well-Govern'd People, and that some Angel or their Genius should lay before them a Scheme or Draught, where they might see, on the one side all the Riches and real Advantages, that would be acquired by Navigation in a Thousand Years, and on the other, the Wealth and Lives that would be lost, and all the other Calamities, that would be unavoidably sustain'd on Account of it, during the same time, I am confident, they would look upon Ships with Horrour and Detestation, and that their Prudent Rulers would severely forbid the making and inventing all Buildings or Machines to go to Sea with, of what shape or denomination soever, and prohibit all such abominable Contrivances on great Penalties, if not the pain of Death.

But to let alone the necessary consequence of Foreign Trade, the corruption of Manners, as well as Plagues, Poxes, and other Diseases, that are brought to us by Shipping, should we only cast our Eyes on what is either to be imputed to the Wind and Weather, the Treachery of the Seas, the Ice of the North, the Vermin of the South, the Darkness of Nights, and Unwholesomness of Climates, or else occasion'd by the want of good Provisions and the Faults of Mariners, the Unskilfulness of some and the Neglect and Drunkenness of others; and should we consider the losses of Men and Treasure swallow'd up in the Deep, the Tears and Necessities of Widows and Orphans made by the Sea, the Ruin of Merchants and the consequences, the continual Anxieties that Parents and Wives are in for the safety of their Children and Husbands, and not forget the many

Pangs and Heartakes that are felt throughout a Trading Nation by Owners and Insurers at every blast of Wind: should we cast our Eyes I say on these things, consider with due attention and give them the Weight they deserve, would it not be amazing, how a Nation of thinking People should talk of their Ships and Navigation as a peculiar Blessing to them, and placing an uncommon Felicity in having an Infinity of Vessels dispers'd through the Wide World, and always some going to and others coming from every part of the Universe?

But let us once in our consideration on these things confine our selves to what the Ships suffer only, the Vessels themselves with their Rigging and Appurtenances, without thinking on the Freight they carry or the Hands that work them, and we shall find that the damage sustain'd that way only is very considerable, and must one Year with another amount to vast Sums: The Ships that are founder'd at Sea, split against Rocks and swallow'd up by Sands, some by the fierceness of Tempests altogether, others by that and the want of Pilots, Experience and Knowledge of the Coasts: The Masts that are blown down or forc'd to be cut and thrown Over-board, the Yards, Sails and Cordage of different sizes that are destroy'd by Storms, and the Anchors that are lost: Add to these the necessary repairs of Leaks sprung and other Hurts receiv'd from the rage of Winds, and the violence of the Waves: Many Ships are set on Fire by carelessness, and the effects of strong Liquors, which none are more addicted to than Sailors: Sometimes unhealthy Climates, at others the badness of Provision breed Fatal Distempers that sweep away the greatest part of the Crew, and not a few Ships are lost for want of Hands.

These are all Calamities inseparable from Navigation, and seem to be great Impediments that clog the Wheels of Foreign Commerce. How Happy would a Merchant think himself, if his Ships should always have Fine Weather, and the Wind he wish'd for, and every Mariner he employ'd, from the highest to the lowest, be a knowing experienc'd Sailor, and a careful, sober, good Man! Was such a Felicity to be had for Prayers, what Owner of Ships is there or Dealer in *Europe*, nay the whole World, who would not be all day long teazing Heaven to obtain such a Blessing for himself, without regard what detriment it would do to others? Such a Petition would certainly be a very unconscionable one, yet where is the Man, who imagines not that he has a right to make it? And therefore, as every one pretends to an equal claim to those Favours, let us without reflecting on the impossibility of its being true, suppose all their Prayers effectual and their Wishes answer'd, and afterwards examine into the Result of such a Happiness.

Ships would last as long as Timber Houses to the full, because they are as strongly Built, and the latter are liable to suffer by high Winds and other Storms, which the first by our supposition are not to be: So that, before there would be any real occasion for New Ships, the Master Builders now in being and every body under them, that is set to Work about them, would all die a Natural Death, if they were not starv'd or come to some Untimely End: For in the first place, all Ships having prosperous Gales, and never waiting for the Wind, they would make very quick Voyages both out and home: Secondly no Merchandizes would be Damag'd by the Sea, or by stress of Weather thrown Over-board, but the entire Lading would always come safe a Shore; and hence it would follow, that Three Parts in Four of the Merchant-men already made would be Superfluous for the present, and the stock of Ships that are now in the World, serve a vast many Years. Masts and Yards would last as long as the Vessels themselves, and we should not need to trouble *Norway* on that score a great while yet. The Sails and Rigging indeed of the few Ships made use of would wear out, but not a quarter part so fast as now they do, for they often suffer more in one Hour's Storm, than in Ten Days Fair Weather.

Anchors and Cables there would be seldom any occasion for, and one of each would last a Ship time out of mind: This Article alone would yield many a tedious Holy-day to the Anchor-Smiths and the Rope-Yards. This general want of Consumption would have such an Influence on the Timber-Merchants and all that Import Iron, Sail-Cloth, Hemp, Pitch, Tar, &c. that four parts in five of what, in the beginning of this Reflection on Sea-Affairs, I said, made a considerable Branch of the Traffick of *Europe* would be entirely Lost.

I have only touch'd hitherto on the consequences of this Blessing in relation to Shipping, but it would be detrimental to all other Branches of Trade besides, and destructive to the Poor of every Country, that Exports any thing of their own Growth or Manufacture. The Goods and Merchandizes that every Year go to the Deep, that are spoyl'd at Sea by Salt Water, by Heat, by Vermin, destroy'd by Fire, or lost to the Merchant by other Accidents, all owing to Storms or Tedious Voyages, or else the neglect or rapacity of Sailors; such Goods I say and Merchandizes are a considerable part of what every Year is sent abroad throughout the World, and must have employ'd great Multitudes of Poor before they could come on Board. A Hundred Bales of Cloth that are Burnt or Sunk in the *Mediterranean*, are as Beneficial to the Poor in *Englund*, as if they had safely Arriv'd at *Smyrna* or *Aleppo*, and every Yard of them had been Retail'd in the Grand Signior's Dominions.

The Merchant may break, and by him the Clothier, the Dyer, the Packer and other Tradesmen, the Midling People may suffer, but the Poor that were set to Work about them can never lose. Day Labourers commonly receive their Earnings once a Week, and all the Working People, that were Employ'd either in any of the various Branches of the Manufacture it self, or the several Land and Water Carriages it requires to be brought to perfection from the Sheeps Back to the Vessel it was enter'd in, were paid, at least much the greatest part of them, before the Parcel came on board. Should any of my Readers draw Conclusions *in infinitum* from my Assertions that Goods sunk or burnt are as beneficial to the Poor as if they had been well sold and put to their proper Uses, I would count him a Caviller and not worth answering: Should it always Rain and the Sun never shine the Fruits of the Earth would soon be rotten and destroy'd; and yet it is no Paradox to affirm, that, to have Grass or Corn, Rain is as necessary as the Sunshine.

In what manner this Blessing of Fair Winds and Fine Weather would affect the Mariners themselves and the Breed of Saylors may be easily conjectured from what has been said already. As there would hardly one Ship in four be made use of, so the Vessels themselves being always exempt from Storms, fewer Hands would be required to Work them, and consequently five in six of the Seamen we have might be spared, which in this Nation, most Employments of the Poor being overstock'd, would be but an untoward Article. As soon as those superfluous Seamen should be extinct, it would be impossible to Man such large Fleets as we could at present: But I do not look upon this as a detriment, or the least Inconveniency: for the Reduction of Mariners as to Numbers being general throughout the World, all the consequence would be, that in case of War the Maritime Powers would be obliged to Fight with fewer Ships, which would be an Happiness instead of an Evil: and would you carry this Felicity to the highest pitch of Perfection, it is but to add one desirable Blessing more, and no Nation shall ever Fight at all: The Blessing I hint at is, what all good Christians are bound to pray for, *viz.* that all Princes and States would be true to their Oaths and Promises, and Just to one another, as well as their own Subjects; that they might have a greater regard for the Dictates of Conscience and Religion, than those of State Politicks and Worldly Wisdom, and prefer the Spiritual Welfare of others to their own Carnal Desires, and the Honesty, the Safety, the Peace and Tranquillity of the Nations they Govern to their own love of Glory, Spirit of Revenge, Avarice and Ambition.

The last Paragraph will to many seem a Digression, that makes little for my purpose: But what I mean by it is to demonstrate that Goodness, Integrity and a Peaceful Disposition in Rulers and Governors of Nations are not the proper Qualifications to Aggrandize them, and encrease their numbers any more, than the Uninterrupted Series of Success that every Private Person would be Blest with, if he could, and which I have shewn would be Injurious and Destructive to a large Society, that should place a Felicity in Worldly Greatness, and being envied by their Neighbours, and value themselves upon their Honour and their Strength.

No Man needs to Guard himself against Blessings, but Calamities require hands to avert them. The amiable qualities of Man put none of the Species upon stirring: His Honesty, his love of Company, his Goodness, Content and Frugality are so many Comforts to an Indolent Society, and the more Real and Unaffected they are the more they keep every thing at Rest and Peace, and the more they will every where prevent Trouble and Motion it self. The same almost may be said of the Gifts and Munificence of Heaven, and all the Bounties and Benefits of Nature: This is certain that the more extensive they are, and the greater plenty we have of them, the more we save our Labour. But the Necessities, the Vices and Imperfections of Man, together with the various Inclemencies of the Air and other Elements contain in them the Seeds of all Arts, Industry and Labour: It is the Extremities of Heat and Cold, the Inconstancy and Badness of Seasons, the Violence and Uncertainty of Winds, the vast Power and Treachery of Water, the Rage and Untractableness of Fire, and the Stubborness and Sterility of the Earth that rack our Invention, how we shall either avoid the Mischiefs they may produce, or correct the Malignity of them and turn their several Forces to our own Advantage a Thousand different ways; whilst we are employ'd in supplying the infinite variety of our Wants, which will ever be multiply'd as our Knowledge is enlarg'd, and our Desires encrease. Hunger, Thirst and Nakedness are the first Tyrants that force us to stir: afterwards our Pride, Sloth, Sensuality and Fickleness are the great Patrons that promote all Arts and Sciences, Trades, Handicrafts and Callings; whilst the great Task-masters, Necessity, Avarice, Envy and Ambition, each in the Class that belongs to him, keep the Members of the Society to their Labour, and make them all submit, most of them chearfully, to the Drudgery of their Station; Kings and Princes not excepted.

The greater the Variety of Trades and Manufactures, the more operose they are, and the more they are divided in many Branches the greater Numbers may be contain'd in a Society without being in one another's way, and the more easily they may be render'd a Rich, Potent and Flourishing People. Few Vertues employ any Hands, and therefore they may render a small Nation Good, but they can never make a Great one. To be strong and laborious, patient in Difficulties, and assiduous in all Business are commendable Qualities; but as they do their own Work so they are their own Reward, and neither Art nor Industry have ever paid their Compliments to them; whereas the Excellency of Human Thought and Contrivance has been and is yet no where more conspicuous than in the Variety of Tools and Instruments of Workmen and Artificers, and the multiplicity of Engines, that were all invented either to assist the Weakness of Man, to correct his many Imperfections, to gratifie his Laziness, or obviate his Impatience.

It is in Morality as it is in Nature, there is nothing so perfectly Good in Creatures that it cannot be hurtful to any one of the Society, nor any thing so entirely Evil, but it may prove beneficial to some part or other of the Creation : So that things are only Good and Evil in reference to something else, and according to the Light and Position they are placed in. What pleases us is good in that regard, and by this Rule every Man wishes well for himself to the best of his Capacity, with little Respect to his Neighbour. There never was any Rain yet, tho' in a very dry season when Publick Prayers had been made for it, but somebody or other who wanted to go abroad wish'd it might be Fair Weather only for that Day. When the Corn stands thick in the Spring, and the generality of the Country rejoyce at the pleasing Object, the Rich Farmer who kept his last Year's Crop for a better Market, pines at the sight and inwardly grieves at the prospect of a plentiful Harvest. Nay, we shall often hear your Idle People openly wish for the Possessions of others, and not to be injurious forsooth add this wise Proviso, that it should be without Detriment to the Owners : But I'm afraid they often do it without any such Restriction in their Hearts.

It is a Happiness that the Prayers as well as Wishes of most People are insignificant and good for nothing; or else the only thing that could keep Mankind fit for Society, and the World from falling into Confusion, would be the Impossibility, that all the Petitions made to Heaven should be granted. A dutiful pretty young Gentleman newly come from his Travels lies at the *Briel*[60] waiting with Impatience for an Easterly Wind to waft him over to *England*, where a dying Father, who wants to embrace and give him his

60. A Dutch seaport. – Ed.

Blessing before he yields his Breath, lies hoaning[61] after him, melted with Grief and Tenderness: In the mean while a *British* Minister, who is to take care of the Protestant Interest in *Germany*, is riding Post to *Harwich*, and in violent haste to be at *Ratisbon* before the Diet breaks up. At the same time a rich Fleet lies ready for the *Mediterranean*, and a fine Squadron is bound for the *Baltick*. All these things may probably happen at once, at least there is no difficulty in supposing they should. If these People are not Atheists, or very great Reprobates, they will all have some good Thoughts before they go to Sleep, and consequently about Bed-time they must all differently pray for a fair Wind and a prosperous Voyage. I don't say, but it is their Duty, and it is possible they may be all heard, but I am sure they can't be all serv'd at the same time.

After this I flatter my self to have demonstrated that, neither the Friendly Qualities and kind Affections that are natural to Man, nor the real Virtues, he is capable of acquiring by Reason and Self-Denial, are the foundation of Society; but that what we call Evil in this World, Moral as well as Natural, is the grand Principle that makes us Sociable Creatures, the solid Basis, the Life and Support of all Trades and Employments without exception: That there we must look for the true origin of all Arts and Sciences, and that the moment, Evil ceases, the Society must be spoil'd if not totally dissolv'd.

I could add a Thousand things to enforce and further illustrate this Truth with abundance of Pleasure; but for fear of being Troublesome I shall make an End, tho' I confess, that I have not been half so Sollicitous to gain the Approbation of others, as I have study'd to please my self in this Amusement; yet if ever I hear, that by following this Diversion I have given any to the Intelligent Reader it will always add to the Satisfaction I have receiv'd in the Performance: In the hope my Vanity forms of this, I leave

61. Yearning. – Ed.

him with regret, and conclude with repeating the seeming Paradox, the Substance of which is advanc'd in the Title Page; that Private Vices by the dextrous Management of a skilful Politician may be turn'd into Publick Benefits.

THE END

THE

INDEX[62]

A.

Air and *Space* no Objects of Sight, Pag. 331.

Acknowledgment due to Ancestors, 324.

Alexander the Great. The Recompence he had in View, 90. Proved from his own Mouth, *ibid*. Another Demonstration of his Frailty, 338.

America, what the Conquest of it has cost, 210.

Anger defined, 216. Conquered by Fear, *ibid*. and 220. The operation of Strong Liquors imitates that of Anger, 225.

Apology (an) for several Passages in the Book, 240, 241, 242. An Apology for recommending Ignorance, 297.

Atheism has had its Martyrs, 227.

Avarice, 131. The reason why it is generally hated, *ibid*. Why the Society stands in need of it, 132. Is equally necessary with Prodigality, 135, 258.

B.

Beards, The various Modes concerning them, 332.

Beggars, Their Policy, 267, 268. What sort of People complain of them most, *ibid*.

Behaviour of modest Women, 103. Of a Bride and Bridegroom, 106. Of undisciplin'd Soldiers, 221.

Belief, when we deserve it, 178.

Benefits that accrue from the worst of People, 118, till 126.

Blessings, Prejudicial, 238.

Brandy-Shops, the Qualifications required to keep them, 122.

62. The Index was added in 1723. Page references are to the present. – Ed.

P.

S.

The Index

A

Vindication of the Book,[63]

from the Aspersions contain'd in a
Presentment of the Grand Jury of *Middlesex*

AND

An Abusive Letter to Lord C.

63. The 'Vindication' was added in 1724. – Ed.

That the Reader may be fully instructed in the Merits of the Cause between my Adversaries and my self, it is requisite that, before he sees my Defence, he should know the whole Charge, and have before him all the Accusations against me at large.

The Presentment of the Grand Jury
is worded thus

We the Grand Jury for the County of Middlesex have with the greatest Sorrow and Concern, observ'd the many Books and Pamphlets that are almost every Week Published against the Sacred Articles of our *Holy Religion*, and all Discipline and Order in the *Church*, and the Manner, in which this is carry'd on, seems to us, to have a Direct Tendency to *propagate Infidelity*, and consequently Corruption of all Morals.

We are justly Sensible of the Goodness of the Almighty that has preserved us from the *Plague*,[64] which has visited our Neighbouring Nation, and for which great Mercy, his Majesty was graciously pleased to command by his Proclamation that Thanks should be returned to Heaven; but how provoking must it be to the Almighty, that his Mercies and Deliverances extended to this Nation, and our Thanksgiving that was publickly commanded for it, should be attended with such flagrant Impieties?

We know of Nothing that can be of greater Service to

64. This was the great plague at Marseilles, which lasted from 1720 to 1722. – Ed.

his Majesty and the Protestant Succession (which is happily established among us for the Defence of the *Christian Religion*) than the Suppression of Blasphemy and Prophaneness, which has a direct Tendency to subvert the very Foundation on which his Majesty's Government is fixed.

So Restless have these *Zealots for Infidelity* been in their Diabolical Attempts against Religion, that they have,

First, Openly blasphemed and denied the Doctrine of the Ever *Blessed Trinity*, endeavouring by specious Pretences, to revive the *Arian Heresy*, which was never introduced into any Nation, but the Vengeance of Heaven pursued it.

Secondly, They affirm an Absolute *Fate* and deny the *Providence* and Government of the Almighty in the World.

Thirdly, They have endeavoured to subvert all Order and Discipline in the Church, and by vile and unjust Reflections on the *Clergy*, they strive to bring Contempt on all Religion; That by the Libertinism of their Opinions they may encourage and draw others into the Immoralities of their Practice.

Fourthly, That a General Libertinism may the more effectually be established, the *Universities* are decried, and all *Instructions of Youth* in the Principles of the Christian Religion are exploded with the greatest Malice and Falsity.

Fifthly, The more effectually to carry on these Works of Darkness, studied Artifices and invented Colours have been made use of to run down Religion and Vertue as *prejudicial* to Society, and detrimental to the State; and to recommend Luxury, Avarice, Pride, and all kind of Vices, as being necessary to *Publick Welfare*, and not tending to the *Destruction* of the Constitution : Nay the very *Stews* themselves have had strained Apologies and forced Encomiums made in their Favour and produced in Print, with Design, we conceive, to debauch the Nation.

These Principles having a direct Tendency to the Subversion of all Religion, and Civil Government, our Duty to the *Almighty*, our Love to our *Country*, and Regard to our *Oaths*, oblige us to Present,[65]

[*Edmond Parker*, at the Bible and Crown in Lombard street] as the Publisher of a Book, entituled, The *Fable of the Bees*, or Private Vices Publick Benefits, 2d Edit. 1723.

And also [*T. Warner* at the Black Boy in Pater-Noster Row,] as the Publisher of a Weekly Paper, called the *British Journal*, Numb. 26, 35, 36, and 39.[66]

The Letter I complain of is this;

My Lord,

'Tis Welcome News to all the King's Loyal Subjects and True Friends to the Estabish'd Government and Succession in the *Illustrious House of* Hanover, that your Lordship is said to be contriving some *Effectual* Means of securing us from the Dangers, wherewith His Majesty's happy Government seems to be threatned by *Catiline*, under the Name of *Cato*; by the Writer of a Book intituled, *The Fable of the Bees*, &c. and by others of their *Fraternity*, who are undoubtedly useful Friends to the *Pretender*, and diligent, for his sake, in labouring to subvert and ruin our Constitution, under a specious Pretence of defending it. Your Lordship's wise Resolution, totally to suppress such impious Writings, and the Direction already given for having them *Presented*, immediately, by some of the *Grand Juries*, will effectually convince the Nation, that no Attempts against *Christianity* will be suffer'd or endured here. And this Conviction will at once rid Men's Minds of the Uneasiness

65. Mandeville omitted the two names and addresses in brackets here, although they appeared in the original presentment. – Ed.

66. These numbers of the *British Journal* contained letters by 'Cato' (John Trenchard and Thomas Gordon) attacking the clergy and the charity schools. – Ed.

which this flagitious Race of Writers has endeavour'd to raise in them; will therefore be a firm Bulwark to the *Protestant Religion*; will effectually defeat the Projects and Hopes of the *Pretender*; and best secure us against any Change in the *Ministry*. And no *faithful Briton* coud be unconcern'd, if the People should imagine any the least Neglect in any single Person bearing a part in the Ministry, or begin to grow *Jealous*, that any thing could be done, which is not done in defending their Religion from every the least Appearance of Danger approaching towards it. And, my Lord, this *Jealousy* might have been apt to rise, if no Measures had been taken to discourage and crush the open Advocates of *Irreligion*. 'Tis no easy Matter to get Jealousy out of one's Brains, when 'tis once got into them. Jealousy, my Lord! 'Tis as *furious* a Fiend as any of them all. I have seen a little thin weak Woman so invigorated by a Fit of *Jealousy*, that five Grenadiers could not hold her. My Lord, go on with your just Methods of keeping the People clear of this cursed *Jealousy*: For, amongst the various Kinds and Occasions of it, that which concerns their *Religion*, is the most violent flagrant frantick Sort of all; and accordingly has, in former Reigns, produced those various Mischiefs, which your Lordship has faithfully determined to prevent, dutifully regarding the Royal Authority, and conforming to the *Example* of his Majesty, who has graciously given *DIRECTIONS* (which are well known to your Lordship) *for the preserving of Unity in the Church, and the Purity of the Christian Faith*. 'Tis in vain to think that the People of *England* will ever give up their *Religion*, or be very fond of any *Ministry* that will not support it, as the Wisdom of this Ministry has done, against such audacious Attacks as are made upon it by the *Scriblers*; for *Scribler*, your Lordship knows, is the just Appellation of every Author, who, under whatever plausible Appearance of good Sense, attempts to undermine the Religion, and therefore the Content and Quiet, the Peace and Happiness of his Fellow-Subjects, by subtle and artful and fallacious Arguments and Insinuations. May Heaven avert those insufferable Miseries, which the Church of *Rome* would bring upon us! *Tyranny* is the Bane of Human Society; and there is no Tyranny heavier than that of the *Triple Crown*. And therefore, this free and happy People has justly conceived an utter Abhorrence and Dread of Popery, and of every thing that looks like Encouragement or Tendency to it; but they do also abhor and dread the Violence offer'd to *Christianity* itself, by our British *Catilines*, who shelter their treacherous Designs against it, under the false Colours of Regard and Good-will to our blessed Protestant Religion, whilst they demonstrate, too *plainly* demonstrate, that the Title of *Protestants* does not belong to them, unless it can belong to those, who are in Effect Protesters against *all Religion*.

And really, the People cannot be much blamed for being a little unwilling to part with their Religion: For they tell ye, that there *is* a *God*; and that *God* governs the World; and that he is wont to bless or blast a Kingdom, in Proportion to the Degrees of *Religion* or *Irreligion* prevailing in it. Your Lordship has a fine Collection of Books; and, which is a finer thing still, you do certainly understand them, and can turn to an Account of any important Affair in a trice. I would therefore fain know, whether your Lordship can show, from *any Writer*, let him be as *profane* as the *Scriblers* would have him, that any one Empire, Kingdom, Country or Province, Great or Small, did not dwindle and sink, and was confounded, when it once fail'd of *providing* studiously for the *Support of Religion*.

The *Scriblers* talk much of the *Roman* Government, and *Liberty*, and the *Spirit* of the *Old Romans*. But 'tis undeniable, that their most plausible Talk of these Things is all *Pretence*, and *Grimace*, and an *Artifice* to serve the Purposes of

Irreligion; and by consequence to render the People *uneasy*, and ruin the Kingdom. For if they did in *Reality* esteem, and would faithfully recommend to their Countrymen, the Sentiments and Principles, the main Purposes and Practices of the wise and prosperous *Romans*, they would, in the first place, put us in mind, that *Old Rome* was as remarkable for *observing* and promoting *Natural Religion*, as *New Rome* has been for corrupting that which is *Reveal'd*. And as the *Old Romans* did signally recommend themselves to the Favour of Heaven, by their faithful *Care of Religion*; so were they abundantly convinced, and did accordingly acknowledge, with *universal* Consent, that their Care of Religion was the *great Means** of *God's* preserving the Empire, and crowning it with Conquests and Success, Prosperity and Glory. Hence it was, that when their *Orators* were bent upon exerting their utmost in moving and persuading the People, upon any Occasion, they ever put them in mind of their *Religion*, if *That* could be any way affected by the Point in debate; not doubting that the People would determine in their *Favour*, if they could but demonstrate, that the Safety of *Religion* depended upon the Success of their *Cause*. And indeed, neither the *Romans*, nor any other Nation upon Earth, did ever suffer their *Establish'd Religion* to be *openly* ridiculed, exploded, or opposed: And I'm sure, your Lordship would not, for all the World, that this Thing should be done with *Impunity* amongst *Us*, which was never endured in the World before. Did ever any Man, since the blessed Revelation of the *Gospel*, run Riot upon *Christianity*, as some

---

* *Quis est tam Vecors qui non Intelligat, Numine hoc tantum Imperium esse Natum, Auctum, & Retentum?*—Cicer. Orat. de Harusp, Respons.[67]

67. 'Who is so witless that he does not understand that it is by the divine power that the Empire has been created, extended and sustained?' Cicero, *De Haruspicum Responsis Oratio*, ix, 19. – Ed.

Men, nay, and some few Women too, have lately done? Must the *Devil* grow rampant at this Rate, and not to be call'd *Coram Nobis*?[68] Why should not he content himself to carry off People in the common Way, the Way of Cursing and Swearing, Sabbath-breaking and Cheating, Bribery and Hypocrisy, Drunkenness and Whoring, and such kind of Things, as he us'd to do? Never let him domineer in Men's Mouths and Writings, as he does now, with loud, tremendous Infidelity, Blasphemy and Prophaneness, enough to frighten the King's Subjects out of their Wits. We are now come to a short Question: *God*, or the *Devil*? that's the Word; and Time will shew, who and who goes together. Thus much may be said at present, that those have abundantly shewn their Spirit of Opposition to Sacred Things, who have not only inveighed against the *National* Profession and Exercise of Religion; and endeavour'd, with Bitterness and Dexterity, to render it *Odious* and *Contemptible,* but are sollicitous to hinder *Multitudes* of the Natives of this Island from having the very *Seeds* of *Religion* sown among them with Advantage.

Arguments are urged, with the utmost Vehemence, against the Education of poor Children in the *Charity-Schools*, tho' there hath not one just Reason been offer'd against the Provision made for that Education. The Things that have been objected against it are *not*, in Fact, true; and nothing ought to be regarded, by serious and wise Men, as a *weighty* or *just* Argument, if it is not a *true* one. How hath *Catiline* the Confidence left to look any Man in the Face, after he hath spent more Confidence than most Men's whole Stock amounts to, in saying, that *this pretended Charity has, in Effect, destroy'd all other Charities, which were before given to the Aged, Sick, and Impotent.*

It seems pretty clear, that if those, who do *not* contribute to any *Charity-School*, are become more Uncharitable to any

68. Before us (as a defendant). – Ed.

other Object, than formerly they were; their want of Charity to the one, is not owing to their Contribution to the other. And as to those who *do* contribute to these Schools; they are so far from being more sparing in their Relief of other Objects, than they were before, that the poor Widows, the Aged and the Impotent do plainly receive more Relief from *Them*, in Proportion to their Numbers and Abilities, than from any the same Numbers of Men under the same Circumstances of Fortune, who do *not* concern themselves with the *Charity-Schools*, in any Respect, but in condemning and decrying them. I will meet *Catiline* at the *Grecian* Coffee-House any Day in the Week, and by an Enumeration of particular Persons, in as great a *Number* as he pleaseth, demonstrate the Truth of what I say. But I do not much depend upon his giving me the Meeting, because 'tis *his* Business, not to encourage *Demonstrations* of the Truth, but to throw *Disguises* upon it; otherwise, he never could have allowed himself, after representing the Charity Schools as intended *to breed up Children to Reading and Writing, and a sober Behaviour, that they may be qualified to be Servants*, immediately to add these Words; *A sort of idle and rioting Vermin, by which the Kingdom is already almost devoured, and are become every where a publick Nusance, &c.* What? Is it owing to the *Charity Schools*, that Servants are become so *Idle*, such *rioting Vermin*, such a publick *Nusance*; that *Women*-Servants turn *Whores*, and the *Men*-Servants *Robbers*, *House-breakers*, and *Sharpers*? (as he says they commonly do). Is this owing to the *Charity-Schools*? or, if it is *not*, how comes he to allow himself the Liberty of representing these Schools as a *Means* of *increasing* this Load of Mischief, which is indeed too plainly fallen upon the Publick? The *imbibing Principles of Vertue* hath not, usually, been thought the chief Occasion of running into Vice. If the early Knowledge of *Truth*, and of our *Obligations* to it, were the surest Means of *departing* from it, no Body would doubt, that the Knowledge of Truth was instill'd into *Catiline* very *Early*, and with the utmost Care. 'Tis a good pretty Thing in him to spread a Report, and to lay so much Stress upon it as he does, that *there is more Collected at the Church Doors in a Day, to make these poor Boys and Girls appear in Caps and Livery-Coats, than for all the Poor in a Year.* O rare *Catiline!* This Point you'll carry most swimingly; for you have no Witnesses against you, nor any living Soul to contradict you, except the Collectors and Overseers of the Poor, and all other principal Inhabitants of most of the Parishes, where any Charity-Schools are, in *England.*

The Jest of it is, my Lord, that these *Scriblers* would still be thought *good moral Men.* But, when Men make it their Business to *mislead* and *deceive* their Neighbours, and that in Matters of *Moment*, by *distorting* and *disguising* the Truth, by *Misrepresentations*, and *false* Insinuations; if such Men are not Guilty of *Usurpation,* whilst they take upon them the Character of *good moral Men*, then 'tis not Immoral, in any Man, to be *false* and *deceitful*, in Cases where the *Law* cannot touch him for being so, and *Morality* bears no Relation to *Truth* and *Fair Dealing.* However, I shall not be very willing to meet one of these *moral Men* upon *Hownslow-Heath*, if I should happen to ride that Way without Pistols. For I have a Notion, that They who have *no* Conscience in one Point, don't much abound with it in another. Your Lordship, who judges accurately of *Men*, as well as *Books*, will easily imagine, if you had no other Knowledge of the Charity-Schools, that there must be something very *excellent* in them, because such *kind of Men* as These are so warm in *opposing* them.

They tell you, that these Schools are Hinderances to *Husbandry* and to *Manufacture*: As to Husbandry: the Children are not kept in the Schools longer than till they are of Age and Strength to perform the principal Parts of it, or to bear constant Labour in it; and even whilst they *are* under this Course of Education, your Lordship may depend upon it, that they shall never be hindered from working in the Fields, or being employ'd in such Labour as they are capable of, in any Parts of the Year, when they can get such Employment for the Support of their Parents and themselves. In this Case the Parents in the several Countries are proper Judges of their several Situations and Circumstances, and at the same time, not so very fond of their Childrens getting a little *Knowledge*, rather than a little *Money*, but that they will find *other* Employment for them than going to School, whenever they can get a Penny by so doing. And the Case is the same as to the *Manufactures*; the Trustees of the Charity-Schools, and the Parents of the Children bred in them, would be thankful to those Gentlemen who *make* the Objection, if they would assist in *removing* it, by subscribing to a Fund for joyning the Employment of *Manufacture* to the Business of learning to *Read* and *Write* in the Charity-Schools: *This* would be a *noble* Work: 'Tis already effected by the Supporters of some Charity-Schools, and is aimed at, and earnestly desired by all the rest: But *Rome* was not built in a Day. Till this *great* Thing can be brought about, let the Masters and Managers of the Manufactures in the several Places of the Kingdom be so charitable as to employ the poor Children for a certain Number of Hours in every Day in their respective Manufactures, whilst the Trustees are taking Care to fill up their other Hours of the Day in the usual Duties of the Charity-Schools. 'Tis an easy Matter for *Party-men*, for designing and perverted Minds, to invent colourable, fallacious Arguments, and to offer *Railing* under the Appearance of *Reasoning* against the best Things in the World. But undoubtedly, no *impartial* Man, who is affected with a *serious* Sense of *Goodness*, and a *real* Love of his Country, can think this proper and just View of the Charity-Schools liable to any *just, weighty* Objection, or refuse to contribute his Endeavours to improve and raise them to that *Perfection* which is propos'd in them. In the mean time, let no Man be so *weak* or so *wicked* as to deny, that when poor Children cannot meet with Employment in any other honest Way, rather than suffer their tender Age to be spent in Idleness, or in learning the Arts of Lying and Swearing and Stealing, 'tis true *Charity* to *Them* and good Service done to our Country, to employ them in learning the Principles of *Religion* and *Vertue*, till their Age and Strength will enable them to become Servants in Families, or to be engag'd in Husbandry, or Manufacture, or any kind of Mechanick Trade or Laborious Employment; for to these *laborious* Employments are the Charity Children generally, if not always turn'd, as soon as they become capable of them: And therefore *Catiline* may be pleas'd to retract his Objection concerning *Shop-Keepers* or Retailers of Commodities, wherein he has affirm'd, that *their Employments* which he says *ought to fall to the Share of Children of their own Degree, are mostly anticipated and engross'd by the Managers of the Charity-Schools.* He must excuse my acquainting your Lordship, that this *Affirmation* is in Fact directly *false*, which is an Inconvenience very apt to fall upon *his* Affirmations, as it has particularly done upon one of 'em more, which I would mention: For he is not asham'd roundly to assert, *That the Principles of our common People are debauch'd in our Charity Schools, who are taught as soon as they can speak to blabber out* HIGH-CHURCH *and* ORMOND,[69] *and so are bred up to be Traytors before they know what Treason signifies.* Your *Lordship*, and other Persons of *Integrity*, whose Words are the faithful Representatives of their Meaning, would now think, if I had not given you a Key to *Catiline's* Talk, that he has been fully convinced, that the Children in the Charity-Schools *are bred up to be Traytors.*

69. The Duke of Ormond (1665–1745), one of the leading Jacobites. – Ed.

My Lord, If any one Master be suffer'd by the Trustees to continue in any Charity-School, against whom Proof can be brought, that he is disaffected to the Government, or that he does not as faithfully teach the Children *Obedience* and *Loyalty* to the King, as any other Duty in the Catechism, then I will gratify *Catiline* with a License to pull down the *Schools*, and hang up the Masters according to his Heart's Desire.

These and such things as these are urg'd with the like *Bitterness* and as *little Truth* in the Book mention'd above, viz. *The Fable of the Bees*; or, *Private Vices, publick Benefits*, &c. *Catiline* explodes the fundamental Articles of *Faith*, impiously comparing the Doctrine of the Blessed Trinity to *Fee-fa-fum*: This profligate Author of the *Fable* is not only an Auxiliary to *Catiline* in Opposition to *Faith*, but has taken upon him to tear up the very Foundations of *Moral Vertue*, and establish *Vice* in its Room. The best Physician in the World did never labour more to purge the *Natural* Body of *bad* Qualities, than this Bumble-Bee has done to purge the Body *Politick* of *good* ones. He himself bears Testimony to the Truth of this Charge against him: For when he comes to the Conclusion of his Book, he makes this Observation upon himself and his Performance: 'After this I flatter my self to have demonstrated, that neither the friendly Qualities and kind Affections that are *natural* to Man, nor the real *Virtues* he is capable of acquiring by *Reason* and Self-denial, are the *Foundation of Society*; but that what we call *Evil* in this World, *Moral* as well as *Natural*, is the *Grand Principle* that makes us sociable Creatures, the *solid Basis*, the *Life* and *Support* of all Trades and Employments without Exception: That there we must look for the true Origin of all Arts and Sciences, and that *the Moment Evil ceases, the Society must be spoil'd, if not totally dissolv'd.*'

Now, My Lord, you see the *Grand Design*, the main

Drift of *Catiline* and his Confederates; now the Scene opens, and the secret Springs appear; now the Fraternity adventure to speak out, and surely no Band of Men ever *dared* to speak at this Rate before; now you see the *True Cause* of all their Enmity to the poor Charity Schools; 'tis levell'd against *Religion; Religion*, my Lord, which the Schools are instituted to promote, and which *this Confederacy* is resolved to destroy; for the Schools are certainly one of the greatest Instruments of *Religion* and *Vertue*, one of the firmest Bulwarks against *Popery*, one of the best Recommendations of this People to the Divine Favour, and therefore one of the greatest Blessings to our Country of any thing that has been set on Foot since our happy *Reformation* and Deliverance from the Idolatry and Tyranny of *Rome*. If any trivial Inconvenience *did* arise from so excellent a Work, as some little Inconvenience attends all human Institutions and Affairs, the Excellency of the Work would still be Matter of *Joy*, and find *Encouragement* with all the *Wise* and the *Good*, who despise such *insignificant* Objections against it as *other* Men are not asham'd to raise and defend.

Now your Lordship also sees the *true Cause* of the *Satyr* which is continually form'd against the *Clergy* by *Catiline* and his Confederates. Why should Mr *Hall's* Conviction and Execution be any more an Objection against the Clergy, than Mr *Layer's* against the Gentlemen of the *Long Robe*?[70] why, because the Profession of the *Law* does not immediately relate to *Religion* : and therefore *Catiline* will allow, that if any Persons of *that* Profession should be Traytors, or otherwise *vicious*, all the rest may, nothwithstanding the Iniquity of a Brother, be as loyal and vertuous as any other Subjects in the King's Dominions : But because Matters of *Religion* are the profess'd *Concern* and the *Employment* of the *Clergy*, therefore *Catiline's* Logick makes it out as

70. Christopher Layer (1683–1723) was executed for complicity in a Jacobite plot. – Ed.

clear as the Day, that if any of *them* be disaffected to the Government, all the rest are so too; or if any of *them* be chargeable with *Vice*, this Consequence from it is plain, that All or Most of the rest are as vicious as the Devil can make them. I shall not trouble your Lordship with a particular Vindication of the Clergy, nor is there any Reason that I should, for they are already secure of your *Lordship*'s good Affection to them, and they are able to vindicate themselves wheresoever such a Vindication is wanted, being as *faithful* and *vertuous* and *learned* a Body of Men as any in *Europe*; and yet they suspend the *Publication* of Arguments in a solemn Defence of themselves, because they neither *expect* nor *desire* Approbation and Esteem from *impious* and *abandon'd* Men; and at the same Time they cannot doubt that all Persons, not only of great *Penetration* but of *common Sense*, do now clearly see; that the Arrows shot against the *Clergy* are intended to wound and destroy the *Divine Institution* of the Ministerial Offices, and to extirpate the *Religion* which the sacred Offices were appointed to preserve and promote. This was always *supposed* and *suspected* by every honest and impartial Man; but 'tis now *demonstrated* by those who before had given Occasion to such Suspicions, for they have now openly declared that *Faith* in the Principal Articles of it, is not only needless but ridiculous, that the *Welfare* of human Society must sink and perish under the Encouragement of *Vertue*, and that Immorality is the only *firm* Foundation whereon the Happiness of Mankind can be built and subsist. The *Publication* of such Tenets as these, an open avow'd Proposal to extirpate the *Christian Faith* and all *Vertue*, and to fix *Moral Evil* for the *Basis* of the Government, is so stunning, so shocking, so frightful, so flagrant an Enormity, that if it should be imputed to us as a *National* Guilt, the *Divine Vengeance* must inevitably fall upon us. And how far this Enormity would become a *National Guilt* if it should pass disregarded and unpunished, a *Casuist* less skilful and discerning than your Lordship may easily guess: And no doubt your Lordship's good Judgment in so plain and important a Case has made you, like a wise and faithful Patriot, resolve to use your utmost Endeavours in your high Station to defend Religion from the bold Attacks made upon it.

As soon as I have seen a Copy of the *Bill for the better Security of his Majesty and his happy Government, by the better Security of* Religion *in* Great-Britain, your Lordship's *just Scheme of Politicks*, your *Love of your Country*, and your *great Services* done to it shall again be acknowledg'd by,

My Lord,
Your most faithful humble Servant,
Theophilus Philo-Britannus.

These violent Accusations and the great Clamour every where raised against the Book, by Governours, Masters, and other Champions of Charity-Schools, together with the Advice of Friends, and the Reflection on what I owed to my self, drew from me the following Answer. The candid Reader, in the perusal of it, will not be offended at the Repetition of some Passages, one of which he may have met with twice already, when he shall consider that to make my Defence by it self to the Publick, I was obliged to repeat what had been quoted in the Letter, since the Paper would unavoidably fall into the Hands of many who had never seen either the Fable of the Bees, or the Defamatory Letter wrote against it. The Answer was Published in the *London Journal* of *August* 10, 1723, in these Words:

Whereas in the Evening-Post of Thursday *July* 11, a Presentment was inserted of the Grand Jury of *Middlesex*, against the Publisher of a Book, entitled, *The Fable of the Bees; or, Private Vices Publick Benefits*; and since that, a passionate and abusive Letter has been publish'd against the same Book and the Author of it, in the *London Journal* of *Saturday* July, 27. I think my self indispensably oblig'd to vindicate the abovesaid Book against the black Aspersions that undeservedly have been cast upon it, being conscious that I have not had the least ill Design in Composing it. The Accusations against it having been made openly in the publick Papers, it is not equitable the Defence of it should appear in a more private Manner. What I have to say in my Behalf, I shall address to all Men of Sense and Sincerity, asking no other Favour of them than their Patience and Attention. Setting aside what in that Letter relates to others, and every thing that is Foreign and Immaterial, I shall begin with the Passage that is quoted from the Book, *viz. After this, I flatter my self to have demonstrated that, neither the friendly Qualities and kind Affections that are natural to Man, nor the real Vertues he is capable of acquiring by Reason and Self-denial, are the Foundation of Society; but that what we call Evil in this World, Moral as well as Natural, is the grand Principle that makes us sociable Creatures, the solid Basis the Life and Support of all Trades and Employments without Exception. That there we must look for the true Origin of all Arts and Sciences; and that the Moment Evil ceases, the Society must be spoil'd, if not totally dissolv'd.* These Words I own are in the Book, and, being both innocent and true, like to remain there in all future Impressions. But I will likewise own very freely, that, if I had wrote with a Design to be understood by the meanest Capacities, I would not have chose the Subject there treated of; or if I had, I would have amplify'd, and explain'd every Period, talk'd and distinguish'd magisterially, and never appear'd without the Fescue[71] in my Hand. As for Example; to make the

71. A school rod. – Ed.

Passage pointed at intelligible, I would have bestow'd a
Page or two on the Meaning of the Word *Evil*; after that I
would have taught them, that every Defect, every Want was
an Evil; that on the Multiplicity of those Wants depended
all those mutual Services which the individual Members of a
Society pay to each other; and that consequently, the greater
Variety there was of Wants, the larger Number of Indi-
viduals might find their private Interest in labouring for
the good of others, and united together, compose one Body.
Is there a Trade or Handicraft but what supplies us with
something we wanted? This Want certainly, before it was
supply'd, was an Evil, which that Trade or Handicraft was
to remedy, and without which it could never have been
thought of. Is there an Art or Science that was not invented
to mend some Defect? Had this latter not existed, there
could have been no occasion for the former to remove it. I
say, p. 368. *The Excellency of human Thought and Con-
trivance has been, and is yet no where more conspicuous
than in the Variety of Tools and Instruments of Workmen
and Artificers, and the Multiplicity of Engines, that were
all invented, either to assist the Weakness of Man, to correct
his many Imperfections, to gratify his Laziness, or obviate
his Impatience.* Several foregoing Pages run in the same
strain. But what Relation has all this to Religion or In-
fidelity more than it has to Navigation or the Peace in the
North?

The many Hands that are employ'd to supply our natural
Wants, that are really such, as Hunger, Thirst, and Naked-
ness, are inconsiderable to the vast Numbers that are all
innocently gratifying the Depravity of our corrupt Nature; I
mean the Industrious, who get a Livelihood by their honest
Labour, to which the Vain and Voluptuous must be beholden
for all their Tools and Implements of Ease and Luxury. *The
short sighted Vulgar, in the Chain of Causes, seldom can
see farther than one Link; but those who can enlarge their*

View, and will give themselves Leisure of gazing on the Prospect of concatenated Events, may in a hundred Places see Good *spring up and pullulate from* Evil, *as naturally as* Chickens *do from* Eggs.

These words are to be found p. 123 in the Remark made on the seeming Paradox; that in the grumblng Hive

> *The worst of all the Multitude*
> *Did something for the Common Good:*

Where in many Instances may be amply discover'd, how unsearchable Providence daily orders the Comforts of the Laborious, and even the Deliverances of the Oppress'd secretly to come forth not only from the Vices of the Luxurious, but likewise the Crimes of the Flagitious and most Abandon'd.

Men of Candour and Capacity perceive at first Sight, that in the Passage censur'd, there is no Meaning hid or express'd that is not altogether contain'd in the following Words: *Man is a necessitous Creature on innumerable Accounts, and yet from those very Necessities, and nothing else, arise all Trades and Employments:* But it is ridiculous for Men to meddle with Books above their Sphere.

The *Fable of the Bees* was design'd for the Entertainment of People of Knowledge and Education, when they have an idle Hour which they know not how to spend better: It is a Book of severe and exalted Morality, that contains a strict Test of Vertue, an infallible Touch-stone to distinguish the real from the counterfeited, and shews many Actions to be faulty that are pawm'd upon the World for good ones: It describes the Nature and Symptoms of human Passions, detects their Force, and disguises and traces Self-Love in its darkest Recesses; I might safely add, beyond any other System of Ethicks: The Whole is a Rhapsody void of Order or Method, but no Part of it has any thing in it that is sour or pedantick; the Style I confess is very unequal, sometimes very high and rhetorical, and sometimes very low and even very trivial; such as it is, I am satisfied that it has diverted Persons of great Probity and Virtue, and unquestionable good Sense; and I am in no fear that it will ever cease to do so whilst it is read by such. Whoever has seen the violent Charge against this Book, will pardon me for saying more in Commendation of it, than a Man not labouring under the same Necessity would do of his own Work on any other Occasion.

The Encomiums upon Stews complain'd of in the Present-ment are no where in the Book. What might give a Handle to this Charge, must be a Political Dissertation concerning the best Method to guard and preserve Women of Honour and Virtue from the Insults of dissolute Men, whose Passions are often ungovernable: As in this there is a Dilemma be-tween two Evils, which it is impracticable to shun both, so I have treated it with the utmost Caution, and begin thus: *I am far from encouraging Vice, and should think it an un-speakable Felicity for a State, if the Sin of Uncleanness could be utterly banish'd from it; but I am afraid it is impossible.* I give my Reasons why I think it so; and speaking occasion-ally of the Musick-houses at *Amsterdam,* I give a short Account of them, than which nothing can be more harmless; and I appeal to all impartial Judges, whether what I have said of them is not ten times more proper to give Men (even the voluptuous of any Taste) a Disgust and Aversion against them, than it is to raise any criminal Desire. I am sorry the Grand-Jury should conceive that I publish'd this with a design to debauch the Nation, without considering that in the first Place, there is not a Sentence nor a Syllable that can either offend the chastest Ear, or sully the Imagination of the most vicious; or in the second, that the Matter com-plain'd of is manifestly address'd to Magistrates and Poli-ticians, or at least the more serious and thinking Part of Mankind; whereas a general Corruption of Manners as to

Lewdness, to be produced by reading, can only be apprehended from Obscenities easily purchas'd, and every Way adapted to the Tastes and Capacities of the heedless Multitude and unexperienced Youth of both Sexes; but that the Performance, so outragiously exclaim'd against, was never calculated for either of these Classes of People, is self-evident from every Circumstance. The Beginning of the Prose is altogether Philosophical, and hardly intelligible to any that have not been us'd to Matters of Speculation; and the Running Title of it is so far from being specious or inviting, that without having read the Book itself, no Body knows what to make of it, whilst at the same Time the price is five Shillings. From all which it is plain, that if the Book contains any dangerous Tenets, I have not been very sollicitous to scatter them among the People. I have not said a Word to please or engage them, and the greatest Compliment I have made them has been, *Apage vulgus.*[72] *But as nothing* (I say p. 241) *would more clearly demonstrate the Falsity of my Notions than that the Generality of the people should fall in with them, so I don't expect the Approbation of the Multitude. I write not to many, nor seek for any Wellwishers, but among the few that can think abstractly, and have their Minds elevated above the Vulgar.* Of this I have made no ill Use, and ever preserv'd such a tender Regard to the Publick, that when I have advanced any uncommon Sentiments, I have used all the Precautions imaginable, that they might not be hurtful to weak Minds that might casually dip into the Book. When, *pag.* 239. I own'd, *That it was my Sentiment that no Society could be rais'd into a rich and mighty Kingdom, or so rais'd subsist in their Wealth and Power for any considerable Time, without the Vices of Man,* I had premised, what was true, *That I had never said or imagined, that Man could not be virtuous as well in a rich and mighty Kingdom, as in the most pitiful Commonwealth.*

72. Away with the rabble. – Ed.

Which Caution, a Man less scrupulous than my self might have thought superfluous, when he had already explain'd himself on that Head in the very same Paragraph, which begins thus: *I lay down as a first Principle, that in all Societies, great or small, it is the Duty of every Member of it to be good; that Virtue ought to be encourag'd, Vice discountenanc'd, the Law obey'd, and the Transgressors punish'd.* There is not a Line in the Book that contradicts this Doctrine, and I defy my Enemies to disprove what I have advanced, p. 241 that *if I have shewn the Way to worldly Greatness, I have always, without Hesitation, prefer'd the Road that leads to Virtue.* No Man ever took more Pains not to be misconstrued than my self: Mind p. 241 *when I say that Societies cannot be rais'd to Wealth and Power, and the Top of Earthly Glory without Vices; I don't think that by so saying I bid Men be vicious, any more than I bid them be quarrelsome or covetous, when I affirm, that the Profession of the Law could not be maintain'd in such Numbers and Splendor, if there was not abundance of too selfish and litigious People.* A Caution of the same Nature I had already given towards the End of the Preface, on Account of a palpable Evil inseparable from the Felicity of *London.* To search into the real Causes of Things imports no ill Design, nor has any Tendency to do harm. A Man may write on Poysons and be an excellent Physician. Page 367. I say, *No Man needs to guard himself against Blessings, but Calamities require Hands to avert them.* And lower, *It is the Extremities of Heat and Cold, the Inconstancy and Badness of Seasons, the Violence and Uncertainty of Winds, the vast Power and Treachery of Water, the Rage and Untractableness of Fire, and the Stubbornness and Sterility of the Earth, that rack our Invention, how we shall either avoid the Mischiefs they produce or correct the Malignity of them, and turn their several Forces to our own Advantage a thousand different Ways.* Whilst a Man is enquiring into the Occupations of vast Multitudes, I cannot see why he may not say all this and much more, without being accused of depreciating and speaking slightly of the Gifts and Munificence of Heaven; when at the same time he demonstrates, that without Rain and Sunshine this Globe would not be habitable to Creatures like ourselves. It is an out of the way Subject, and I would never quarrel with the Man who should tell me that it might as well have been let alone: Yet I always thought it would please Men of any tolerable Taste, and not be easily lost.

My Vanity I could never conquer, so well as I could wish; and I am too proud to commit Crimes; and as to the main Scope, the Intent of the Book, I mean the View it was wrote with, I protest that it has been with the utmost Sincerity, what I have declared of it in the Preface, where at the bottom of the third Page you will find these Words. *If you ask me, why I have done all this,* cui bono? *And what good these Notions will produce; truly, besides the Reader's Diversion, I believe none at all; but if I was ask'd, what naturally ought to be expected from them? I would answer, that in the first Place the People who continually find Fault with others, by reading them would be taught to look at home, and examining their own Consciences, be made asham'd of always railing at what they are more or less guilty of themselves; and that in the next, those, who are so fond of the Ease and Comforts of a great and flourishing Nation, would learn more patiently to submit to those Inconveniencies, which no Government upon Earth can remedy, when they should see the Impossibility of enjoying any great Share of the first, without partaking likewise of the latter.*

The first Impression of the Fable of the Bees, which came out in 1714, was never carpt at, or publickly taken Notice of; and all the Reason I can think on why this Second Edition should be so unmercifully treated, tho' it has many Precautions which the former wanted, is an Essay on Charity and Charity-Schools, which is added to what was printed before. I confess that it is my Sentiment, that all hard and dirty Work ought in a well-govern'd Nation to be the Lot and Portion of the Poor, and that to divert their Children from useful Labour till they are fourteen or fifteen Years old, is a wrong Method to qualify them for it when they are grown up. I have given several Reasons for my Opinion in that Essay, to which I refer all impartial Men of Understanding, assuring them that they will not meet with such monstrous Impiety in it as is reported. What an Advocate I have been for Libertinism and Immorality, and what an Enemy to *all Instructions of Youth in the Christian Faith*, may be collected from the Pains I have take on Education for above seven Pages together: And afterwards again, *page* 311, where speaking of the Instructions the Children of the Poor might receive at Church: *from which* I say, *or some other Place of Worship, I would not have the meanest of a Parish that is able to walk to it, be Absent on Sundays. I* have these Words, *It is the Sabbath, the most useful Day in Seven that is set apart for Divine Service and Religious Exercise, as well as resting from bodily Labour; and it is a Duty incumbent on all Magistrates to take a particular Care of that Day. The Poor more especially, and their Children, should be made to go to Church on it, both in the Fore and the Afternoon, because they have no Time on any other. By Precept and Example they ought to be encouraged to it from their very Infancy: The wilful Neglect of it ought to be counted Scandalous; and if downright Compulsion to what I urge might seem too harsh and perhaps impracticable, all Diversions at least ought strictly to be prohibited, and the Poor hindered from every Amusement Abroad, that might allure or draw them from it.* If the Arguments I have made use of are not convincing, I desire they may be refuted, and I will acknowledge it as a Favour in any one that shall convince me of my Errour, without ill Language, by shewing me wherein I have been mistaken: But Calumny, it seems, is the shortest Way of confuting an Adversary, when Men are touch'd in a sensible Part. Vast Sums are gather'd for these Charity Schools, and I understand human Nature too well to imagine, that the Sharers of the Money should hear them spoke against with any Patience. I foresaw therefore the Usage I was to receive, and having repeated the common Cant that is made for Charity Schools, I told my Readers, page 276. *This is the general Cry, and he that speaks the least Word against it, is an uncharitable, heard-hearted and inhuman, if not a wicked, profane and Atheistical Wretch.* For this Reason it cannot be thought, that it was a great Surprise to me, when in that extraordinary Letter to Lord C. I saw my self call'd *profligate Author; the Publication of my Tenets, an open and avowed Proposal to extirpate the Christian Faith and all Virtue,* and what I had done *so stunning, so shocking, so frightful, so flagrant an Enormity,* that it cry'd for the Vengeance of Heaven. This is no more than what I have always expected from the Enemies to Truth and fair Dealing, and I shall retort nothing on the angry Author of that Letter, who endeavours to expose me to the publick Fury. I pity him, and have Charity enough to believe that he has been imposed upon himself, by trusting to Fame and the Hearsay of others; For no Man in his Wits can imagine, that he should have read one quarter Part of my Book, and write as he does.

I am sorry if the Words *Private Vices, Publick Benefits,* have ever given any Offence to a well meaning Man. The Mystery of them is soon unfolded when once they are rightly understood; but no Man of Sincerity will question the Innocence of them, that has read the last Paragraph, where I take my Leave of the Reader, *and conclude with repeating the seeming Paradox, the Substance of which is advanced in the Title Page; that private Vices by the dextrous Management of a skilful Politician, may be turn'd into publick*

Benefits. These are the last Words of the Book, printed in the same large Character with the rest. But I set aside all what I have said in my Vindication; and if in the whole Book call'd, *The Fable of the Bees*, and presented by the Grand-Jury of *Middlesex* to the Judges of the *King's-Bench*, there is to be found the least Tittle of Blasphemy or Profaneness, or any Thing tending to Immorality or the Corruption of Manners, I desire it may be publish'd; and if this be done without Invectives, personal Reflections, or setting the Mob upon me, Things I never design to answer, I will not only Recant, but likewise beg Pardon of the offended Publick in the most solemn Manner; and (if the Hangman might be thought too good for the Office) burn the Book my self at any reasonable Time and Place my Adversaries shall be pleased to appoint.

The Author of the Fable of the Bees

Textual Appendix

ALL passages, of at least a sentence in length, which Mandeville added to *The Fable of the Bees* in 1723 and 1724, have been noted at the foot of the appropriate page and are not repeated here. I have listed below all other substantive variants (differences in actual wording) found in the *London Journal* (*LJ*), *The Grumbling Hive* (1705), and the editions of the *Fable* of 1714, 1723, 1724 and 1725 described on pages 48-9 above, except for obvious misprints and those corrected in the errata lists of the various editions. The letters referring to the remarks were added to *The Grumbling Hive* in 1714 and the addition of Remarks *N* and *T* to the *Fable* in 1723 required a change in alphabetization throughout the book; in both cases these minor alterations can be inferred without further notice. The first notation below, as an example of the rest, means the following: on page 54, line 25, of the present edition the words 'point to' printed there appeared in the editions of 1723, 1724 and 1725, replacing the words 'point at' in the first edition of 1714. The second edition of 1714 possesses no textual authority and has therefore been ignored throughout.

THE PREFACE

54:25 point to] *23-25*; point at *14*. 57:9 time] *23-25*; times *14*. 57:20 and the] *14, 23*; the *24, 25*. 57:24 swarms] *23-25*; swarm *14*. 57:30 'tis] *25*; it is *14-24*. 58:17-18 Thus much I had said... in the Second.] *24, 25*; Thus much I have said to the Reader in the First Edition; what I have further to say to him he will find in the Additions I have made since. *23*.

THE GRUMBLING HIVE

65:6 refreshing] *14-25*; retaining *05*. 66:6 The] *24, 25*; Some *05-23*. 68:5 'em] *05*; them *14-25*. 68:17 oth'r] *05*; other *14-25*. 71:7 be'ng] *14-25*; being *05*. 71:26 'em] *05*; them *14-25*. 76:13 shabby crooked] *14-25*; crooked, shabby *05*.

AN ENQUIRY INTO THE ORIGIN OF MORAL VIRTUE

81:24 has] *24-25*; have *14, 23*. 83:13 Pleasures] *14-24*; Pleasure *25*. 83:26 Passions] *14-24*; Passion *25*. 86:1 stood... way] *24, 25*; were so obnoxious to them *14, 23*. 88:32 Sir *Richard Steele*] *24, 25*; Mr *Steele 14*; Sir *Rd. Steele 23*. 90:31 To define then] *23-25*; For, to define *14*. 91:4 Toils] *23-25*; Exploits *14*. 92:28 of the Divine] *23-25*; of Divine *14*.

REMARK A

94:14 the Children] *14-24*; their Children *25*.   95:7 any] *24, 25*; every *14, 23*.

REMARK B

97:14 came] *24, 25*; was come *14, 23*.

REMARK C

99:17 Women] *24, 25*; Woman *14, 23*.   101:34 were] *25*; was *23, 24*.   105:14 that the Man] *24, 25*; the Man *23*.   105:22 which] *24, 25*; what *23*.   106:12 Submission] *24, 25*; Submissions *23*. 107:2 sate] *24, 25*; set *23*.   108:5 no other Shift] *23*; no Shift *24, 25*.   110:8-9 Complaisance] *25*; Complaisency *23, 24*.   113:9 that it is] *23, 25*; that is *24*.

REMARK D

113:19 *won't*] *24, 25*; *don't 14, 23*.   113:20 *than*] *24, 25*; *then 14, 23*.   113:21 of] *25*; for *14-24*.   114:4 ask'd] *14-24*; ask *25*.

REMARK E

115:24 Leg] *14, 23*; Legs *24, 25*.   116:5 that very Reason] *24, 25*; that Reason *14, 23*.

REMARK F

118:8 but] but that *14-25*.

REMARK G

118:18 root] *24, 25*; rout *14, 23*.   121:16 Juniper] *25*; Juniper-Berries *23, 24*.   122:16 it's] *25*; it is *23, 24*.   122:22 than] *25*; then *23, 24*.   122:31 make] *24, 25*; makes *23*.   124:3 that] *23, 24*; the *25*.

REMARK H

126:14 Sentiments] *14-24*; Sentiment *25*.   129:3 endeavour] *24, 25*; endeavours *14, 23*.   130:24 (to whom I owe the last Paragraph)] *23-25*.

REMARK K

133:14 Chimney] *23-25*; Chimneys *14*.   134:22 in a few years] *23-25*; in few years *14*.   134:34 thus shews] *23-25*; shews *14*.

REMARK L

139:14 Benefit] *23-25*; Benefits *14*.   139:23 we shall] *24, 25*; we'll *14, 23*.   139:24 and only be] *24, 25*; we only shall be *14, 23*.   140:14 sent] *23-25*; send *14*.   141:21 Manufacture] *14*; Manufactures *23-25*.   143:23 a] *24, 25*; our *14, 23*.   144:4 *Tockay*] *24, 25*; *Tockay* Wine *14, 23*.   145:7 requires] *14, 23*; require *24, 25*.

413

145:28 o'Bed] *14, 23*; a-bed *24, 25*.   146:23 the first] *23-25*; one
14.   148:18 *th*'] *23-25*; *the 14*.

REMARK M

150:18 their] *23-25*; his *14*.   150:31 were] *14*; was *23-25*.   151:28
beholden] *23-25*; beholding *14*.   152:19 *Whatsun*] *24, 25*; *Whit-
suntide 14, 23*.   155:10 ridiculous] *25*; a ridiculous *14-24*.   156:24
sleek] *24, 25*; slick *14, 23*.

REMARK N

158:23 what] *24, 25*; which *23*.   159:33 their] *25*; the *23, 24*.   162:3
but to] *24, 25*; but *23*.   163:2 latter] *25*; first *23, 24*.   168:17 which
it is] *23*; which is *24, 25*.

REMARK O

173:20 like] *24, 25*; as *14, 23*.   173:29 Pleasures] *23-25*; Pleasure
14.   173:32 ever] *24, 25*; never *14, 23*.   178:11 upon] *24, 25*; on
14, 23.   181:6-7 unreasonable] *14*; reasonable *23-25*.   181:15-16
all the Symptoms] *24, 25*; a great share *14, 23*.   181:23-24 has not
Strength...to] *24, 25*; can't *14, 23*.   183:35 in a Magnificence] *25*;
in Magnificence *14-24*.   184:14-16 Those pageant Ornaments...
but] *24, 25*.   185:2 their own Appetites] *23-25*; themselves *14*.
186:29 *would be thought*] *23-25*; *would be 14*.   187:2 but] *23-25*;
than *14*.   187:25 'em] *25*; them *14-24*.

REMARK P

188:21 to what] *23-25*; what *14*.   191:9-10 was a Funeral for
Slaves, or made a Punishment] *23-25*; was a Punishment *14*.   191:21
it is] *23-25*; is it *14*.   193:17 extirpation] *14, 23*; Extirpations *24,
25*.   194:23-24 the countenance...Beast] *24, 25*; his countenance
14, 23.   195:30 'em] *24, 25*; them *14, 23*.   195:34 if Man] *14, 23*;
if a Man *24, 25*.   196:6 belong] *23-25*; belongs *14*.   196:35 worst]
23-25; worse *14*.   198:15-16 as soon as...can] *23-25*; what Mortal
can, as soon as the wide Wound is made, and the Jugulars are cut
asunder *14*.

REMARK Q

200:16 are] *23-25*; is *14*.   202:6 their] *23-25*; this *14*.   203:26 a
wonder] *23-25*; wonder *14*.   203:33 the same] *23-25*; same *14*.
204:7 further improve our] *23-25*; keep up the Price of *14*.   204:10
those] *23-25*; they *14*.   205:19 proportion] *23-25*; part *14*.   205:23
since] *23-25*; ever since *14*.   205:28 it is] *23-25*; is *14*.   205:32-33
Burthen...lies] *23-25*; Burden lies of all Excises and Impositions
14.   208:5 in such a] *23-25*; in a *14*.   208:7 by] *24, 25*; up *14, 23*.
208:10-11 (what...) that] *23-25*; that (which is yet impossible)

14. 208:17 would] *23–25;* should *14.* 209:22 whatever] *24, 25;* whoever *23.* 209:23 Labourers] *24, 25;* Labour *23.* 210:2 prompted to it] *23–25;* prompted *14.* 210:4 powerfully influenc'd] *23–25;* influenc'd *14.* 210:7 the labouring Man] *23–25;* Man *14.* 210:21 there were] *23–25;* were *14.*

REMARK R

219:33 noxious] *24, 25;* obnoxious *14, 23.* 220:12 by] *23–25;* with *14.* 220:13–14 to consult ... Method] *23–25;* in a different manner to act toward *14.* 221:4 how civiliz'd ... may] *23–25;* as civiliz'd as Men can *14.* 222:12 whom they] *24, 25;* they *14, 23.* 222:33 comes] *24, 25;* becomes *14, 23.* 224:27 this] *14–24;* there *25.* 226:10 when] *23–25;* and *14.* 226:11 ghastly] *23–25;* ghostly *14.* 226:12–13 with all ... and] *23–25;* mangled Carcasses, with all the various Scenes of *14.* 227:1 cannot] *23–25;* can *14.* 227:19 silly] *24, 25;* horrid *14, 23.* 228:10–11 instead of Valour ... himself] *23–25;* and even by himself be mistaken for a Principle of Valour *14.* 228:31–32 without laughing ... Finery] *23–25;* upon a Man accoutred with so much paultry Gaudiness and affected Finery, without laughing *14.* 228:34 it is in] *23–25;* it is *14.* 229:4 *Bedlam*] *23–25; Bethlem 14.* 230:12 grew] grow *14–25.* 230:18 it is] *23–25;* is it *14.* 230:18 without it] *23–25;* without *14.* 230:19 beholden] *23–25;* beholding *14.* 230:22 who] *24, 25;* which *14, 23.*

REMARK S

234:28 and ask'd] *23–25;* ask'd *14.* 234:31–32 that of the *Weavers*] *23–25;* those *14.* 234:32 *Silk*] *24, 25; Silks 14, 23.*

REMARK T

236:22 that the] *23;* the *24, 25.* 239:5 poorly] *24, 25;* but poorly *23.* 240:31 the last] *24, 25;* this *23.* 242:17 very scarce ... wanted] *24, 25;* scarce, if not almost useless *23.* 243:10 a shift] *24, 25;* shift *23.*

REMARK V

248:21 for] *24, 25;* to *14, 23.* 248:28 an Eye] *23–25;* a Look *14.* 249:33 Speed] *24, 25;* Expedition *14, 23.* 252:17 a] *14–24; for a 25.* 252:18 *Hand*] *23, 24; Hands 14, 25.* 252:27 Person] *23–25;* Persons *14.*

REMARK X

254:15 Harshness] *23–25;* Rigour *14.* 255:11 Men] *23–25;* Man *14.*

REMARK Y

255:18 has] *23–25;* as has *14.* 258:21 difference in] *25;* difference of *23, 24.* 259:3 turns] turn *23–25.*

AN ESSAY ON CHARITY AND CHARITY-SCHOOLS

266:12 are] *24, 25;* were *23.* 271:8 sometimes] *23, 24;* sometime *25.* 274:6 a hundred] *25;* hundred *23, 24.* 274:33 Mens] *24, 25;* Mans *23.* 278:19 those] *25;* these *23, 24.* 278:34–35 Snuff Box] *25;* a Snuff Box *23, 24.* 279:21–22 the taking] *23, 24;* taking *25.* 280:9 'em] *23;* them *24, 25.* 280:32 not have] *23, 24;* have *25.* 282:3 It is not then the want] *25;* It is then not want *23;* It is then not the want *24.* 286:17 it] *24, 25;* of it *23.* 286:25 denying] *23;* denying it *24, 25.* 287:14 most] *23, 24;* the most *25.* 288:13 seem] seems *23–25.* 290:25 enjoyns] *23, 24;* enjoys *25.* 293:27 make up] *24, 25;* make *23.* 294:29 these] *24, 25;* those *23.* 295:7 are] *25;* is *23, 24.* 296:16 I never] *24, 25;* that I never *23.* 297:1 Methinks] *24, 25;* my thinks *23.* 301:28 discourage] *23;* discharge *24, 25.* 301:34 'em] *24, 25;* them *23.* 303:12 th' other] *23, 24;* the other *25.* 304:2 the] *25;* their *23, 24.* 305:23 Tradesmen] *24, 25;* Tradesman *23.* 305:28 neglectful] *25;* negligent *23;* neglecting *24.* 308:17 or] *23, 24;* and *25.* 311:5 to 't] *24, 25;* to it *23.* 314:4 'em] *24, 25;* them *23.* 315:7 'em] *23;* them *24, 25.* 315:10 'em] *24, 25;* them *23.* 315:21 have call'd] *23, 24;* called *25.* 315:23 'em] *24, 25;* them *23.* 322:35 of] *25;* on *23, 24.*

A SEARCH INTO THE NATURE OF SOCIETY

329:6 expect] *25;* expects *23, 24.* 332:17 but] *25;* bar *23, 24.* 332:30 Carnation] *24, 25;* Coronation *23.* 332:35 a vast] *23;* vast *24, 25.* 333:9 'em] *24, 25;* them *23.* 340:2–3 This bears a fine gloss] *24, 25;* This is great Stress laid upon *23.* 340:3 and is] *24, 25;* and *23.* 343:5 'em] *24, 25;* them *23.* 343:14 a Clock] *23;* a'Clock *24, 25.* 350:2 Man] *25;* Men *23, 24.* 353:3 cannot] *24, 25;* shall not *23.* 358:14 great] *25;* brave *23, 24.* 359:17 *West-Indies*] *23, 24;* *East-Indies 25.* 360:10 Ship-wreck] *24, 25;* a Ship-wreck *23.* 361:31 makes] *23, 24;* make *25.* 366:24 should] *25;* would *23, 24.* 368:21 Trades] *25;* Trade *23, 24.* 368:31 nor] *25;* or *23, 24.*

THE INDEX

372:1 Sight, Pag.] *24, 25;* Sight *23.* 372:17 most] *24, 25;* the most *23.* 375:5 Their policy] *24, 25;* The policy *23.* 383:15 ibid.] *23;* ib. *24, 25.*

A VINDICATION OF THE BOOK

403:5 those] *25;* the *LJ, 24.* 411:14 Adversaries] *24, 25.* Adversary *LJ.*